OLIVER P. RAFFERTY

Catholicism in Ulster
1603–1983

An Interpretative History

GILL & MACMILLAN

Published in Ireland by
Gill & Macmillan Ltd
Goldenbridge
Dublin 8
© Oliver P. Rafferty, 1994
0 7171 2174 7
Printed in Hong Kong

A catalogue record is available for this book from the British Library.

In Memoriam
Cecelia Doherty (née Rafferty)
1953–1976

CONTENTS

PREFACE AND ACKNOWLEDGEMENTS

This work is primarily intended for the non-specialist general reader, though I hope it is not too much of a vanity to think that it might also be of some use to the student of Irish history. In such an enterprise, the author inevitably incurs enormous debts to those who have previously worked over the available material. Although I have tried to keep footnotes to a minimum I trust that both there and in the bibliography the labours of those on whom I have drawn in shaping the present essay have been sufficiently acknowledged. My attention to the twentieth-century phase of Ulster catholic history will I am sure disappoint those whose interests lie in other periods but I hope the weight given to events of the last eighty years does not seem disproportionate.

I am conscious that this work is very much an introduction and can in no sense claim to be an exhaustive study of the complex issues which the topic involves. There is much work still to be done expounding and interpreting the history of the Ulster catholic community. That task must be left to pens both weighter and more accomplished than mine. I have endeavoured to give a preliminary sketch of the terrain. It is for the reader to judge whether this has been a worthwhile exercise.

I should like to take this opportunity to thank those who have assisted and encouraged me in the preparation of this volume. It was Dr Sean Loughlin of the University of Rotterdam who first suggested that I should attempt to write the history of the catholic community in Ulster, and put me in touch with the publisher Christopher Hurst, who boldly commissioned this work and used his editorial skills to good effect upon the completed manuscript. Dr Paolo Morisi of the University of Bologna encouraged me to persevere at a time when I was beginning to think I should never have undertaken the project.

For their kindly interest throughout I must also mention Patricia Bowden, Claire O'Brien, Maire Duddy, Nick Hammersley, Dr Mary O'Connor and Dr Myra Skipper. I have also received much support in all the stages of this enterprise from various Jesuit colleagues, too numerous to list but whose friendship and interest have been a source of inspiration and encouragement. However I should like to mention Ray Lawler, SJ, who assisted with the proofreading and whose expert eye saved me from many inaccuracies.

The staff of various libraries and institutions have, despite insistent demands on my part, always treated me with patience and courtesy. Among these I should like to thank the staff of the British Library in

London, the Bodleian Library in Oxford, Belfast Central Library, the Linen Hall Library in Belfast and especially Ms Mary Hughes, the library of the Queen's University, Belfast, the diocesan library in St Malachy's College, Belfast, and the Public Records Office of Northern Ireland. I owe a special debt of gratitude to Dr Patrick Walsh, the bishop of Down and Connor, for permission to use the archival material in his care and to the archivist of his diocese, the Rev. George O'Hanlon. My thanks also to Cardinal Cahal Daly for access to the archives of the archdiocese of Armagh and to the Rev. S.J. Klyne and his successor the Rev. Eugene Sweeney for their help in ferreting out the material I needed. I should also like to thank the cardinal's household for all the hospitality I received on my frequent trips to Ara Coeli, and Dr Raymond Murray and his fellow clergy at the parochial house in Armagh for their generosity on many occasions.

The following have read and commented on individual chapters: Mgr Michael Dallat, Dr John McCavitt, Dr Eamon Phoenix, and Dr Bob Purdie. Dr Norman Tanner, SJ, read the entire manuscript and pronounced it free from theological error. In addition, he suggested a number of refinements, which I have incorporated. Needless to say any remaining errors of fact and interpretation are entirely my own responsibility. Dr Ambrose Macaulay drew to my attention material relating to catholic attitudes to the 1798 rising.

I must also record my gratitude to various friends in Oxford who in the final stages of my work on this book listened with much forbearance and good humour to my endless droning on Ireland and Ulster catholicism. In particular Liam McIlvanney, Ray Ryan and Peter Smith lent sympathetic ear, above and beyond the ordinary demands of friendship and good neighbourliness.

Finally my greatest debt of all is to my family who have tolerated my idiosyncracies over a long period, and from whom I have learnt much about faith and Ulster Catholicism. I hope that they will not be too disappointed with what I have written and will recognise the story here presented as very much their own.

15 August 1993   OLIVER P. RAFFERTY, SJ
Campion Hall and Christ Church Oxford

MAPS OF IRELAND

DIOCESES OF THE ROMAN
CATHOLIC CHURCH 1831–1974

Dioceses united before 1831
Cathedrals 1974
Boundaries of the provinces of
Armagh Cashel Dublin and Tuam

K.M.Davies

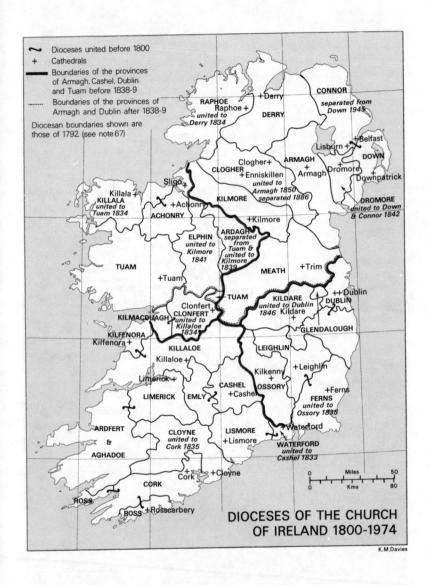

DIOCESES OF THE CHURCH
OF IRELAND 1800-1974

K.M.Davies

Legend:

~ Dioceses united before 1800
+ Cathedrals
— Boundaries of the provinces of Armagh, Cashel, Dublin and Tuam before 1838-9
...... Boundaries of the provinces of Armagh and Dublin after 1838-9

Diocesan boundaries shown are those of 1792 (see note 67)

Map labels:

RAPHOE Raphoe + united to Derry 1834
+Derry
DERRY
CONNOR separated from Down 1945
Clogher+ CLOGHER
+Enniskillen united to Armagh 1850 separated 1886
ARMAGH +Armagh
Lisburn + +Belfast
DOWN
Dromore+ Downpatrick
DROMORE united to Down & Connor 1842
Sligo+
Killala + KILLALA united to Tuam 1834
+Achonry ACHONRY
KILMORE
+Kilmore
ELPHIN united to Kilmore 1841
ARDAGH separated from Tuam & united to Kilmore 1839
TUAM
+Tuam
MEATH
+Trim
++Dublin DUBLIN
TUAM
Clonfert+ CLONFERT united to Killaloe 1834
KILMACDUAGH
KILDARE united to Dublin 1846 Kildare
GLENDALOUGH
KILFENORA
Kilfenora +
KILLALOE
Killaloe+
LEIGHLIN
+Leighlin
Kilkenny + OSSORY
+Ferns FERNS united to Ossory 1835
Limerick +
LIMERICK EMLY
CASHEL +Cashel
+Waterford
ARDFERT & AGHADOE
CLOYNE united to Cork 1835
LISMORE +Lismore
WATERFORD united to Cashel 1833
+Cork +Cloyne
CORK
ROSS +Rosscarbery

Miles 0 50
Kms 0 80

Derry
LONDONDERRY
ANTRIM
Ballymena
Lifford
DONEGAL
TYRONE
Omagh
Belfast
ULSTER
FERMANAGH
Enniskillen
Armagh
Downpatrick
Sligo
LEITRIM
Monaghan
MONAGHAN
ARMAGH
DOWN
SLIGO
Cavan
CAVAN
LOUTH
MAYO
Carrick
on Shannon
Dundalk
Castlebar
ROSCOMMON
Longford
LONGFORD
Navan
Roscommon
MEATH
CONNACHT
Mullingar
GALWAY
WESTMEATH
Galway
LEINSTER
DUBLIN
Dublin
OFFALY
(KING'S
COUNTY)
Tullamore
Naas
KILDARE
Port Laoise
CLARE
Nenagh
LAOIS
(QUEEN'S COUNTY)
WICKLOW
Wicklow
Ennis
TIPPERARY
(NORTH RIDING)
Carlow
CARLOW
Limerick
Kilkenny
LIMERICK
TIPPERARY
(SOUTH RIDING)
KILKENNY
WEXFORD
Tralee
Clonmel
MUNSTER
Wexford
KERRY
Waterford
WATERFORD
CORK
Dungarvan
Cork

Miles   50
Kms   80

PROVINCES, COUNTIES AND COUNTY TOWNS 1976

K.M. Davies

INTRODUCTION

The aim of this essay is to tell the story of the Roman Catholic community in north-east Ulster from the final defeat of the Ulster Irish chieftains O'Neill and O'Donnell in 1603, at the hands of the English, to the remarkable electoral success of Sinn Fein, the political wing of the IRA, in the Westminster elections of 1983. By that time Sinn Fein had captured 100,000 votes from the catholic-nationalist population and looked as if it might become the biggest single catholic party in the State.

Among the characteristics of northern Ireland catholics one might list a sense of inferiority, alienation from the state, and a conservatism in religious belief and practice. But these features are not the result of partition. The seeds of northern catholic discontent, its unease with itself and the tenacity of its attachment to catholicism were sown in the Ulster Plantation of the early seventeenth century. To understand the Ulster catholic community it is necessary to appreciate that it sees itself as a community under siege—a mentality which, ironically, it shares with the protestant-unionist population of the six north-eastern counties of Ireland. For the catholic community this mentality is the product of the success of the plantation and the attempt to displace catholicism and the catholic population with English and Scots protestants. Bereft of political power and economic security, and with a gradual erosion of the cultural *mores* dependent on these factors, the community had only catholicism left to preserve its identity. This is not to suggest that the practice of the faith was always of a high order or that the content of religious belief was recognisably that of post-Tridentine catholicism. Nonetheless an attachment to the idea of catholicism and the recognition of a sense of belonging to a wider religious community gave a cohesion to Ulster catholics which, arguably, they have never lost.

That cohesion did not arise merely from the internal dynamics of the community which increasingly identified itself over against a protestantism which was manifestly a 'foreign creed'. The chief difficulty which catholics faced was the pervasiveness of protestantism in Ulster as a whole. Within some thirty years of the Plantation, Ulster catholics had developed a lingering hostility to Reformation christianity which less protestantised areas of Ireland to some extent managed to escape. The bloody Ulster uprising of 1641, for example, represented not only a desire for revenge over the question of land and displacement but also a spontaneous outpouring of hatred against protestantism and all it stood for. This element however was not to prove an enduring

1

feature of Ulster catholic attitudes to its reformed neighbours, and by the nineteenth century many leading Ulster churchmen were personally well disposed to protestants and championed government initiatives in education which sought in effect to lessen sectarian animosities. The relationship between the catholic community and the protestant Churches in Ulster is not a story of unmitigated hostility. This is also clearly seen in the nineteenth century when northern catholicism was dependent on the benefactions of indulgent protestants for the growth of its infrastructure. Nor should one disregard individual friendly relationships which form as much a part of the general tone of inter-community contact as does internecine hostility.

This is not to attempt to undermine the fact that the community's dealings with protestants remained a crucial element in Ulster catholicism's defining characteristics. On the other hand, the antipathy to the reformed religion was as much a reaction to protestant political power and dominance as it was a rejection of a theological system which sat uneasily within a Gaelic outlook and mode of life. One underlying trait of Ulster catholicism's self-understanding is that it has its own version of the Calvinist doctrine of the elect. It is important however to be aware that, unlike certain strands of Northern Ireland calvinism, Northern Ireland catholics do not regard the religion of their political opponents as essentially evil, or its practices as blasphemous. Nonetheless catholics in Ulster have, in the absence of political or economic prosperity, historically placed their hope in a sort of 'eschatological vindication', believing that their reward for the suffering endured at the hands of protestants would be a blissful union with God in heaven. The community saw itself, too often perhaps, as an island of catholic piety in a harsh sea of protestant heresy. To some extent their clergy encouraged Ulster catholics in this attitude.

A note of caution should be sounded when using the term 'Ulster catholicism'. It would be too easy to assume that there is historically a single unified body which had a central identity, purpose and will. Clearly one must be sensitive to divisions of ideas and opinions within any given group, and this is especially true of Ulster catholicism as becomes apparent if one compares the Ulster catholic experience in the seventeenth century with the community's vicissitudes in the nineteenth century. It is most marked in the divergent social and political ambitions of the ecclesiastical hierarchy as opposed to the middle-class laity. Church leaders on the whole were primarily concerned for order and stability within the state, irrespective of government policy or political arrangements, provided certain minimum freedoms for catholicism were guaranteed.

This raises the serious difficulty of the role and influence of the clergy in the community, and the leadership given to the community by the bishops. There are three aspects to be looked at here. First, one could suggest that with the collapse of the Confederation of Kilkenny in 1650, in the closing stages of which two of the Ulster bishops played a prominent military role, the bishops were effectively depoliticised and tended to seek only religious as opposed to political freedoms. Such a policy had surprising and even incongruous results. The seventeenth-century archbishop of Armagh, Oliver Plunkett, was a model post-Tridentine prelate whose apostolate in south Armagh and mid-Ulster was distinctly apolitical. Yet he was put to death for treason at Tyburn in 1681, one of the last victims of the Titus Oates plot. On the whole the bishops distrusted radical political movements, since they could not control them, and preferred to concentrate on pastoral activity. But the dependence of bishops on the patronage of the house of Stuart up to the death of the Old Prentender served to ensure that, well into the eighteenth century, they were never regarded as purely religious leaders. It is also true that some individuals showed a devotion to the Stuart cause which could not but jeopardise their pastoral ministry. Equally it was the Ulstermen who first realised the uselessness of hoping for a Stuart restoration and sought to proclaim their loyalty to the Hanoverian regime.

Secondly, while as a caricature this might be true of the generality of bishops, the same cannot be said of the of the lower clergy. Certainly by the nineteenth century some at least of the Ulster clergy were celebrated political agitators, a charism they shared with their anglican and presbyterian colleagues. Their actions not only occasioned tensions between themselves and the bishops but also met with disfavour from Rome.

Finally Ulster catholicism has long been marked by internal division in the struggle between clergy and laity over the question of who had the right to speak for the catholic population. In the 1640s the Ulstermen sided with the clergy in arguing for a full restoration of catholicism in Ireland, and acknowledged the clergy's right to have a specifically political role in the state. In so far as there was a political agenda in the eighteenth century, this was dominated by the bishops and priests given the social disadvantages under which the community existed. The nineteenth century and most of the twentieth tell a similar story, but clerical dictation in political life had begun to break down in the late nineteenth century, and in some catholic political circles in the north there were signs of anti-clericalism. One of the effects of partition was again to restore the clergy to positions of political dominance which was finally broken by the emergence of the Social Democratic and Labour Party in 1970, determined as it was not to be susceptible to clerical influence. More menacingly from the church's perspective was the rise of Sinn Fein with an agenda for a secularised and socialist Ireland. The inability of the Church to control the politics of the community from the onset of the troubles at the end of the 1960s was abundantly illustrated at the time of the IRA hunger strikes in 1981, when even the intervention of pope John Paul II could not prevent ten members of the Provisional IRA and the INLA from starving themselves to death. That event generated enormous support for the IRA in the catholic community, exactly the contingency the hierarchy wanted to avoid. That was but one round in a long fight by politicians to wrest control of the community from the clergy. The clergy have therefore been forced to reassess their own role in the community, and there are signs that a depoliticised mode of operation is not entirely to their liking.

The longest section of this work is that dealing with the twentieth century, and the concentration needs some justification. The church resisted for as long as possible the idea of partition, fearing as it did the dominance of a protestant ethos in the north-east. The separation from their fellow-catholics in the rest of the island by virtual imprisonment within the borders of the new Northern Ireland state was acutely felt by nationalists in counties Fermanagh and Tyrone and in Derry city, where nationalists had a small majority over the protestant-unionists. However the relative numerical superiority of the nationalists did provide some consolation for the community in those areas. The catholics in Antrim and Down, and especially in Belfast had no such comfort and found themselves under constant physical and psychological threat in the new 'protestant state'. The latest 'troubles' are, as much as anything else, a product of the isolated frustration that the border brought about. Since they were cut off from the catholic-nationalist majority in the rest of Ireland, oppressed by the protestant-unionist majority in the 'new' Ulster through political gerrymandering and social and economic discrimination, and ignored by the Westminster government, it seemed that violence was the only means open to the community to realise their political aspirations. The events of the war years, 1939–45, and the IRA campaign of the late 1950s were forebodings of the greater traumas to come. The Church, not unusually, was completely unprepared for the civil rights movement and the subsequent violence.

The border intensified the Ulster catholics' penchant for introspection and self reliance, attributes which have long been one of their particular distinguishing marks. The community has come to look warily on all outsiders—even fellow-catholics. However this is no new phenomenon and is an attitude of mind which was marked even in O'Neill and O'Donnell. The Ulster community is convinced that no one really understands it and that only those born in the situation can come to terms with its complexities. The distrust of the outsider and the social difficulties which catholics faced were matched only by their propensities for self-destruction. It is one of the paradoxes of the history of Ulster catholicism that a strong sense of unity around the identity of faith has co-existed so readily with internal dissension.

1

ULSTER IN THE SEVENTEENTH CENTURY

Submission and flight

The surrender of Hugh O'Neill to the lord deputy Mountjoy in the grounds of the suppressed Cistercian monastery of Mellifont, Co. Louth, on 30 March 1603 did not of itself mark the passing of the remnants of Gaelic Ulster, with its celtic customs and catholic religion. O'Neill had not only styled himself as the 'lieutenant of the Church and of the Catholic faith'[1] but had secured from Pope Clement VIII in April 1600 a Bull of indulgence which gave all who fought with him the same spiritual privileges as the crusaders against the godless Turk.[2] Yet O'Neill for all his brash display of fidelity to the old faith was first and foremost a politician concerned as much for the promotion and status of his own family as for the progress of religion. This might seem a harsh judgement, but it is one that was shared by at least some of his contempories. When the final ignominy came there was not one catholic member of the Irish House of Commons who defended this champion of catholic belief against the bill of attainder in 1613.[3]

In the aftermath of the defeat O'Neill and Rory O'Donnell, his companion in arms, were both presented at Wantage to king

---

[1] This at least is what the papal commissary in Flanders, Innocenzo Malvasia, wrote to Cardinal Aldobrandini on 25 July 1595. Cf. 'Catalogue of material of Irish interest' in the Collection *Nunziatura di Fiandra*, Vatican Archives: part 1, vols. 1-50, in *Collectanea Hibernica*, vol. 1 (1958), p. 49.

[2] '. . . to all of you who follow and the said Hugh and the Catholic army, if you truly repent and confess, and if possible receive the holy communion, plenary pardon, and remission of all sins, as usually granted to those setting out to the war against the Turks, for the recovery of the Holy Land' is granted. Cf. Calendar of Carew MSS., 1589-1600, p. 523. In the following year O'Neill found it necessary to write again asking not only for the Pope's continued prayers for the success of the war against Elizabeth but also for the same powers of ecclesiastical patronage as his ancestors had enjoyed. He further pleaded with Clement to excommunicate those who took up arms against him, and who refused to assist him.

[3] It must be noted however that in that parliament the catholic representation from Ulster was precisely one out of sixty-four. This was to increase only slightly in 1634 to three out of sixty-six, and in 1640 to four. At the beginning of the period catholics outnumbered protestants in the country by about forty to one.

James VI and I who conferred on them the earldoms of Tyrone and Tyrconnell respectively. As a further mark of esteem he appointed O'Neill lord lieutenant of Tyrone with a yearly emolument of £600. Tyrone, by the terms of his surrender, was given unprecedented powers in Ulster amounting virtually to the status of a palatine-prince.[4] James's obvious benevolence and the fact that he was the son of Mary Queen of Scots led many in Ireland to suppose that he would be favourably disposed to catholicism. This 'feel good factor' was further strengthened with the passing of the Act of Oblivion in the spring of 1603, which enabled Irish rebels to have their past offences against the crown blotted out. They were also allowed to recover their lands provided they swore an oath of allegiance to the king and his successors. Francis Bacon, the English lord chancellor, was known to favour a religious settlement along the lines of that reached in France with the edict of Nantes. The king himself asserted that as for the catholics he would not 'persecute any that will be quiet and give but an outward obedience to the law, neither will I spare to advance any of them that will by good service worthily deserve it.'[5] The difficulty was that catholic church law would not permit attendance at divine service in the established church not even for the sake of 'outward obedience'. Such practice was specifically forbidden by pope Paul V in a brief issued on 22 September 1606.

Mountjoy as the king's representative in Ireland was prepared to operate a policy of tolerance so long as that was in accord with the political disposition of the king. The Irish Privy Council as a whole however sought the king's permission in July 1605 to pursue a stronger policy against catholicism. This and pressure on the king in England caused him to issue his 'proclamation' against religious toleration. In this James declared that he would never 'do any act that may confirm the hopes of any creature, that they shall have from him any toleration to exercise any religion than that which is agreeable to God's word, and is established by the law of the Realm'.[6]

Of the proclamation itself there was little direct impact in Ulster, and even at the time it was seen as being aimed against the Dublin recusants. It did however pinpoint the crux of the matter. Catholicism was for the reformed an iniquitous, sinful and blasphemous system with which there could be no compromise. Catholics of course took much the same attitude towards the state church, at least where theology was concerned. In Ireland, as in the rest of Europe in the

---

[4] R.F. Foster, *Modern Ireland 1600–1972* (London, 1988), p. 43.

[5] Quoted in R. Dudley Edwards, 'The Penal laws in Ireland 1534–1691', unpurbe, Ph.D. thesis, University of London, 1933, p. 438.

[6] *Calendar of State Papers Ireland* (hereafter *Cal.S.P.Ire.*), 1603–25, pp. 301 ff. In addition all catholic priests were to depart from the Kingdom by 10 December of that year.

seventeenth century, it was difficult to separate politics and religion into discrete blocks. The real problem however concerned the issue of catholic loyalty to the state. After all, the Ulster rebels had enlisted the help of catholic Spain in their rebellion against Elizabeth. What was to prevent them from doing so again? Furthermore had not the pope relieved catholics of their obligations of obedience to the English monarch in the excommunication of Elizabeth?

On the other hand it is clear that Peter Lombard, the absentee archbishop of Armagh (1601–25), had persuaded the authorities in Rome that they might adopt a different policy towards James from one of outright hostility. He himself wrote to the king in 1608 urging him to restore 'true religion'. In addition he complained that the condition of catholics had actually become worse since James's succession. He told the king that he had written a book which he hoped would convince James of the truth of catholicism and had dedicated it to him.[7] Such sentiments did not find a ready acceptance with James, who not only personally disliked Lombard but actually railed against him in parliament. Nonetheless the primate of Armagh managed to convince Rome that for the present the best course for catholic Ireland lay with acceptance of James as the lawful sovereign, in the hope that the church would not be persecuted. By 1607 the government in London felt sufficiently secure to instruct the Dublin administration to moderate the policy of strict uniformity.

By then political factors had dictated the course of the administration's outlook on Ulster. So long as the old chieftains, for all their conformity with English titles and ways, retained power and influence over the native Old Irish they remained a potential danger to the good government of the country. While it is not possible to discern any systemic strategy to displace them, nonetheless government and family dynamics in the months before September 1606 served to undermine Tyrconnell and Tyrone and made 'the flight of the earls' inevitable.

James's declaration against catholicism was promulgated in Tyrone's manor of Dungannon. Simultaneously there was a threat that the crown would reclaim old ecclesiastical properties for purposes of endowment connected with the appointment of George Montgomery as Church of Ireland bishop in three of the northern dioceses—Clogher, Derry and Raphoe.[8] In his somewhat autocratic

---

[7] The test of this letter is given in *Archivium Hibernicum*, vol. 3 (1914), pp. 273–84.

[8] The lord deputy wrote to the Earl of Salisbury in July 1606 pleading with him 'hasten [the bishop] to his charge' since 'the north hath great want of him'. *Cal. S. P. Ire.*, 1603–05, p. 510.

style Tyrone asserted what he took to be his rights as overlord over his son-in-law Donal O'Cahan in Co. Coleraine. O'Cahan objected that he had surrendered himself to Elizabeth and received his lands back from her hand, therefore Tyrone had no rights over him since his first loyalty lay with the crown. In fact Sir Arthur Chichester, the lord deputy in 1505–16, had encouraged the king to assert publicly that the Irish owed no obedience to local chiefs since they were the direct subjects of His Majesty. The Dublin government had also made it known that it favoured a president in Ulster who would exercise authority in the king's name. This further hightened the tensions not only between Tyrone and his son-in-law but also between himself and those Ulster chiefs such as Cahir O'Doherty and Niall Carbh O'Donnell, who had gone over to the English in 1602.

In traditional Gaelic style Tyrone mounted a cattle-raid on O'Cahan's land in October 1606. An appeal for justice was made directly to James and in the run-up to the case being heard Sir John Davies, the Irish attorney-general 1606–19, prepared the case against Tyrone. Tyrconnell too had his share of difficulties. He endured the rebellion of one of his lesser chiefs Sir Nial O'Donnell, a substantial landholder near Lifford, and the increasing attempts of the administration to destabilise his position in Ulster. Also he, but not O'Neill, was later to stress religious persecution as a factor in his decision to quit the country. The general air of insecurity then prevailing rather than a specific threat was perhaps the cause of Tyrconnell and Maguire, the Fermanagh chieftain, making preparations to flee.

It was the actions of Tyrconnell which also precipitated Tyrone's flight, since had he remained he would have clearly been under suspicion of plotting to overthrow the government. His brother-in-law Sir Patrick Barnell had already been arrested and committed to the Tower of London, although proceedings against him were subsequently dropped. In August Tyrone visited the house of his friend Sir Garrett More at Slane and there bid a solemn farewell to the whole household, which gave them all some cause for concern 'because in general it was not his manner to use such compliments'. On 5 September Tyrone, Tyrconnell and about 100 others boarded ship at Rathmullen and sailed into exile, reaching Normandy after twenty-one days at sea.

The government reacted immediately and assuming that the earls were guilty of treasonably plotting against the crown—since why else would they flee—confiscated their land. The subsequent bill of attainder, along with the judgements of the summer assizes of 1608, provided the legal basis for the confiscation. Almost immediately the government put into action plans for the plantation of those counties over which the earls had exercised control. The outline of the scheme had already been drawn up by Chichester in 1605–6. The decisive action of the administration in confiscating tracts of land beyond the immediate jurisdiction of the departed earls led to the rebellion in April 1608 of Sir Cahir O'Doherty, an otherwise loyal man and son-in-law to lord Gormanston, who ironically was one of the commissioners appointed to govern the former territory of the earls. Doherty was joined in the revolt by Neil O'Donnell, members of the O'Cahan family (Donal O'Cahan was already being held in Dublin under suspicion of treason) and the O'Hanlons.

On the very day the rebellion began, 18 April, the London government showed its appreciation for Sir Cahir, who had been proclaimed the 'Queen's O'Doherty' and knighted in 1602 at the age of sixteen, by restoring to him his ancestral patrimony in Inishowen. The rebel force, estimated at that stage to be no more than 100 strong, took Derry. They burnt some 2,000 'heretical books', which belonged to bishop Montgomery. The campaign took the rebels to Coleraine fort, Tyrone, Armagh, and then back to Donegal. O'Doherty was killed in battle near Kilmacrenan. The revolt was at an end, although seventy men were to be hanged for treason. This little local difficulty having been ironed out, the redistribution of land began in earnest.

The Plantation

The formal colonisation of Ulster under James chiefly concerned the counties of Armagh, Cavan, Coleraine (soon to be renamed Londonderry), Donegal, Fermanagh and Tyrone. Monaghan had been ceded to Elizabeth in 1591 by the MacMahons and was already parcelled out by this stage to trusted individuals. The division of Antrim and Down between various English and Scots settlers had been going on since a little after the turn of the century, furthered in part by the financial difficulties which many of the Old Irish were experiencing and which forced them to sell tracts of land to the Hamiltons, the Montgomerys, to Chichester himself, who had been governor of Carrickfergus before his promotion, and even (as with the MacQuillans) to their Scots catholic co-religionists the MacDonnells. In 1603 the king made further provision for Montgomery and Hamilton by dividing 60,000 acres in north Down between them and Con O'Neill of Clandeboye. The Scots influence in north-east Ulster had been prominent from time immemorial given the proximity of the Antrim and Down seabord to the Scottish islands and mainland.

The church 'as by law established' was to gain from the plantation, as was Trinity College Dublin, and Chichester was granted the land of the barony of Innishowen for his loyal service. Certain classes of 'deserving natives' were to be granted land, or allowed to retain an interest in their own lands. This was deliberate policy. It was decided by the Dublin government that 'the severity of the treatment of leading families must be offset by greater lenience towards others.'[9] Those native Irish chiefs excluded from the effects of plantation included Conor Roe Maguire in east Fermanagh, Sir Turlough McHenry O'Neill, and the heirs of the Tyrone and Armagh estates of Sir Henry Og O'Neill who gave his life fighting for James in the suppression of O'Doherty's rebellion.

For the rest, the land was to be divided between the remainder of the loyal natives, English and Scots 'undertakers' brought to Ulster for the purpose of receiving the land, and the 'servitors'—army officers who had served in the late wars. There were strict conditions for taking possession of the land:

'Everyone of the said Undertakers, before he be received as an Undertaker, shall take the Oath of Supremacy, either in the Chancery of England or Scotland . . . and shall also conform themselves in Religion according to his majesties laws. . . . the said undertakers, their heirs and assignies, shall not Alien or demise their portions or any part thereof to the mere [i.e. native] Irish or to such persons as will not take the said Oath of Supremacy . . .'[10]

This last was under pain of forfeiture. The servitors on the other hand were permitted to take native Irish tenants on the payment of a 50 per-cent surcharge. The natives were not obliged to take the oath of supremacy but they did have to 'use tillage and husbandry after the manner of the English Pale', and pay double the rent of protestant tenants.

The land was to be parcelled out into grants of 1,000, 1,500 and 2,000 acres. The actual division of the land when it finally came resembled nothing like the modesty that these holdings suggest. An annual rent of £5 6s 8d was payable on each 1,000 acres and there was a minimum residence requirement of five years. A number of the native Irish were removed from their land and the status of others was reduced to that of tenant at will, perhaps not so very different from what they enjoyed under the rule of the old Gaelic chieftains. In all there were perhaps 100 undertakers, less than half of them Scots, who enjoyed possession of a quarter of all the land available. For their part the servitors, who numbered about fifty, were given one-fifth of the land between them. As much again was exempt from plantation.

[9] Aidan Clarke with R.D. Edwards, 'Pacification, plantation and the catholic question, 1603-23' in T.W. Moody, F.X. Martin, and F.J. Byrne (eds), *A New History of Ireland*, vol. 3 (Oxford, 1976 and 1978), p. 201.

[10] *Conditions to be Observed by the British Undertakers of the Escheated Lands in Ulster* (London, 1610).

Because of what was taken to be its strategic importance, the county that became known as Londonderry was marked out for special treatment. Twelve London companies were to have the exclusive land rights to the new county which consisted of the old Co. Coleraine, the barony of Loughlinsholin except for its south-west corner, Derry and its north-west liberties, and Coleraine town with its north-east liberties. The total land involved was probably more than 400,000 acres. Ecclesiastical property was exempt from this settlement, as was 4 per cent of the land which went to Sir Thomas Phillips, a servitor, and a further 10 per cent was reserved for the mere Irish.[11] In return the companies were not only to develop the land but were to rebuild the garrison towns of Coleraine and Derry. Except for the land allotted to them in that county, catholics were excluded from being tenants.

To say that the plantation was a success is perhaps to state the obvious or rather to understate it. By 1630 there were 14,500 adult male settlers, not to mention women and children, in the escheated counties. Equally one should not underestimate the difficulties they faced, not least that of making a profit from the lands which they held under stringent terms from the crown. One of their difficulties was the disgruntlement and resentment of the native Old Irish. As early as September 1610, Chichester was writing to Salisbury that 'the natives of these counties . . . are generally discontented, and repine greatly at their fortunes, and the small quantity of land left to them upon the division.' Toby Caulfield had already reported to Chichester in June of that year of the Ulster native population that 'there is not a more discontented people in Christendom.' The previous year Chichester had tried to cope with some of the disagreeable Ulstermen by arranging for them to be shipped overseas as mercenaries to fight in the Swedish wars. At one point he claimed that as many as 6,000 had thus left the Province. This was despite the opposition of the Ulster priests who said that the whole enterprise was a pretence, and that the English government had no intention of deporting them to Sweden but wanted to get every able-bodied swordsman out to sea where they intended to drown them. The clergy in the rest of the country advanced a theological argument against the arrangement, arguing that since the king of Sweden was a heretic, catholics could not lawfully fight for him.[12]

To cope with the difficulties of living among a discontented populace but more particularly to ensure the profitability of their

---

[11] Cf. Clarke and Edwards, 'Pacification, plantation and the catholic question', p. 199. The full story is vividly told by T.W. Moody in his *The Londonderry Plantation, 1609–41: The City of London and the Plantation of Ulster* (London, 1939).

[12] *Cal.S.P.Ire.*, 1608–10, p. 300.

holdings, some of the undertakers and, in their turn, the London companies began to let some of the land to catholic tenants. The precedent for this was probably set by the government which had already admitted some few individual catholic Scots among the planters.[13] Even so, this did not distort the general picture of hostility to catholicism, nor did it offset the native discontent which in time would give rise to open hostility and intrigues to change the politico-religious settlement of the country by force. The settlers in general were to prove their worth in their adherence to the reformed faith and the defence of the protestant crown and constitution in the periods of crisis in the seventeenth and eighteenth centuries. But what of the catholics?

The state of catholicism

Pope Paul V's *Clero nobilitati et Populo fidelis Regni Hiberniae*, possibly written in 1606, acknowledged the sufferings the Irish had undergone for the sake of catholicism. He urged them to persevere in their adherence to the Roman faith which they should do nothing to injure, and assured them of a 'heavenly crown' as the outcome of their life of devotion. In addressing catholic Ireland with such rhetorical vigour, Paul was perhaps unaware that he was addressing not one Church but two.

The catholicism of the Pale and of the major towns such as Galway differed in many ways from that practised in the rest of the country and especially in Gaelic Ulster. In Ulster catholicism had failed in its civilising influence, and christianity was but precariously integrated into a distinct Celtic understanding of life in both its spiritual and its material dimensions.

Ulster catholicism of the early seventeenth century had yet to succumb to many of the aspects of Tridentine reform. Not only was there a married clergy in some places, but the Celtic penchant for divorce was still much in evidence. As with Ireland generally, the parish was not yet the centre of religious life. In this respect Ulster was more reminiscent of medieval than modern catholicism. The family and clan provided the focus for religion and nurtured the spiritual development of its members often with the help of the regular clergy. The Franciscans, but also the Dominicans in Derry and counties Antrim and Down, played an especially important part in facilitating Gaelic Ireland's approach to catholicism and this is obviously the case in the North where the newer orders such as the Jesuits, Capuchins and the reformed Franciscans made little impact. The activity of

[13] *Cal.S.P.Ire.*, 1625–32, pp. 510–13.

the 'unreformed' Franciscans outside the country was also to have
a considerable bearing on Ulster's affairs. St Anthony's college at
Louvain, founded in 1607, was to become an important centre for
rallying the flagging morale of Ulstermen in continental exile. The
college was made up almost exclusively of Franciscans from the north
and there the exiles 'met with the stark doctrines of the Counter
Reformation, especially the idea that Ireland was being run by
heretics'.[14] It was from St Anthony's that pope Paul V selected three
priests to work in Scotland in 1618. The importance of this work was
again highlighted by Urban VIII in 1630. Urban, in appointing the
Franciscan Bonaventure Magennis as bishop of Down and Connor,
also gave him responsibilites for the Scottish missions. For their part
the diocesan priests were heavily dependent for support on the laity.
In practice this often meant their own families, which had the effect
of making them relatively independent of their bishops and of the
diocesan structure in so far as this existed at the time.

The 'rites of passage' were by far the most important occasions for
religious practice, and these served to strengthen both social and
familial bonds. At times this was literally the case since the Old Irish
were much given to marriage within the forbidden degrees of kinship.
The tradition of the wake at funerals was long to be a running sore
in the relationship between reformed and Celtic catholicism, and
funerals were also to give rise to much dispute between the secular and
regular clergy because of the Irish fondness for burial in monastic
sites.

Confession was probably not a frequent sacrament in seventeenth-
century Ireland, and in Ulster it was common to impose a money
penance on those making confession in preparation for the Easter
religious festival. John Bossy is therefore convinced that this sacrament was seen to be 'primarily a social act, mediating between overt
offences and overt acts of "satisfaction" and owing more to a compensation theory than to a recognized need for repentance'.[15]

The synod of Drogheda of February 1614 claimed that the decrees
of the Council of Trent (1545–63) had been received and promulgated
in Ireland at a meeting of the bishops of the Armagh Province held
for that purpose at Clogher in 1587. In issuing the 'Statutes of
Armagh' the Drogheda synod believed itself simply to be confirming
and furthering the process which Clogher had begun. The synod was
under the impression that if Ireland was to be saved for catholicism
it must conform itself to the reformed and updated Church of post-

---

[14] Raymond Gillespie, *'Conspiracy' Ulster Plots and Plotters in 1615*, p. 52.
[15] 'The Counter-Reformation and the people of Catholic Ireland, 1596-1641.' in
Historical Studies, VIII, p. 166.

Tridentine Europe. Michael Rothe, Lombard's vicar in Ireland, presided at the meeting which was attended by the vicars-general and vicars forane (equivalent to rural deans) of the Province as well as representatives of the Cistercians, Jesuits, and Franciscans 'of the strict observance'. The synod was important as much for its political agenda as for the hopes it treasured of Tridentine reform in the Armagh province. It upheld the teaching of the council of Toledo on treason against the state, since the catholic Church 'always abhorred treason and conspiracy.' It nonetheless affirmed that it was inadmissible for catholics to take either the oath of allegiance or the oath of supremacy. Priests were exhorted not to meddle in politics and to endeavour not to make themselves in any way obnoxious to the civil authorities, but to render 'unto Caesar the things that are Caesar's and unto God the things that are God's'.

The synod in its Tridentine enthusiasm sought to regulate every department of catholic life, from reminding priests that they must only hear the confessions of their own parishioners, to enjoining the faithful to observe the sabbath. It is also interesting that it goes to some lengths to warn the clergy off drink. The Armagh statutes are at pains to castigate the widespread custom of challenging others to feats of alcohol consumption. Ecclesiastics were expressly forbidden from accepting such challenges, under pain of suspension, still more for giving them, and lay people guilty of such 'crimes' were to be excluded from the sacraments until they had made confession to the ordinary of their diocese.

The synod's theological agenda was to assert, against the encroachment of state protestantism in Ireland, the strict teaching of Trent. It not only quotes extensively the Tridentine decree concerning the real presence of Christ in the eucharist but also forbids priests to keep company 'with heretics' except of course in trying to convert them. The Tridentine catechism is recommended for instruction, as is that of Peter Canisius. The statutes also lay down the number of holy-days to be observed as well as regulating days of fast and abstinence, of which there were a considerable number. Apart from warnings against superstitions connected with holy wells and trees, its most significant regulations concerned the administration of the sacrament of matrimony.

Clandestine marriages were forbidden, and the sacrament was to be preceded by confession for both parties. If for any reason the couple refused to comply with this request there was to be no mass at the wedding, or nuptial blessing. On the other hand the synod, recognising the peculiar state under which catholicism laboured in the country, did not enforce the full rigours of Trent's teaching on marriage. Any available priest could perform the ceremony since in the absence of one's parish priest 'frequent concubinage would . . . result'. In this regard it was also accepted that while not all the reforms could be observed, those that could be kept should be.

We have spent some time examining the statutes of Armagh since they give a fascinating insight into the religious conditions of Ulster and the rest of the Armagh province. But they are also important as they set the tone for the way in which the major ecclesiastics wanted catholicism to develop in the following decades. But it is also clear that there were great tensions within the Irish catholic community. These strains had immense effect on the religious and political situation in the years immediately following the Synod. The power blocks within the community came under very different influences. The Old English (i.e. the Anglo-Norman Irish) catholics, along with the Jesuits and the Capuchin Franciscans, looked to French and English catholics for support and guidance. The Old Irish and thus Ulster looked to the alliance with Spain in conjunction with the unreformed Franciscans and the Dominicans for a model of church and church-state relations.

Spain offered a view of a catholicism without compromise. It was after all the home of the Inquisition. France however was even then trying to come to terms with the religious pluralism in its midst.[16] Although their father general Vitelleschi had written to the Irish Jesuits 'Your Ulster is very dear to me', and by the 1640s they had actively tried to recruit more members from the north of the country,[17] the order was never to exercise much influence in Ulster. The same is true of the Capuchins. This left the field clear for the older orders. They too were trained in the new model continental seminaries and were determined to keep an unflinching face against the advance of heretical government in Ireland. This gave to Ulster catholicism not merely an ardent papal ethos but also a less bending political complexion. It is also true that the northern Franciscans looked more kindly on the Celtic traits endemic in northern catholicism than other orders.

The freedom to practise the faith varied greatly. In 1613 the inter-nuncio to Flanders sent Rome a very optimistic report on the state of religion in Ireland. He claimed that the penal laws were not being enforced and that nearly all the population were openly professing their religion. He also mentioned that there were 800 secular priests in the country, along with 130 Franciscans and twenty Jesuits with a

[16] Brendan Fitzpatrick, in his *Seventeenth Century Ireland: The War of Religions* (Dublin, 1988), is among many historians who attempt to analyse this phenomenon. However, later in the century, as the reforming clergy tried to impose Tridentine reform on the Irish Church more rigorously, a combination of theological and political factors would make the French approach more acceptable to Gaelic Ulster.

[17] Louis McRedmond, *To the Greater Glory: A history of the Irish Jesuits* (Dublin, 1991), p. 60.

few Dominicans and Benedictines. Eight years earlier Chichester, in reporting to London on the affairs of the north, said that he found in Armagh a number of priests 'holding their dignities and prebends by Bills from Rome'. The cathedral in the town was however 'much ruined and fallen into decay.' At the same time the lord deputy complained that there was not one of these priests willing to celebrate 'divine service and sacraments according to His Majesty's laws'.[18] The lords justices who governed Ireland in the years 1629–33 turned their attention at one point to the pilgrimage centre of St Patrick's Purgatory on Lough Derg, Co. Donegal. The site was held by James Magrath the son of the Church of Ireland archbishop of Cashel, and former catholic bishop of Clogher. The justices issued a proclamation binding the owner of the shrine under a penalty of £1,000 to

> . . . .pull down and utterly demolish that monastery of fame called St. Patrick's Purgatory, with St. Patrick's bed, and all the vaults, cells and all other houses and buildings, and to have all the other superstitious statues and materials cast into the Lough, and that he should suffer the superstitious chapel in the island to be pulled down to the ground, and no boat to be there, nor pilgrimage . . . during James Magrath's life willingly or wittingly.[19]

In 1613 a report was sent to the king of Spain telling him that fines were being imposed for non-attendance of the established Church. Catholic schoolmasters were forbidden and it was prohibited to send children abroad for education. In other words the penal laws were being applied.[20] The correspondent gives the intelligence that the penalty for hearing mass was 200 crowns on a first offence rising to 800 for a third offence and life imprisonment. He added that the imprisonment might be escaped by bribery but there was no chance of escaping the fines. At the other end of the scale, as it were, failure to attend the protestant services commanded a one shilling fine. As R. Dudley Edwards remarks, this was at a time when the wages for a labouring man might not exceed five shillings a week.[21]

---

[18] *Cal.S.P.Ire.*, 1601–3, p. 322. Whatever the religious outlook, the social conditions of the Province were very grim. In the same report Chichester spoke of the 'great wastes and desolation' he had observed giving it of course a theological dimension since in his view the bleakness was 'God's just judgement upon this people for their stubbornness and rebellion'.

[19] Ramsey Colles, *The History of Ulster from the earliest times to the present Day*, 4 vols (London), 1919–20); here vol. 2, p. 239.

[20] This document is given in full in *Archivium Hibernicum*, vol. 6, (1917), pp. 48–54.

[21] Edwards, *The Penal Laws in Ireland*, p. 503, note 1. Edwards fails however to mention that the cost of administering the fine had also to be borne by the offender. This could be as much as ten shillings. He observes however that 'One of the complaints at a later date against the recusancy fines was that poor people were thereby reduced to beggary' (*ibid.*).

By 1614 Chichester had received orders from London to proceed against the recusants throughout the country with all possible severity. The full force of the law had already been meted out to several individuals since the beginning of the century. In 1604 Redmond O'Gallagher, the bishop of Derry and vice-primate, had been put to death by a troop of cavalry. The guardian of the Franciscan convent in Donegal, Nigel O'Boyle, suffered the supreme penalty for his faith in 1607. The following year saw the ninety-year-old Dominican prior Donatus Oluin hung drawn and quartered in the market-place in Derry along with several secular priests and his brother William, also a Dominican. From that period the most celebrated execution was that of the eighty-year-old bishop of Down and Connor, Cornelius O'Devany, OSF.

The privy council in London had in 1611 sent instruction to Dublin that it would be expedient if a catholic bishop could be apprehended and punished as a deterrent to others. It was also emphasised that such action must stress not the religious but the political nature of the individual's crimes.[22] O'Devany and his chaplain, a fellow-Franciscan Patrick Loughlain, were seized on an island in Lough Neagh in the same year and brought to Dublin to stand trial for treason. O'Devany had been a close associate of O'Neill and it was suggested that he had counselled O'Neill's flight. He was further accused of having assisted the rebellion by administering the sacrament to O'Neill's troops. While the bishop did not deny his association with the great earl, his defence was that the liaison was not treasonable. He also appealed to the Act of Oblivion. These defences were rejected and even though the one catholic member of the jury found him not guilty the decision of the majority was accepted and he was sentenced to death along with his chaplain. On the scaffold the bishop made clear that he was being executed for his faith and not a political offence, since the government had offered to spare his life if he conformed to the state Church and took the oath of supremacy. From the time of his death in April 1612, he was venerated as a martyr and there were reports of miraculous occurrences even at the scaffold.

Peter Lombard used O'Devany's death to underline his moderate policy of living in the world of *realpolitik* in relation to Rome's overall dealings with London and Dublin. He argued that only bishops acceptable to the government ought to be appointed. He wanted O'Neill deprived of his powers of episcopal nomination, emphasising that individuals recommended by him would simply antagonise the English government. Whatever the transcendental benefits of O'Devany's death may have been, the immediate effect

[22] *Cal.S.P.Ire.* 1611–14, p. 97.

was to create a vacuum in the episcopal leadership of the Church in Ulster. Although the Holy See moved quickly to appoint Patrick Hanratty as vicar apostolic in Down and Connor, through Peter Lombard's influence, in 1614 four years later there was not a resident bishop in the country. By 1625 the situation had improved very slightly in the other provinces but Ulster was still without a bishop, although John O'Cullenan had been appointed vicar apostolic of Raphoe in 1621.[23]

The earls of Tyrone and Tyrconnell, fearing for the state of religion in the province, petitioned Urban VIII to appoint three bishops in 1625. The death of Peter Lombard in Rome that year enabled Tyrone to have his nominee Fr Hugh MacCaghwell, a Franciscan from Co. Down, made archbishop of Armagh. He was consecrated in April 1626 but died of fever in Rome in September when preparing to set out for Ireland. Tyrone and Tyrconnell again wrote to the pope in that year and argued that the Armagh vacancy must be filled by none other than an Ulsterman. In a letter they recommended Bonaventure Maguire, OSF, a near relative of O'Neill, for the job. Instead Urban translated the bishop of Kilmore, Hugh O'Reilly, to Armagh in August 1628. O'Reilly governed the Armagh Church till 1651 but within two years of his death episcopal leadership had reverted to the same level as in 1618, with only one resident bishop in the country.

Instability and intrigue

A basic premise of the government of Ireland in the early seventeenth century was that the influence of the catholic clergy was almost wholly traitorous. There were good grounds for the authorities to take such an attitude. It has been suggested that bishop Cullenan of Raphoe was active in a movement in 1625 to try to persuade Spain to invade Ireland. The Vatican itself was not averse to such a policy, indicating that it had forsaken Lombard's policies of conciliation. Catholic hostility to English government in Ireland crystallised around the lack of freedom to practice the Roman Catholic faith. Such resentment was fuelled by the penal laws, not always acted on, which from time to time inflicted serious hardship and even death on clergy and laity

[23] O'Cullenan was made bishop of Raphoe in 1629. He unsuccessfully petitioned the Holy See to be transferred to the Derry diocese in a letter of 5 September 1636. In that letter he describes the state of Raphoe as 'wretched' with only sixteen priests who were reduced to circumstance of indigence. The English and Scots protestants had 'driven out' the catholics and he claimed that there were hardly 700 individuals of 'any note' left in Donegal. The bishop was captured in 1643 and almost put to death. He was saved by Sir James Askin but later imprisoned and tortured, ending his days in exile. He died in Brussels on 24 March 1661.

alike. In Ulster the plantation, though ultimately successful in bringing the native population to heel, nonetheless failed in the main to
graft the essentially foreign shoot of the reformed faith on to the native
plant of catholicism. Indeed in Ulster Irish the word used for a protestant made all too clear the non-native character of the religion which
the English tried to force on the people, *albanach*. In the circumstances,
not surprisingly, the underlying antipathy to the outsiders, and their
religion, was prone to erupt into violence and bloodshed. Or perhaps
more accurately in the years before 1641 there was a growing desire
on the part of the Ulster Irish to reassert themselves in what over time
became the only way of achieving their purposes—war, an art more
talked about than practised in the decades following the collapse of the
Ulster armies in 1603. Some of the momentum for a radical approach
to the problems Ulster faced was provided by the clergy.

It is reported of the friar Tirlough McCrudden that he preached
rebellion to a crowd 1,000 strong on the last Sunday of May 1613.
The congregation had assembled in the open on the borders of
Fermanagh and Tyrone to attend mass. In urging his audience to
rebellion McCrudden told the people that he had a message from the
pope that they were to persevere in their religion and resist the
onslaught of anglicanism. The pope, be it said, did not urge rebellion;
this was doubtless McCrudden's preferred way of preserving
catholicism. He drew down the wrath of heaven on the 'English
service' which had replaced the mass saying that it 'proceeded from
the sediment of the devil'. The congregation was also informed that
Tyrone would return at the head of a Spanish army of 18,000, and
when the English had been driven from the land he would rule
Ireland. It is the peculiar mixture of religious sentiment and political
virulence, not uncommon in sixteenth- and seventeenth-century
religious strife, which makes such calls to arms so striking.[24]

This attempt to incite disloyalty and rebellion fell on deaf ears.
However, like other such incidents, it did help to keep flowing the
streams of rumour which fed the sea of discontent in catholic Ulster
in those decades. The plot to seize the garrison towns of Coleraine,
Carrickfergus and Derry in 1615 was on the face of it a more realistic
attempt by catholics to reclaim their ancestral heritage. Yet when the
lord deputy announced in the Irish parliament on April 18 that he had
indeed uncovered such a conspiracy his disclosure was treated with
a good deal of scepticism. The government was having difficulties
passing a money bill and it looked simply like a ploy to hasten

---

[24] A report of the sermon is given in Constantia Maxwell, *Irish History from Contemporary Sources* (London, 1923), pp. 150–1.

that procedure and suppress the assembly which was proving uniquely irritating to the Irish administration.[25]

The ringleaders of the plot were not native Ulster Irish but the catholic Scots Alexander MacDonnell, his brother Sorley and cousin Lundar. The main issue was one of personal grievance between Alexander and his uncle Sir Randal MacSorley MacDonnell who had been granted very large tracts of land in Co. Antrim. In time the conspiracy was to involve seventeen leaders in all, including Loughlin O'Laverty, Alexander's chaplain and the friar Edmund Mullarkey. Mullarkey, in trying to persuade Cormac Maguire to join the conspirators, assured him that his soul would be sure to go to heaven, and that anyone killed in the rising would have a place in eternity. The plot was joined by Rory Og O'Cahan, desperate to recapture his ancestral lands near Limavady from Sir Thomas Phillips. He had wild ideas of a general rising with help from Spain and the Hebrides. It was an ill-fated and hopeless affair, scarcely a real plot and more an impetuous outburst of envy brought on by too much drink. The irony of the whole business was that Alexander the chief culprit was acquitted, and was to become a baronet in 1627, while six of the seventeen, including the hapless chaplain and Fr Edmund, were sentenced to death. By the early twentieth century they were to be venerated as martyrs for the catholic faith and their cause for canonisation was introduced at Rome.

Concessions, toleration and plans for revolt

Apart from the determined efforts to rid the land of catholicism between Cromwell's arrival and 1660, Dudley Edwards was convinced that the seventeenth-century penal laws as a system operated only between 1603 and 1623.[26] By the 1620s there was something of a revival of the fortunes of Ulster catholics, linked in part to Randall McDonnell the earl of Antrim. He was accused in 1621 of harbouring priests and though arraigned for this crime he was acquitted thanks to the intervention of the king—thus serving to illustrate that the really powerful lords were immune to the full effects of penal legislation even in Ulster. Although James had given an order to the lord deputy in December 1623 to move against catholics, this was quickly retracted. However, when his son prince Charles failed to secure the hand of the daughter of the king of Spain, suspicions were once again

---

[25] The full story of the plot and the circumstance surrounding it is told by Raymond Gillespie in *Ulster plots and plotters in 1615*.

[26] Edwards, *The Penal Laws in Ireland*, p. iv. Except of course for attempts to drive the clergy from Ireland, which continued until the end of the century and into the next.

aroused and further measures were taken against catholics. All
bishops and seminary priests along with the Jesuits were ordered out
of the country by mid-March 1624.

Priests in the north tended to go about in disguise, carrying swords
and pretending to be soldiers. But by 1629 the ministrations of bishops
and priests were more public than ever before. The religious situation
in the Derry diocese was precarious but not desperate. Although he
was known to be favourably disposed to catholics, Richard Kirby held
the office of sheriff of Derry in 1630-7. In some parts of the county
it is true that the sacraments were celebrated 'in the woods or hills or
private houses', but the London companies had by 1631 built six
mass-houses on their estates. Taken as a whole catholics had a relative
degree of freedom on the Londonderry plantations. Clergy were in
some instances regarded as important and valuable members of the
community who helped to keep order among the catholic populace.
In return they received a certain amount of protection from the
vicissitudes of their own flock. It is recorded that the Sheriff of
Limavady heard cases brought by a catholic priest against members
of his congregation who had failed to pay their contribution to his
upkeep. The sheriff found for the priest.[27] In other parts of the province catholicism was openly practised. Downpatrick with its population of 8,000 was by 1630 almost wholly catholic. The sacramental
needs of the inhabitants were met by secular and regular clergy alike.

The mere presence of the catholic clergy and their exercise of the
ministry, however trying the circumstances, did not always succeed
in turning back the tide of protestantism or prevent its encroachments
on their flock. Carrickfergus was an especially fruitful field for the
harvest of protestant divines, and the people of that town took to the
reformed religion with great aplomb. Sir John Davies pointed to
the reformation's success in Carrickfergus as a paradigm of what
could be achieved with a strict adherence to the penal code.[28] Derry
also saw a number of priests and laypeople conforming to the new
religion thanks in part to the sustained efforts at proselytising by
bishop Hugh Montgomery. When it became clear that such efforts
would not ultimately succeed, the established church in Ulster would
in time develop a theology of the 'elect' under influence from Scottish
Calvinism which would absolve it from the need to see itself as an
evangelising instrument for the conversion of catholics. The elect
alone would be saved while the rest, those who refused to have the

[27] W.P. Burke, 'The Diocese of Derry in 1631', *Archivium Hibernicum*, vol. 5 (1916),
p. 5.
[28] The fact that Carrickfergus was a garrison town meant that it was easier to propagate the reformation than in other areas which lacked the strong arm of the state to
ensure conformity.

gospel preached to them, were lost, so that the community would hence forth concentrate its efforts on the improvement of its own lot in this world having been assured of salvation in the next. However the wish to convert the natives was never wholly surrendered but here the protestants vacillated in their desires and motives.

Despite the fragility of its position and the fact that catholics had to pay stipends to protestant clergy to have their own sacraments administered, the catholics still found plenty to argue about among themselves. One particular grievance between the regular and secular clergy concerned the burial of the dead. Irish tradition dictated that interments should take place on monastic sites. The problem arose as to who should perform the ceremony. Since officiating at burials was a source of income, the secular clergy naturally wanted to perform such services and attract the revenue that would accrue. The same held good for the friars and monks. Eventually Rome gave judgement for the secular clergy in 1626 but this hardly settled the matter and the dispute was to drag on till the end of the century and into the next.

Concession to catholics was to be the order of the day from the accession of Charles I in 1625. His marriage to Henriette Marie of France made him more favourably disposed to catholics than his father. More important, he was at war with Spain and needed security in Ireland, especially because Spain might invade that country as a means of weakening his position. He was also virtually penniless. From this confused amalgam of circumstances there arose the granting of 'the Graces' in 1626. In return for an increase in the standing army in Ireland to be paid for by a voluntary subsidy raised by the Irish, the recusancy fines were dropped. Soon after Charles's ascent of the throne pope Urban VIII issued a Bull urging catholics to lay down their lives rather that take the oath of supremacy. It was agreed therefore that catholics could take an oath of allegiance rather than that of supremacy. This would enable them to hold certain offices.

In the immediate aftermath of the proposal to grant these concessions the bishops of the Church of Ireland led the opposition of what appeared to them at times, to be something near to a restoration of popery. Archbishop Ussher of Armagh and the other protestant bishops issued a statement on 20 November in which they did not mince their words. 'The religion of the papists', they declared, 'is superstitious and idolatrous, their faith erroneous and heretical, their church, in respect of both, apostatical. To give them therefore a toleration, or to consent that they may freely exercise and profess their faith and doctrine is a grievous sin.'[29] The following April the bishop of Derry again attacked any notion of concessions in a sermon at

[29] Lawrence F. Ranehan, *Collections on Irish Church History* (Dublin, 1861), p. 35.

Christ Church Dublin. He saved his greatest vituperation for the idea of suspending the recusancy fines and suddenly 'the whole Church almost shaked with the great sound their loud Amens made.'[30]

By 1628 Charles was again prepared to entertain the possibilities of concessions. An agreement was entered into whereby in return for a grant of £40,000 a year for three years the king granted fifty-one concessions. Among these, once again, the oath of supremacy was replaced for catholics by an oath of allegiance. Proceedings against catholics in the case of the illegal celebration of the sacraments was to be undertaken by officials of the state rather than the established Church, and the Ulster planters were to be indemnified for having failed to keep the terms of the plantation by allowing catholics as tenants on planted land.

Various events conspired to reduce the effectiveness of these concessions and raised rather than reduced tension. Abroad the most important was the 'Peace of Suza' negotiated with cardinal Richelieu in May 1629. It was agreed that if England withdrew its support from the protestants of La Rochelle, France would no longer dabble in the affairs of catholics in Ireland and England. Sir Francis Annesley complained in 1628 and 1629 that the concessions were having disastrous consequences in Ulster and causing great insecurity. The Undertakers were in his view so discouraged by the turn of events that 'they were leaving the new colonies and returning to England.'[31] On 21 March 1629 he had argued that it was necessary 'without entering upon an anti-catholic crusade, to execute moderately the laws in force for the maintenance of the king's supremacy in ecclesiastical causes, to use ecclesiastical censures and suppress by degrees all public mass-houses.'[32] Even under these conditions there was still a grudging tolerance of catholics. However the proclamation against the seminary priests and the religious orders was reissued on 1 April 1629 and by the time the subsidy agreed to with Charles was at an end, the protestants argued for the reimposition of recusancy fines. Their behaviour in this regard was really quite disgraceful, but owed little to religious ideology. Having no wish to pay for the army from their own resources they argued that the recusancy fines could be used for this purpose.

The situation as it developed in the 1630s would totally change the hopes and expectations of the whole of catholic Ireland. The impetus for this came from those Ulstermen willing to seize on the king's difficulties in the neighbouring kingdom. The main problem was within

[30] *Cal.S.P.Ire.*, 1625–32, pp. 239–40.
[31] *Cal.S.P.Ire.*, 1625–32, p. xxxviii.
[32] *Cal.S.P.Ire.*, 1625–32, p. 441.

the established Church itself and concerned events in Scotland and England, and then Ulster because of the predominance of Scottish influence. The refusal of the Scots to have bishops imposed upon them received puritan support in England. This produced a crisis for Charles who was determined to have a unified Church policy with a strict hierarchical structure and himself at the top as head and supreme governor. The Scots entered into a 'covenant' whereby they swore not to have prelacy forced upon them. The Ulster Scots joined in this movement as a protest against the establishment; of course the irony was that they themselves had benefited so handsomely from establishment. By the late 1630s they had most of the churches and tithes in the province in their possession.

To deal with this rapidly worsening situation in Ulster the lord lieutenant, Wentworth, imposed the 'oath of abjuration', or 'black oath' as it became known, in the summer of 1639. It was administered to all Ulster Scots over the age of sixteen and bound them to loyalty to the king and repudiation of the covenant. Many escaped to Scotland rather than take it. It was clear that the internal tensions within the state Church in Scotland and England would lead to war and the Ulster catholics prepared for this contingency, hoping that in demonstrating their loyalty to the king they would have their religion and land restored to them. By April 1639 the bishop of Down and Connor was writing to Rome to inform the pope of the cherished hope of northern catholics that they might be enrolled in a royal army to fight against the Scottish puritans.[33] This dangerous policy which Charles pursued came to grief, but he was to have some relief temporarily when he agreed to the treaty of Berwick in June 1639. He was however determined in the long run to force his will on Scotland and if necessary to use as his instrument an Irish army. He sent for Wentworth in March and commissioned him to raise such a force. The Irish catholic army, of some 9,000 men, was stationed in the north. But under pressure from the English parliament it was disbanded in 1640 and Wentworth, by now the earl of Strafford, was executed having been arraigned by Parliament. The king's position even at that stage was such that he could do nothing to save his loyal servant. Nonetheless the general instability of the three kingdoms was to precipitate a general call to arms in Ulster by October 1641.

---

[33] P.F. Moran (ed.), *Spicilegium Ossoriense* (3 vols, Dublin, 1874–84), here vol. 1, p. 237. It seems that three Jesuits, Thomas Maher, Michael Chamberlain and Matthew Hartegan, had been assigned to act as chaplains in this force.

The rise and fall of the Ulster rebellion and the confederation

There was a general assumption that Charles had intended his Irish
army to bolster his flagging authority in Scotland and England.
Parliament however had compelled the king to abolish the force. But
Charles did not give up so easily. Although what happened next
cannot be proved beyond reasonable doubt, the strong suspicion is
that the king requested the earl of Antrim and the duke of Ormond
to reassemble the force and take Dublin castle. In the event this did
not prove possible but it did inspire others to take matters into their
own hands.

On the execution of Strafford the government of Ireland passed to
the lord justices Sir William Parsons, a puritan, and Sir Robert
Borlase. Parsons had resolved that within a year no catholic would be
left in the country. In January 1641 the English House of Commons
asked the king to enforce the penal code and Charles promised a proclamation against the catholic clergy. These proposed measures found
a ready audience in Ireland and the Privy Council in Dublin pressed
for tougher action against Irish catholics. A letter began to circulate
in the north stating that a Scottish covenanting army was preparing
to go to Ulster under the leadership of general Leslie 'to extirpate the
Roman Catholics of Ulster, and leave the Scots as the sole possessors
of that Province'.[34] This combination of circumstances helped bring
about the rising in Ulster in October 1641.

Sir Phelim O'Neill forged a document purporting to come from the
king 'under the Great Seal of Scotland' ordering the Irish to defend
themselves against the oppression they were to face. There was a
reluctance to do so but a local pogrom in the Island Magee area
of Co. Antrim tipped the balance in Sir Phelim's favour. The conspiracy to rebel had been months in the making. Conor Maguire Lord
Enniskillen, Rory O'More (in many ways the overall leader),
Turlough O'Neill, Philip O'Reilly and Hugh Og MacMahon were
among the representatives of the leading Ulster families who took part
in the preparations for the rising. Neil O'Neill, recently arrived from
Spain, met O'More in Ulster in April with a message from the earl
of Tyrone to say that cardinal Richelieu would offer support. On
Tyrone's death however the leadership passed to Owen Roe O'Neill
who likewise indicated his approval of the scheme.

On Friday 22 October the Ulstermen began their bloody work.
Very quickly fort Charlemont was taken, then Dungannon and
Mountjoy castle in Tyrone. The forts at Tandragee, Newry,
Castleblaney and Carrickmacross in Co. Monaghan quickly followed

---

[34] Thomas Carte, *Life of James, first Duke of Ormonde* (Oxford, 1851), vol. 1, p. 160.

in surrendering to the insurgents. There was less success in other areas. Rory Maguire failed to take Enniskillen, lord Chichester held Belfast and Lisburn, and Sir William Stewart and his brother Sir Robert prevented Derry from falling to the Ulster catholics. Sir Phelim proclaimed in Dungannon that it was not a rebellion against the king's authority but rather in defence of their own liberty and freedom for their religion. The earl of Antrim held aloof from the proceedings and was later to claim that the impulsiveness of O'More and his band brought the whole enterprise to ruin. 'The fools . . . well liking the business would not expect our time or manner for ordering the work, but fell upon it without us, and sooner, and otherwise than we should have done taking to themselves, and in their own way, the managing of the work, and so spoiled it.'[35]

There is some suggestion that Charles, if in fact he was behind the insurrection, desired an alliance between the Scottish presbyterians and the Ulster catholics as a means of threatening the English parliament. Such an unlikely combination was not altogether an impossibility. After all it was the equally unlikely marriage of Ulster protestant and Old English interests in the Irish parliament which had seen the downfall of Strafford in the summer of 1640. There is some indication that when the northern rising began the Ulster chiefs instructed their troops not to interfere with the Scots but to move against the English settlers.[36]

The extent of the violence is difficult to gauge accurately. There was not the wholesale slaughter so beloved of legend and sectarian mythology. But the human tragedy in terms of the numbers of dead and displaced should not therefore be underplayed. Such savagery as did occur, the massacre at Portadown being a case in point ('where Protestants in multitudes [were] forced over the bridge' into the river), resulted perhaps from a 'lack of discipline, . . . private vengeance . . . or religious fanaticism'.[37] It is estimated that between 4,000 and 12,000 perished in the uprising, including those put to death and those who died of hunger, disease and cold.

The accounts of the atrocities contained in the 'depositions' taken under oath from the survivors are chilling. Alice Gregg of Armagh testified that 300 protestants were stripped naked and put into the church at Loughgall. A number of these were murdered in the church including John Gregg who was 'quartered alive', and his remains

[35] Quoted in Sir Richard Cox, *History of Ireland* (London, 1689), part II, Appendix XLIX, p. 208.
[36] Thomas L. Connan, *The Irish Catholic Confederacy and the Puritan Revolution* (Dublin, 1954), p. 102.
[37] *A New History of Ireland*, vol 3, p. 291.

were then exhibited before his father Richard who himself was then put to death in front of his wife. The rest were released from the church to 'beg amongst the Irish' and many of these were also done to death. Another horrific tale records how in the parish of Kilmore, Co. Armagh, twenty-two protestants were herded into a thatched cottage which was then put to the torch. All inside were burnt to death.

The depositions also stress the religious motivation of the rebels. Matthew Browne from Monaghan testified that he heard Peter Bath say 'that they looked to have the king to put out the words "Defender of the faith"; for none was the supreme (head) of the Church, and Defender of the faith, but the Pope.'[38] Such an assertion of course had both religious and political overtones. More surprisingly a number of the respondents suggested that purely political considerations were uppermost in the minds of some of the insurgents. It was reported by a number of witnesses that the rebels were determined to have a king other than Charles. However they did not agree precisely on whose head the crown would rest. The candidates varied from the Earl of Tyrone to Phelim O'Neill and Rory Maguire. Such a possibility seems most unlikely. These suggestions may well be the result of a court plot to distance Charles from the rebels as a means of again trying to reassure the puritans that he was not in league with Irish catholics. Later in the decade this problem was again to raise its head with the publication in 1645 of *Disputatio Apologetica de Jure Regni Hiberniae* by the Jesuit Cornelius O'Mahony. Among other things the book tried to make out a case for an Irishman to be king in Ireland. This was taken as further evidence of treachery, a judgment which was not disabused by the observations of the papal nuncio archbishop Rinuccini that Owen Roe O'Neill was the only 'natural' and 'vernacular' Irishman fit to be king.

Another factor in the rising may have been resentment over further protestant annexation of catholic landholdings. By 1639 half the native freeholds on the Londonderry plantations were held by settlers in defiance of the arrangement made for the 'mere Irish'. Whatever its origin the rising of 1641, coupled with the English civil war, was to have profound significance not only for Ulster but for the whole country in the next decade.

The attitude of Irish catholics outside Ulster was at first hostile to the activities of the Ulstermen. The Old English of the Pale offered to assist the Irish administration in suppressing the rebellion. In

---

[38] *An Abstract of Cerain Depositions, By virtue of His Majesties Commission, taken upon Oath, Concerning the Traitorous intention of the Rebels in Ireland* . . . (London, 1642), p. 2.

dealing with them the Dublin government made an initial serious blunder. It had condemned the outbreak of violence in October as a 'most disloyal and detestable conspiracy intended by some evil-affect Irish papists'. On 29 October this was amended to read 'the Old mere Irish of the Province of Ulster'. But the government had too readily shown its hand. It was the policy of the lords justices to force all Irish catholics into the same camp, showing in effect that they were all disloyal, and thereby to identify catholicism as such as the enemy of stability and order, and so take the appropriate measures for its suppression. It was this failure of trust, the refusal by the government to allow the Old English to demonstrate their unquestioning allegiance to the English throne, which caused them to reassess their position. Having been assured that the Ulstermen were indeed taking the king's part against the puritans, the Old English found themselves drawn into the conflict on the side of Gaelic Ulster.

For its part the English parliament did not stand idly by and watch a rebellion in Ireland purportedly in defence of the king's prerogatives. The 'Act of Adventures' of February 1642 set about to raise £1,000,000 for an army to quell the Irish rebellion against parliamentary rule. In exchange for the monies the adventurers of capital would be indemnified with 2,500,000 acres of Irish land, to be confiscated when the war was at an end. The Act declared all Irish papists to be rebels.

In the following month the rebel forces were given an enormous boost to their morale and fortunes. A synod of the northern ecclesiastical province met on 22 March under the presidency of Hugh O'Reilly, the archbishop of Armagh, and declared the war to be just and undertaken for the defence of the catholic faith. The synod asserted that the war was waged against those who plotted 'the destruction of Catholics, the slavery of the Irish, and the abolition of the King's prerogatives.' A three-day fast was ordered throughout the Armagh Province at the end of which all were to confess their sins and receive communion so as to call down the assistance of divine Providence on the war.

Of a more practical nature all clerics above a given status were to contribute funds to the war effort. It was declared sinful to join in the campaign simply from motives of personal gain or private revenge. The synod proclaimed excommunicated all those who engaged in murder or plunder, or who illegally confiscated land and property. Churches which fell into rebel hands were exempt from this prohibition as the tenth decree of the synod makes plain. 'In churches where Mass was not hitherto celebrated, the parish priests are authorized to officiate with portable altars, as they have hitherto done on hills, in

woods, and in private houses, till the country shall enjoy peace.'[39]
Those who aided puritans 'or other enemies of King and country'
were similarly dealt with. Each regiment of the army was to have three
chaplains who were instructed to preach frequently. Most important
of all, the synod called for an assembly of laymen and clerics to rule
the country for the duration of the emergency. Thus was born the
'Confederation of Kilkenny'.

The groundwork for the proposed confederation was laid at a
special meeting of the representative laity and clergy of the whole
country held at Kilkenny on 10–13 May. Not only did this general
congregation reiterate much of the work of the synod of the Armagh
province but it made absolutely explicit that the war was for the
defence of the king's rule in Ireland. 'Whereas the war is undertaken
for the preservation of our sovereign King Charles, and his just rights
and prerogatives, for the defence of our most serene Queen and the
royal progeny, for the defence of the Catholic religion, the protection
of our lives and fortunes . . . and the liberty of this nation against
unjust oppressors and invaders, especially the puritans, we judge it
on the part of the Catholic side to be lawful . . .'[40] The original oath
of association was also drawn up at this time. Each individual was to
swear 'in the presence of God and of his angels and saints, to defend
the liberty of the Roman Catholic and Apostolical Church, the
person, heirs and rights of his majesty King Charles, and the freedom
and privileges of this kingdom against all usurpers and at the peril of
my life and fortune.'[41]

It was decided that the general assembly of the confederation should
meet in October. Meanwhile the war was to be prosecuted, and
events moved rapidly. Owen Roe O'Neill arrived in Ireland from
Flanders at the end of July to take charge of the Ulster army. There
was no overall commander of the confederation's forces owing to
personal differences between O'Neill and Thomas Preston, the latter
also a veteran of continental wars and the general of the Leinster
army.[42] The situation in Ulster was hampered by the fact that the

---

[39] J. O'Rourke, *The Battle of the Faith in Ireland* (Dublin, 1887), p. 162.

[40] Thomas Burke, *Hibernia Dominicana Sive Historia Provinciae Hiberniae Ordinis Praedicatorum* (1762), p. 648.

[41] John Lynch, *Cambrensis Eversus* (ed. with translation and notes by Matthew Kelly, Dublin, 1848–52), vol. I, pp. 14–5.

[42] Oddly enough there is some suggestion that the Spanish authorities actually tried to prevent O'Neill, Preston and another Irish commander, John Bourke, from leaving Flanders. At least this is what was reported to Rome by the nuncio, because 'more regard [was] had to the relations desired with England than to the interests of Christianity and the Catholic Faith.' Cf. G.D. Burtchaell and J.M. Rigg (eds), *Historic Manuscripts Commission, Report on Francisan Manuscripts* (Dublin, 1906), p. 124.

king's opponents held large stretches of land in Antrim, Down, Londonderry and Armagh. Their position was considerably strengthened by the arrival at Carrickfergus of general Munro in April at the head of a large army, which quickly recaptured several of the towns lost to the catholics the previous autumn and winter.

The position of the Ulster protestants was further reinforced later that year with the meeting at Carrickfergus of the synod of Ulster. This marked not only the effective foundation of the presbyterian Church in Ireland but gave a religious and ideological coherence to Ulster nonconformity which it has never lost. The will to fight all the manifestations of 'Popery' was further intensified in 1644 with the preaching in Ulster of the 'Solemn League and Covenant'. This had been contracted between the English parliament and the Scots in September 1643 and bound the covenanters 'to root out of the empire, all heretics and enemies of the true worship of God'. The covenant was quite clear about who these enemies were. Those who believed in 'the idolatrous sacrifice for the sins of the quick and the dead, blasphemous litanies, [and] justification by works'. Not unexpectedly the Pope was condemned as 'the Roman Antichrist' along with his 'five bastard sacraments, his devilish Mass, his blasphemous priesthood'.

Munro and his officers took the covenant in April 1644 despite the king having proclaimed it 'a traitorous and seditious combination against him and the established religion and laws of the kingdom'. The fervour of the 'Scots ministers' for the covenant knew no bounds. They preached that the covenant was as necessary to salvation as the sacrament of the Lord's Supper, and deprived of the sacrament those who would not swear it. Consequently soldiers and civilians alike took it 'as if it were the only means of preserving both their souls and bodies'.[43]

Long before events took such an intense theological turn the confederationists at Kilkenny had issued a statement reasserting their loyalty to Charles. They declared on 31 July 1642 that their only aim was to have 'the just freedom of subjects, independent of any jurisdiction not derived from your majesty'. 'His majesty's Roman Catholic subjects . . . now in arms' conveyed their hopes through the duke of Ormond, Charles's representative in Ireland. In October the general assembly convened at Kilkenny and appointed a supreme council of twenty-four, six representatives for each of the Provinces. To curb their political power the clergy were made to sit and vote with the 'lords temporal' and the elected representatives. The supreme council was to direct all operations of the confederation including the

---

[43] Carte, *Ormonde*, vol. 1, p. 490.

army engagements. Owen Roe, perhaps the best army strategist the confederation had, began to take a more independent military line after his defeat at the battle of Clones on 13 June 1643, which he had entered against his better judgment but at the behest of the Council.

Despite the grand alliance between the Old English and the Old Irish they had very different purposes in going to war. At most the catholics of the Pale sought security to practise their religion albeit in the comfort of their own homes. The Ulstermen, supported in this by the clergy, wanted nothing less than a full restoration of catholicism. Such a restoration would have implied a return of monastic lands to their historic owners, much to the disadvantage of many of the Old English who had profited from the spoliation of the monasteries in the sixteenth century. The authorities in Rome, surprising as it may seem, were not disposed to be sympathetic to the plight of the monks and friars. Cardinal Barberini writing to the papal nuncio to France, complained bitterly about the Irish clergy in this regard. He argued that instead of squabbling about the ownership of property they should be working to ensure the security of catholicism.[44] The religious dispositions of the Ulster leaders were doubtless shaped in part by the influence of continental counter-reformation catholicism. Yet it remains true that an unreformed Irish ecclesiastical system, based as it was on monastic rather than diocesan structures, suited their religious and social needs better than the episcopal and parish organisation favoured by the catholics of the Pale and the council of Trent. These differences in religious tastes were compounded by the fact that the Ulstermen were simply not trusted by their fellow-confederates. The Gaelic Irish soldiers were not given direct access to weapons or ammunition, a source of much resentment. The differences and hostilities between the two catholic groups would become more important as time wore on.

The war was waged against Puritans and Royalists alike. By the middle of January 1643 the king gave instructions to Ormond to meet representatives of the confederation, listen to their grievances and write to him about them. A meeting was arranged from Trim on 17

---

[44] Cf. *Archivium Hibernicum*, vol. 1 (1912), p. 115. He also suggested in the same letter that none of the O'Neills should claim lordship of Ireland as this would make matters difficult for the English king and queen. In another letter the following week, 12 June 1642, he complains in the most vociferous terms about Bonaventure Conny of St Isidore's College, Rome. Conny without consulting either the Pope or Barberini wrote to contacts in England that it was hoped in Rome to make one 'of the house of O'Neill prince of Ulster'. It was reported to Rome that the king had this letter published to demonstrate again not only the true nature of the Irish insurrection but to prove that he was not in league with Irish catholics. Such posturing on Charles's part was a necessary piece of insidious adroitness if he was to survive.

March, which Ormond did not attend. Among other things the insurgents demanded the abolition of discriminatory laws against catholics and a promise that acts of the English parliament should not apply in Ireland. This was followed in April by Charles's request to Ormond to sue for a one-year truce, but the terms of this were to be kept secret. The outcome was ultimately successful but was not reached till September. No concessions were given to the confederation except for the promise of safe conduct to England where their representatives could put their case in person to the king, in the hope of a settlement with the protestants of Ulster. Each side was to retain the territory it held at the time of signing the accord and there was to be an exchange of prisoners. The king was also to receive £30,000 compensation for his loss of revenue.

The confederation meanwhile had been recognised by France, Spain and the Holy See. Pope Urban VIII sent as his personal representative to the confederates Pietro Scarampi, an Oratorian priest. Scarampi argued passionately against the peace but his pleas were ignored. By March 1644 Charles was losing much of his control over affairs, and parliament ordered the protestant armies in Ireland to resume hostilities, which they did in Ulster and Munster. By the following year the king was under severe pressure and was anxious for a permanent peace in Ireland. He was willing to grant sufficient concessions to the confederation in order to obtain an Irish army to assist his flagging fortunes in England. In May the internuncio to Flanders met the earl of Antrim in Brussels, and urged him to join the confederate army in defence of the catholic faith. Antrim was disinclined to do so but did promise to secure continental arms and munitions for the confederates. The new pope Innocent X (elected on 15 September 1644) decided to send a nuncio to Ireland, with full powers of excommunication, to strengthen the hand of the clerical faction. The archbishop of Fermo, Giovanni Battista Rinuccini, arrived in October 1645 as the papal ambassador. This and the arrival of the earl of Glamorgan, a devout catholic, in August to negotiate a secret peace was to open up a new and painful chapter in the fortunes of the confederation and the hopes of Ulster.

The brief for Rinuccini's mission was based on the reports that the previous papal agent in Ireland, Fr Scarampi, had sent back to Rome. Innocent instructed the nuncio to ensure that the Irish 'subject themselves to the mild yoke of the Pontiff, at least in all spiritual affairs'. The problem in Ireland by the mid-seventeenth century, and since, was the difficulty of disentangling spiritual and political affairs. King Charles did not in principle object to the papal nuncio's presence in Ireland, and in fact wrote to him saying he hoped Rinuccini would give all possible assistance to the earl of Glamorgan's mission and that he looked forward to further correspondence with the 'minister of the Pope'.

The nuncio arrived to find that Glamorgan had already concluded a peace with the confederation.[45] Charles had given Glamorgan the authority to grant whatever concessions might be necessary to obtain a cessation. All the terms were to be kept secret but the king promised to stand by Glamorgan's treaty 'on the word of a King and a Christian'. The terms of the peace agreed on 25 August ensured that catholics would have the full public exercise of their religion and that they could keep any churches not actually in the possession of protestants. In return the catholics were to provide an army of 10,000 men for the king's use in England. This was ratified by the general assembly of the confederation within a few days of the terms being signed.

The nuncio repudiated the Glamorgan treaty in December because it did not fully establish catholicism as the religion of Ireland. He forced another treaty from Glamorgan since among other things he did not wish the terms to be kept secret, fearing that the king could privately abrogate the agreement if there was a turn for the better in Charles's fortunes. Rinuccini made Glamorgan promise that in future the lords lieutenant of Ireland would be catholic and that catholic bishops would sit in parliament, if not the first after the peace then in all subsequent ones. Charles reacted violently to the nuncio's interference in this way. He asserted that Glamorgan was acting without authority, whereupon Ormond had him arrested on a charge of treason.

Events in the other kingdoms made the king's position vulnerable. Chester fell to the parliamentary army in February and in May the king surrendered Scotland at Newark. Meanwhile he had again given instructions to Ormond to conclude a peace with the representatives of Kilkenny. This was arrived at on 28 March 1646 but owing to the situation in England and Scotland it was not made public till 30 July. No new concessions were made to the catholics. A general pardon was promised, the oath of allegiance would replace that of supremacy and the confiscations under Strafford would be made good.

The nuncio again rejected the peace, claiming that it maintained the protestant supremacy. The Supreme Council of the confederacy refuted Rinuccini's comments pointing out, not unnaturally or untruthfully, how much they had suffered for their religion and that

---

[45] In his subsequent report to Rome Rinuccini was to claim that while the Ulster Irish welcomed him as 'a minister of God', the 'old party' (the Anglo-Irish catholics) saw him as 'the treasurer of a Prince'. Cf. G.B. Rinuccini's *Embassy in Ireland*, translated with introduction by Annie Hatton (Dublin, 1873), p. 490.

they were not likely to abandon the interests of catholicism at this stage of the game. They claimed that the nuncio underestimated the forces of protestantism and that they were persuaded that the Ormond peace was their only 'salvation.' The sticking point was the question of the public restoration of catholicism. It had been impressed upon the nuncio before he left Rome that his chief aim must be the right of the catholics to exercise their religion publicly. For their part the Irish theologians argued among themselves whether the public exercise of catholicism was an essential need for the practice of the faith. Many alluded to the fact that Christ had presided at the first eucharist in a private house. The nuncio was appalled at such talk.

Rinuccini's accounts of the state of religion in the country are filled with examples of what he takes to be indications of the inadequacies of church life and ecclesiastical practice. Doubtless, judged against the background of Italian catholicism, the predicament in which Irish catholicism found itself must have seemed scandalous. His report on Irish church affairs in March 1646 was designed to strike horror into the hearts of all post-Tridentine clerics. Because the Irish bishops were accustomed to administering the sacraments in private houses they had 'an abhorrence of ceremonial' and officiated like ordinary priests. They did not even wear mitres or stoles when administering confirmation. He did however have praise for some including the bishop of Clogher, Heber MacMahon. The younger bishops in general, like MacMahon, were more vigorous in the defence of catholicism. The greatest revulsion he recorded was in connection with the celebration of mass. 'Even the lowest artisan wishes in sickness to hear Mass at his bedside; but often, to our great scandal, on the very table from which the altar cloth has been but just removed, playing cards or glasses of beer together with food for dinner are at once set.'[46]

The nuncio had the clergy convene a special meeting at Waterford in August. There the peace was declared to be contrary to the oath of association. Rinuccini placed all towns and cities which accepted the peace under an interdict, so that neither the sacraments nor any religious ceremonies could be celebrated. On 12 August the bishops issued a declaration that 'Having received the opinions and reasons of each, and having moreover, consulted the writings of the most approved theologians, it has been unanimously decreed, that all and each of the confederate Catholics who shall adhere to this peace, or give assent to its supporters are absolutely to be considered as perjurers.'[47] A new oath of association was proposed which made even more explicit the demand to restore catholicism to the status it

[46] Rinuccini, *Embassy in Ireland*, p. 142.
[47] M.J. Brennan, *An Ecclesiastical History of Ireland* (1864), p. 459.

enjoyed in the days of Henry VII. On October 5 a sentence of excommunication was pronounced against those who supported Ormond's peace.

The Ulstermen sided with the clergy against the Old English and decided against the new peace. This was partly for religious reasons but it was also because the peace held out little hope for the restoration of their position in Ulster. They had suffered most in the previous forty years and their grievances were all the more acute. Their determination to have all or nothing was also reflected in their commitment to fight. This was recognised immediately by Rinuccini who initially wanted to devote all the papal monies to the defence of Ulster, a proposal overruled by the supreme council. In fact because they were accustomed to greater hardship and privations, the Ulstermen in the confederate army were paid only half what the others received. On mature reflection in later years the nuncio deeply regretted that he had not followed his immediate instincts. If the sums bestowed on Thomas Preston, viscount Tara, the confederate army commander, had been diverted to O'Neill, 'Ulster could have been completely freed from the Scotch.' The doggedness of the Ulster army did not endear itself to all in the confederate cause. The nuncio himself was forced to admit that 'during the whole war the Ulster soldiery had treated the people with such harshness that they had excited a very bitter hatred against them'.[48]

Among their number the nuncio's strongest supporter was Owen Roe O'Neill who by then was in a particularly powerful position, having routed the parliamentary forces, led by Munro, at Benburb on 5 June. Rinuccini had not always either liked or trusted O'Neill. On April 10 he had reported to Rome that O'Neill was once again to command the Ulster army, and expressed the reservation that 'he is a strange and grasping man but it would be impossible to remove him.' There is no doubt however that O'Neill saw himself as an instrument of heavenly visitation. Before the battle he had declared to his men that they were fighting against the 'enemies of God'. Such sentiments were far from unusual; even Munro was to see his defeat at Benburb in starkly theological terms saying that 'the Lord of Hosts had a controversy with us to rub shame on our faces . . . till once we shall be humbled.' Munro reported that he had lost 5–600 men; the Ulstermen claimed it was more in the region of 3–4,000. On June 14 the nuncio wrote to cardinal Pamphili in a somewhat exaggerated tone that Benburb was 'a victory so signal, that in the memory of man no greater has ever been known here'.[49] A few days later he wrote to

[48] Rinuccini, *Embassy in Ireland*, p. 517.
[49] Rinuccini, *Embassy in Ireland*, p. 172.

the Pope that the arms and aid Innocent had sent had occasioned the destruction of almost the whole puritan army in Ulster.[50]

From this time O'Neill began to refer to his troops as 'the Catholic Army of Ulster'. It was with this catholic army that the papal nuncio entered Kilkenny on the 18 September and imprisoned lord Muskerry the general of the Munster army, Bellings the secretary of the council, Edmond Mountgarret and sundry other of his opponents. Thomas Preston was forced into support of the nuncio very much against his will, he and his men having been threatened with excommunication.

The result of the debacle over the Ormond peace was that the clergy emerged as the real power-brokers in the country. A new supreme council was formed which included four bishops, Preston, Sir Phelim and Owen Roe O'Neill (these two having made up their differences), and the nuncio as president. Rinuccini, who declared that he had sought no jurisdiction in temporal affairs, accepted the job with alacrity.

Meanwhile the decision was taken to order the army to march on Dublin. It arrived within a few miles of the city, but by this time the relationship between O'Neill and Preston had again deteriorated to the point where it was doubtful if a sustained attack could be made on the capital in the absence of harmony in the army. The nuncio summoned the commanders to a meeting which was hastily abandoned on receiving a report that a parliamentary expedition had landed in Dublin. This was not entirely true but it succeeded in forcing the confederates to retreat. By the following June the city had indeed been surrendered to the roundheads. The failure to take it had forced the nuncio to rethink his policy. On returning to Kilkenny he released his former enemies from prison and a reconciliation of sorts was entered into and yet another oath of association was pronounced in January 1647.

Later that year O'Neill was made the commander of the Connaught army in addition to his responsibilities for the Ulster troops. In November another meeting of the general assembly convened at Kilkenny. The Old English, finding themselves in a majority, reconstituted the confederation along lines favourable to themselves including appointing a new supreme council. As a means of trying to weaken O'Neill's position further, they ordered bishop Heber MacMahon of Clogher, a very close associate and one of the main

---

[50] This contrasts with a more recent opinion on the matter that O'Neill's victory 'had a merely negative effect on the military position; it prevented the Scots from marching south to attack Kilkenny, but it did not open the way for a general confederate victory.' J.C. Beckett, 'The Confederation of Kilkenny Revised', *Historical Studies*, II, p. 38.

supports to Owen Roe, to undertake a mission to the French king in December, as a means of getting him out of the country. MacMahon declined the commission on the grounds that he could speak neither English nor French.

The armies continued to sustain heavy losses in engagements with the parliamentary forces, leading the more conciliatory in the Confederate camp to attempt once more to come to terms with the king, judging that their prospects for religious toleration were greater with the monarch than with his enemies. Their representatives visited the queen and Ormond, by then in Paris exile, in April 1648 and a treaty was concluded along the lines of that reached in 1646.

Meanwhile in Ireland itself lord Inchiquin, one of the parliamentary commanders disillusioned with his treatment at the hands of the English parliament, declared for the king in April, and thus made it more acceptable for the confederates to do a deal with him. A peace accord was duly concluded in May. The nuncio immediately condemned it, excommunicated all who adhered to it and laid all towns supporting it under an interdict. The excommunication of the theologians who had approved the peace was fixed to the doors of the cathedral in Kilkenny on 27 May. The Old English did not take these censures lying down and immediately dispatched an envoy to the pope claiming that the nuncio had overstepped his powers. The archbishop of Armagh, Hugh O'Reilly, and fourteen other bishops issued a statement that the peace with Inchiquin would inexorably lead to the overthrow of catholicism in Ireland. Several other bishops rallied to the Old English side, although the only Ulster prelate to do so was the bishop of Dromore Oliver Darcy, OP.[51] These bishops questioned the legitimacy of Rinuccini's actions. The problem was not so much the principle of whether or not it was legitimate to enter into an alliance with a heretic but whether or not the nuncio's actions were compatible with ecclesiastical law.

The confederation decided to call a special meeting with the clergy to determine these matters. The questions raised lingered on for several years and it was not till 1665 that pope Alexander VII finally absolved from censure those who had been condemned. Rinuccini fled

---

[51] Darcy, a native of the diocese of Meath, distinguished himself as the only Ulster bishop of his day able to preach in both Irish and English. It was no surprise to the nuncio that he should side with the Old English. In fact Rinuccini had reservations about appointing him to Dromore but was pressurised into doing so. He had served as the 'chief chaplain in the Catholic army in Ireland' and the episcopacy was a reward for his labours. As we have seen, in an earlier generation Tyrone and O'Donnell had tried to impress on Rome that only native Ulstermen should be appointed to bishoprics in the Province. Darcy was one of eleven bishops appointed to various dioceses in March 1647.

from Kilkenny on May 7, placing himself under the protection of O'Neill. The supreme council accused him of causing division in the confederation which promptly fell apart and was reduced to a shambles. The nuncio summoned a synod to be held at Galway but confederate forces prevented it from taking place, and arrested clergy on their way to the meeting. Finally Sir Richard Blake, the speaker of the supreme council, ordered Rinuccini out of the country in October and he departed from Galway in February 1649.

A final peace treaty was drawn up between the confederates and Ormond, who arrived back in Ireland in January 1649. The terms were not unfavourable to the church and several bishops approved, although the confederation was thereby brought to a formal end. The country was to be ruled by a twelve-man commission under Ormond's direction. However, this agreement was scarcely worth the paper it was written on since the king was executed at the end of the month. The English parliament was in no mood to be lenient to Irish catholics and the Ormond treaty was set aside. In the following year Charles II, when proclaimed king of Scotland, repudiated Ormond's peace as the price of having Scottish support for his claim to the throne.

For his part O'Neill, fearing that he would be severely disadvantaged by his former confederate colleagues, threw in his lot with the parliamentary army in Ulster, an aberration which brought him some temporary relief but did not last six months. O'Neill had been under enormous pressure from his underlings, many of his soldiers having simply deserted in the last months of 1648. He sent his agent to London to negotiate with a parliamentary commission. In return for his support he sought an act of oblivion, religious freedom, and restoration of the estates in Ulster of those who served in his army. Already in August the confederation had declared against him and Preston had sent word to Jones the commander of the parliamentary army describing O'Neill as 'that perfidious enemy of the British nation.' In the following month Kilkenny had issued a formal declaration denouncing him as a 'manifest traitor and rebel.' All officials were ordered to proceed against him under pain of treason. He died in November 1649 having again returned to the Royalist side. From his death-bed he wrote to Ormond:

> I call my saviour to witness that as I hope for salvation, my resolution, ways and intentions from first to last of these unhappy wars tended to no particular ambition or private interest of my own, notwithstanding what was or may be thought to the contrary, but truly and sincerely to the preservation of my religion, the advancement of His Majesty's service, and [the] just liberties of this nation.

He had given his life for the defence of catholicism in Ireland and for the royal cause. That cause was effectively at an end and another chapter had opened up in Irish affairs—one that was to be long remembered. It was associated with a man who was to leave his mark more firmly rooted in the popular imagination than Owen Roe O'Neill ever would: Oliver Cromwell.

From Cromwell to the Restoration

Cromwell arrived in Dublin on 15 August 1649 to begin the subjection of Ireland to the authority of the English parliament. Perhaps no other military leader had such a highly developed religious sense of the mission that he was undertaking. His butchery at Drogheda he described to the speaker of the House of Commons as a 'righteous judgement of God upon these barbarous wretches who have imbrued their hands in so much innocent blood . . .' He was determined as far as was humanly possible to rid Ireland of catholicism. Although he boasted that he would not interfere with any man's conscience, he also made clear that freedom of religion did not extend to the free practice of catholicism. Cromwell set the tone for the treatment of catholics over the next decade. As Clarendon was to observe:

> The Parliamentary Party . . . grounded their own authority and strength upon such foundations as were inconsistent with any toleration of the Roman Catholic religion, and even with any humanity to the Irish nation, and more especially to those of the old native extraction, the whole race whereof they had, upon the matter, sworn to extirpate.[52]

Although he encountered his only defeat in Ireland at the hands of an Ulsterman, Hugh O'Neill, the nephew of Owen Roe, at Clonmel, he did not himself venture north but left the task of subduing the Ulster forces to Sir Charles Coote and colonel Robert Venables; an assignment which they completed with effortless skill and expertise. Newry surrendered without much loss of blood, and Belfast, a Royalist town, collapsed within four days of Venables taking up position outside it. Londonderry, which had been outside the control of the confederation, provided the support needed to take Coleraine. By the end of November the only sizeable garrisons not under the control of parliament were Carrickfergus, Charlemont and Enniskillen but by the end of December they too had fallen.

    The events of 1649 had left the catholics more deeply divided and mistrustful of one another than perhaps at any time in Irish history.

---

[52] Edward Hyde (Lord Clarendon), *History of the Rebellion and Civil Wars in Ireland* (London, 1720), p. 182.

The advent of Cromwell on Irish soil, O'Neill's untimely death and the bitterness left as a result of the fiasco over the nuncio forced the bishops once again to attempt the role of reconciler between the Old English and the Ulster catholics. It was now beyond doubt that the alliance with Ormond was the only hope for the Church. The bishops 'and other prelates' met at Clonmacnois on 4–13 December, under the direction of Hugh O'Reilly archbishop of Armagh, to set about the work of national reconstruction and to call for a united effort 'to avert God's wrath fallen on the nation.' The divine anger was, in their view, manifested in the famine and plague then ravaging the country but it was given more direct expression in the person of Cromwell.

The bishops warned, if such notice were necessary, that the people could not expect from the English rebels any toleration of themselves, their property or religion. They 'prohibited' any division between 'the various peoples that go to make up the Irish nation'. Unity was the essential quality in the face of the common enemy. Preachers were to preach charity, and if any prelate served to undermine charity or harmony then he would answer for it not only to the civil magistrate but before God himself. Furthermore they stressed the need for toleration of those English and Scots protestants loyal to the king, and they reminded soldiers that they were not to oppress the people by plundering. For all these protestations of national and religious unity, the catholics of Ireland were to remain as divided as ever. At this stage however the question of Ormond's leadership of the forces loyal to the king was not an issue.

A more immediate problem was to find a replacement for O'Neill as the general of the Ulster army. Before his death Owen Roe had left instruction that the new general of the army was to be elected by the nobility of Ulster and that their choice was to be ratified by Ormond. The voters gathered at Belturbet on 18 March 1650 to make their selection. Daniel O'Neill, a nephew of Owen Roe and himself a candidate for the generalship, caused much indignation by proposing Ormond. Ormond's nomination was turned down on the grounds that as a protestant he could not command 'the catholic army of Ulster'. Hugh Duff O'Neill might have been elected had he attended the meeting, but instead the lot finally fell to Heber MacMahon who, whatever his abilities as a bishop and politician, was no military commander. It was something of an irony that the bishop of Clogher, and former bishop of Down and Connor, should don the armour of a soldier and fight for the privileges of the Holy See 140 years after the last bishop of Rome had personally led troops into battle. MacMahon was not the only bishop to fight in the Ulster army. The otherwise kindly Cistercian Arthur Magennis held the rank of colonel but probably saw little fighting.

Ormond confirmed the selection and commissioned MacMahon on April Fool's Day. Initially the number of soldiers increased under the bishop to a total of 6,000. In the early days of his campaign he had some limited victories, taking Toome, Dungivern and Ballycastle, although the latter offered no resistance. However, because of his inexperience and inability to listen to military advice he finally came to grief at the battle of Scariff Hollis near Letterkenny on 21 June, scarcely three months after his appointment. He engaged the combined forces of Coote and Venables and although he had a numerical superiority he surrendered his tactical hillside advantage to engage the Parliamentary army on low-lying ground. The result was a near massacre: the Ulster army was devastated and the casualties amounted to 3,000, Coote suffering the loss of 100 soldiers and one officer.

MacMahon himself escaped with a small party and rode south-east. They were overtaken by the forces of major King, the governor of Enniskillen, and although they fought bravely enough the bishop's troops were forced to surrender. He was taken to Enniskillen and there tried for treason, suffering the due penalty prescribed by law for all traitors. His head was placed on a pike and set up on the walls of the town as an example for all to see.

The bishops once more grew restive with Ormond's leadership and after the synod of Jamestown in August 1650 sent a deputation headed by the bishop of Dromore asking him to resign. Ormond had already obtained from Charles II permission to leave Ireland if he felt his own position to be sufficiently under threat. He went into voluntary exile in December, leaving the marquis of Clanricard in charge of the king's affairs. The archbishop of Armagh wrote a most extraordinary letter to the papal internuncio at Brussels in October 1651 claiming that the bishops had driven Ormond from the country and deprived him of his authority.

Cromwell too had departed, in May 1650, and his command was taken by his deputy Ireton who systematically weeded out the opposition that remained. But the conflict dragged on and in time Clanricard himself, though a catholic, was to fall foul of the bishops, and a decree of the provincial synod of Armagh was issued against him in 1652. The Ulster bishops then sought help directly from the Duke of Lorraine claiming him as the protector of the people and soldiers of Ulster. But by early 1652 their position was quite hopeless. In that year the parliamentary government began the policy of banishing the clergy except for those against whom a definite crime could be proved, who were subjected to the full rigours of the law. By an order issued on 6 January 1653 all priests were to leave the country within twenty days; any found after this time would be regarded as traitors. It is estimated that between 1650 and 1654 as many as 1,000 priests went into exile. Carrickfergus became the main centre for the transportation of priests and civilians such as schoolmasters whom the authorities regarded as dangerous. Many of these were shipped to the West Indies. As late as 1659 a group of priests and lay people were held in Carrickfergus castle awaiting deportation. They had been there for three years in conditions of great hardship, and some of their number had obtained relief by converting to protestantism.

The 1650s were *par excellence* the age of the mass rock. The Act of Settlement of August 1652 deprived catholics of their land in three provinces, Connaught alone being thought fit for their abode. But this was a strategic rather than an economic consideration since throughout the Commonwealth period Ulster was still regarded as the least prosperous area of the country. In general the conditions for both priests and people were intolerable. Clergy were hunted relentlessly. By the second half of 1654 the only bishop left in the country was in the Armagh province, Eugene MacSweeny, whose decrepitude made him no risk to the parliamentary religious policy in Ireland. Between 1652 and 1655 neither the sacrament of orders nor that of confirmation was administered anywhere in the country. The celebration of the sacraments, when it took place at all, was at night and in remote areas, rarely in towns. The condition of religion was very low with widespread ignorance of the faith. As for the priests, the superior of the Jesuit mission testified that they lived 'generally in the mountains, forests and inaccessible bogs, where the . . . trooper at least cannot reach us'. There they ministered to the people who 'flocked in crowds'. But even these areas were not always safe and when they were discovered by the soldiers 'the wild beast was never hunted with more fury'.[53]

By 1657 bishop Anthony MacGeoghegan testified that the cathedral of St. Patrick and the Holy Trinity in Armagh had fallen into ruins. Nonetheless some priests continued to administer the sacraments in the town. But the dangers of arrest and imprisonment if not death were still very great. Although it is generally regarded that the Commonwealth was more disposed to exile catholic priests than to kill them after 1654, there were a number of instances when priests were put to death. John Flaverty, the prior of the Dominican house in Coleraine, was stoned to death in 1656 and his body was thrown into the Bann. Another member of the Coleraine community, James O'Reilly, died the same year from ill-treatment at the hands of the soldiers. The Dominicans lost the prior of Derry John O'Loughlin to a similar fate the following year: he was beheaded. It was said of him

---

[53] *Cambrensis Eversus*, p. 81.

that he could be seen to levitate at prayer, although this particular charism was often attributed to members of the Derry priory. Meanwhile the government continued to pay money for the apprehension of priests and friars. In November 1658 lieutenant Edward Wood received £25 from William St George, a justice of the peace in Co. Cavan, for having apprehended five priests '. . . who upon examination, confessed themselves to be both priests and friars'.[54]

Between 1651 and 1654 the Congregation of Propaganda in Rome appointed a number of vicars apostolic to administer the affairs of the Irish dioceses. But even by the end of the century diocesan and parish organisation was little better than chaotic. Derry was in an especially bad state of administration and Down and Connor had to wait till 1717 before regular episcopal administration became the norm. Armagh was to be more fortunate. Pope Alexander VII appointed Edmund O'Reilly, the former vicar-general of Dublin, to be its new archbishop. On the same day he appointed vicars-apostolic to Clogher and Down and Connor ordering them to be in Ireland within four months. By June he had made similar provision for Raphoe.

O'Reilly tried to land in Ireland in 1658 but was captured. He was however permitted, under Cromwell's protection, to visit England. In his report to Propaganda Fide he intimated that catholics had not enjoyed such freedom of worship since the time of Queen Mary. He also reported that the religious affairs of Ireland were in a deplorable state but that there was some ground for thinking that an improvement might be forthcoming. O'Reilly finally managed to take up the duties of his see in 1659, but his ministry in Ireland was to be brief. His political sympathies were judged to be at best ambiguous and he was once more forced into exile.

That catholicism survived at all was a remarkable attestation to the attachment of the Irish to the old religion. Despite the determined efforts of the roundheads most of the natives remained true to the religion of their forebears, thus indicating the ability of the individual to maintain a sense of catholicism without the support of formal ecclesiastical structures. This is not to belittle the efforts of the clergy, many of them heroic, to maintain a sacramental system in conditions of extreme social and religious disruption and indeed persecution.

By the late 1650s many priests had begun to drift back to the country. By the time of the Restoration there were three bishops in Ireland, all in the Armagh province. Ulster could boast of a total of 121 priests, but these were widely scattered and there were great variations between the dioceses. The diocese of Dromore had only twelve clergy,

---

[54]Myles O'Reilly, *Memorials of those who suffered for the Catholic Faith in Ireland in the Sixteenth, Seventeenth, and Eighteenth Centuries* (London, 1868), p. 344.

Down and Connor fifteen and Derry seventeen. Clogher was perhaps the best off with thirty. It was still difficult at this stage for the clergy to function openly. Consequently many went about in disguise and took secular employment not only as a means of concealment but for material support. Very few native Irish landowners in Ulster escaped the Cromwellian confiscations. In the whole of Fermanagh only one, Brian Maguire of Tempo, did so. The clergy having no large benefactors had to support themselves. The mere fact of the restoration of the king to government did not improve the lot of Irish catholics, but it held out the hope that improvement might not be far off.

The struggle to survive

If the stability of the church depended on a smooth and uninterrupted line of episcopal succession, then the Ulster church would virtually have ceased to exist in the turbulent atmosphere of political upheaval in seventeenth-century Ireland. Only the Armagh diocese preserved any competent episcopal supervision and even here, of the three archbishops who laboured there from the mid-century on, one, Edward O'Reilly, was to spend most of his episcopate in exile, and another, Oliver Plunkett, had his ministry cut short owing to the attentions of the executioners at Tyburn. Archbishop Dominic Maguire had only eight years of service among his flock before he too went into exile in 1691, dying in Paris in 1707. Derry was without due episcopal administration for 125 years, until the appointment of Fergus Lawrence Lea in 1694 on the recommendation of the deposed king James II, and the other Ulster dioceses had long periods of government by vicars-general.

The reports emanating from Ulster on the state of religion in the Province in the second half of the seventeenth century give a wearying testimony of a church in serious decline. Apart from the obvious political dangers concomitant with government hostility, at times spilling over into overt persecution, the inability to enact Tridentine reform and the low moral and intellectual calibre of the clergy combined, with a wretched ecclesiastical infrastructure, to make the administration of the sacraments an at best haphazard and often widely neglected activity. Clerical vice among both seculars and regulars was so endemic as to have become a way of life. Archbishop Plunkett complained to the Franciscan provincial chapter in 1672 that 'some of your fathers cannot avoid offending, by their over-indulgence in whiskey.'[55] On another occasion the future martyr

[55] John Hanly (ed.), *Letters of St Oliver Plunkett* (Dublin, 1979), p. 340.

declared that an Irish priest without the vice of drunkenness was assuredly a saint.

A weakness for *aqua vitae* was not the only besetting sin among the Ulster clergy of these decades. Open concubinage was no rarity. The visitation reports for the diocese of Down and Connor in October 1670 mention several priests who were 'suspect as regards to chastity'. Some, such as James O'Hara who in his early years as a priest fathered children, had in later life mended their ways; still others like Cormac O'Heale, who 'but ten years ago . . . sent away his mistress', had nonetheless taken to drink as a substitute. In this Down and Connor was by no means exceptional. In Raphoe the following year both Hugh Nan and Gregory Ultagh had maintained common law wives till the visitation. The most celebrated case of all was perhaps that of Terence O'Kelly, the vicar-general of the Derry diocese, who for thirty years had quite openly kept a concubine. He was finally deposed by the provincial synod of Armagh, held at Clones in September 1670. This was not the first attempt to deprive him of his position. A previous action by Ronan Magin, vicar-general of the Dromore diocese, ran into various legal difficulties. It was unclear in ecclesiastical law if Magin had the authority to remove O'Kelly from his post. The redoubtable Derry man took no chances and alerted the secular authorities to Magin's purpose in Derry, and he was promptly arrested on a charge of praemunire.[56] The unfortunate vicar of Dromore was taken to Dublin for trial but subsequently released.

Because of the conditions in which the church operated there was a widespread ignorance of the catholic faith, not just among the laity. Very few priests had a proper education in the sacred sciences. At best they were the product of hedge schools, in addition to which they had some training in ceremonial and for the brighter candidates a brief course in Latin.[57] When the Jesuits opened their school at Drogheda in July 1670, the primate insisted on sending twenty-five priests to receive a basic education and instruction in theology. In time Plunkett came to believe that there were too many priests in Ireland, some of whom were little more than chaplains to their own families, and he pleaded with Rome not to allow the practice of ordaining men '*extra tempora*', who had little or no educational formation.[58]

[56] The statute of praemunire 1362 placed a theoretical brake on the exercise of papal power in the kingdom, even in ecclesiastical matters. Individuals could not be sued to answer before the papal court if the matter could be dealt with by English or Irish law. In effect O'Kelly's action amounted to a charge that Magin was acting contrary to the king's jurisdiction in Ireland.

[57] Ef. Benignus Millet, *A History of Irish Catholicism* (ed. P.J. Corish), vol. 3, no. 8 (Dublin, 1968), p. 15.

[58] This is the substance of a letter he wrote to the internuncio at Brussels on 18 August 1673.

In the decades after the restoration of the monarchy the Ulster church did mke strenuous efforts to reform its life and practice. The synods in Armagh in 1670 and 1672, in Clogher in 1677, and the provincial synods at Clones in 1670 and Ardpatrick, Co. Louth, in 1678 give ample testimony to this fact. These clerical gatherings sought to regulate the religious life of Ulster and as far as possible to stamp out abuses. Various decrees were enacted which prohibited priests from frequenting drinking houses and markets, and a ten shilling fine was fixed for a violation of these precepts. It was further stipulated that alcohol was not to be consumed at wakes, either by clergy or laity, and all-night wakes were to be forbidden. For their part parish priests were to have a fixed abode, and vicars general were not to move outside their diocese except with the expressed permission of the archbishop of Armagh.

To guard against clerical avarice, priests were forbidden to resort to the law courts to stake a claim for benefices, under pain of suspension, and any lay person who assisted a priest in such a venture would suffer the punishment of excommunication. It was further regulated that parish priests were to hold a collection at the altar only four times a year. But it was also stipulated that each family was to give the priest in the parish at least two shillings a year, and mass stipends were fixed at one shilling. No priest was to set amounts smaller than those laid down by the synods. Stipends were also expected at christenings and marriages. For poorer catholics these were generally set at the level of a shilling. Even this could represent severe economic hardship for some, given that catholics were also obliged to pay the tithes of the established Church, whose ministers also expected to receive shilling stipends when the catholic sacraments were administered. To oversee the proper administration of the sacraments two masters of ceremonies were to be appointed in each diocese and a licence to preach had to be obtained; this was not to be readily given, especially to those who had received insufficient training. Penalties were fixed for priests who said mass without having fasted from the previous midnight. Priests were forbidden to say more than one mass a day even on Sundays and Holydays except when they had received episcopal dispensation, and this was to be rarely given.

One source of enormous strain, felt perhaps more acutely in the Ulster catholic community than elsewhere in Ireland, was to be found in the relationship between the secular and regular clergy. It was a not infrequent allegation that Franciscans and Dominicans exercised parochial functions *contradicente episcopo*. This became the subject of a decree in 1678 to the effect that no member of a religious order was to engage in parochial activity without the written approval of the bishop in the diocese concerned. Henceforth members of religious

orders were not to beg for money in parishes where they did not perform some pastoral activity or if they did not live in community. So
as to reduce the influence of the religious orders and avoid unseemly
squabbles at funerals it was decreed in 1670 that no lay person was to
be buried in the habit of a religious order (a special privilege
customarily accorded to those with special connections to an order,
such as benefactors). It was hoped thereby to encourage the laity to
have the secular clergy perform the obsequies at funerals, the stipends
from which continued to be an important source of income for priests.

The houses of religious orders continued however to be a focus for
the complaints of the diocesan clergy. The main problem was lack of
discipline and the fact that most such institutions tended to be too
small and informal to give proper training to new recruits. Such
charges applied principally to the 'unreformed' Franciscans and the
Dominicans. At times too in Ulster, particularly in the dioceses of
Armagh, Clogher, Down and Dromore, there were disputes between
the Dominicans and Franciscans about their respective spheres of
influence. In a celebrated and prolonged contretemps after the
Cromwellian dispersal, the Franciscans returned to a number of sites
in Ulster and set up house in former Dominican friaries. When the
Dominicans returned to their previous habitations, not only would the
sons of St Francis not admit them but they challenged the rights of
the Dominicans to beg for alms in districts such as Carlingford,
Downpatick and the area around the old priory of Gaula in Co.
Tyrone. Oliver Plunkett as archbishop was asked to settle these continuing grievances and when he did, in 1672, in favour of the
Dominicans, the Franciscans appealed to the pope and began a
whispering campaign against him. The disputes dragged on and there
are recorded instances of fighting between both groups in Co. Tyrone
even during the celebration of mass.

In contrast to the practice in the rest of the country where mass
could often be said in the private houses of the well-to-do, the celebration of the sacraments in Ulster tended to be carried out in the open
with little protection from the elements for either clergy or people.
Churches, in so far as they existed, were more often than not in
atrocious states of disrepair and tended to be in the possession of the
protestants. In such circumstances it was impossible to operate the
standard parochial system, apart from the cultural and political considerations which mitigated against it. This fact was recognised by the
internuncio Sebastiano Tanari in Brussels when he informed the Congregation of Propaganda in August 1677 that in the Derry diocese
there were no fixed parish boundaries or clerical revenues. Each priest
was assigned the care of a certain number of families in the hope that

these would provide a sufficient living for him.[59]

The often miserable condition of Ulster catholicism did not prevent it from exercising a care for those even less fortunate. The highlands and islands of Scotland fell under the jurisdiction of the primate of Armagh, and successive bishops struggled to find the wherewithal to support this mission. The marquis of Antrim also took a benevolent interest in the work, often supporting up to three clergy out of his own resources. Such internal difficulties as lack of resources must never obscure the fact that catholicism in those decades fought to keep its head above water in the most complex and antipathetic political circumstances, which required the greatest sensitivity from Church leaders. The Ulster churchmen gave expression to this at the Ardpatrick synod. The fathers there assembled deemed it prudent to issue a statement defining the purpose of their gathering. On 28 August 1678 they declared that they intended only to promote 'the glory of God, and the advancement of the Catholic Faith, the salvation of souls, the tranquillity of the kingdom, rendering to Caesar the things which are of Caesar, and to God the things which are of God'.[60]

Political difficulties and lack of resources restricted Ulster catholicism's ability to function as a Church able to meet the varying needs of all the faithful. However at the heart of its struggle to survive in the midst of the external threat from English and protestant animosity, there raged in Ulster catholicism a vicious ideological battle with serious political and theological implications. The struggle centred on a doctrine which had been formed around the teaching of a professor at the University of Louvain, Cornelius Jansen, who became bishop of Ypres in 1636, and it was certainly one of the elements that caused the downfall of the archbishop of Armagh Oliver Plunkett, since as a good Roman he was one of its most dogged opponents. This was Jansenism.

Jansenism and the loyal formulary

Jansenism was essentially concerned with the nature of grace. The doctrine as derived from Jansen's book *Augustinus* taught that in the absence of special grace the performance of God's will was impossible for man. Equally the operations of God's grace were irresistible.

---

[59] Cf. 'Catalogue of Material of Irish Interest in the Collection *Nunziatura di Fiandra*', *Collectanea Hibernica*, vol. 3 (1960).

[60] Quoted in P.F. Moran, *Memoir of the Ven. Oliver Plunkett* (2nd edn, Dublin, 1895), p. 149. Cf. also Hanley, *Letters of St. Oliver Plunkett*, p. 517.

Humanity was therefore deprived of free will. The doctrine also suggested that only very few were saved and tended to promote an over-rigorous spirit in disciplinary and sacramental matters. Jansen's teaching was condemned by the Sorbonne in 1649 and pronounced heretical by Innocent X in May 1653 and by Alexander VII in October 1656. In France, where it attracted its greatest following, it was also allied with that anti-papal strand in catholicism which emphasised the prerogatives of the local church against the centralising claims of Rome. The Jansenists also taught that the Pope was not infallible and that the authority of St Augustine was greater than that of papal pronouncements.

The Irish Franciscans at Louvain, many of them from Ulster, had a certain sympathy for the doctrine and it was probably through them most of all that it found its way to Ireland. Jansenist books circulated there, including *On Holy Communion* and the New Testament in French and English, which at points varied from the authorised Vulgate version. The text of the mass in French and English was also in circulation. All of this created an independence from official Roman teaching which made the English government not indisposed to those who propagated such doctrine since, as Ormond indicated in 1666, devotion to the pope actively prevented the Irish from 'giving their allegiance to the Crown'.[61] Among those who were to prove most useful for government purposes in helping to divide the catholic community in their respective loyalties to king and pope was the Franciscan Peter Walsh.

Walsh came to prominence as the result of archbishop O'Reilly being *persona non grata* with Charles II owing to his too close association with Oliver Cromwell. O'Reilly was suspected of having betrayed the royalist forces to Michael Jones, one of the parliamentary commanders. He was forced into exile and rumours persisted that he was trying to land an expeditionary force in Ireland with the aim of bringing down the restored monarchy. To counter these persistent rumours and to advocate the needs of Irish catholics at court, O'Reilly appointed Walsh as his agent in London. Walsh managed to persuade him to issue a declaration of loyalty and this broadened out into a general campaign by the Franciscan to encourage all catholics to sign what became known as the 'Loyal Formulary', in the hope that such a demonstration of loyalty would persuade the king to grant further concessions to his Irish catholic subjects.

Already in 1663 the vicar general of Armagh, Dr Patrick Daly, had written a letter to the lord lieutenant stating that the king was 'to be worshipped in temporals next to God, a thing glorious, yea,

<hr />

[61] *Cal.S.P.Ire.*, 1666–9, p. 132.

even divine'.[62] Such was Walsh's persuasiveness that he convinced Ormond of the need to hold a national synod in Dublin so that the Remonstrance could receive full ecclesiastical approval. He even went further and managed to secure permission for the return of the exiled archbishop of Armagh for the meeting. By May 1662 the remonstrance had already attracted the supporting signature of sixty-one Irish clerics, most of them Franciscans, including one prelate Oliver Darcy the Dominican bishop of Dromore. The pope however had made his displeasure known to Darcy and his fellow-signatories. They riposted by telling the pope that he had been wrongly advised on the nature and implications of the formulary.[63] In the event the synod, meeting in Dublin on 11–25 June, rejected the Remonstrance as proposed by Walsh since it repudiated any role for the pope in temporal affairs, and a compromise formula that most were prepared to sign was rejected by Ormond. The lord deputy, furious at this setback to his plans, ordered the arrest of all the bishops present at the synod. O'Reilly was once again banished from the kingdom on 27 September and died three years later.

The formulary had connected to it certain 'Gallican propositions' of obvious French and, by this time, Jansenist flavour. The three propositions were concerned to deny papal authority in temporal matters in Britain or Ireland. For the upholders of the Counter Reformation such a denial was entirely unacceptable. Every reforming synod in the country in those years took the opportunity to repudiate any diminution of papal authority. In particular the Ardpatrick synod rejected such favourite Gallican ideas as the view that papal teaching or appointments depended *ab acceptatione cleri et populi*, or that the people had the right to elect their own pastors. However the papal cause had been seriously weakened by exposure to continental ideas. Plunkett's at times misguided reforming zeal brought him into conflict on practical and ideological grounds more than once with those not disposed to accept high papal and Tridentine doctrine. His imprudence was also noted in Rome which reprimanded him in several instances for interfering in matters outside his jurisdiction.[64]

What has been described here as the 'ideological' conflict in the Ulster church at this time was also reinforced by outright racism. The Ulster Irish tended to resent the practice of having 'Old English' bishops foisted on them by Rome. This was true in Plunkett's case and in that of Patrick Tyrell, bishop of Clogher in 1676–87. In spite

---

[62] *The History and Vindication of the Loyal Formulary* (London, 1674), pp. 490–1.

[63] Cf. *Collectanea Hibernica*, vol. 1 (1958), p. 124.

[64] Canice Mooney, 'Accusations against Oliver Plunkett', *Seanchas Ardmhacha*, vol. 2 (1956), pp. 119–40, gives details of these occurrences.

of his being a Franciscan, Tyrell's Old English outlook gave him little sympathy for the native Irish and his appointment was widely resisted by the clergy and people of his diocese, who instead wanted the Gaelic Irish Franciscan Phelim O'Neill, son of Owen Roe.[65] Not only did Tyrell suspend several priests who refused to accept his authority, but he responded in kind by petitioning the Holy See to be transferred to the diocese of Meath.

Plunkett too tried to curb the influence of the Ulster friars in the affairs of the Church by recommending the Holy See to avoid appointing friars to bishoprics in Ireland. He claimed that such appointments in the past had never been successful; '. . . they may get on well in Catholic countries, but not here.'[66] The Titus Oates plot when it came was to engulf Plunkett, and his departure to a saintly end was quickened with the connivance of several Franciscans. The conventional wisdom is that the individuals concerned were unrepresentative of the order as a whole. Nonetheless one should not underestimate the dislike in Ulster for the type of Church and outlook that Plunkett represented. The sharp divisions within the Church were continually exploited by the government in Dublin and London as it sought to keep catholicism firmly under control.

In the rush for reform in the Irish and Ulster Church in the mid-to late seventeenth century there was an attempt to impose a standardisation of catholicism to bring it into line with the continental reforms, the idea being that wherever one went in the catholic world common recognisable elements of belief and practice would be evident. Local diversity was thereby destroyed. The aim, from a centralising point of view, was the laudable one of constructing a dynamic and irrefutable counter-attack on the inroads which protestantism had made in Europe. The effect in Ulster however was gradually to weaken those elements in the Celtic temperament which had helped to give a clear sense of Ulster Gaelic identity, and which enabled the Old Irish to set themselves over against English and Scots protestant influence.

This was a very different agenda from the catholicism of the Pale. There the cultural identity, while from a religious viewpoint catholic, had historically been dependent on the English connection. The Anglo-Norman ascendancy looked to an English rather than a Gaelic past for a sense of itself. The reforming Tridentine clergy such as the Jesuits, the discalced Carmelites, the Capuchins and the Roman-trained prelates like Plunkett operated from a cultural context which was as much the enemy of Gaelic Ulster catholicism as was protestan-

[65] Cf. Tomas O'Fiaich, *Clogher Record*, vol. 1, no. 3 (1955), pp. 10–11.
[66] Plunkett to Cardinal Baldeschi, 23 July 1673.

tism *per se*. The attempted imposition of a religious standardisation undermined Gaelic Ulster's way of life, and thus severely and even mortally impaired its ability to resist the political and religious onslaught of English rule. This process was long and tenacious but we see here at this stage of the seventeenth century the important, indeed decisive first battles. Meanwhile the Ulster catholic community had also to contend with a fast changing and complex set of political events which more immediately continued to threaten its very existence.

Further decline

The report on the state of the diocese of Down and Connor in 1671 is a reasonable summation of the conditions of Ulster catholics and their clergy as a whole in the post-Restoration area. The protestants had all the church revenues, all the native Irish were catholics, 'the bishop dresses in lay attire and performs the duties of his office in secret; he has no income on which he can depend.'[67] Despite this the ecclesiastical authorities did their best to appear as loyal members of the body politic. However throughout the reign of Charles II, the reiterated injunction of the clergy to pray for the royal family brought little change in the official government attitude of belligerence towards catholicism. Political unrest in Ulster made a greater impression on government strategy than catholic supplication to the deity for the health and long life of the king.

By the time of the Restoration the government had to contend not only with catholic unrest in Ulster but also with that of the dissenters, who were enraged by the reestablishment of episcopal government and who now began to suffer under some of the same disabilities as catholics.[68] The Act of Uniformity 1662 while enacting no new measure against the catholic clergy nevertheless sought to restrain the work of catholic schoolteachers. The land question remained of primary importance and after much rumour about the possibility of an Ulster rising, fomented by the Friars, a local outbreak did occur under the leadership of Mulmore O'Reilly in 1665; it was quickly suppressed.[69] The previous December an order had been issued for the

[67] Quoted in Cathaldus Giblin, 'The "Processus Datariare" and the Appointment of Irish Bishops in the Seventeenth Century' in *Father Luke Wadding: Commemorative Volume* (Dublin, 1957), p. 588.

[68] Raymond Gillespie, 'The Presbyterian Revolution in Ulster, 1660–90' in W.J. Sheils and Diana Wood (eds), *The Churches, Ireland and the Irish* (Oxford, 1989), outlines some of the difficulties under which presbyterians lived and worshipped at this period.

[69] It is clear that the government knew about this well in advance, since it had been looking for O'Reilly, O'Doherty, Sarle, and Nugent for some time. Cf. *Cal.S.P.Ire.* 1663–65, pp. 551 and 553.

arrest of certain priests suspected of plotting against the government and talk of such conspiracies was reinforced by this rising. An earlier report in July 1664 had archbishop O'Reilly land in Ireland with an army of 15,000 men, to be assisted by Philip MacHugh mac Shane and a further 10,000 troops from Flanders. The Franciscans too were alleged in 1663 to be plotting to overthrow the king. It was reported that Anthony Dogherty, the guardian of the friars in Co. Tyrone, and fifteen of his confreres attracted the attention of the government, between June and August that year, on being accused of such traitorous behaviour. Unfortunately one of the witnesses to the plot admitted to receiving the intelligence of the intrigue when he was in a state of intoxication.[70]

By 1668 the authorities had again moved against the clergy and some friars and others were imprisoned in Carrickfergus and Downpatrick. Still others were kept under close scrutiny by government agents. There was no absolutely consistent policy towards the clergy in the decades from the Restoration on. Ormond was in favour of excluding clergy whose loyalty could not be shown to be unimpeachable; on the whole he disliked catholicism and was disinclined to tolerate it. He was deeply suspicious of its role as a rallying point for discontent, especially in Ulster. In 1669 he again complained of the troublesome 'Old Irish rebels' in the north. They had carried out much vandalism and robbery, Co. Tyrone yet again seeing more than its share of such lawlessness, which included burning property; in one infamous incident a whole town was held, the sheriff was taken prisoner and the insurgents threatened to hang him.[71] Such disorder posed a challenge to the authority of both state and Church. Landless bands of robbers, general known as Tories, were a common feature in many parts of Ulster and occasionally they would be accompanied by a priest, most often a friar. These catholic peasants, victims of previous government policies, had now returned with a vengeance to menace their fellow-citizens and government officialdom. The Church as the avowed enemy of all disorder issued a degree against the Tories in 1668. Once more Plunkett was behind the move. Not content with this general decree, he sought out many of them and with a general pardon he had obtained for them from the viceroy induced many to go into exile.

An order for the expulsion of catholic priests from England in 1671 was not applied to Ireland, but there did follow a period of more intensive persecution, which the Ulster clergy seem largely to have escaped. A general order was however promulgated by the lord

---

[70] William P. Burke, *The Irish Priests in the Penal Times* (Waterford, 1914), p. 10.
[71] *Cal.S.P.Ire.*, 1666–9, p. 261.

lieutenant, the earl of Essex, on 27 October 1673 ordering all bishops and priests out of Ireland by 31 December. In the following months a number of northern clergy were caught and imprisoned including the dean of Raphoe and a Franciscan companion. As was to be expected, the Titus Oates scare at the end of the decade saw many Ulster clergy in prison. Between May 1680 and August 1683 the Dominicans in Derry were regularly rounded up and imprisoned. Dean Brian McGuirk was also arrested in Derry in May 1682 and charged with 'extolling foreign jurisdiction', being the 'titular' vicar-general of the Armagh diocese although he is sometimes described as the 'vicar general of the Irish papist clergy in Ulster'. The government made determined efforts to secure his conviction, having him arraigned at the assizes in Armagh, Dungannon and Monaghan. He was however acquitted in each instance. His defence was that he was technically a vicar-capitular having been selected by his fellow-priests to fulfil that office and thus was not an appointee of the pope. This became a standard defence in such cases. He also testified to the unvarying practice in the Armagh diocese of informing the local justices of any gathering of clergy, thus negating any intimation of conspiratorial intent in these meetings.[72] In all McGuirk spent more than a year in prison.

The trials of clergy and laity in Ulster in those years are full of testimony to self-sacrifice and heroism. The ability to endure such hardship was not given to everyone. Dominic McLerinon, the youngest priest in Down and Connor when he was ordained in 1697, was unable to meet the demands that the penal laws placed upon him, and conformed to the established Church. There is a tradition preserved in the parish of Ahoghill, Co. Antrim, that McLerinon did present himself to the parish priest, and to the bishop of Down and Connor Dr James Shiel asking to be reconciled to the Church. McLerinon felt himself unable to fulfil the conditions Shiel imposed for his return to the bosom of the Church and seems to have died outside the faith.[73]

As was to be expected the accession to the throne of the catholic James II, proclaimed king on 6 February 1685, marked the beginning of an improvement in the conditions of Irish catholicism. James allowed the bishops to resume their accustomed dress in public but they were not to wear pectoral crosses. Two Ulster bishops Dominic Maguire and Patrick Tyrell travelled to England to congratulate him on behalf of the Irish Church and to plead for the appointment of a

---

[72] Carte, *Ormonde*, vol. 6, pp. 384–5.
[73] His story is partly told in *A Digest of the historical account of the Diocese of Down and Connor* (Belfast, 1945), p. 103.

catholic viceroy. James was prepared to make some concessions to catholic Ireland; he appointed Richard Talbot earl of Tyrconnell to the post of lieutenant-general of the army but not till January 1687 was he made lord deputy. However, James's general restoration of catholicism was to proceed with some caution. Although he wrote to the Irish bishops in March 1686 assuring them of his royal protection and favour, the king initially made it abundantly clear that he would not restore catholics to their land whatever might be his policy over the open practice of the faith. Eleven catholic bishops were give a state allowance of between £150 and £300, and in addition the archbishop of Armagh received £2,190 annually for 'secret service' to the king. These monies were paid out of vacant Church of Ireland bishoprics. By the autumn of 1688 'Catholics had received enough encouragement', especially concerning appointments in the army, 'to enable them to restrain their impatience for a complete reversal of the previous position.'[74] What they really wanted was a full restoration to the pre-reformation position—something which James could simply not do. Ultimately his religious policy satisfied neither catholics nor protestants and the birth of a catholic heir in June 1688 was the final straw for protestant forbearance.

[74] J.G. Simms, *Jacobite Ireland, 1685-91* (London, 1969), p. 43.

2

THE EIGHTEENTH-CENTURY
EXPERIENCE

The penal laws: an explanation?

Even today there is some controversy among historians concerning the purpose of Irish penal legislation in the late seventeenth and early eighteenth centuries. As the eighteenth century wore on, Irish protestants mostly seemed content to allow catholics to practise their religion free from restraint while adhering to the social and political aspects of the popery laws, which prohibited the catholic community as a whole from enjoying the position in society to which its wealth and numerical strength might have entitled it. The question at issue however is: what was the intention of the framers of the penal laws? Did they see them as a means of extirpating catholicism from the country, as a necessary first step in converting Ireland to protestantism,[1] or simply as a means of securing the position of a protestant élite?[2]

Maureen Wall typifies the view prevalent in some historical circles that it was not the intention of the legislators to secure the conversion of all Irish catholics to protestantism. Like Dr Brady she argued that such a contingency would have undermined the position of the ruling protestant élite, since it is presumed that the latter would thereby have

[1] Thus Robert E. Burns observes that the Irish Popery laws 'comprised one of the most persistent legislative efforts ever undertaken by a western European state to change a people.' Cf. 'The Irish Popery Laws: A study of Eighteenth-Century Legislation and Behaviour', *The Review of Politics*, vol. 26 (1962) p. 485. Cf. also S.J. Connolly, 'Religion and History', *Irish Economic and Social History*, vol. 10 (1983), p. 77, who thinks this view deserves more credence than it has been given.

[2] This is the broad consensus adhered to in such diverse works as Maureen Wall, *The Penal Laws, 1691-1760* (Dundalk, 1961, 1967), John Brady and Patrick J. Corish, 'The Church under the Penal Code' in *A History of Irish Catholicism*, vol. 14 (Dublin, 1971), and Patrick J. Corish, *The Irish Catholic Experience* (Dublin, 1985). E.M. Johnston has written that the penal laws 'perpetuated a racial division upon religious grounds and ensured the political social and to an extent economic ascendency of a small minority . . .' Cf. 'Problems common to both Protestant and Catholic Churches in Eighteenth-century Ireland' in Oliver MacDonagh (ed.), *Irish culture and Nationalism 1750-1950* (London and Canberra, 1983), p. 14. R.E. Burns, 'The Irish Penal Code and Some of Its Historians', in *The Review of Politics*, vol. 21 (1959), gives an account of views on the question from a representative sample of nineteenth-and early twentieth-century historians.

been forced to share its privileges with Irish catholic converts to the state religion. S.J. Connolly has, rather harshly, characterised such an analysis as the union of 'conservative Catholic tradition and schoolboy Marxism'.[3] He rightly points out that the whole of European society was based on ruling élites and from this viewpoint Ireland was no different from any other contemporary society. Irish protestants would not have been at a disadvantage had the general populace gone over to the state religion; the ruling élite would still have maintained its status as an élite. Elsewhere he concludes that 'the real flaw in the structure of eighteenth-century Irish society was not that it excluded a large section of the population from democratic freedoms. It was rather that it debarred them from taking on as fully as they might otherwise have done the role of deferential subordinates.'[4] He is further convinced that the purpose of the popery laws was ostensibly what they claimed to be, the means of destroying catholicism in Ireland.[5]

However the 'schoolboy marxist' approach cannot be entirely dismissed. It is clearly the case that élites by their very nature are closely contained. It is in the interests of the élite to restrict access to its privileges, otherwise they are dissipated. The controlling élite in Ireland was protestant. Members of the eighteenth-century Irish catholic élite were excluded from positions of influence and authority. Those members of the growing catholic middle class with flair and resourcefulness were prevented by the operation of the penal laws from the opportunity shared by their protestant equivalent of progressing into the élite. Had all such classes conformed, the élite could not have survived as such.

Connolly is as aware as anyone of the danger of ascribing a single explanation for the gradual and piecemeal process that gave Ireland its anti-popery laws in the late seventeenth and early eighteenth centuries. Irish protestants after all had the example of England to look to. If anything, English anti-catholic legislation was in many ways harsher that the Irish measures, yet in dealing with a relatively insignificant minority for a period of more than 150 years the English government was not able to rid that country of catholicism. It is perhaps stretching credulity to think that the framers of the Irish popery laws actually believed they could achieve from a numerically inferior position what English protestants had been unable to do in much more advantageous circumstances.

---

[3] Cf. 'Religion and History', p. 75.
[4] *Religion, Law and Power: The Making of Protestant Ireland 1660–1760* (Oxford, 1992), p. 43.
[5] *ibid*, p. 290.

There were other factors which made the ascendency hesitant about catholic conversions. R.E. Burns draws attention to the correspondence between Edward Synge, the Church of Ireland bishop of Raphoe, and archbishop William Wake of Canterbury in which Synge outlines the pros and cons of attempting to convert the Irish to protestantism.[6] The catholics, he tells Wake, were notoriously insincere converts, many of them reconverting on their deathbeds. Further, mass conversions would give the legal right to hold guns to a vast number of recent Jacobite sympathisers, whose loyalty in the face of any future invasion from France could not be relied upon. Synge saw the catholic clergy as the real menace. If they could be definitively dealt with, then there might be some hope for wholesale conformity but not otherwise. It is obvious even at this stage that the Banishment Act of 1697 and the Registration of the Clergy Act of 1704 were not having their desired effect. For Synge and those like him, the penal laws were conceivably more a guarantee of political stability than a means of subduing catholicism.[7] Later in the century John Wesley concluded that it was no wonder 'those who are born Papists generally live and die such, when the protestants can find no better way to convert them than the penal laws and acts of parliament.'[8]

However it would be a mistake to suppose that the anglican Church showed no interest in converting catholics. Efforts were made to train clergy in the Irish language and there were periodic attempts to preach salvation to lower-class catholics. The difficulty was that the authorities lacked a systematic strategy for bringing the whole catholic population into the protestant fold. Dr King, archbishop of Dublin in 1703–29, records that it was plain to him that 'by the methods that have been taken since the reformation and which are yet pursued by both the civil and ecclesiastical powers that there never was nor is any design that all should be Protestants.'[9] The presence of so many dissenters in the north-east caused internal problems for the established church, between the Tory wing which viewed such protestant non-conformity with loathing and the Whigs who would have been

---

[6] Cf. 'Thoughts on Converting the Irish 1715', in *The Irish Ecclesiastical Record*, vol. 98 (1962), pp.142–4.

[7] *ibid.*, p. 144.

[8] *John Wesley's Journal*, vol. 3, p. 314. Quoted in Brady and Corish, *The Church under the Penal Code*, p. 5.

[9] Francis Finegan, 'The Irish "Catholic Convert Rolls"', *Studies* (1949), p. 75. By 1787 the anglican bishop of Clonfert, taking a more ecumenical line, had decided to circulate among catholics in his diocese, who outnumbered protestants twenty to one, booklets and tracts by 'some of the best of their own authors . . . unable to make the peasants about me good Protestants, I wish to make them good Catholics, good citizens, good anything' (*ibid.*, p. 82).

content to concentrate on eliminating catholicism but who distrusted the motives and dispositions of their Tory brethren. This division also had political implication, especially towards the end of Anne's reign when it was apparent the Tories would have restored the Stuarts to the British throne had the pretender been willing to become a protestant.[10] In the circumstances of mutual distrust within the established Church it was unlikely that any real consensus on how to deal with Irish catholicism would emerge.

Connolly draws attention to the fact that the political fears which catholicism evoked in Irish protestants continued well into a period when the full rigours of the penal laws were not implemented.[11] Indeed it is often suggested that the religious aspects of the penal laws were not rigorously enforced except in times of crisis—as in 1708, 1714, 1719, 1723, 1734, and 1739. Equally it could be argued that the laws were enforced as rigorously as government resources allowed given the constraints under which the early eighteenth-century Irish administration laboured. Communications were difficult, those parts of the country where catholicism was strongest were the least accessible, and little cooperation could be expected from the native population in tracking down clergy who were operating illegally in the country.

One can see that there is no single explanation for the purpose of the penal laws. The complexity of the Irish administrative system was such that precision remains elusive.[12] As a minimum we can say that the laws were directed against catholics and catholicism as a means of bolstering the position of the protestant ascendancy. For the latter to achieve its purpose it was not in itself necessary that catholicism should be completely abolished. But it needed to be severely curtailed and the activities of the clergy in particular restricted. However at root the threat posed by catholicism was not religious but political. It is therefore perhaps best to see the enactments as the means for the emasculation of catholicism as a political force in Ireland. Had the laws been completely successful catholicism would have died. That it did not is as much a testimony to the tenacity with which the native Irish held on to the faith of their forebears as to the failure of the government to devise means for the full implementation of the laws.

---

[10] Wall, *The Penal Laws*, p. 57.

[11] Quoting from the correspondence of the wife of the Dean of Down he demonstrates that protestant trepidation centred around the fact the 'the pope might be prevailed upon by foreign powers to order them [the Catholics] into rebellion against their inclinations.' *Religion, Law and Power*, p. 258.

[12] Thomas Bartlett, *The Fall and Rise of the Irish Nation: The Catholic Question, 1690–1830* (Dublin, 1992), p. 20.

Thus far we have looked at the intentions of the laws; it is now time to look at the legislation itself.

The Williamite settlement and penal law enactments

Only with the usurpation of the throne by William and Mary did James II show himself disposed to make concessions on the land question in Ireland as a means of trying to raise an Irish catholic army in an attempt to secure his crown. Whatever the European dimension of the Williamite campaign, in Ireland the struggle between the two kings was as much as anything else concerned with the security of protestant landholdings and the established nature of protestantism.[13] The activities of the Earl of Tyrconnell as James's lord deputy in Ireland had greatly strengthened the political position of Ulster catholics, and in the war of 1689-91 the Ulstermen fought tenaciously to hold on to their gains. The protestants went down to defeat in such diverse areas as Antrim, Carrickfergus and Coleraine. Although Belfast surrendered without a fight, Enniskillen resisted all attempts to take it, and most celebrated of all Derry saw off the catholic armies in a heroic resistance to James's forces. For their part the Ulster catholics had little to lose in the ensuing comprehensive defeat of James. The earl of Antrim was one of but a handful of substantial catholic landholders in the province and he was regarded as an unrepentant Jacobite.[14] There was some confusion whether or not under the terms of the treaty of Limerick he should be deprived of his lands. The difficulty lay partly in the question of the validity of the much-debated clause 2 of the treaty. Antrim was camped on a hillside outside Limerick, and it was unclear if he fell within the terms of the protection offered to the garrison forces of several counties deemed to be under the protection of Sarsfield's army. Antrim forfeited his lands in 1691 but regained them towards the end of the decade having appealed on the basis of the Limerick treaty. Despite the failure to uphold the second clause it seems that in this catholics were less disadvantaged by William's failure to stand by his agreement than might otherwise have been expected.

The failure to ratify the full terms of the treaty of Limerick was not

---

[13] Cf. W.A. Maguire, 'The Land Settlement' in Maguire (ed.), *Kings in Conflict: The Revolutionary War in Ireland and its Aftermath, 1689-1750* (Belfast, 1990), p. 139.

[14] J.G. Simms, *The Williamite Confiscations in Ireland, 1690-1703* (London, 1956), p.23. Other substantial Ulster catholic landholders included the fourth earl of Abercorn, Sir Neil O'Neill and in Fermanagh Cuchounact Maguire. The last-named was killed at the battle of Aughrim and his lands forfeited to the Crown. However they were regained by his son Brian in 1700 who argued that his father had only possessed a life interest in the family estates. cf. Maguire, 'The Land Settlement' p. 155.

entirely William's fault. The continuation of the continental war inclined him to follow a policy of reasonable toleration towards Irish catholics—under pressure, as he was, from his catholic European allies. The Irish parliament, having a more direct interest in the matter, was less disposed to leniency and was supported in this attitude by the English House of Commons, which complained to William in February 1693 at the favour he had shown to catholics in Ireland. The sight of 10,000 troops, together with sundry clergy including the archbishop of Armagh, sailing into exile with Sarsfield was a salutary reminder of the political menace that catholicism still posed. As if to underline the disloyal nature of catholicism to the new political arrangements, some of the most senior clergy continued to be retainers in James's court at St Germain.[15] The continuing Jacobite threat made the declarations of religious liberty in the Limerick accords so much beating of the wind.[16]

It would be misleading to suggest that all members of the Irish parliament were equally conscious of the need to renege on the promises given at Limerick. When the bill to ratify the treaty was finally presented to parliament in 1697, seven Church of Ireland bishops along with seven peers signed a protest regretting that the ratification fell short of the terms agreed. Although it is often suggested that some of the lay peers who signed this remonstrance were recent converts to the established religion and thus harboured a residual sympathy for the religion they had so recently abandoned, their main concern was financial. Their protest asserts: 'We apprehend that many Protestants may and will suffer by this Bill, by reason of their having purchased and lent money upon the credit of the said Articles.'[17] By that time parliament had already begun to enact that *ad hoc* series of statutes which have become know as the 'penal laws'.

Anthony Dopping, the anglican bishop of Meath, had in a famous sermon six weeks after the agreement at Limerick made known the resentment of many Irish protestants at what was perceived as a sell-out to catholic interests. The administration retaliated by dismissing Dopping from the privy council for his outspoken contempt for government policy. But not all such opposition was as easily sup-

---

[15] Many soldiers did not go into exile. The bands of Rapparees who terrorised south Ulster well into the 1720s were mostly former members of Sarsfield's army. Cf. Jonathan Bardon, *A History of Ulster* (Belfast, 1992), p. 167.

[16] At its most liberal interpretation the Treaty guaranteed catholics the same privileges as they enjoyed under Charles II.

[17] Cf. *A Collection of the Protests of the Lords of Ireland from 1634–1770* (London 1771), p. 221. This prompted the earl of Shrewsbury to remark that there was 'nothing more suprising than to see an Irish house of parliament making difficulties over a bill because it was not sufficiently favourable to Catholics.' Quoted in Simms, *The Williamite Confiscations*, p. 62.

pressed and Irish protestants began to retaliate against both the government and the catholic community. It is indicative of the insecurity of many protestant landholders at that time that they deemed it necessary to move against catholicism, as if their position could only be ensured if firm wraps were placed upon the catholic population. A further motive for the enactment of penal legislation was the straightforward one of revenge.[18] However the Irish parliament's first act of political muscle-flexing was to reject an English money bill in 1692 on the constitutional grounds that it had been foisted on parliament by the executive and had not originated in the House of Commons.

By September 1695 parliament had enacted legislation which prevented catholics from having an education either at home or abroad, and had diminished the military threat from the community by forbidding catholics to bear arms or to own a horse of more than five pounds in value. The education measures were designed to reduce catholics as a whole to illiteracy, but also to prevent candidates for the priesthood from being trained abroad. Parliament also tried in that year to expel members of religious orders, the regular clergy, from the country but this was prevented, only temporarily as it turned out, by the intervention of the emperor Leopold I with king William. However, Leopold's ambassador to William, count Auersperg, urged the regulars not to make too many demands on the populace and to restrict the number of those whom they received into their orders. But in general there could be no hope of reducing Ireland to protestantism as long as the clergy remained at large in the country.[19] More important politically at a time when the possibility of a Jacobite invasion was still seriously entertained, it was clear that the loyalty of the clergy lay with James. By 1697 a move against the clergy had become inevitable.

The act to banish the clergy was originally intended to apply only to members of religious orders, but it was extended to include the bishops and all clergy who exercised jurisdiction in the kingdom. The precise reason for including the bishops is unclear.[20] There was some

---

[18] J.G. Simms, 'The Establishment of Protestant Ascendancy, 1691–1714' in T.W Moody and W.E. Vaughan (eds), *A New History of Ireland IV: Eighteenth Century Ireland 1691–1800* (Oxford, 1986), p. 16.

[19] This was the substance of a report which the bishop of Meath made to the government in October 1693, in which he recommended that the regulars at least should be banished.

[20] J.G. Simms, *War and Politics in Ireland, 1649–1730*, ed., D.W. Hayton and Gerard O'Brien (London, 1986), p. 235. On the other hand this proposal had first emerged in 1693 but was rejected by the London government probably once more owing to pressure from the Emperor. Cf. Seamus Creighton, 'Innocent XII and Early Irish Penal Legislation' in *Irish Ecclesiastical Record*, vol. 98 (1962), p. 215.

disagreement even among Irish protestants over whether the secular or regular clergy constituted the greater threat; some argued that the secular clergy were too much given to factionalism and their desire for the preferments dispensed by Rome and the court of St Germain (the house of Stuart had the right of nomination to Irish bishoprics until the Old Pretender died in 1766) kept them beholden to foreign and dangerous powers. Much the same argument was made against the regulars but for different reasons.

In view of the proposal to expel the clergy the papal internuncio at Flanders wrote to Leopold's chief minister pleading with him to have William's government deflect the Irish parliament from its course. Auersperg wrote to the Secretary of State denouncing the proposed measure. Blathwayte replied on 16 September explaining that the religious were being expelled at the request of the secular clergy. This intelligence seems to have been accepted by Auersperg at face value but the idea was repudiated by the nuncio.[21] A document was circulated in Ireland, purporting to have the assent of the secular clergy, which denied that they had asked for any such expulsion. Under the terms of the Banishment Act all bishops, clergy exercising jurisdiction, and regulars were to leave Ireland by 1 May 1698. Of the thirteen Irish bishops still alive at the time of the passing of the act five were already in exile, five others left the country in accordance with the law and three remained, illegally, to minister to their flocks. In all some 400 priests were deported from the country. Some of the regulars did stay on acting as parish priests, and given that there were 1,367 secular clergy the spiritual needs of the faithful could not be said to have been neglected as a consequence of the expulsion.

The expulsion of the regulars taken in conjunction with the prohibition on bishops would have killed off the priesthood in Ireland within a generation.[22] That William agreed to the measure was perhaps a mark of his growing impatience with his friends in the imperial alliance. The conclusion of the peace of Ryswick in that year also meant that he could pursue a more independent religious policy in Ireland. On the other hand the evidence would suggest that the English government both in William's reign and in that of Anne tended to exercise a restraining hand on the otherwise strong-armed

[21] Creighton, 'Irish Penal Legislation', p. 216

[22] Some papers preserved in the Vatican archives contain contingency plans for the preservation of the priesthood in Ireland in the absence of bishops. It was suggested that two bishops might be sent to the country, one an Irishman and the other a foreigner, with the title of patriarch. They would not only ordain priests as they saw fit but also consecrate suitable candidates to the episcopacy without reference to Rome. These ideas were never acted upon. It is difficult to know how serious such proposals were. Cf. Cathaldus Giblin (ed.), 'Miscellaneous Papers', *Archivium Hibernicum*, vol. 16 (1951), pp. 70–3.

inclinations of the Irish parliament and administration in its dealings with catholics. The proposal to have catholic children raised as protestants was rejected by the London government, as was the 1719 proposal of the Irish Commons that unregistered priests caught in the country should be branded on the face with the letter P, a punishment amended by the Irish privy council to that of castration.

'The Act to Prevent the Further Growth of Popery' of 1704 has been described as the 'most notorious and comprehensive of all the penal laws'.[23] Its provisions ensured that by that year catholics might not have any profession save that of medicine, and that they could not inherit property. Additionally they might not marry a protestant nor in law could one become the guardian of minors. The right of catholics to sit in parliament had already been removed in 1691. By 1709[24] only those catholics prepared to repudiate the Jacobite claim to the throne might vote and by 1727 all catholics, whatever their political opinions, were deprived of the franchise. One other statute which deserves some consideration for its bearing on the continued existence of the Church in Ireland was the act requiring the catholic clergy to register with the clerk of the peace at their local quarter sessions.

The Registration Act was a logical corollary of a 1703 measure (2 Anne, c.3) which forbade any catholic priest from entering Ireland after 1 January 1704. The act was intended to furnish a list of individual clergy legally operating in the country. Such a list would be useful for future reference as a help in making sure that the previous measures were not being violated. A priest was obliged to register his name, address, age, parish, and the date and place of his ordination and the name of the ordaining prelate, and in addition to have two sureties of £50.[25] Those not prepared to register were ordered to leave the country. On the other hand registered priests were free to administer the sacraments unmolested provided they did not officiate outside their own parish. As an inducement to the clergy to convert it was also provided that any priest conforming to the established Church would receive a pension of £20 a year. One further stipulation that no priest might keep a curate was an attempt to impose yet another restriction on clerical numbers and helps to confirm the general impression that altogether the intention of the Irish

[23] J.G. Simms, 'The Making of a Penal Law (2 Anne, c.6), 1703–4', in *War and Politics in Ireland*, p. 264.

[24] J.G. Simms has written of his conviction that from this year 'the penal laws began in earnest and there was a steady increase in the number of heirs to landed estates who decided that conforming to the established Church was the lesser of two evils.' *War and Politics in Ireland*, p.276.

[25] Tomas O Fiaich in 'The Registration of the Clergy in 1704', *Seanchas Ard mhacha*, vol. 6 (1971), p. 50, noted that some protestants, especially in Ulster, acted as sureties.

parliament was, in principle at least, to rid Ireland of the catholic clergy.

It has been necessary to give a general indication of the scope and effects of the Williamite settlement and the subsequent penal laws as the background to the progress of the Ulster catholic community in the eighteenth century. Catholics of the northern province, because of their relative poverty and the greater concentration of protestants in their midst,[26] were to feel the constraints of those aspects of the penal laws which affected religious observance more penetratingly than any other group in the country.[27] Their plight was compounded, as we shall see, by the increasing difficulty of encouraging clergy returning to Ireland from their continental training to settle in Ulster because of the social and economic hardships they were expected to endure.

Ulster catholicism and the penal laws

The immediate effect of the penal laws in Ulster was to make a difficult ecclesiastical situation very much worse. Except in Armagh there was no regular episcopal succession in the Ulster dioceses before the 1730s. By 1703 there were 189 priests in the province and on average this gave a ratio of about one to every 1,000 catholics, a reasonably satisfactory level of clerical support. However by 1714 the bishop of Clogher, Hugh MacMahon, was complaining of a shortage of pastors in his diocese. Ministry to the spiritual needs of the faithful was conducted rather haphazardly, even when there was no overt persecution. Places of worship were few, and conditions were hard for clergy and people alike.

A constant theme in reports to Rome or to the internuncio in Brussels in these years was the difficulty of ministering in an area so much under the dominance of 'Scotch Calvinists'. MacMahon accused the presbyterians of coming to Ulster almost daily in large numbers from Scotland and of 'occupying the towns and villages, seizing the farms in the richer part of the country and expelling the natives'.[28] Four years earlier Dr Patrick Donnelly, the bishop of

---

[26] As Wall, *The Penal Laws*, p. 9, points out, there was little sympathy between catholics and dissenters in Ulster before the 1760s. At the same time Dr Wall maintained that presbyterian influence on Ulster catholics served to make them 'more critical, more contentious, and less tolerant of authority.' *ibid.*, p. 38.

[27] Louis Cullen, 'Catholics under the Penal Laws', in *Eighteenth Century Ireland*, vol. 1 (1986), p. 24, indicates that Ulster catholics were 'distinctively more disadvantaged than their fellow-catholics in material and cultural terms' well into the later decades of the century.

[28] Cf. The bishop of Clogher, Hugh MacMahon, report to the internuncio in Brussels in 1714, in Moran, *Spicilegium Ossoriense*, vol. 2, pp. 470ff. A translation of this

Dromore, had similarly complained that the natives of Ulster were more abandoned than any other catholics in Ireland:

> On account of the great number of Scotch Presbyterians . . . Those (catholics) who remain living in the middle of the presbyterians, are reduced to such poverty that they have not the means to encourage or support missionaries—in fact they have more need of help themselves than have the priests. The result is that the missionaries prefer to go to other parts where they get better support. . . .[29]

By this time the government had already acted to tighten the penal laws. The Popery Act of 1709 had ordered all registered clergy to take the Oath of Abjuration which repudiated James III's right to the throne and professed loyalty to the protestant succession. In Ulster only one or two priests and in the country as a whole only thirty-three swore the oath.[30] There was some dispute as to whether or not it was legitimate for the clergy to take the oath of abjuration. A Dr Moore of the University of Paris had declared that it did not violate catholic teaching or practice, and this view was given wide circulation in Ireland. Pope Clement XI ruled that the oath was inadmissible and forbade the clergy to take it.[31] Strictly, priests refusing to take the oath lost their legal status but the government faced with such widespread disaffection found it a wiser course not to move against the clergy in this broad fashion. The abjuration act also empowered magistrates to compel, under oath, any catholic over sixteen years old to reveal where and when he had last been to mass and the name of the priest saying the mass.

These restrictions gave rise to eccentric manoeuvring to protect clerical identity. Priests began to veil their faces when saying mass, so that they would not be known to their congregations, or alternatively the priest would say mass in one room while the congregation gathered in another. The need for secrecy was paramount, and parishioners in various areas developed an elaborate sign system to

---

document is given by Patrick J. Flanagan, 'The Diocese of Clogher in 1714' in *The Clogher Record*, vol. 1 (1953), pp. 39ff. and 125ff. Here p. 40.

[29] O'Donnell to Mgr Grimaldi, 28 March 1710, quoted in Michael McRory, 'Life and Times of Dr Patrick O'Donnelly, 1649–1716, "the Bard of Armagh"', *Seanchas Ardmhacha*, vol. 5 (1969), p. 26. This point is also borne out by MacMahon in his 1714 report.

[30] MacMahon in the document already cited reports that the Ulster clergy preferred to face suffering rather than be false to their religion and 'their king', which is perhaps further evidence that catholicism did in fact pose a political threat to the state and that the penal laws were an attempt to deal with that danger rather than catholicism *per se*.

[31] Cf. MacMahon-Grimaldi correspondence in Giblin, *Collectanea Hibernica*, vol. 5 (1962), p. 18.

indicate to one another the times at which mass was being said. But such was the danger that often they would simply come together to pray at the time when they knew mass was being celebrated elsewhere. The environment of secrecy and the activity of priesthunters and denouncers led to distrust between neighbours, which made the job of the clergy more hazardous. Bishop MacMahon reported to the nuncio the practice of saying mass at night with only the head of a household and his wife, since parents in such circumstances could not trust their own children not to betray them.

Although the general pattern was one of the oppression of catholicism, there were some areas of Ulster where even at this period the faith could be practised with relative freedom. Up to 1720 catholics and protestants in Loughlinisland, Co. Down, worshipped in the same church on the island. The catholics had mass in the morning and the protestants had their service early in the afternoon. This premature experiment in 'church sharing' came to an end when one Sunday the catholics remained in the church sheltering from a storm. The protestants were kept waiting outside and were not only deprived of their service but suffered the full effects of the storm. Consequently they decided to build a church of their own at Seaforde, and used the roof of the Loughlinisland building for the new church. The faith was also openly practised at Lough Derg, where even the local protestants seemed to find some edification in what otherwise many of them regarded as barbarous superstitions. One element in this may have been the fact that the boat to the island was operated by a protestant family who charged pilgrims sixpence to ferry them there and back. But the island did not entirely escape the attentions of the authorities. Pilgrimages to St Patrick's Purgatory were expressly forbidden by the 1704 Popery Act, and a raid in 1715 resulted in three priests being arrested—but they were released without charge. Significantly the spiritual needs of pilgrims were catered for by Franciscan friars, despite the fact that they were banned from the country. The Rev. Terence McRory ministered unhindered in Draperstown, Co. Tyrone, in the first and second decades of the century. He was a man of considerable wealth and this may have influenced local officialdom in their attitude to him.

These instances of local toleration are offset by the many examples of overt persecution of the clergy. By March 1708 there were only seven catholics in Belfast, including the priest Philomy O'Hamill who was then in gaol although he was sixty-four years old and posed no threat to the authorities; indeed the mayor reported to Dublin that the priest was a harmless fellow who had been good to protestants. In the whole barony of Belfast there were less that 150 catholics. The nearly senile dean of Armagh Brian McGurk was imprisoned at the age of ninety in 1712. When the magistrate Thomas Dawson, on arriving to apprehend the dean, tried to compel some dissenters to assist him, they refused to do so and were prosecuted for their offence.[32] Such was the outrage in Armagh that Dawson, who had collected £50 reward for the dean's capture, wrote to Dublin on 4 October that McGurk's imprisonment was bad publicity for the penal code, and that even protestants complained about the inhumanity of the old man's treatment. This remonstrance had no effect and the dean died in prison early in 1713. For some time after his death the city was without a priest.[33]

By June 1714 the mayor of Derry could report that there were no priests in the city except one, and he hoped to have him in prison soon. In the same year the sheriff of Donegal tried to round up the unregistered priests in that county but found the task almost impossible. From time to time parishioners would prevent the sheriff's forces from doing their work, and on occasion this had disastrous consequences for all concerned. The bishop of Raphoe, James Gallagher, reported to the internuncio in Brussels in July 1734 that the civil authorities had tried to apprehend Charles Kerighan the parish priest of Kilgarvan, Co. Donegal. Kerighan's parishoners mounted a rescue bid in which many were injured on both sides including the unfortunate parish priest who died from his wounds. A number of people were imprisoned for their part in the fracas, and others had to flee to escape arrest.[34] If a priest was taken it sometimes happened that his parishioners would mete out reprisals on the arresting officers. When the archdeacon of Down, James Hanna, was arrested in Downpatrick in February 1713 the local clergy and people caused such ill-feeling towards the man who captured him that the magistrate Henry Maxwell was obliged to issue the captor with arms to protect himself and his family. Two years earlier it is reported that James O'Hegarty, the Dominican, parish priest of Fahan, Co. Donegal, was summarily executed by a party of soldiers. It was suggested that he had been betrayed by his brother-in-law.[35] The infamous priest-hunter Edward Tyrrell made several forays into Ulster and had a notable success in 1712 when he captured several priests, but his main prey Hugh MacMahon managed to elude his attentions.

For catholicism to function effectively, given the hierarchical and

---

[32] John Brady, 'Catholics and Catholicism in the Eighteenth Century Press', *Archivium Hibernicum*, vol. 16 (1951), p. 19

[33] Burke, *The Irish Priests in Penal Times*, p. 282.

[34] Giblin, *Collectanea Hibernica*, vol. 9 (1966), p. 42.

[35] O'Fiaich, 'The Registration of the Clergy', p. 52, accepts the authenticity of this oral tradition; Wall, *The Penal Laws*, p. 30, is more sceptical of it.

sacramental nature of the Church, it was essential to have to hand a steady supply of priests and if possible bishops. By the time of the registration of the clergy in 1704 there was but a single bishop in Ulster, Patrick O'Donnelly. He lived on the slopes of Sliabh Gullion, working as a farmer as part of his disguise and also as a means of financial support. O'Donnelly registered as the parish priest of Newry but he was well known to the authorities, who rightly suspected that he was in fact a bishop. He was arrested in 1706 and taken to Dundalk. There he made a declaration under oath that he had received no holy orders other than those of a priest, and that he had never performed any function that in essence belonged to the office of a bishop. This declaration has led some historians to conclude that O'Donnelly was not in bishop's orders at this time but it is more likely that this was a perfectly legitimate instance of casuistry, since in catholic theology, in a tradition going back to St Jerome, it can be argued that the distinction in orders between a priest and a bishop is one of jurisdiction and not of orders.[36]

O'Donnelly was released from prison in May 1707 at which time he consecrated three others to the episcopacy, including Hugh MacMahon. O'Donnelly's brother Terence was made Vicar Apostolic of Down in 1711, and the diocese of Connor was given to his jurisdiction three years later. Terence was finally appointed bishop of Derry in 1720. The tradition of dominant clerical families was by no means unusual in Ulster. MacMahon was promoted to Armagh in 1715, and was succeeded in Clogher by his nephew Bernard, who in turn bequeathed the diocese to his brother Ross. Both Bernard and Ross followed their uncle in the primacy of Armagh, in 1737 and 1748 respectively.[37]

The supply of priests was maintained by the practice of ordaining men who had little education beyond the ability to read Latin. After several years of ministry they usually went to the continent to be educated in philosophy and theology,[38] and were financed either by bursaries established for that purpose or by stipends for saying masses for the dead. Hugh MacMahon confessed to ordaining a number of men of inferior intellectual ability in order to ensure a sufficient

---

[36] Cf. St Jerome, Letter 146 *ad Evangelium*, in J.P. Migne (ed.), *Patrologia Latina*, vol. 21, pp. 1192ff.

[37] W. Maziere Brady, *The Episcopal Succession in England Scotland and Wales, A.D. 1400–1875*, 3 vols (Rome, 1876). Here vol. 1, pp. 213ff.

[38] Thus for example the college at Alcala, which in future years became absorbed into that at Salamanca, catered solely for students from the north of Ireland.

[39] This is dispite the fact that he told the internuncio Mgr Santini in 1718 that he always took the greatest care in promoting men to the priesthood, notwithstanding all the persecutions. Moran, *Spicilegium Ossoriense*, vol. 3, p. 131

number of priests for his diocese.[39] By mid-century the Holy See became increasingly unhappy with this practice and restricted the number of such priests to twelve in each diocese, despite the protests of a number of Irish bishops.

Ulster catholics have long had a reputation of being fractious and in the early eighteenth century, despite the level of official hostility towards the faith and perhaps even because of it, much energy was expended on internal squabbling. Owing in part to presbyterian influence and the intermittent nature of direct episcopal oversight, parishes often asserted what they took to be their right to select their own pastors. This was in open defiance of the principle that it was the bishop who made clerical provision for the parishes in his diocese. Normally some sort of compromise had to be arrived at.

A serious dispute arose in Armagh on the death in exile of archbishop Dominic Maguire. The clergy of the diocese elected the parish priest of Drogheda, John Verdon, as the ecclesiastical superior, or vicar-capitular, pending the appointment of a replacement for Maguire. Bishop O'Donnelly declared the election illegal and using what he took to be his authority as vice-primate in the absence of any other bishop, appointed Patrick Dowdall as the administrator of the diocese. Verdon refused to back down. The dispute in turn led to recrimination in the other Ulster dioceses. On the death of the vicar-capitular of Kilmore in 1710, both Verdon and Dowdall made provision for his successor and the same thing happened in Derry the following year. Bishop O'Donnelly, writing to Grimaldi in 1709, accused Verdon of having blessed and distributed the holy oils used in the various sacraments before Holy Thursday that year, which was contrary to ecclesiastical law, and according to the bishop a source of great scandal in the diocese.[40] MacMahon, writing in the same year on the dispute, remarks that 'the internuncio can judge whether such things help the progress of the mission or ruin it completely throughout the province of Armagh, which is full of [anglican] bishops and presbyterians who are overjoyed when they see the priests divided among themselves'.[41] The irony of all this was that as early as 1698 Verdon had been described as the only person in the ecclesiastical province of Armagh worthy of a bishopric.[42] Acting on this advice and doubtless hoping to resolve the matter, Rome appointed Verdon bishop of Ferns in 1709, but even then he refused to give up his position in Armagh and the dispute dragged on till 1714.

One other recurring feud which again surfaced in 1719 was a

---

[40] *Collectanea Hibernica*, vol. 4 (1961), p. 125
[41] *ibid.*, p. 209
[42] *Archivium Hibernicum*, vol. 16 (1951), p. 67

disagreement between the archbishops of Armagh and Dublin over which see exercised ultimate jurisdiction in the country. This wrangle produced one of MacMahon's few major writings, the tract *Ius Primatiale Armacanum*. This sets out to justify the claims of the arch- bishop of Armagh to the title *Totius Hiberniae Primatialis*. The Holy See, at first reluctant to adjudicate on the matter, was finally forced to issue two briefs in favour of the claims of Armagh.

More significant was the concern Rome expressed for orthodoxy in Ireland. We have seen above that Jansenism was already a force in the country by the 1680s. There was some suspicion that bishop O'Donnelly was a Jansenist sympathiser and had actually ordained several clergy for the Jansenist Church in Utrecht. O'Donnelly was innocent of the charge and Dr Fagan of Meath seems to have been the culprit. Rome was anxious that the anti-Jansenist bull *Unigenitus Dei Filius* (8 September 1713) should be promulgated in Ireland. MacMahon cautioned against this. He wrote to the internuncio in April 1714 that talk of any commission from the Holy See served only to excite further the hostility of Irish protestants.[43] As late as February 1718 the nuncio wrote to the Secretary of State at the Vatican saying that it was still not possible to promulgate *Unigenitus* in Ireland. But even by this time there was a growing confidence in the Ulster Church and MacMahon issued a pastoral letter in April warning against the dangers of Jansenism and stating on behalf of his suffragan bishops their acceptance of the papal teaching on this issue. Such was MacMahon's abhorrence of Jansenism that he even tried to prevent Irish students from going to study in Paris, which he regarded as a seedbed of the heresy. In this instance he was overruled by his fellow-bishops.

From the year 1712, perhaps to capitalise on the internal difficulties in Armagh and the Ulster Church as a whole, some efforts were made in the Armagh diocese to convert the natives to anglicanism. The Church of Ireland primate set aside £130 yearly to train ministers in the Irish language, and thus equipped with the vernacular they would preach and read prayers to catholics. The ministration of the pastors of the established Church were at times well received. Thus the primate reported that on occasion in the city of Armagh 'above 200 persons have attended at prayers and sermons, and behaved themselves very decently with great attention and seeming devotion and did express great satisfaction for having prayers and scriptures read and explained to them in a language they understood.'[44] This

---

[43] *Collectanea Hibernica*, vol. 5, (1962), p. 80

[44] Quoted in Burke, *The Irish Priests in the Penal Times 1660–1760* (Dublin, 1914), p. 284

was at a time when the catholic clergy tended to administer the sacraments hurriedly with little preaching or instruction. When catholics had the benefit of preachers of their own denomination they often flocked to hear them. Thus on Good Friday, 26 March 1725, William Smith attracted a crowd of 2–4,000 in a remote townland in south Derry.[45] Notwithstanding the attempts at conversion, half-hearted though they were, in the period 1703–99 less than 460 catholics in the ecclesiastical province of Armagh conformed to the established Church.

By the late 1720s it was obvious that the penal laws were not having their desired effect. The number of bishops and others exercising ecclesiastical jurisdiction was increasing. The friars were returning in greater numbers from the continent and augmenting their number from local recruits. The ineffectual attempts at conversion, as we have seen, produced results that were all but negligible. Catholics were receiving an education of sorts in various parishes and parents continued to send children abroad for schooling. Having been deprived of the opportunity to enter the professions, catholics were now competing on equal terms with protestants in trade, and some—though few in Ulster—were beginning to accumulate wealth. The adminstration became increasingly uneasy and decided to inquire into the strength of catholicism with a view to determining how to contain what was perceived as the continuing catholic menace.

Seeds of recovery and growing turmoil

The Irish House of Lords in 1731 ordered that high sheriffs and chief magistrates were to make a survey of the state of catholicism within their own areas and report on the number of friars and nuns. Similarly the archbishops, bishops and ministers of the established Church were instructed to state the 'number of Mass Houses and Popish Chapels, and the number of priests officiating in each, and also the number of reputed Friaries and Nunneries and Popish schools' in each of their parishes.[46] The 1731 returns show catholicism in Ulster to be worse off than in the rest of the country. Armagh boasted twenty-five mass

---

[45] Smith is scarcely typical. He was an odd character, a lay person who was nonetheles, usually, licensed to preach. He may not have been entirely orthodox either, since he was tried for blasphemy by the civil authorities despite using a copy of a book of sermons by John Tillotson, archbishop of Canterbury in 1691–4, which had been translated into Irish. Cf. the collection of documents edited by Patrick J. Larkin ' "Popish Riot" in South Co. Derry 1725', in *Seanchas Ardmhacha*, vol. 8 (1975–6), pp. 97–110, here p. 110.
[46] 'Report on the State of Popery, Ireland, 1731, *Archivium Hibernicum*, vol. 1 (1912), p. 10

houses but of these only seven were in the Ulster part of the diocese, while the rest were in Co. Louth. Of the forty parishes in the diocese of Derry only twenty-three had resident priests. The Church of Ireland bishop does however say in his report that the diocese was 'frequently infested with strolling Friars and Regulars, who say Mass from parish to parish as they pass, in ye open fields or in mountains, and gather great numbers of people about them'. Raphoe diocese had but four mass houses, one of which was a cabin and another simply 'a shed'. In fact none of the Ulster dioceses was especially well provided with either mass-houses or schools.

The rather dilapidated state of Ulster catholicism in the 1730s must be set against a certain resilience as well as intensity with which people held onto their faith, and the determination of the clergy as far as possible to conduct a 'business as usual' policy in ecclesiastical administration. The anglican bishop of Down and Connor reported that Dr John Armstrong 'who takes upon him to be Bishop' held regular visitations in the diocese, and that the clergy 'teach boldly that there is no salvation outside their communion'. The law forbidding curates was so flagrantly disregarded by this time that James Hackett, the sheriff of Newry, could maintain in somewhat exaggerated tones that in his district the number of young priests was daily on the increase.

That the 'popery report' for Ulster in 1731 should paint such a dismal portrait of the physical state of the Church is hardly surprising. The reasons for this were the now traditional ones of a greater concentration of protestantism and nonconformity in the province, and the lack of material resources at the disposal of the catholic community. One of the few remaining catholic landed families, the earls of Antrim, had gone over to protestantism in 1721,[47] as did the Savages of Portaferry. A few Ulster catholic landed families did manage to survive such as the O'Reillys in Cavan, but this had little impact on the overall social and economic standing of the Ulster community. From a structural, and to some extent organisational, viewpoint Ulster catholicism continued to lag behind the rest of Ireland throughout the eighteenth century. There is even some suggestion that the penal laws were more strictly applied in Ulster than elsewhere in the country and that the established Church in the north deliberately encouraged sectarian bitterness. The Church of Ireland archbishop of Armagh, writing in October 1745, instructed his clergy 'to raise in your people

---

[47] Alexander, the fifth earl, was eight years old at the time of his father's death. His grandmother Rachel Hungerford, dowager Lady Massereene, and his uncle, the third Viscount Massereene, became his guardians. Lady Massereene determined that the young earl should henceforth be brought up in her own protestant faith. Cf. George Hill, *An Historical Account of the MacDonnells of Antrim* (Belfast, 1873), p. 269.

a religious abhorrence of the Popish government and polity (for I can never be brought to call Popery in the gross a religion) . . .'[48]

The general view among historians is that from the 1740s there was a growing acceptance of catholicism by protestant Ireland. But from the 1750s one can detect growing sectarian animosities. At times protestants would complain at the impudence of catholics, whom they regarded as little better than negro slaves or north American Indians.[49] Even in the earlier decade there were many signs of intolerance, at least in Ulster. As late as 1744 there was a general proclamation ordering mass houses to be closed. Dr Francis Stuart, the catholic bishop of Down and Connor, was driven from his home in Hillsborough, Co. Down, in 1742 and his chapel was burnt by a protestant mob. The bishop of Raphoe, James Gallagher, had been forced to flee from his diocese in 1734, because he had removed a priest from a parish who then reported him to the authorities. Similarly Bernard MacMahon archbishop of Armagh went into hiding in 1741 to escape from the authorities, having been denounced to the magistrates by a priest whom he had refused to promote to a parish.

Further intolerance is evinced by the reaction to the attempt of catholics in Downpatrick to build a chapel at Struell. This was pulled down by the local Church of Ireland curate and some of his parishioners.[50] The building of mass houses in Ulster even in the 1760s was a source of tension with protestants who tended to complain about what was seen as further catholic defiance. For the hierarchy, however, the provision of such establishments was increasingly seen as a priority. In 1764 archbishop Blake was thanked by his canons for building a number of mass houses in parishes where pastors had been indolent in the matter of church provision. The point of the mass house was that it guaranteed mass at fixed times and came to be the centre of parish life, and so made for greater order in the administration of the sacraments.[51]

Protestant and state hostility was not confined to resentment about the building of places of catholic worship. The penal laws although falling into disuse could still, on occasion, be directed against the clergy. Archbishop O'Reilly and eighteen of his priests were arrested at Killcurley, Co. Louth, in late April 1756 and taken to Dundalk for questioning before James Hamilton, viscount Limerick. Limerick

[48] Brady, 'Catholics and Catholicism', pp. 69–70.

[49] R.B. MacDowell, *Irish Public Opinion 1750–1800* (London, 1944), p. 72

[50] James O'Laverty, *An Historical Account of Down and Connor, Ancient and Modern*, 5 vols (Dublin, 1878–95), here vol. 1, p. 101.

[51] Patrick J.Corish, *The Catholic Community in the Seventeenth and Eighteenth Centuries* (Dublin 1981), p. 106.

had them all released on ascertaining the reason for their meeting, which seems to have had no other conspiratorial intent than to distribute holy oils and try to regulate the number of religious holidays. As a result of their deliberations eighteen such festivals were dropped from the calendar. As *Faulkner's Dublin Journal* reported on 11 May that year, the proposal must be 'very pleasing' to the public since such days were 'great inlets into all idleness and vices'. The holidays tended to be celebrated as days of 'debauchery and drunkenness; not of religion but of vice and immorality; so that one nominal saint or holiday makes thousands of real sinners.'[52]

Government authorities had long seen the Church as a means for helping to control a wayward populace. Clergy often stressed the need for order, and to abstain from drunkenness and miscreant behaviour. The Church's role as an instrument of order in society was singularly important as the possibility of unrest was heightened in periods of social disintegration. Spectacular instances of violence or disorder were carefully monitored by both state and Church. The papal inter-nuncio reported from Brussels to Rome in October 1736 of a skirmish in the previous month between a detachment of dragoons and 200 'rebels' in Dungannon. The insurgents had taken the mayor and burghers hostage, demanding that a ransom be paid for their release. No ransom was forthcoming, and instead the soldiers mounted a rescue operation in the process of which they killed eighteen of the marauders. Later in the century the Whiteboy movement which had begun as an agitation against the tithes of the Church of Ireland soon turned its attention on the exactions of the catholic clergy. Given the oath-bound nature of their organisation, the Whiteboys were opposed by the official Church. It was not a movement popular in Ulster despite the poverty of the people. This may be indicative of a greater bond between the Ulster clergy and their people because of their minority status in the province and the solidarity this engendered. However by the end of the century this cohesion was beginning to break down and Ulster catholics too began to complain of clerical exactions.

In the 1740s the Church was not the only instrument of social con-trol. In the famine years of 1739–41 as many as 300,000 people died from hunger and disease, and those who suffered most in Ulster were poor catholics. Because of the demoralisation of this experience and its aftermath there was no support for the Scottish Jacobite rising in 1745 in favour of Charles Edward the Young Pretender. It has been suggested that by this stage many of the richer catholics were more interested in the maintenance of the *status quo* to protect their vested

[52] Brady, *Archivium Hibernicum*, vol. 16, p. 90.

interests than in the restoration of the house of Stuart.[53] But such considerations were hardly to the fore in Ulster. Here it is more likely that a lack of leadership coupled with the demoralisation adverted to above was the main cause of the failure of the Ulstermen to turn out for Charles Edward. This should not be taken as an indication of general alienation or of lack of support for the Stuart cause. On his appointment as bishop of Down and Connor in 1740, Dr Francis Stuart wrote to thank James III for his appointment to that see. Stuart of course was a committed Jacobite. As Franciscan provincial in Ireland he opposed the scheme of some catholic lords to present an address of loyalty to George II in 1727, on the grounds of adherence to the Old Pretender. But Stuart was not the only Irish bishop to insist on maintaining loyalty to the old order of things. Daniel O'Reilly also wrote in effusive terms to James after his appointment to episcopacy in September 1747.[54]

Whatever advantages catholicism might have as a stabilising influence on the catholic underclass in the 'protestant nation', it still aroused deep suspicion in many members of the ascendancy. Towards the end of the 1750s further attempts were made to regulate the relationship between catholicism and the Irish state. The 1757 bill for the registration of the clergy, would have allowed 200 more priests into the country, and a further fifty to act as personal chaplains to wealthy catholics. Each clergyman would have to take an oath that he was not a regular, and, as with queen Anne's registration act, parish priests would not be allowed to officiate outside their parishes. The bill was rejected by the House of Lords where the Church of Ireland bishops rallied to defeat it. This was not the act of tolerance on the part of the bishops which it might ostensibly appear to be; the new registration bill was linked to a proposal to reform the Church of Ireland in an effort to undermine catholicism further, and the bishops thought that the proposed reforms were too expensive to introduce.[55]

One of the most remarkable attempts by the Irish church in the eighteenth century to come to terms with the reality of its position was spearheaded by several of the Ulster bishops in 1757. Under the careful stage management of the leading lay catholic lord Trimleston, archbishop O'Reilly of Armagh, along with MacColgan of Derry (who also represented Nathaniel O'Donnell of Raphoe[56]) and

[53] F.J. McFlynn, ' "Good Behaviour": Irish Catholics and the Jacobite Rising of 1745' in *Eire-Ireland*, vol. 16 (1981), p. 50.

[54] *Archivium Hibernicum*, vol. 14 (1949), p. 90.

[55] Cf. John Brady, *Irish Ecclesiastical Record*, vol. 97. 1962, pp. 220-1.

[56] O'Donnell may have stayed away from this meeting because of problems between his predecessor and the primate. In 1751, much to O'Reilly's chagrin, bishop Anthony O'Donnell had opposed the idea of calling a provincial synod because he thought it

O'Reilly of Clogher, met at Tremblestown, Co. Meath, to discuss the factors which had led to the proposal for the 1757 clergy registration bill. To counter the claims of catholic disloyalty, a pastoral letter was drawn up which provided for prayers to be said after mass on Sundays and holy-days for the king and members of the royal family. In addition the bishops added a declaration to be read at mass four times a year, stating that it was not catholic teaching that the pope or a general council of the Church could depose kings or release subjects from their duty of allegiance to their sovereign. The declaration also rejected the idea that the pope had any power over the temporal jurisdiction of princes. It asserted that the pope could not permit catholics to take false oaths, and furthermore that it formed no part of catholic teaching that members of the Church might injure heretics with impunity.[57]

Although this pastoral letter was issued over the signatures of the Ulster bishops concerned, it is important to stress its unrepresentative nature. The prelates in the other ecclesiastical provinces rejected it almost as soon as it became public, as did the absent Ulster bishops O'Doran of Down and Connor and Garvey of Dromore. The document represents a uniquely Irish brand of gallicanism which some historians detect as an essential feature of Irish catholicism from the 1750s on,[58] but its clear rejection of the Stuart pretensions to the throne served to ensure that it would be less than sympathetically received in the Irish Church as a whole.

From the mid-century there was something of a shortage of clergy in Ulster, partly because of the rising population but also because the Holy See had decided, after many complaints, to take action against the friars in Ireland. Even the House of Lords had complained in 1731 of the fact that the friars fought among themselves over their individual rights to quest for money in different parishes. Archbishop Michael O'Reilly was convinced that the conduct of the friars was an impediment to the reform of the Irish Church, and frequently complained to Rome of the abuses the regulars made of their privileges of exemption from diocesan control.

Another source of contention was that when friars were placed in positions of authority they did not always live up to the standards expected from membership of the hierarchy. Laurence Taaffe, canon of Armagh, protested bitterly to cardinal Antonelli of Propaganda in April 1784 at the conduct of Denis Maguire, the Franciscan bishop of Kilmore, who appointed fellow Franciscans to the best parishes

---

might give rise to suspicion on the part of the government and become the pretext for further persecution.

[57] Cf. Brady, *Irish Ecclesiastical Record*, vol. 97 (1962), p. 217.

[58] R.B. McDowell, *Irish Public Opinion 1750-1800* (London, 1944), p. 14.

in his diocese. The diocesan clergy became so frustrated with his conduct that they killed his horse and set fire to his house in retaliation. The historian of the friars in Ireland, Hugh Fenning, comments that Taaffe was an influential Ulster priest and far from being an eccentric.[59] Bishop John MacColgan of Derry also complained of difficulties with the frairs, and this despite the 1751 rescript from Propaganda which forbade the orders from receiving recruits in Ireland, and which made the regular clergy subject to diocesan control.

In some areas the regular clergy had sufficient levels of personnel to ensure some continuity. The Franciscan community survived to minister in the district of Donaghmore, north-west of Dungannon, into the early nineteenth century. The parliamentary returns for 1764 mention that there was a friary there with six members, but by the end of the century there was only a single friar acting as curate to the diocesan parish priest.[60] The policy of no native training was to have a devastating effect on the number of friars in the northern Church. By 1766 James MacDonnell the Franciscan provincial was writing to Rome that in Ulster the friaries at Dromore, Down, Carrickfergus, Derry and Strabane were all vacant. By the following year the Dominicans had less than fifteen friars in the province, including Patrick McHenry who lived on his own in Coleraine as both 'prior and pastor'.[61]

Coupled with the problem of the friars, and the relative shortage of clergy was the issue of the calibre of individuals ordained to the priesthood. When they eventually arrived on the continent for training having had experience on the mission they were often inimical to collegiate discipline. Dr John Bourke, 'privisor' of the Irish College in Paris, wrote to James III in June 1735 that priests in such 'age of manhood, can neither have learning nor good behaviour, and who instead of learning or manners bring only along with them hither a certain wrong turn of wit [or] brain and a stubbornness, with which they think to cover their other defects, and are easily drawn in by a few artful men to enter into their fractious views'.[62]

Later in the century the shortage of priests was made worse by the closure of continental colleges. To remedy this in his own diocese the

---

[59] *The Undoing of the Friars of Ireland a study of the Novitiate Question in the eighteenth century* (Louvain, 1972), p. 53, note 1.

[60] Canice Mooney, 'The Franciscan First Order Friary at Dungannon', *Seanchas Ardmhacha*, vol. 1 (1955), pp. 72–93, traces the history of this friary for most of the eighteenth century.

[61] Hugh Fenning, 'Some Problems of the Irish Mission, 1773–1774', *Collectanea Hibernica*, vol. 8 (1965), p. 88.

[62] Hugh Fenning (ed.), 'Clerical Recruitment, 1735–1783: Documents from Windsor and Rome', *Archivium Hibernicum*, vol. 30 (1972), p. 4. A 'privisor' was one who recommended candidates to the benefactor who paid for their clerical education.

bishop of Raphoe turned his house in Letterkenny into a seminary, the first such establishment in Ulster. By 1794 he had fourteen students living with him, nine of whom were already ordained.[63] Bishop Troy however reported to Rome in 1781 of the increase of the clergy in the Armagh diocese from 1776 onwards, but this may have been confined to Co. Louth and therefore perhaps had little impact in Armagh and Tyrone. The question of shortage of clergy is not unrelated to the issue of how much use the faithful made of them. There is some controversy over the precise levels of practice of the faith in the mid- to late eighteenth century. Patrick Corish is perhaps inclined to overestimate the level of practice, and there are grounds for suspecting that in Ulster it may have been lower than in the rest of the country.[64]

In its dealings with Ireland the Holy See, despite the often intolerable circumstances under which the local Church existed, was still concerned to uphold its own authority at every level. It was also anxious to stamp out abuses. Ulster catholics continued to attract a certain amount of notoriety, to some extent because of the lack of quality in the clerical leadership of the community. This had serious repercussions not just for the internal coherence of the community but also in its dealings with the universal Church. In 1749 John Brullaghan the parish priest of Coleraine was appointed bishop of Derry, partly through the machinations of a close relative, a Dominican friar, who was an adviser to the congregation of Propaganda in Rome. Brullaughan was a most unsuitable character for any ecclesiastical office, least of all that of a bishop. He was accused by the archbishop of Armagh of being violent and a drunkard, and in addition seems to have kept a concubine. Rome admitted that it had made a mistake and following the personal intervention of pope Benedict XIV his nomination was withdrawn, but not before more than eighty pages of evidence had been taken against him.

At times however Rome displayed a lack of sensitivity in its dealings with the Irish Church. It is true that a certain licence was permitted to Ireland which was denied elsewhere. On several occasions in the earlier decades of the century archbishops of Armagh were permitted to exercise metropolitan authority although they had not received the pallium. By 1782 however Rome reprimanded the Ulster bishops for holding a synod which, it claimed, was not properly constituted; the diocesan chapter of Armagh had not been invited to take part in the proceedings. The Holy See took a dim view of this neglect of ecclesiastical procedure. In the early 1740s Rome had erected a

[63] Fenning, *The Undoing of the Friars in Ireland*, p. 43.
[64] *The Catholic Community in the Seventeenth and Eighteenth Centuries*, pp. 108ff.

canonical chapter in Armagh in an attempt to start bringing Ireland under the Tridentine model of ecclesiastical government. The then primate Bernard MacMahon, who disliked any interference in his conduct of the government of the diocese, objected with the claim that the individuals thus promoted were unworthy of the honour. Future archbishops were no less antipathetic to the idea of having to consult the lesser clergy in the administration of their diocese.

The synod of Drogheda had, however, committed an even greater breach of ecclesiastical protocol. The assembled bishops decided that it was costly and time-consuming to refer appeals of first instance to Rome. They therefore concluded that it would be much easier to settle disputes locally as far as possible. Rome moved swiftly to disabuse the Ulstermen of the idea that it should not hear such appeals, and were told unambiguously that 'The S[acred] Congregation will never suffer this.'[65] The changes they advocated smacked too much of gallicanism for the centralising tastes of Rome.

Concern for the proper administration of the sacrament of marriage remained an abiding issue throughout the century, particularly in Ulster where the clergy were convinced that under protestant influence catholics tended to sit lightly to marriage within the forbidden degrees of consanguinity. A typical request for dispensation was that sent by Bartholomew Hanlon, the parish priest of Drumcree Portadown, Co. Armagh, in the summer of 1764. The petition was made on behalf of Arthur MacMahon and Rose MacGranald who were related in the second degree of affinity. MacGranald was the sister of MacMahon's dead wife; they had lived together for seven years and had three children. The parish priest had persuaded them to marry so as to legitimise the children and 'avoid scandal'. The internuncio in Brussels, in forwarding the request to Rome, commented that 'the petitioners are poor people who live by the work of their hands.'[66] This anxiety for regularity in the observance of the regulations of the sacrament of marriage was a constant problem well into the nineteenth century.

Considering the trouble taken over marriage questions, remarkably little effort was made to provide for proper instruction in the basics of catholic belief. Bishop Gallagher of Raphoe published sixteen Irish sermons, which because of their novelty had enormous circulation. Most dioceses did have manuals of Sunday sermons, but these tended to be foreign imports and were in either French or Latin. Teaching the faith was mostly confined to Sunday instruction from the catechism; in the Clogher diocese this task was often given to someone

[65] Moran, *Spicilegium Ossoriense*, vol. 3, p.397.
[66] Giblin, *Collectanea Hibernica*, vol. 10 (1967), p. 138.

preparing for the priesthood or to a layman. In 1726 Archbishop Blake of Armagh had published a catechism which circulated in both Irish and English, but there was little effort to improve upon it, and it was still in use in the north of Ireland in the 1940s.[67]

As we have seen, the poverty of the Ulster community was a grave inpediment in its ability to make progress in religious matters, but with the many legal restrictions which either actively discouraged or blatantly prevented economic prosperity, what could be done? James Gallagher, bishop of Raphoe, wrote to the nuncio in September 1736 asking whether a book by the bishop of Killala, *A short view of the practice of giving money at interest* . . . , was orthodox. Some of the ideas in the book were apparently causing distress among the clergy. Was taking interest on a loan the sin of usury or not? If it was not, then—as Gallagher pointed out—this could be of great benefit to better-off catholics who, while excluded for other professions, might be able to prosper as money-lenders.

The rise of a catholic middle class, which occurred mostly outside Ulster, was facilitated through trade, both domestic and international. In Ulster most overseas trade was carried on by dissenters. One of the factors in the rise of Belfast to the prosperity it was beginning to enjoy from the mid-century on was the trade with Ulster presbyterians in America. That presbyterians had gone to America in such large numbers is perhaps attributable to a failure to prosper rather than direct persecution. For their part Ulster catholics were without money or inclination to follow suit.[68] In catholic circles overseas trading contacts tended to be with Europe and affected the areas of the country outside the northern province.[69]

By the middle decades of the century Rome was frequently vexed by the fact that Irish bishops would not reside in their dioceses. Many spent long periods in Dublin, and, although circumstances were undoubtedly harsh, such metropolitan residence was hardly justifiable on the grounds of persecution. One of the most celebrated examples of the abuse of non-residence was that of archbishop Anthony Blake of Armagh. Blake had had a vigorous ministry in Galway, where he was 'Warden' (priest in charge of all the parishes, with certain episcopal privileges and responsibilities), and was made bishop of Ardagh whence he was translated to Armagh in 1758. It has been suggested that he could have been promoted because he had remained a staunch Jacobite at a time when other bishops in the

---

[67] *A Digest of the historical account of the Diocese of Down and Connor*, p.284.

[68] Bardon, *A History of Ulster*, p. 177.

[69] Wall, 'The Rise of the Catholic Middle Class in Eighteenth-Century Ireland', *Irish Historical Studies*, vol. 11, 4, pp. 114–15.

Armagh province considered declaring loyalty to the house of Hanover.[70]

Blake would seem initially to have been an effective pastor, much given to reforms such as regularising times and places of worship and trying to stamp out abuses among the clergy. He convoked a diocesan synod in 1761 which aimed to give full ecclesiastical authority to his reform programme, and included a reassertion of the rights of the bishop in appointments to parishes.[71] One enactment of the synod urged the primate 'to disposses any priest of his parish, and of any other charge . . . who is a drunkard, or who will stay to drink whiskey, or any other spirituous distilled strong liquors, at any one place, time or meeting, exceeding the measure of what is commonly called a noggin, or double that quantity in punch'.[72] Soon, however, Blake's episcopal administration was dogged by factionalism. That he was an 'outsider' did not commend him to the Ulster clergy in his diocese. From the days of the O'Neill, as we have seen, Ulstermen had insisted that only one of their own was sufficiently understanding of the needs of the Ulster Church to be archbishop of Armagh. Such parochialism could at times be even more restrictive. In 1779 a group of Armagh priests wrote to cardinal Castetelli complaining that 'it was the unhappy lot of this diocese that for seventy years past it should be governed by bishops who did not spring from the diocese . . .'

Blake generated enormous opposition to his episcopacy through greed. He imposed exorbitant financial dues for religious services such as visiting parishes, appointments of parish priests, ordaining men to the priesthood—all this in addition to the ordinary diocesan taxes required annually of each parish. Failure to pay resulted in the suspension of the parish priest concerned. He also showed his contempt for the diocese by refusing to have a permanent place of residence, arguing that since he spent so much of his time visiting the remote parts of the diocese he could not justify such expense. In reality he spent much of his time living at his family home in Carrowbrowne, Co. Mayo.

Ironically the cause of the first round of sustained opposition to Blake from his clergy came when he suspended Peter Markey, the parish priest of Kilsaran, for having absented himself from his parish for several days, although Markey had secured the services of another priest to look after it in his absence. Blake's non-residence and

---

[70] Cf. pp. 77–8 above for an account of the Tremblestown meeting; also Patrick Whelan, 'Archbishop Anthony Blake of Armagh, 1758–1787', in *Seanchas Ardmhacha*, vol. 5 (1970), p. 259.

[71] Renehan, *Collections on Irish Church History*, p. 103.

[72] *ibid.*, p. 105.

consummate neglect were so infamous that he was satirised in a collection of late eighteenth-century Irish verse as 'a Connaught gentleman who came to Armagh on his visitations'.[73]

There were persistent complaints about Blake's non-residence and neglect of Armagh, even from his fellow-bishops. Factions arose owing to his attempt to create a coterie of supporters, by promoting his camp-followers to the wealthier benefices. The Holy See was prevailed upon to suspend Blake from his episcopal duties in April 1776, pending a full inquiry into all the charges against him. The investigation of the affair was placed in the hands of Dr John Troy, OP, then bishop of Ossory and subsequently archbishop of Dublin—who restored Blake to his duties in July the following year. Even after his restoration Blake was determined to cause further mischief for himself and the Ulster Church. On resuming his duties he set about suspending those priests whom he regarded as the ringleaders of the opposition to his episcopal administration. Eventually however he was persuaded to accept a co-adjutor—Richard O'Reilly a man of great independent wealth, and after some initial ill-feeling from the clergy in Counties Armagh and Tyrone, the diocese returned more or less to normal. O'Reilly administered the diocese while Blake lived the life of a country gentleman in his native province until death overtook him in advanced old age in 1787.

The Blake debacle is revealing; it shows that despite the church's adverse position in Ulster society the clergy, even including the highest-ranking prelates, often did not have a well-developed sense of mission. There is no suggestion that Blake was more avaricious than the average clergyman; in his will he left only £26 of disposable income,[74] despite having an annual pension of £150 between 1780 and 1787, but concern for a secure financial position was a growing phenomenon in the period as the general prosperity of the country increased the number of middle-class catholics.

The improvement in economic conditions which affected even some Ulster catholics contributed partly to the raising of catholic political demands and expectations. More especially it gave rise to the Catholic Committee in 1758, one of whose aims was to achieve gradual catholic integration into the political life of the nation. Although in the 1760s Ulster participation was almost negligible, by the 1780s northern catholics were electing their representatives to what was a strongly Dublin-based pressure group. By that time other groups were also at work in Irish society seeking a more radical transformation of the

[73] *Abhrain Airt Mhic Chubhthaigh*, p. xvii. Cf. also Whelan, *Seanchas Ardmhacha*, p. 300.

[74] William Corrigan (ed.), 'Catholic Episcopal Wills in the Public Record Office Dublin 1683–1812', *Archivium Hibernicum*, vol. 1 (1912), pp. 157–9.

socio-political order. In the propagation of radical ideas Ulster was to give the lead.

Catholic relief and the Volunteer crisis

One of the causes of Ulster's emerging economic fortunes was the 'linen triangle' which included Dungannon, Lisburn and Newry, with north Armagh at its heart. The growing population sustained by the linen industry in that county was almost equally divided between catholics and protestants. Greater financial security combined with the relaxation of the penal laws, brought in its wake renewed tensions between the two communities. The sectarian violence which became a feature of Ulster life from 1780s is partly explained by the fear of poorer protestants and presbyterians that their social and economic position was under threat.[75] Rather than a relaxation of the popery laws, they wanted them reinforced. If the government was unwilling to do this, they were quite prepared to take the law into their own hands.

Ulster's economic landscape was greatly influenced by the development of Belfast as the major industrial centre of the region. Another influence was the improvement in agricultural holdings in the east of the province to the relative disadvantage of mid-Ulster. The political aspirations of Ulster presbyterians were shaped by these economic gains. The outlook of the prosperous protestant bourgeoisie of Belfast and its environs was decidedly more liberal and democratic than that of their mid-Ulster co-religionists. Presbyterians in the east exhibited greater openness to American and French ideas of liberty and the rights of man, and so were more inclined to cast a benevolent eye on catholics and their need to be included in some way in the political nation. However, sectarian division was still an important constituent of Ulster life. Indeed one explanation for the liberal attitudes of presbyterians in the east of the Province was that the catholics, being in such a clear minority, could pose no economic or political threat to them. This contrasts sharply with the circumstances of mid-Ulster where the adherents of the established Church were forced to come to terms with more evenly balanced social and economic circumstances.

Yet intercommunal hostility and violence cannot, in the context of the north of Ireland, be reduced simply to social and economic

[75] Cf. Peter Gibbon, *The origins of Ulster Unionism: the formation of popular Protestant politics and ideology in nineteenth-century Ireland* (Manchester, 1975), pp. 22–43. See also David W. Miller, 'The Armagh Troubles, 1784–95' in Samuel Clarke and James S. Donnelly, Jr. (eds), *Irish Peasants: Violence and Political Unrest 1780–1914* (Manchester, 1983), pp. 162–3.

components. Ulster's bloody and turbulent history is based on those religious antipathies which arose from the central doctrines of the protestant reformation and the catholic counter-reformation.[76] Despite evidence of growing tolerance for catholics among some members of the protestant and presbyterian communities, overall there appeared to be a hardening of religious attitudes. Religious hatreds were to some extent aggravated by a revival of evangelical fervour, which had been making advances in Ulster from the 1740s. One of the effects of this was to help give a sharper edge to the anti-catholic nature of much protestant and calvinist theological speculation.[77] Some at least of the catholic-protestant violence in the closing decades of the century had this renewed religious fervour as its base.

The mid-1770s had witnessed yet more presbyterian emigration to America. Bad harvests and rent increases early in the decade caused living standards to tumble and the resulting social instability made emigration across the Atlantic an attractive alternative for many Ulster presbyterians. The political ferment in America aroused much sympathy and support in presbyterian Ulster for the colonists. The catholics by contrast supported the London government's North American policy,[78] partly because further concessions were in the offing and the community had therefore no wish to upset the establishment by espousing revolutionary causes either at home or abroad.

By the time the French had declared their support for the American colonists the political temperature in Ireland was at fever point. A militant and expansionist France could conjure up among many protestants nothing but the ghost of catholic domination and rekindled images of the Seven Years War, when the French under General Thurot took Carrickfergus in February 1760. Given the possibility of French invasion, and absorption of so much of the London government's resources in the prosecution of the American war, Ireland was thrown back on its own efforts to defend itself. But this was the defence of protestant Ireland and the interests to be protected were those of the ascendancy and, in Ulster, of the presbyterians. It is essential to recognise that by this time in its history presbyterianism was for all

---

[76] On this Marianne Elliott has remarked: 'It has become unfashionable to reiterate the importance of religious divisions in modern Irish history.' See 'The Origins and Transformation of Early Irish Republicanism', in *International Review of Social History*, vol. 22 (1978), p. 407.

[77] David Hempton and Myrtle Hill, in *Evangelical Protestantism in Ulster Society, 1740–1890* (London and New York, 1992), p. 44, suggest that in the 1780s and '90s Evangelicalism 'imbued the Ulster Protestant Community with a sense of divine approval in its continued resistance to assimilation into the wider culture in which the Roman Catholic religion was regarded as the most central and pernicious element.'

[78] R.B. McDowell, *Ireland in an Age of Imperialism and Revolution, 1760–1801* (Oxford, 1979), p. 241.

practical purposes part of the protestant nation, despite the efforts of Belfast presbyterianism to make it otherwise.[79]

The birth of the Volunteer movement must be seen then as an essentially protestant reaction to what was perceived as a renewed danger from the catholic quarter. The Volunteers in Ulster at times recruited *en masse* from among the 'Peep o' Day Boys' but it is a mistake to see, as R.E. Burns does, recruitment from the ranks of the Freemasons as necessarily indicative of sectarianism.[80] At this period there were many catholic Masons and this was a determinant unifying factor in the harmony of some catholics and Volunteer groups.[81] In general though the possibility of a French war, fear of government relaxation of the penal laws, and the worsening economy all fused to cause Irish protestants to turn on their 'historic enemies—Irish Catholics'.[82]

For their part the catholics were only too anxious to express their loyalty to the crown and constitution, but membership of the Volunteers as a means of doing this was denied to them. We have the testimony of the Rev. William Steele, presbyterian minister of Portaferry, that offers by Ulster catholics to join the Volunteers were for the most part rejected. The Volunteers were at times used for policing activities, and in some areas helped to put down Whiteboyism. After the crisis of 1778–9, when it was abundantly clear that Irish catholic loyalty lay with George III, the Volunteers were used by the Irish parliament as a lever in obtaining redress for the grievances of the protestant nation in its ongoing struggle with London over Poyning's Law, which required all Irish legislation to be approved by the Westminster government. In Ulster by the end of the 1770s there were perhaps as many as 20,000 Volunteers, some companies of which from the early 1780s admitted catholics, but the number of such companies must not be exaggerated.[83] Catholics

---

[79] As Hempton and Hill remark, 'To say that Presbyterians were to the forefront of Belfast radicalism is not the same thing as saying that Belfast radicalism was the dominating feature of Ulster Presbyterianism,' *Evangelical Protestantism*, p. 24.

[80] 'The Belfast Letters, the Irish Volunteers 1778–79 and the Catholics', *Review of Politics*, vol. 21 (1959), p. 687. Like many such organistions in Ulster, the Peep o' Day Boys' were a band of marauders who engaged in sectarian violence against the Catholic community. Although it was often claimed for such groups that they were a response to a perceived threat, the element of 'recreational violence' was also present in their attacks.

[81] Patrick Rogers, *The Irish Volunteers and Catholic Emancipation, 1778–1793: A neglected phase of Ireland's history* (London, 1934), p. 62.

[82] R.E. Burns, 'The Belfast Letters', p. 684.

[83] The Belfast Volunteers were certainly less sectarian in origin than Volunteer companies elsewhere and were the first to admit catholics to their number in 1783.

were still seen as a threat to the ascendancy, and even as late as October 1791 the Armagh grand jury was complaining of 'the rage among Roman Catholics for illegally arming themselves'.[84]

The Volunteers were however increasingly given approval by the Ulster catholics, and feelings of mutual admiration were allowed to come to the surface. Volunteer support for the new catholic mass-house in Belfast is well known. In Derry by July 1782 Volunteer companies were being inspected by catholic clergy who were 'politely entertained' by them. Two years earlier the catholic bishop of Derry, Philip McDevitt, and some thirteen of his priests had presented the Strabane Volunteers with a sum above £39, conscious as they were 'of the advantages that may arise to the Kingdom from the union of so many brave men, conducted by commanders of tried experience and known integrity and patriotism . . .' The money was used, with the bishop's approval, to buy gunpowder.[85]

Thus we can see that by 1780 the Volunteers had developed into something more than a mere defensive force. Henry Grattan was determined to use them as a bargaining counter in wringing concessions from the London administration. In December 1779 the Newry Volunteer company resolved that Ireland needed its legislative independence in order to protect its commercial interests. The Dungannon Volunteer convention in February 1782 resolved in favour of further catholic relief. It did so as the result, it must be said, of prompting from Grattan, who had advised the convention that it would be 'impolitic' to refuse to deal with the issue of catholic expectations of greater liberty in 'patriot' Ireland. This was followed a year later with a resolution by the First Belfast Volunteer Company in favour of full catholic emancipation. By this time Grattan had won his 'constitution' from Westminster, and English parliamentary and administrative restraint on Irish legislation and trade had been repealed. But it is questionable how much the British government's hand had been forced by events in Ireland into conceding the 1782 measures. Gerard O'Brien has indicated that 'The constitution of 1782 was primarily the product of [English] government policy and a set of political circumstances over which neither the patriots nor the Volunteers had any direct control.'[86] This is not to deny that

---

[84] McDowell, *Ireland in the age of Imperialism*, p. 382.

[85] Brady, *Archivium Hibernicum*, vol. 17 (1953), pp. 209 and 216. This is in contrast to episcopal attitudes elsewhere in the country. Bishop Troy was completely opposed to the Volunteers, and the financial contribution to them by Bishop Sweetman of Ferns had been coerced under threat of violence. Cf. Burns 'The Belfast letters', p. 688.

[86] Gerard O'Brien, *Anglo-Irish Politics in the Age of Grattan and Pitt* (Dublin, 1987), p. 171.

the London government feared armed opposition in the shape of the Volunteers. Of more significance and importance perhaps was the possibility of further enhancing catholic dependence on London in a way that would ensure catholic loyalty, in opposition to the patriotic tendencies of the Irish parliament.[87] At most we can say that the pace of political reform was speeded up under the influence of the Volunteers, rather than determined by them.

The Catholic Relief Acts of 1778 and 1782 removed most of the restrictions on catholic education and regulations on land ownership and inheritance. These acts were not necessarily pledges of government trust in the catholic community, but the reaction of catholics gave the Dublin and London governments grounds for hope that in time catholics could be relied on. The *London-Derry Journal* of 3 September 1782 reported that bishop McDevitt, his dean Dr O'Donnell and sundry other of the catholic clergy, appeared before Mr Justice Lill and in open court took the oath of allegiance as demanded by the 1782 act which regularized the presence of catholic clergy in the country. A typical reaction to the measure was that of Hugh O'Donnell the parish priest of Belfast. On 22 March he preached a sermon in which he praised the government for its enlightened and liberal policy. At the same time he hoped that the effect of the act would be to enable catholics 'to be of use to their king and country'. In O'Donnell's view catholics would be inclined to give 'every testimony of gratitude and allegiance'.[88] He was not unaware of hostility to the relief acts from some sections of protestant and presbyterian opinion, but he adverted to a resolution passed by the Presbytery of Bangor welcoming the growing toleration of catholics, which he took to be indicative of presbyterian feeling in general. The Bangor vote in favour of catholic relief was followed by a similar declaration from the Presbytery of Killyleagh in May. These were not the posturings of eccentric pockets of presbyterian opinion. In June that year the synod of Ulster debated the Killyleagh declaration and in an address to the king approved the idea of universal toleration in religious matters.[89]

The relief acts, though welcome, did not remove all the grounds for catholic grievances. Under the terms of the 1782 act catholics were still excluded from the political nation, although both Edmund Burke in England and Grattan in Ireland worked to change this state of affairs. Yet more concessions were granted in the 1793 Catholic Relief Act, forced by Pitt on the Irish parliament in the face of further economic

---

[87] Cf. Thomas Bartlett, *The Fall and Rise of the Irish Nation*, pp. 98–101.
[88] Brady, *Archivium Hibernicum*, vol. 17, p. 219.
[89] Rogers, *The Irish Volunteers*, pp. 71–2.

catastrophe and renewed war with France. The lord lieutenant, lord Westmoreland, had seen what was on the horizon the previous year, and revealingly told the home secretary Dundas: 'If concession be found advisable and we can manage the business in a manner not to alienate the Protestants, it will not be so dangerous, though it will certainly be very hazardous; and at the very least every step of conciliating the two descriptions of people that inhabit Ireland diminishes the possibility of the object wished—a union with England.'[90] But, as was to become clear by the end of the decade, the concessions achieved what the government had hoped for, namely the complete loyalty of the catholic community.

The difficulties in Armagh and mid-Ulster gave rise to two organisations which in their own way helped to fuel sectarian bitterness between catholics and protestants. Attacks on catholic homes by gangs of protestants ostensibly looking for arms—the 'Peep o' Day Boys'—saw the advent of the Defender organisation in Ulster. Initially the ascendancy party were inclined to be sympathetic to the catholic plight. One correspondent to the *Dublin Chronicle*, however, argued that catholics invited violence through their own provocative behaviour. He complained that they were accustomed to gathering in large groups, especially on the eve of May Day, 'to the great terror and alarm of the Protestant inhabitants of Armagh'. This line of argument was repudiated by a fellow Armagh protestant who wrote to the *Chronicle* that had the previous correspondent

> . . . been as vigilant in observing the real errors of our party, as he has been in noticing the imaginary misdemeanours of an other, he might have had opportunities during the winter of frequently seeing within two miles of Armagh some hundreds assembled under the denominations of Break of Day Men, for the illaudable purpose of concerting schemes to harass their Roman Catholic neighbours, many of whom, except when they were sheltered by their more humane Protestant friends, were obliged to commit themselves to the cover of caves during the night. . . .[91]

Violent incursions into the catholic districts made the community increasingly dependent on the Defenders for its protection. Although initially, in the 1780s, the Defenders were non-denominational (there is even some suggestion that they were armed by the Volunteers), they soon began to retaliate in kind, attacking protestant homes and centres of population. Their militancy caused general alarm among

---

[90] Quoted by John Healy, *Maynooth College: Its Centenary History* (Dublin, 1895), p. 89.
[91] Brady, *Archivium Hibernicum*, vol. 17, p. 255.

the ascendancy whose members began to change their minds about catholics, and instead of offering succour started to support the protestant insurgents. The threat to order from the Defenders was real. With its hierarchical and lodge-based system, its oath and catechisms, Defenderism[92] took on many of the characteristics of later secret revolutionary societies.[93] In fact the Defenders modified French revolutionary tastes for Irish palates. Marianne Elliott has found evidence that by 1792–3 the Defenders were negotiating with the French over possible assistance for a revolution in Ireland, almost two years before they began to be subsumed wholesale into the ranks of the United Irishmen.[94]

The absorption of the Defenders into the United Irishmen movement was in part a reaction to the emergence on the Ulster scene of the Orange Order.[95] The Armagh troubles had been growing more intense in the late 1780s and early 1790s, when it seemed as if the protestants were determined on a campaign to rid north Armagh of catholics altogether. It has been estimated that as many as 7,000 were driven from the county in the space of only two months in 1795, and that large numbers of these ended up settling in Connaught. One of the difficulties which increased bitterness was the fact that given relative catholic prosperity they were able at times to offer higher rents for tenancies than their protestant neighbours. Growing catholic strength was interpreted as a direct assault on protestant supremacy.

By the mid-1790s Defenderism had grown to the proportions of a national movement, and the revolutionary disposition of the catholic peasantry so excited protestant fears that the need to demonstrate domination became all the more pressing. Orangeism was to provide the forum in which this was to be accomplished. Building on certain traditional groupings already in existence, it was to give 'a kind of moral sanction to the subjugation of catholics . . . [an activity which had] a special attraction to the protestant peasantry . . . in border areas of south Ulster.'[96] The birth of the Order in September 1795 as

---

[92] Michael Beames, *Peasants and Power: The Whiteboy Movements and their control in Pre-Famine Ireland* (Brighton and New York, 1983), p. 26.

[93] Bardon, *A History of Ulster*, p. 225, says that the Defenders were a genuinely revolutionary organisation. In intent and motivation they were inspired by the American and French revolutions. This is at variance with David W. Miller, in 'The Armagh Troubles', p. 178, who is inclined to regard them as not revolutionaries in the strict sense. He points to evidence of the fact that some of the oaths used pledge allegiance to George III.

[94] Elliott, 'Early Irish Republicanism', p. 461.

[95] Stewart, *The Narrow Ground*, p. 103.

[96] Hereward Senior, *Orangeism in Ireland and Britain, 1795–1836* (London, 1966), p. 22.

a result of the battle of the Diamond in Loughall, Co. Armagh, helped to consolidate sectarian division at a stage in Ulster history when there appeared to be the possibility of greater catholic-protestant rapprochement than at anytime before.

The United Irishmen

It is perhaps best to see the United Irishmen, founded in Belfast in 1791, as an essentially protestant reform movement which nonetheless needed catholic support for its objectives.[97] Many of the leaders of the movement still tended to think of catholics as brutalised and illiterate.[98] The United Irishmen were to learn from the suppression of the Volunteers in 1793, the rejection of parliamentary reform by the Irish legislature, and the grudging nature of the Catholic Relief Act of 1793 that constitutional agitation would not bring about the Ireland they wanted. The only course left open was that of revolution.[99] By then the Catholic Committee had split into its radical and conservative factions, the latter supported by the hierarchy and the former infiltrated by United Irishmen. The committee was to dissolve in 1793, the more conservative element having judged that the concessions enacted that year made its continued existence unnecessary. The bishops were also worried by the continued extremist infiltration on to the board of the Catholic Committee.

Meanwhile the Irish church was forced to respond to the international crisis facing catholicism. Given the unstable situation on the continent, the bishops pleaded with the government to make provision for clerical education in Ireland. They were also much concerned that Irishmen studying abroad would be contaminated by the revolutionary social theories then so prevalent. The bishops presented a number of petitions to lord Westmoreland in 1794 pleading for a seminary in Ireland. When it was suggested that students for the priesthood might be trained at Trinity College Dublin, the bishops responded that a distinct place of education was necessary because 'the regulations of the Roman Catholic Church enjoin that candidates for Holy Orders shall be proficient in certain branches of learning, which are not included in the exercises of the University of

---

[97] Cf. Maureen Wall, 'The United Irish Movement' in J.L. McCracken (ed.), *Historical Studies V* (London, 1965), p. 122.

[98] Marianne Elliott, *Partners in Revolution: The United Irishmen and France* (London and New Haven, 1982) p. 14.

[99] Edith M. Johnston, *Great Britain and Ireland 1760–1800* (London, 1963), pp. 6–7. Elliott, in *Partners in Revolution*, p. 47, dates the United Irishmen's 'conversion' to republicanism to 1795.

Dublin.'[100] Moreover, they objected to Trinity as a centre of 'atheism and Jacobinism'.[101]

The bill to establish a catholic seminary—later to become the Royal College of St Patrick, Maynooth—was given the royal assent in the summer of 1795. A number of government officials were to be among the trustees and three bishops from each ecclesiastical province were also to act in this capacity. The first two Ulster bishops to be trustees were O'Reilly of Armagh and McDevitt of Derry. The trustees, professors and students were all obliged to swear the oath of allegiance as prescribed in the 1782 relief act. In return the government was to build and endow the college. The price to be paid was undoubtedly the restriction of the Church's freedom of action in its dealings with the state. But given the events of the French revolution the catholic Church was only too happy to ensure state support and cooperation wherever it could be found. Yet, as Edmund Burke had warned the churchmen, 'If you consent to put your clerical education, or any other part of your education, under their control [i.e. government supervision] then you will have sold your religion for their money.'[102]

The harmony of government and catholic interests was such that by 1799 the episcopal trustees of Maynooth could record that 'in the appointment of the Prelates of the Roman Catholic Religion to vacant sees within the kingdom, such interference as may enable it to be satisfied of the loyalty of the person to be appointed is just and ought to be agreed to.'[103] This document, while signed by only the Maynooth trustees, indicates nonetheless the thinking of the most important bishops in the country, including the archbishop of Armagh who was one of the instigators of the whole scheme. When however its contents were made public by Grattan in 1808, it raised a storm of protest in the Irish Church, and the bishops were forced to back down. As late as 1814 the topic was again discussed at Rome in the light of a proposal to grant Catholic emancipation; Cardinal Litta of Propaganda accepted in principle that an oath of allegiance to the monarch, and even a government veto in episcopal appointments, was not incompatible with catholic teaching provided there were some safeguards. The main cause for concern in 1799 had obivously been the conduct of rebellious catholics the previous year, prompting a desire among the bishops as representatives of the catholic community to demonstrate their ultra-loyalty. But how had catholics behaved in 1798?

[100] Moran, *Spicilegium Ossoriense*, vol. 3, p. 463.
[101] *ibid.*, p. 474.
[102] Quoted in Healy, *Maynooth College*, p. 101.
[103] Moran, Spicilegium Ossoriense, vol. 3, p. 614.

The rising

'The ninety-eight' in the south-east degenerated into little more than sectarian slaughter. In Ulster by contrast the rising was aimed directly against government forces, and despite the near decimation of the United Irishmen by lieutenant-general Gerard Lake the previous year, they remained strong enough for the rising to have some successes in its early phase in June. The insurgents counted the taking of Ballymena, Randalstown and Saintfield among their prizes. It is striking, however, that the Ulster rebellion was generally a presbyterian affair. Catholics did participate but their numbers and influence outside the eastern seaboard were not significant. Yet even in Antrim and Down the impression is of catholics deserting the movement.[104] Indeed one of the most treacherous individuals from the whole period was the young catholic farmer from Saintfield, Nicholas Magin, who for eighteen months before the rising systematically betrayed his revolutionary colleagues to the Dublin Castle authorities.[105]

The failure of catholics to support the rebellion in Ulster inevitably contributed to the hopelessness of the enterprise. The reasons for catholic reluctance to take part are not hard to find. Ulster catholics had suffered much brutality at the hands of the yeomanry which had been raised in 1796 largely from among Orangemen, and which even in the year of rebellion continued to terrorise catholics in mid-Ulster. By the end of the rebellion protestants and catholics were more divided than at any time in the previous fifty years. If catholics felt cowed by the Orange yeomanry, fear of catholicism ensured the enduring success of the Orange Order. Despite the clear political differences between the anglican-based Order and the presbyterian community, as joint heirs of the reformation, they had sufficient community of interests to regard catholicism as the chief obstacle to their liberties. On the other hand thirteen presbyterian ministers were implicated in the rising, and of these three were executed.[106] More typical however of the general sentiments of Ulster presbyterians was the motion adopted at the autumn meeting of the synod of Ulster, condemning the behaviour of 'those few unworthy members of our Body whose conduct we can only view with grief and indignation'; it went on to reaffirm the Church's 'fidelity to the crown' and 'attachment to the constitution'.[107]

---

[104] Thomas Pakenham, *The Year of Liberty: The History of the Great Irish Rebellion of 1798* (London, 1969), p. 219.

[105] *ibid.*, p. 170. Pakenham points out that Magin like so many others had been blackmailed into spying for the government. That said he took to his task with alacrity and was well rewarded by his paymasters.

[106] Louis Cullen, *The Hidden Ireland: Reassessment of a Concept* (Mullingar, 1988), p. 33.

[107] Quoted in Hempton and Hill, *Evangelical Protestantism*, p. 25.

Ulster catholic failure to support the rebellion was not solely the result of demoralisation arising from protestant oppression. Church authorities had no wish to encourage rebellion, which however political in intent would inevitably call into question the authority of the Church and the relationship between Church and state. There is after all some suggestion that Defenderism had become somewhat anti-clerical before its virtual amalgamation with the United Irishmen, and that it had begun to concern itself with Whiteboy issues such as offerings made to priests for the administration of the sacraments. Aware of this danger the Ulster clergy acted decisively to counteract rebellious ideas. In an address published by the *London-Derry Journal* on 5 March 1793, bishop McDevitt and the clergy of Derry warned of the dangers, both temporal and spiritual, and the concomitant disregard for all lawful authority, which were the direct result of membership of revolutionary organisations:

> At a time when the public mind seems to be much agitated, when sentiments inimical to good government, hostile to civil society and subversive of all order and regularity begin to be manifested by unlawful and tumultuous associations and to be carried into execution by riotous and unwarrantable proceedings, we feel it to be our indispensable duty to remind you of your obligations both civil and religious . . . conjure you by everything that is most dear to you not to let yourselves be misled under any pretence whatsoever from the line of loyalty due to your sovereign and of obedience to the laws of your country. . . . We cannot here omit to assure you that any individual under our care who shall be so unhappy, so imprudent and so foolhardy as to deviate from the line of conduct here pointed out to him shall upon conviction be forthwith branded by us an enemy of the community at large and shall be and is hereby declared altogether unworthy of our communion.[108]

This carefully worded denunciation of lawlessness and rebellion was by no means exceptional in Ulster. In January of the 'Year of Liberty', the Dominican parish priest of Carrickfergus, James Matthew MacCary, preached and wrote a lengthy pamphlet against the United Irishmen, again warning of the dangers of rebellion and drawing attention to the rewards of loyalty. Certain strands of Irish historiography tend to dismiss MacCary and his fellow priests such as William Taggart of Saintfield and Patrick MacArtan of Loughlinisland, because there is some suggestion that they were paid informers.[109] Equally the exemplary nature of their views is treated

[108] P.R.O.N.I., *Aspects of Irish Social History*, pp. 109–10.
[109] Cf. John Gray, 'A Loyal Catholic Sermon of 1798', *The Linen Hall Review*, vol. 14, 4 (1987), p. 13. Gray notes that MacCartan also gave evidence against the

by some with scepticism especially because MacCary became something of an ecclesiastical renegade and although he died reconciled to the Church he was suspended for many years.

It is also possible to amass evidence for the alternative view that the catholic clergy were fomenters of United Irish disturbances. In all, fourteen priests were involved in revolutionary activity and six of them were executed. This does not include the case of James O'Coigly, a United Irishman, a native of the parish of Kilmore and priest of the Armagh diocese, who was captured at Maidstone in Kent on his way to France. He was tried for treason and sentenced to death in May 1798 and has the distinction of being the last catholic priest to be executed in England for treason. The curate of Rathlin Island, Edward MacMullen, was likewise a revolutionary and although arrested and brought to Ballycastle he escaped flogging by promising never to set foot again in Co. Antrim. St Patrick's College Maynooth also had its share of United Irish sympathisers. In all some seventeen students were expelled after confessing to having taken the United Irish oath, mostly before they joined the college. All this took place before the rebellion in May had got under way.

The compliance with governmental authority shown by the overwhelming majority of the clergy in Ulster was more typical. Their loyalty was further demonstrated in the following year when the proposals for union with Britain were unveiled. One allurement for the Church in considering its attitude to the union was the fact that Pitt had promised Catholic emancipation if the United Kingdom were brought into being. It is difficult to estimate just how much this was a factor in the bishops' deliberations on the matter. What did occupy them was the concern not to be seen to obstruct government proposals in a way which might give any grounds for suspicion that they were not wholly devoted to the authority of the crown. Also, there were still sporadic attacks on Ulster catholics, and instances of mass-house burning in counties Down and Tyrone. This took place like the persecutions earlier in the decade under the rule of the 'patriot parliament'. There was no reason to think that catholics would be any worse off under a United Kingdom government; on the contrary there was some indication that their lot would improve. After all, 'England had always proved a better friend to the Catholics than had their fellow

---

1803 rebel leader Thomas Russell. The compiler of *A Digest of the historical account of the Diocese of Down and Connor* suggests that MacCartan did so against his will. Gray also records the name of a 'Father Devenney' of Ballygowan near Larne who was also a paid informer. Gray here gives his source as Robert M. Young, *Ulster in '98* (Belfast, 1893) p. 44. However I can find no record of any priest of that name having served in the diocese. The failure may of course be mine rather than that of Gray or Young.

countrymen.'[110] Even Wolfe Tone, for all his rhetoric on liberty, had views on the catholic position in society which could seem far from enlightened.[111]

Early in 1799 archbishop Troy of Dublin wrote to Rome that because of the 'criminal action' of some priests in the rebellion it was only right that some demonstration of loyalty to the crown be offered by catholic officials; he was thinking primarily of government approval of bishops and parish priests before they assumed office.[112] But what greater token of fealty to the state could there be than support for the union? For his part the primate of Armagh, Richard O'Reilly, indicated his vigorous support for the proposal of legislative union. He went so far as to persuade his fellow-archbishop, Dr Dillon of Tuam, to sign the resolution in favour of union at a time when Dillon was wavering. The senior clergy supported the Union in the hope of better conditions for Roman Catholicism in the United Kingdom, than they had come to expect in 'patriot' Ireland.

J.C. Beckett has written of eighteenth-century Ireland that it was a protestant kingdom, 'governed under a Protestant constitution; and the whole Protestant population, from the members of parliament at College Green to the linen weavers of County Armagh, was convinced of its right to a position of ascendancy. . . .'[113] It was largely to refute the claims to that ascendancy that catholics acquiesced in the union. The eighteenth century had seen the development of the church from a position where it was actively persecuted to one where external barriers to its existence and development had been removed. It did not thereby become a completely free agent, able to evolve inexorably according to its own internal constitution. Its position in Ulster was, at the very least, precarious. With comparatively few resources and with religious practice not always of a high or regular order, it faced an uphill struggle in confirming the faith of its adherents. The point however is that by the end of the century it could hope to peruse its mission on its own terms, though still battling against the legacy which its frequently bitter experience in the eighteenth century had bequeathed to it.

---

[110] Marianne Elliott, *Wolfe Tone: Prophet of Irish Independence* (New Haven and London, 1989), p. 131.

[111] Elliott, 'Early Irish Republicanism', p. 422.

[112] Margaret Gibbons, *Glimpses of Catholic Ireland in the Eighteenth Century* (Dublin, 1932), p. 266.

[113] *The Anglo-Irish Tradition* (London, 1976), p. 81.

3

THE SOCIAL AND RELIGIOUS
CONDITION OF ULSTER CATHOLICS
TO 1850

The background

The circumstances of Ulster catholicism in the early to mid-nineteenth century cannot be described as particularly propitious. The north was slow to recover from the effects of penal legislation. Church accommodation was not nearly sufficient to meet the needs of the people and religious instruction and catechesis were at an especially low ebb. This was partly the result of lack of education among the clergy.

Maynooth, when it was founded in 1795, could not provide for all the needs of the country. French seminaries were closed to Irish students so that often, as in the eighteenth century, aspirants to the priesthood received rudimentary education either as 'apprentice' priests picking up the basics '*in situ*' or, as in the Clogher diocese, attending a hastily constructed seminary in which the bishop himself admitted that the level of instruction was at best 'tolerable'. As a remedy bishops introduced 'monthly conferences' with the purpose of giving priests an ongoing formation in philosophy and theology with particular emphasis on scripture and moral theology. Such conferences may not entirely have made up for a basic lack of sound education in the sacred sciences but priests were nonetheless compelled to attend meetings and contribute to the expenses.

While it is true that Maynooth began to offer better education in both quality and quantity, it had to deal at times with relatively poor abilities in its students. Theodore Hoppen believes that Maynooth as 'a power house of ideas . . . was a failure'.[1] A less antagonistic view, probably nearer the mark, was that the college was 'more a school of piety and ecclesiastical discipline . . . than an intellectual centre where minds were stretched by the philosophical and theological issues of the age'.[2] The Church in Ulster produced more than its fair

[1] K. Theodore Hoppen, *Elections, Politics and Society in Ireland, 1832–85* (Oxford, 1984), p. 103.
[2] Donal A. Kerr, 'Under the Union Flag: The Catholic Church in Ireland 1800–70' in *Ireland after the Union* (Oxford, 1989), p. 35.

share of the leading lights of Maynooth, but even so there remained
in parts of Ulster the practice of bishops ordaining priests who had
not completed the full course of their studies. Occasionally this
meant sending individuals abroad to fill the lacunae some time after
ordination.

Historians are divided on whether northern catholics were worse
off than those in the rest of the country in the way in which they
understood their religion. What is clear is that many were almost
entirely ignorant of the content of the christian faith and practised
what was often little more than a folk religion. Superstitions were rife
even, at times, among those aspiring to the priesthood. William
Carleton records one such would-be Melchizedek threatening that
when he finally received the panoply of sacerdotal power he would
'translate all the protestants into asses and then we'll get our hands
rid of them altogether'.[3] Such notions of the magical powers of the
catholic clergy were at times shared by protestant peasants and made
the priest feared by this stratum of society in both communions.

There were instances of rural peasants being tricked into eating
meat on Friday and then believing that they had thereby ceased to be
catholics, and sometimes as a result they conformed to the established
Church. The Derry diocese reported that in the course of the special
services held to mark Gregory XVI's priestly jubilee in 1842,
'thousands thronged the tribunal [i.e. the confessional] . . . among
whom were many who renouncing the errors of Protestantism
embraced the Catholic faith.' This seems to be a reference to people
returning to catholicism having fallen away for these comparatively
trivial reasons. Even explicitly religious festivities and sites had about
them the ring of superstition and debauchery. The holy well in
Letterkenny was known not only for its local saint but also for the local
fairy who was said to reside there; often in popular perception the two
were indistinguishable. Such intermingling of faith and fancy lead
the ecclesiastical authorities gradually to withdraw their blessing
from such sites in many places in the north. Examples range from
St Patrick's well in Struel, Co. Down, to St John's Errigall-Keroge in
Co. Tyrone. The custom at such sites followed a set formula whereby
the visitor made a wish and left some article of clothing attached to a
bush as a reminder to the patron to grant one's request. Holy wells
were believed to have supernatural force which could dispense
remedies for all complaints, not merely spiritual ones. St Bodhan's
pond in Culdaff, Co. Donegal, did a roaring trade in curing cattle
dipped in it.

[3] William Carleton, *Traits and Stories of the Irish Peasantry* (Dublin, 1830–3), vol. 1,
p. 163.

In many places bonfires were lit on St John's Eve accompanied by much feasting. It seems that these activities were reminiscent of pre-christian celtic services to mark the summer solstice. The feast of the Assumption of the Virgin in August was also a time of pilgrimage to the holy places. However, as more than one witness testifies, these excursions were often celebrations of 'the most disgusting drunkenness and debauchery, under the pretence of paying adoration' to the local saint. In the parish of Cloncha in the Derry diocese the saint in question was Moriallagh whom the local Church of Ireland rector observed was not even in the calendar of saints. He furthermore reported that 'the clergy of the church of Rome have, very properly, forbidden the offensive orgies by which [St. Moriallagh] is worshipped: it is, however, to be regretted, that his votaries have not attended to the salutary advice of their pastors on this subject.'[4]

Historically the most famous site in the north of Ireland as a centre of pilgrimage was St Patrick's Purgatory on Lough Derg in the Clogher diocese. Its popularity was at its height in the 1820s when an estimated 6,000 would flock each year to perform what by any standards were gruelling feats of religious endurance consisting of fasting, deprivation of sleep and the constant repetition of the set prayers, the Our Father and Hail Mary, in Latin, a language which very few of the pilgrims understood. The piety associated with the shrine was almost exclusively Marian, although pilgrims were expected to confess their sins and receive the eucharist. However this pilgrimage, though free from the debaucheries of other sites, was also beset with superstitions. Pilgrims urged one another on to even greater acts of austerity believing this would ensure that no request from heaven 'good, bad or indifferent' would fail to be granted. The northern bishops acted to curtail such impieties by insisting that only those pilgrims who had the permission of their parish priests could be admitted to the island to perform the penances and receive the proffered indulgence. As the century progressed the site lost some of its appeal, and by the 1880s attendance had dropped to around 3,000 pilgrims a year.

Two other aspects of catholic practice, one of which endured long into the century and beyond, deserve mention: stations and wakes. The abuses connected with saying mass and administering the sacraments in the home of selected individuals tended to centre around clerical avarice. Only the wealthier farmers could afford to host such gatherings where often the priest would sit down to a hearty

---

[4] William Shaw Mason, *A Statistical Account or Parochial Survey of Ireland*, 3 vols (Dublin, 1814–19). Here vol. 2, pp. 181–2.

meal with the better class of parishioners. Although they were increasingly seen as opportunities to catechise, the practice fell increasingly into disuse after 1850.

Wakes were altogether different and in some respects might be seen as a domestic lying-in-state. Even the poorest households would offer whiskey and other refreshment, with pipes and snuff. Wakes were opportunities for story-telling with fairy stories and ghost stories predominating, but at times too, there were stories of political ferment, especially the rebellion of 1641. Apart from the excessive eating and drinking that accompanied such social gatherings the clergy objected in particular to keening and the wake games. Some of these were of an explicitly sexual nature while others involved parodies of such things as the sacrament of marriage. Certain games involved physical violence.

The clergy waged a long and often bitter struggle against wakes. Already by the late eighteenth century, following the precedent of the decrees of the synod of Drogheda of 1614, there were regulations in several of the northern dioceses against them. 'We wish that abuses and scandals in as much as they are said by the people to be committed by all at vigils of the dead commonly called "wakes" . . . should be vigorouslsly restricted by pastors and eventually abolished.' Thus read the statutes of Clogher of 1789. Further regulations threatened with suspension any priest who performed any religious function at a funeral where a wake had taken place. Because of this prohibition, there was at times the spectacle of family and friends having to bury a corpse themselves without any church service. This was at the cost of some hardship to the priests, since at funerals in the north it was customary to have a collection for the officiating clergyman. The evidence is fairly consistent, from the early nineteenth century on, of a sustained effort to rid funerals of wakes. Success was patchy but by 1814 the priests of Maghera in Co. Derry had managed to have keening abolished and replaced, most surprisingly at this early stage, by the singing of solemn Latin hymns including the *Dies irae*.[5]

By 1832 Arnold McMahon, the parish priest of Tydavent, Co. Monaghan, was still having to insist that no funeral service would take place in the parish unless it could be ensured that no tobacco would be secured for the funeral festivities. He further stipulated that there were to be no all-night dances at wakes, the penalty for violation of this decree being exclusion from the sacraments until public 'satisfaction' was made in the chapel.

If the people were ignorant of their religion, the clergy had to

[5] Mason, *Parochial Survey*, vol. 1, pp. 596–7.

some extent to bear the blame. In too many instances there was little attempt by priests to engage in preaching. Bishops were continually urging clergy to give sermons at church services as is clear from reports sent to Rome in the early years of the century, but these injunctions were often ignored. A Church of Ireland assistant curate reported in 1814 that while the three catholic priests in the two neighbouring chapels 'constantly say Mass' they 'very seldom' preach.[6]

The statutes in force in Clogher between 1789 and 1824 stipulated that if a priest failed to preach on three Sundays in succession he would be *ipso facto* suspended from his duties. It was also regulated that the clergy were to engage lay helpers to instruct parishioners in christian doctrine. This is a general feature of diocesan requirements. The Down and Connor regulations for 1834 stipulated that the vicars-forane were to send a report to the archbishop of Armagh each quarter assuring him that properly qualified lay people had been appointed in each parish to teach catechism, and that christian doctrine had been duly taught on the appointed days. If this had not been done, then the priests concerned were to be identified to the primate.

The church as a whole made sterling efforts to turn back the tide of ignorance. Already by 1838 the Dromore diocese had established religious confraternities some of which were devoted to the propagation of christian doctrine. In 1837 'The Catholic Society of Ireland for the Gratuitous Distribution of Religious books' had dispatched to Ulster 2,097 religious tracts including prayer books and catechisms. The need thus stimulated spread rapidly in the ensuing years with many of the northern bishops expressing the need for diocesan libraries and for christian doctrine confraternities in each parish. By 1842 Derry had a religious lending library of some 400 volumes. Even during the famine year of 1849, the northern dioceses collected more than £153 for the 'propagation of the Faith'.

In the administration of the sacraments the clergy made increasing efforts to curb indifferentism and ignorance of the christian faith. There are many instances of priests refusing absolution to penitents who did not know their catechism. Often, especially at station masses, success in catechetical examination was a *sine qua non* for the reception of the sacrament. Carleton's stories in this regard are most illuminating. 'Andy Lawlor, the Mass-server, in whom the priest had the greatest confidence, stood in a corner examining in their catechism those who intended to confess; and if they were able to stand the test

[6] Mason, *Parochial Survey*, vol. 1, p. 600.

he gave them a bit of twisted brown paper as a "ticket", and they were received at the tribunal.[7] The use of lay catechists as both examiners and instructors in christian doctrine was an important feature of ecclesiastical life. Lough Derg, at least in the early decades of the century, had its fair share of such individuals who attempted to impart sound teaching to the hordes of pilgrims. The catechists gave their services free. The practice of examination before receiving the sacraments became quite widespread towards the mid-century and was much resented by the laity who wanted to avail themselves of these channels of grace without the continuous examination of their beliefs. They often objected that having been put through such interrogation for first communion they should now be exempted from these preliminaries.

Efforts were also made by Church authorities to ensure the strict observance of Church practice in the discipline of the sacraments. Each parish priest was required to inform the bishop *in writing* of those members of the parish who had failed to fulfill their obligations as laid down by the Council of Trent to make their religious duties of confession and communion at least once a year. It was also impressed on clergy that it was their duty to eradicate what was seen as the more grossly unacceptable forms of anti-social behaviour such as illegal associations, quarrelling, violation of the Lord's Day, night wakes, or Sunday dances. The parish priest was to bring all such crimes and misdemeanours on the part of parishioners to the attention of the bishop.

The formal practice of religion in Ulster was not especially popular in the early decades of the century. In Belfast by the mid-1830s the practice rate may have been as low as a quarter but by the late 1840s it was probably more like half. Mass attendance in parts of Donegal and Cavan in the 1830s may have been less than 40 per cent, and in the Newry area less that 50 per cent but Derry, exceptionally in this regard, had a high rate of practice for the diocese as a whole of 74 per cent.[8] Mid-Ulster fared no better than average with a mass attendance rate between 25 and 40 percent. The failure of many to fulfil what was after all an obligation of the faith, to attend mass, may possibly be accounted for by inadequate supply of church accommodation. Until 1844, for example, there were only two churches in Belfast, with at most four priests and a catholic population of 25,000. Many worshippers had to hear mass kneeling outside the church. As late as 1834 the Commissioners of public instruction found open-air

[7] *Traits and Stories* vol. 1, p. 173.

[8] These are the findings of D. W. Miller in 'Irish Catholicism and the Great Famine', *Journal of Social History*, vol. 9 (1975), pp. 81–98.

altars in use in parts of Tyrone. This was also true of Ardclinis, Co. Antrim, in 1819, Portrush in 1835 and Lissan in Co. Londonderry in 1833. A mere insufficiency of churches or mass-houses cannot of course be the only explanation. The diocese of Clogher had by 1864 eighty-two chapels, only four more than in 1844, a number that was to remain fairly constant for the rest of the century, and yet it also suffered from a relatively low rate of turn out for divine services.

One factor may have been the ratio of priests to people. By 1840 Down and Connor had one priest for every 2,654 catholics, and Raphoe one to every 3,381, but Derry had the best in Ulster with a priest to every 2,458. But even in Derry city itself, with a catholic population by 1836 of more than 10,000, the average weekly Sunday mass attendance was 2,500 between three masses, although it is estimated that the chapel could hold 2,000. Given that priests were restricted to saying only one mass daily it would have been physically impossible in some places to serve the religious need of all parishioners every Sunday and holiday. In areas with greater activity by the Ribbonmen the practice rate tended to be lower. The Ribbonmen were successors of the Defenders and their main aim was to defend the interests of the catholic rural peasantry, although they also had a keen political sense often expressed in nationalist aspirations. On the other hand the Church in such regions tended to be relatively under-developed. Undoubtedly however the greatest single obstacle to practice was poverty. It seems that the poorer people are, the less inclined they are to practise formal religion.

Individuals may well not have attended church because they did not have adequate clothing for such a ritualised public occasion. Although it is suggested that catholic living standards in the northeast of Ulster were generally higher than in the rest of the country, there was still widespread poverty and deprivation. In the country many catholics were forced into dwellings that were little more than shacks with neither windows nor chimneys, and in the towns the labouring classes were no better off. Very poor catholics in Derry had to be content with garrets or outhouses in the Bogside, and even there they had to pay a high weekly rent of one shilling and three pence for their hovels. Many families in such circumstances sublet part of their accommodation for as much as sixpence a week. In Belfast the poor of all denominations were, by the early mid-century, crowded into dirty and unhygienic houses mostly consisting of four small rooms with appalling sanitary conditions, which often had to accommodate eighteen to twenty inhabitants. The staple diet was potatoes, porridge and milk. In the country more varied food was available. We are told that in the farmlands of Tyrone even the poorest kept a cow and a pig and could therefore from time to time indulge themselves with a bit of pork or bacon, sometimes supplemented by fish or eels especially during Lent.

In the early nineteenth century the protestant clergy were not averse from exploiting catholic social underdevelopment for propaganda, claiming that catholics were less industrious than their reformed neighbours. Others, more nuanced in their observations, suggested that while both protestants and catholics were industrious, 'the industry of the Scotch [protestants] is steady, patient and directed with great foresight; while that of the Irish [catholics] is rash, adventurous and variable.'[9] Many held to the conviction that the 'ruinous and absurd' practice of dividing land among all the surviving children was an explanation for catholic poverty. The blame for the 'barbarious tastes' and habits of catholics was placed squarely on their Celtic heritage.

But it is also apparent that many of the vestiges of Celtic Ireland were now fast disappearing in the north. Although the Irish language was to survive in some places in Antrim, Armagh and Donegal into the twentieth century, for many its use as the everyday medium of communication was almost extinct by the early nineteenth century. The reasons for this are almost entirely economic. English was the language of trade and for survival in the market-place it had to be mastered. Irish became increasingly associated with poverty and deprivation. This became something of a *bête noire* among the catholic clergy, some of whom came to regard Irish as the chief cause of economic immobility and therefore insisted on the use of English in all transactions where this was permitted rather than Latin. Together with the loss of language, customs and *mores* also altered. Of course the picture varies: by 1837 the catholic inhabitants of Derry were described as 'Scoto-English in everything but name and origin. . . . If any of the peculiar features of the Irish character are still to be found here, strongly marked, it is only among the new comers'—mostly economic migrants from the poorer areas of Donegal.

The devastating effect of the famine on the whole of Ireland produced an improvement in the ratio of priests to people and left the country more disposed to the full effects of Ultramontane catholicism. While parts of Ulster were saved from the worst ravages of the hunger and pestilence, Monaghan, Cavan and Donegal nonetheless suffered greatly and even the more prosperous areas such as Down did not escape unscathed. In Fermanagh it is estimated that a quarter of the population died from disease. In Derry the winter of 1846–7 was particularly severe, and the co-adjutor bishop Edward Maginn reported to his metropolitan that in the barony of Ennishowen only

---

[9] Mason, *Parochial Survey*, vol. 1, p. 307.

5,000 out of 70,000 catholics were not classified as 'destitute'. The towns were greatly affected by the fever which accompanied the famine, and as much as 20 per cent of the population of Belfast suffered from its effects which in the north as a whole was to claim the lives of several priests. Typhus, typhoid and dysentery were the main components of this 'fever'.

To administer some relief soup kitchens were set up in Belfast and elsewhere as the workhouses could not cope with all the demands made on them. The Church in Ulster struggled to deal as best it could with a tragedy of gargantuan proportions. However in some aspects of the Church's life there was a curious otherworldliness about its *modus operandi* in the famine years. Although the building of the cathedral in Armagh was halted for the duration of the great hunger, in 1847–8 the Derry diocese built seven new churches. The northern dioceses contributed between £400 and £1,000 each in February 1849 to a collection to help Pius IX who had temporarily to flee the Roman revolutionary hordes of 1848. Letters from bishops Patrick McGettigan of Raphoe and Michael Blake of Dromore make clear that the Lenten fasts and abstinences would continue with some modification. 'With the exception of the first and last week, in which the strict fast of the Church will be observed, I will permit the use of flesh meat [i.e. the flesh of animals, fish being 'white meat'] on Sundays, Tuesdays, and Thursdays', as Blake rather haughtily told archbishop Crolly of Armagh.

Already in the decades before the famine the catholic community had its share of wealthier middle class families. The foundation of institutions for middle class education in such towns as Belfast, Newry, Derry, and Monaghan from the early mid-century on give ample proof of this. The great majority were however poor. This endemic poverty of the northern Catholic community in the early nineteenth century was complicated by another factor leading to social disintegration, with its concomitant lack of enthusiasm for religion, alcohol abuse. Drunkenness was a common sight in the Victorian town and city with gin costing a penny a pint. In Ireland whiskey was a standard tipple and potheen when it could be had. Illegal stills were numerous in country areas.

Theobald Mathew, the Cork Capuchin friar and 'National Apostle of Temperance', was invited to Ulster in 1841 by bishop Kernan of Clogher and at Whitehill, Co. Fermanagh, some 50,000 gathered to hear him preach. Enniskillen welcomed him with a crowd of 30,000 and Clones was able to call on similar numbers to hear the priest berate the evils of drink. Nationally Mathew helped slash the consumption of whiskey—its production declined from 12,296,000 gallons in 1839 to 5,546,283 in 1844—but his influence in the north was not always welcome. He was regarded by many as a 'healer' and this aura and the hysteria accompaning his revivalist rallies made several of the bishops suspicious of him, including Crolly, Cornelius Denvir of Down and Connor, and Patrick MacLaughlin of Derry. Mathew's movement also became tainted with the spirit of the repeal movement which further increased the hesitancy aroused by his activities. Nonetheless his influence spread, and already in 1841 Dromore could boast that 3,000 had taken the pledge. In the same year Patrick McGettigan of Raphoe asserted that temperance had produced 'a most extraordinary effect in the promotion of peace order and religion'. For the clergy the promotion of religion was perhaps its chief function. However, the more enthusiastic claims of diocesan authorities are hard to credit. In 1843 Kernan was suggesting that in Monaghan town 'a triumphant majority . . . are ardent disciples of Fr Mathew', and in 1844 McGettigan maintained that of the 60,000 people in his diocese who had taken the pledge the previous year he had yet to meet twenty who had broken it. The 1848 *Catholic Directory* records that total abstinence societies embrace 'almost the entire Catholic population' of the diocese of Derry. By that stage the temperance movement was making itself felt even in Down and Connor and Armagh.

Northern catholicism in the nineteenth century exhibited various features which marked it off from catholicism in other areas. One issue was that of congregational control of the parish and clergy. In the Belfast parish in the earlier part of the century, the more prominent individuals formed themselves into an *ad hoc* group know as 'the elders', doubtless reflecting the town's presbyterian ethos, and sought to restrain clerical dominance. A letter from bishop Patrick MacMullan to the agent of the Irish bishops in Rome in 1813 adverts to the fact that he had trouble from some parishes, which 'insisted that I should send them none other than the priest or priests they called for . . . I considered that a compliance with their desires might become a dangerous precedent.'[10] However when the laity of Belfast asked for William Crolly as their new pastor on the retirement of Hugh O'Donnell in 1812, MacMullan advised them to write to Crolly themselves and find out if he would accept the appointment. Other instances of lay patronage are more dramatic. Lady Frances Maguire, a protestant, asserted her rights in 1796 to appoint the Catholic parish priests of Enniskillen and Tempo. At the end of 1816 the parish of Devenish claimed to be empowered to appoint its own parish priest instead of the bishop's nominee. The fighting that resulted from this

[10] Archives of the Diocese of Down and Connor (ADDC), MacMullan to John Connolly, 12 Oct. 1814, B/14.3.

debacle landed the individuals concerned and their supporters in court charged with public order offences.

Such areas of potential conflict were not simply a feature of the relationship between the clergy and the laity. The age-old difficulties of clerical squabbling remained a distinct feature of Church life. Some of these disputes were about the extent of parish boundaries, but sometimes the quarrelling could involve protracted arguments between a bishop and his clergy. More rarely there were interdiocesan feuds. One such was the famous controversy between the dioceses of Derry and Down and Connor over which of them controlled the parish of Coleraine. Priests of the Derry diocese had ministered in the Coleraine area since 1641, and in 1779 the parish was granted to Derry with some privileges reserved to the bishop of Down and Connor. In May 1834 bishop Crolly asserted his right to appoint a Down and Connor priest, John Green, to the town but bishop MacLaughlin promptly responded by putting the town under an interdict. Crolly appealed to Rome and a tribunal was set up in Coleraine headed by archbishop Kelly of Armagh. This tribunal involved more than thirty-five clerics, including five bishops, who sifted through a mass of evidence. The judgement was given in favour of Crolly and was subsequently confirmed by Gregory XVI in February 1835.

An equally acrimonious dispute took place in the 1830s between bishop Edward Kernan of Clogher and his diocesan chapter. Kernan was the first Fermanagh man to be bishop of Clogher since the fifteenth century, but he was handicapped by not being able to speak Irish. Opposition to him began when he was nominated co-adjutor, on the grounds that he was too closely associated with his predecessor James Murphy. As bishop, Kernan tried to abolish the diocesan chapter but it was saved by an appeal to Rome. Clogher had a reputation for factionalism not helped by its bishops often seeing their appointment as opportunities to promote members of their own families, and the rivalry between large clerical families was a source of much scandal. Archbishop Richard O'Reilly, of Armagh, expressed his horror at the situation in Clogher to his own vicar-general in March 1814; religion there he observed, was 'likely to receive a deep wound from the scandalous conditions which prevail between a faction of the clergy and their bishop'. It seems however that Murphy was the last bishop tainted with nepotism.

In general there was a steady progress in the development of Ulster catholicism in the half-century to Cullen's arrival in the see of Armagh. Many areas of the province experienced a veritable explosion of church building. This was most noticeable in the diocese of Raphoe under its indomitable Patrick McGettigan. Bishop Kernan consecrated a catholic burial-ground in October 1840 in the parish of Clogher, the first of its kind in that part of the north since the reformation. An enormous crowd turned up for the event, some travelling great distances, and Kernan used the opportunity to stress the importance of catholics being buried in their own cemeteries. The practice had been to bury individuals in the pre-reformation monastic sites, all of which were in the hands of the established Church. While the increase in catholic Church property and building was doubtless a sign of health, it was but one indication of vitality. The spiritual life of the ordinary catholic was probably centred around less formal acts of piety such as the recitation of the rosary. The Rosary Society had spread as far north as Belfast by 1836. Societies which encouraged devotion to the hearts of Jesus and Mary proved especially popular in Dromore in the 1830s and quickly spread to other parts of the province, as did sodalities aimed at helping 'the holy souls in purgatory'. Such organisations and acts of individual piety and devotion may well have been as popular as they were because they could be carried on without the intervention of the clergy and so enabled lay people to have some control over their spiritual lives.

Involving the clergy in formal sacramental worship, especially at the 'rites of passage', could mean considerable expense. There was a tariff for various services and although the really poor were often excused payment, the clergy none the less tended to make known that such individuals had made no offering. By 1825 the minimum for a baptism was about two shillings and sixpence, and families were expected to pay at least one shilling a year towards the upkeep of their clergy. In Ulster there was no fixed fee for marriages, the stipend being left to local custom. However it was normal for priests to set levies on parishioners to meet the cost of repairs for chapels and schools. It has been suggested that if individual families did not meet these targets spiritual favours, like the 'churching' of women, would be withheld.[11]

Clerical income in Ulster was probably lower than in other parts of the country. Early in the century the income of the primate was in the region of £400, but for archbishop O'Reilly this hardly mattered since his vast personal wealth enabled him to live in a style worthy of his high office. The bishopric of Clogher was worth some £325 per annum and that of Down and Connor about half that amount. Individual clergy of less exalted status could earn considerable sums. Thus John Green of Coleraine-Portrush reported to the bishop in

---

[11] The synod of Thurles forbade the practice of priests withholding the sacraments for non-payment of dues. Clergy who offended against this regulation were to be suspended. Cf. S.J. Connolly, *Priests and People in Pre-Famine Ireland, 1780–1845*, p. 72.

1840 that he had an income of £129. He also mentioned that if the bishop saw fit to appoint another priest to the parish, he had 'a list of subscribers who will pay in the Bushmills district an increased stipend in consideration of attendance being given'.[12] Fifteen years earlier archbishop Curtis had testified that in the whole province there was no parish worth less than £100 per year, although the national average was around £150. Still this was a considerable improvement on only ten years earlier when the income of the clergy in the north averaged around £30–£50. Curates did less well than parish priests. There was no obligation on the pastor to give his curate a fixed revenue but they tended usually to receive about £10 a year plus board and lodging.

Bishops from time to time issued injunctions warning the clergy of the dangers of avarice in their ministries. However one of the main clerical vices was drunkenness, and the bishops mainly tried to stamp out such indelicacies but their efforts were not always successful. Indeed even the aged bishop of Raphoe, Patrick MacGettigan, could be seen drunk in public in his declining years. But in this the clergy did no more than accurately reflect the dispositions of the people at large. Card-playing, often for money, and drinking could be tolerated up to a point, but sexual misdemeanours were more difficult to excuse. Patrick Corish[13] maintains that in sexual matters the north was less rigid than the rest of catholic Ireland, and there were certainly some spectacular lapses among the clergy from this most difficult of virtues. There is the remarkable case of Mr Campbell, the parish priest of Errigal Truagh in the early 1820s, who—if only half the allegations against him were true—led a most profligate life.[14] Such allegations are relatively rare and there is nothing to suggest that the clergy were not largely zealous and conscientious even if they were also somewhat impulsive and hotheaded, especially over politics.

The clergy as a group tended to be drawn from the tenant farmer class although some were of upper-middle class background. The church provided a secure living and for some it represented an ascent in the stratified society of early nineteenth-century catholic Ulster. Not till the 1840s did priests begin to wear distinctive dress, but it was insisted on by the synod of Thurles in 1850. Even then old habits died hard and it was some time before the practice became universal. The general title for a clergyman was 'mister' if he did not have a

[12] ADDC D.40/41
[13] *The Irish Catholic Experience*, p. 189.
[14] Cf. Public Records Office of Northern Ireland (PRONI), DIO(RC) 1/5A/7c. The allegations ranged from his liaison with two sisters who were his cousins, as a result of which one of them 'proved [to be] with child', to his keeping a concubine and abusing his position in the confessional to obtain sexual favours.

doctorate and was not a member of a religious order. In addressing him one would say 'sir' or, in Irish, the vocative '*a shagairt*', was employed.

Nuns, when they finally made their appearance on the Ulster scene, were anomalously known by the civil title 'Mrs'. Although religious sisters were mostly a post-1850 phenomenon, the Poor Clares were in Newry from 1830 running a poor school for 300 girls and an orphanage. By 1838 the community had nine professed sisters. In 1847 a house with a large garden was acquired in Pump Street, Derry, with the hope of attracting either the Sisters of Mercy or the Sisters of Charity. The 'Mercys' duly arrived the next year, four professed, two novices and four postulants under the careful direction of 'Mrs Locke' the superior. They opened a boarding school for girls, with fees of £25 a year 'music extra', and a day school for 100 pupils. They also had some apostlate among the poor of the city, whom they visited and gave 'instruction'. From the protestant community the sisters 'received . . . all that polite attention for which the Dissenters of Derry, notwithstanding the doubtful fame of the locality, are so deservedly remarkable.'[15]

In one sense the effectiveness of the Church continued to depend on the quality of its leadership. The Holy See, long suspicious of Irish episcopal appointments, made clear that it would no longer tolerate the Irish custom of referring to nominees as having been 'elected' by the diocese concerned. Often Irish dioceses would forward the name of a single individual candidate for episcopal office, thus demonstrating that they regarded Rome's involvement as that of 'rubber-stamping' what was essentially a local affair. When the clergy of Dromore diocese 'elected' three possible candidates for the vacant episcopacy in 1825, Rome rejected all three on the grounds that the offending verb had been used. The clergy apologised, the proffered terna was accepted, and the appointment went ahead. But it was the selection of Crolly as the co-adjutor in Down and Connor the previous year that set the precedent for such nominations in Ireland and furnished the custom for the next century. When bishop MacMullan decided to ask for a co-adjutor, the parish priests of the diocese gathered under the presidency of the bishop of Derry, the most senior bishop in the province, to select a list of candidates. Crolly was the clear favourite. This list was subsequently approved by the primate. In the papal rescript of 1829 regulating nominations to the Irish episcopal bench, this procedure was adopted as the norm. The terna however had to be approved by all the bishops of the ecclesiastical province concerned before being forwarded to Rome. There was no

[15] *The Catholic Directory* (Dublin, 1849), p. 325.

obligation for parish priests to keep their votes secret until a rule to that effect was made by the Vatican in 1911.

Catholic-protestant relations

The early nineteenth century witnessed an enormous variety in the social and religious circumstances of Ulster catholics. East of the Bann there was general toleration between individual Catholics and Protestants. This was partly because of the residual sympathy generated by the remnants of the spirit of co-operation which had pervaded certain presbyterian and catholic circles in 1798. Elsewhere in the province, relations were not unfriendly. By 1838 the parish of St Tiernagh Roslea in east Clones could boast of the first purpose-built belltower in the Clogher diocese in 300 years; the cost was £600, and 'protestant labour and protestant money' contributed greatly to the completion of this 'sacred work'. There are repeated references to such magnanimity. Richard Armstrong, a protestant of Ballygawley, Co. Tyrone, bequeathed £25 in 1838 for the relief of the catholic poor of the parish of Errigal Kieran. Lord Cremorne donated a site for the proposed catholic cathedral in Armagh in 1839 and another in Monaghan town the following year for a diocesan seminary. This was matched in Fermanagh in 1839 by the generosity of Sir Arthur Brooke who donated to the catholics of Brookeborough a site for a chapel. Adam McClean, a Belfast protestant, offered land free of charge for the building of a catholic cathedral in the town. When the mayor of Belfast contributed £10 to the building fund he was attacked by a local protestant paper, the *Banner of Ulster*, for being 'an open promoter of Popery, that deadly enemy of all civil and religious liberty'. St Malachy's was opened in 1844 not as a cathedral but as a 'good-sized church'. Also in Belfast the marquis of Donegall in February 1828 donated an acre of ground adjacent to Friar's Bush to enlarge the catholic cemetery. Mr Greer, a Newry protestant, was commissioned by Dr Blake, the bishop of Dromore, to print the Douay version of the New Testament, which within a few months had sold more than 4,000 copies, presumably attesting both to Greer's skill as a printer and salesman and to catholic piety.

In Derry a memorial tablet was placed in the catholic chapel by representatives of both communities to commemorate the work of the Rev. Hugh Monaghan, who died 'of a malignant fever caught in the discharge of his sacred duties'. This was in 1839. Two years earlier it was reported that 300 catholics from the Derry area 'dug five acres of potatoes, and safely pitted them, for the Rev. John Conan,

Protestant Rector, in testimony of their respect for his mild and gentlemanly manners'.[16] The Rev. Patrick Curran, who established the catholic parish of Newtownards in 1811 had in his younger days been a tutor to the marquis of Londonderry and to the Hon. Charles Fitzroy. The Londonderrys maintained some oversight in catholic affairs in Newtownards for the rest of the century. The new chapel of 1875 was built by the dowager marchioness.

If the United Irishmen provided at least some of the impetus for presbyterian-catholic rapprochement, this does not explain the sometimes friendly affinities between catholics and members of the established Church. One instance concerned the old catholic chapel outside the walls of Derry on the site of St Colmcille's hermitage, begun in 1784 and finished two years later. Among the early contributions to the building fund was a donation of 200 guineas from the earl of Bristol, the Church of Ireland bishop of Derry. More surprisingly perhaps the city corporation also came up with 50 guineas for the scheme. In 1810 the protestants of the 'Maiden City' again gave £300 for the renovation of the church.

In areas such as the Glens of Antrim relations were fairly good. Here intermarriage was a factor which tended to promote cross-community harmony. The yeomanry too, surprisingly given its eighteenth-century origins, contained both catholics and protestants. As was so often the case much depended on the outlook of the local priest and minister. The Church of Ireland curate in the parish of Ardclinis near Glenarm, which included Cusendall and Waterfoot, testified in 1819 that 'little or no bigotry prevails, and it must excite very pleasing sentiments that the catholic clergyman, the Rev. Daniel McDonnell, does everything in his power to promote a good understanding among the inhabitants of the parish.'[17]

When the foundation-stone of the new catholic chapel in Hollywood was laid in March 1829, it was attended by protestants and catholics alike. The *Northern Whig* was moved to observe two days later that 'a feeling of liberty, kindness, and cordiality was manifest on this occasion which was highly creditable to both Protestants and Catholics.' It also has to be said that the clear minority status of catholics in most of Antrim, Down and north Armagh meant that the catholic community posed relatively little threat to the majority protestant community. In areas such as Fermanagh and Tyrone, where the communities were numerically more evenly balanced, there was not only a more politicised catholic consciousness but frequently

[16] *Catholic Directory* (Dublin, 1838), p. 435
[17] Mason, *Parochial Survey*, vol. 3, pp. 27–8.

greater tension. One can also see in these areas a greater non-catholic homogeneity and consequently less intra-protestant division.[18]

As we have seen, the promoters of cross-community harmony had their place. The most celebrated of these in the north-west in his day was Charles O'Donnell, catholic bishop of Derry in 1798–1823. He had been educated in Paris and was liberal and tolerant. Indeed his propensities for contact with anglicans and presbyterians earned him the somewhat ambiguous label 'Orange Charlie'. His ready ecumenism was not always appreciated by his flock. Certain sectarian disturbances in Derry in 1813, provoked in part by the parish priest Cornelius O'Mullan over the question of catholic emancipation, caused the bishop to take the not unusual step of depriving O'Mullan of his faculties and suspending him from his duties. O'Mullan's supporters were so outraged that they attacked the bishop in the chapel on 28 November. While 'Orange Charlie' managed to escape with only his dignity affronted, several of his defenders suffered physical injuries. As a result of this outrage O'Mullan was excommunicated and, if that had not been sufficient punishment, he was sentenced by the civil authorities to six months' imprisonment.

William Carleton in the preface to his first series of *Traits and Stories* observes:

> The English reader perhaps, may be sceptical as to the deep hatred which prevails among Roman Catholics in the north of Ireland against those who differ from them in party and religious principles; but when he reflects on what they have suffered perhaps he will grant after all, that the feeling is natural to a people treated as they have been.[19]

The opportunity for such antagonism was to be fuelled even more intensely with the coming of the so-called 'second reformation' dating from the early 1820s. The 'second reformation' was the evangelical revival that swept the whole of Ireland in the early nineteenth century and had particular impact on the religious and political development

[18] Desmond Bowen in his *The Protestant Crusade in Ireland, 1800–70*, advances the thesis that the famine marks the definitive watershed in catholic and pan-protestant animus. His essential view, stated simply, is that the relief which flowed to Ireland from abroad was mainly given by the various churches. With the material assistance there came ultramontane catholicism and hostile evangelical protestantism. The basic idea here is flawed in several ways, not least because ultramontanism was making its way to Ireland and England irrespective of the famine. We have also seen that fundamentalist evangelicalism had contributed to sectarian tensions since the 1740s. Bowen has also given too sanguine an impression of the religious state of Ireland before the famine. All was far from bliss, since the country was capable of giving birth of its own volition to rural sectarian organisations such as the Peep O' Day Boys, the Defenders, Ribbonmen and, most notoriously of all, the Orange Order, without any help from abroad.

[19] Vol. 1, pp. xxiv-v.

elsewhere, on the education issue they were capable of as much rhetorical intransigence as the next. It was said of Patrick Bellew, dean of Clogher, that 'he set himself with all the energy of his soul against *mixed* education for his people, his constant motto was, education exclusively catholic or *none*.'[15] As the century progressed attitudes hardened. The *Derry Journal* for 26 May 1884 reported a sermon that bishop Logue, the future cardinal, delivered at a confirmation service in Ardara. Logue said that he had no complaints to make against the parishioners except in one thing:

> The obstinacy of some of the people in still sending their children to schools not taught by Catholics. He had no fault to find with Protestant teachers, but he believed and impressed upon the congregation that, when schools taught by Catholic teachers were within reach, no Catholic deserving of the name could conscientiously send his children to schools taught by others.

The Christian Brothers did their best to provide an exclusively catholic education. Yet even in Belfast their work did not always progress smoothly. Here however the problem was internal to the Church. St Malachy's College, which had been founded in 1833, was long regarded as the jewel in the crown of catholic education in the town, producing future clerics and professional men alike. With the introduction of intermediate education examinations in 1879, the Christian Brothers began to prepare some of their brighter pupils for them. The bishop felt that such a move would draw pupils away from the diocesan school and a long and bitter wrangle ensued. By the end of the century the work of the Christian Brothers was supplemented by that of the Dc La Salle Brothers, who had also established schools in Belfast, Downpatrick and Keady in Co. Armagh.

The number and variety of religious women continued to expand so much so that by the end of the century most of the main centres of catholic population in Ulster had at least one convent. While the devotion of many of the active religious to the needs of the poor cannot be doubted, it is also clear that the Church authorities were concerned to encourage the growth of the catholic middle classes. The 1861 census revealed that catholics in the north of Ireland made up only 15 per cent of the professional classes. Nuns were to play an important part in the education of the daughters of middle-class families, exceeding in extent that played by diocesan colleges for boys. The education in the middle-class schools run by the sisters was well rounded and genteel, as an advertisement in the *Belfast Morning News* for the 18 March 1874 bears witness. The schooling for any

[15] *Catholic Directory* (Dublin, 1851), p. 210. Emphasis in the original.

young lady presenting herself at the Dominican College, Falls Road, Belfast would comprise 'Religious instruction, the English, French, German and Italian languages, Sacred History, Ancient and Modern History, Geography, Astronomy, . . . Arithmetic, Epistolatory Correspondence (English and French), Natural Philosophy, Botany, Heraldry, . . . and every other accomplishment necessary to complete the education of a young lady'. The Dominican Sisters also opened a National school in the grounds of the convent in which 'they gave a solid and religious education to girls of the humbler classes'.

The Sisters of Mercy made their appearance in Belfast in 1854. They had a day and an evening school in Calander Street and also visited the sick. By 1857 they had moved to a new convent on the Crumlin Road and had already opened a branch house in Downpatrick in 1855. Another convent of the order was opened in Hamilton Street in 1858 and two years later the Sisters were operating from an adjoining site, 'the Belfast Catholic penitentiary'. However in 1867 they handed this work over to the Good Shepherd Sisters, who had arrived in Belfast from Limerick to fulfil the charism of their congregation which was 'to claim fallen females and take care of industrial schools and prisons'. Ten years later the Sisters of Mercy were asked by bishop Dorrian to undertake the training of women National school teachers, a work they finally surrendered to the Dominicans when St Mary's Teacher Training College was opened in 1900.

Among the other religious orders of women active in Down and Connor before the end of the century were the French Sisters of the Sacred Heart who opened a convent school in Lisburn in 1870, the Bon Secours Sisters who worked in Belfast from 1872 visiting the sick, both protestant and catholic, and the Nazareth Sisters who arrived in 1876 and opened a house in Ballynafeigh, east Belfast, where they kept a residence for the old and infirm. The Sisters of Charity were conducting primary schools in Belfast, Downpatrick and Lisburn by 1864. Yet despite all this effort the diocesan authorities regarded the catholic education provision as inadequate and complained that many children still had to attend National schools 'under anti-catholic patrons, in which the course of religious instruction is highly perilous to the faith . . .' We have concentrated thus far on Belfast and its environs because it shows such remarkable expansion of catholic infrastructure in a relatively short time. Most of the religious moved into the diocese within a space of twenty years and there was more than enough work for them all.

Elsewhere there is a similar if not so dramatic picture. The Sisters of the Sacred Heart arrived in Armagh under Dixon's guidance in 1853, although Cullen had negotiated their presence before his departure for Dublin. The Loreto Sisters opened a convent in Omagh in 1856 where seven professed nuns and two novices conducted a boarding school for twenty girls, and a large day school, together with a free school under the careful guidance of Mrs Murray the superior. The Sisters would later open similar establishments in Buncrana. Meanwhile the Mercy Sisters seemed to mushroom. Convents sprang up in Newry and Letterkenny by 1864, the work in the latter being 'the education of the upper and middle classes' carried on by ten nuns. At Ballyshannon in 1867 the sisters were looking after an orphanage and a 'house of mercy', and by 1874 they had also opened a convent in Carndonagh.

The convent of St Clare founded in Keady in 1871 ran a day school and a large night school for girls employed in local factories. Although in its early years the community showed little sign of growth, by 1880 it had almost doubled its numbers to seventeen nuns. By the mid-century the Sisters of St Louis were well established in Carrickmacross, Co. Monaghan, and continued to expand their operations in the Clogher diocese so that by the end of the 1880s they had a second convent in Carrickmacross, another in Monaghan with a reformatory attached, and a house in Clones. By this time they were also in the Armagh diocese where they had built an orphanage and a poor school in Middletown. Their work there also included boarding and industrial schools.

The first house of the Sisters of the Presentation in Ulster was opened at Portadown in 1882 where they had a large day school and a night school for working girls. By this time too the French order of the Holy Family had a convent in Magherafelt, and the Nazareth Sisters had opened an orphanage in Derry. The Mercy Sisters continued to increase in that diocese with a convent in Strabane. While it might seem that expansion was the order of the day from the 1860s on, the bishops continued to complain at the lack of specifically catholic provision in education, nursing and social work. Yet remarkably the increase in the number of priests and religious in the north went hand in hand with a decrease in the population. In the Derry diocese the catholic population fell from 164,475 in 1861 to 132,731 in 1891. A similar picture emerges even in Belfast. Despite the enormous growth of that town in the nineteenth century the proportion of the catholic population declined from 34 per cent in 1861 to 25 per cent by 1911. In the single decade 1871–81 the catholic growth rate by comparison with that of protestants fell by 17 per cent in Belfast and Portadown and by 9 per cent in Lurgan.

There can be little doubt that it was Cullen's presence in Ireland that enabled those latent forces for reform in Irish catholicism to come to the fore. From the 1850s on there is an evident increase in the zealous intensity with which the clergy conducted their religious ministries. The ultramontane programme, if one can call it such, found the north a ready recipient of its religious-political agenda. One symptom of this was a veritable craze for church-building. This phenomenon of course predates both Cullen and even the famine but local factors meant that Ulster had some catching up to do. That it now embarked on such an ambitious church-building programme is indicative of the refusal of Ulster catholicism to be seen as second-best. Adequate church provision was not only a mark of devotion but a statement to the world that catholicism was no longer content to be retiring and elusive in the northern protestant landscape. Although Cullen complained in 1850 that many of the churches in Armagh were in poor condition and had thatched roofs, this was probably something of an exaggeration since in the diocese as a whole between 1800 and 1864 ninety-three new churches had been built. In Raphoe in the same period forty new churches were built at a total cost of more than £90,000, although most of the work was done in the forty-one-year episcopate of Patrick McGettigan. St Peter's church and presbytery in Belfast alone cost £35,900 over the period 1866–85, although as we shall see later Belfast was before this time somewhat under-provided with places of worship. St Eugene's cathedral in Derry was finally dedicated in 1873, having been started in 1851. The total cost was £40,000. Also in 1873 the cathedral in Armagh was opened for liturgical use, although it was still far from complete and indeed was not consecrated till 1905.

We have seen something of the devotional life of northern catholics in the pre-famine era. While it may be exaggerated to see the post-famine period as heralding a 'devotional revolution', nonetheless many paraliturgical devotions such as benediction become popular at this time. There is greater emphasis on devotion to the Virgin, helped in part perhaps by the promulgation of the doctrine of the Immaculate Conception in 1854. Cullen had issued a special pastoral on the Assumption of the Virgin in July 1851, urging 'every preparation' to celebrate the coming festival with appropriate dispositions. Perpetual adoration of the blessed sacrament, novenas, and greater emphasis on confession, the eucharist and the saying of the rosary are all features of the period. So too is devotion to the Stations of the Cross, but it was not till October 1887 that the archbishop of Armagh was granted the general faculty of erecting the Way of the Cross throughout the diocese in churches, convents, cemeteries 'and other proper places'. Before then he had to apply to Rome for permission to erect 'the Stations' in each individual case.

Confraternities and sodalities of all sorts continued to spring up, each promising various spiritual benefits to those who participated in their grace-giving activities. Among the most enduring was that begun by the Redemptorists in Belfast in 1896 with only sixty members, but which was to grow over the next sixty years to have more than 10,000. Of a slightly more ephemeral nature was the confraternity of St Joseph established in the Armagh diocese in the 1860s. Yet with due solemnity the archbishop wrote to the bishop of Beauvais asking that the Armagh chapters might be associated with the archconfraternity of that town in order to gain the 'indulgences' granted by the pope for such affiliation.

Of all the lay organisations which promoted the interests of religion perhaps the most successful and enduring in the north was the Society of St Vincent de Paul. Although its foundational aim was to 'encourage its members, by example and counsel, in piety and religion', it had a distinctly philanthropic approach to christianity. Not only did it distribute books of 'a religious nature' but its members also instructed the poor in christian doctrine, visited the sick and provided material assistance to the needy. By 1856 it had branches in Armagh, Ballymena, Belfast, Enniskillen, Monaghan, Omagh, Portadown and Randalstown. Its work would continue to thrive well into the late nineteenth century and beyond, bringing both aid to the needy and inspiration to its members.

In August 1881 archbishop Daniel McGettigan wrote to Michael Verdon, the vice-rector of the Irish College in Rome, that religion in the country as a whole had never been more flourishing, and indeed judged by some (but by no means all) of the external criteria this seems to have been so. However religion and the spiritual life are also concerned with the internal dispositions of the individual towards God. Of these it is more difficult to judge and the picture varies from region to region as well as from individual to individual and decade to decade. Certainly in the 1850s there is some evidence that while people had a 'great faith' and 'a deep feeling of piety', they were ignorant of such basic tenets of the christian faith as the doctrines of the Trinity and the Incarnation.[16] Ten years later one exasperated missioner declared that 'the people of Ulster seem never to have heard the act of contrition nor [know] how to say the *confiteor*.' There is also evidence from these two decades in Armagh and Down and Connor that catholics were contracting 'unlawful' marriages which the clergy subsequently tried to regularise. A letter from the bishop of Derry to the archbishop of Armagh on 12 January 1860 tells a similar tale for that diocese.

---

[16] These criticisms are levelled against the poor of Crossmaglen in a letter from Fr James Dixon to his brother the primate on 26 May 1855. Cf. AAA, Dixon Archives, VIII.

The clergy at times resisted change and the multiplication of church services and pieties. When Cullen moved to Dublin, some of the Armagh priests dropped his more sentimental devotions from their parish schedules, much to the disgruntlement of their people. Many curates complained to primate Dixon that they were prevented from conducting the new devotions by their parish priests. Dixon himself noted that 'People . . . feel justly alarmed lest the vigour of discipline introduced by Dr Cullen should disappear—lest the devotions established by him should fade away and the opportunities of approaching the sacraments be taken back from them.'[17] More serious was the neglect by individuals of their priestly responsibilities and duties. In Coalisland in June 1861 the local parish priest showed his contempt for the priests conducting the parish mission, which the archbishop had forced him to have, by locking them out of his house, causing them to travel late at night to Dungannon to find shelter. The general picture in some of the northern dioceses in the 1850s and into the '60s is one of indiscipline and faction-fighting among a sizeable minority. On occasion, the misdemeanours involved recourse to the law courts. John O'Donnell, a priest of the diocese of Raphoe, booked into a hotel in Portadown in June 1863 accompanied by an official of the Ulster Railway Company, in which O'Donnell had shares. The priest made off without paying his bill but having enjoyed a thoroughly good time. The owner not surprisingly took a court action to recover the money owed to her, much to the distress of O'Donnell's bishop and the archbishop of Armagh.

The indiscipline was at times sexual but fondness for drink remained an abiding curse among some. There were complaints from various parishes of priests being too drunk to say Mass, and in one instance in March 1866 a report of a clergyman who had died 'from drink'. More typical perhaps was the case of the Rev. Mr Quinn, the parish priest of Donaghmore, who after repeated warning was suspended for having broken the pledge, and Peter Daly of Coalisland who suffered a similar fate for his lack of discipline. The archdeacon of Armagh, on visiting one of his clerical charges Mr Malone, found him looking 'anything but sober'—not an unusual state—and declared that he did not know what to do with the miscreant.

Another problem which served to undermine clerical discipline was overweening family attachments, compounded in certain poorer rural areas such as Donegal by the fact that until well into the late decades of the century some priests continued to live with their families. Bishop McNally of Clogher was reported to Rome

---

[17] AAA, Dixon Archives, VIII, folder 5.

more than once for allowing his family too much say in the affairs of his diocese. While the charge is undoubtedly true, it must be treated with circumspection since by the 1860s he was tending to take an independent line from Rome, accusing the Holy See of 'too much interference in Irish episcopal affairs'. The temptation for the ultra-loyalist in his case was to complain of every infringement of discipline however slight, which in other circumstance might have been over-looked. On the other hand there was an undoubted change of emphasis and tempo in Ulster catholicism in the half-century under discussion. The religious life of the people was more intense, and this was encouraged by a more serious-minded clergy. The older milder and less obviously partisan catholicism was swept away in a rush of ultramontane exuberance. Among those caught in its train was the last example in Ulster of that gentlemanly approach to catholicism Cornelius Denvir, bishop of Down and Connor.

There is little doubt that Cullen and Dixon waged a campaign to force Denvir to resign his see, accusing him of neglecting the Church of Down and Connor through temerity and a refusal to stand up to the hostile onslaughts of presbyterian Belfast. The authorities in Armagh and Rome listened to a stream of invective about Denvir's administration of his diocese for a period of eleven years; as early as 1853 there were allegations that he performed scarcely any liturgical functions, never preached and in the preceding seventeen years had administered the sacrament of confirmation only twice! It was also suggested that he had provided only four priests for the town of Belfast, which at that time still had only three churches, for a catholic population supposedly in the region of 50,000 (this figure however seems to have been an overestimate to make the situation look even worse than it was).

By November 1856 tension between Denvir and his fellow bishops and priests had become so acute that the matter was taken up in a local newspaper, the *Ulsterman* which attributed the lack of church accom-modation to the destitution of Belfast catholics. Still the complaints against Denvir mounted. In the end pope Pius IX summoned him to Rome to give an account of his stewardship. Clearly the Church authorities were worried that Denvir's perceived lack of effort in providing catholic places of worship and educational services was actually playing into the hands of presbyterian proselytisers. Patrick Dorrian complained to archbishop Dixon in odd syntax:

I may state that of some 80 N[ational] Schools in and about Belfast, 70 of these belong to Presbyterians. And it has come to me from a Presbyterian source that, in very many of these the average can be made up only by Catholic children. So that we have been absolutely

thus giving a positive support to, not merely Presbyterian schools, but to proselytism of our own.[18]

Denvir however was more than able to defend himself against all charges. In a long letter to the pope he refuted any suggestion that he had failed to make proper provision for catholic education or that he did not have the interests of his people at heart. However, he stressed the difficulties under which the Church in Down and Connor laboured. 'Orange bigotry is rampant and on the increase,' he wrote and the forces of law and order exercised 'no control over Orange intimidation'. All this argued for caution in the conduct of the Church in this part of Ulster. Denvir was more than conscious that the rapid growth of the catholic community in Belfast, from 2,000 in 1800 to 41,000 in 1861, had caused alarm among certain sections of the presbyterian and anglican population. The growth of the catholic minority fuelled discrimination against them 'because of a Protestant presumption that their flourishing represented a threat to the future of the Protestant community'.[19] In the circumstances Denvir had no desire to jeopardise the catholic position still further. He knew only too well that fear and suspicion of catholicism could easily spill over into violence. He personally helped to save St Malachy's church from a protestant mob during the elections of 1857, contracting bronchitis in the process from exposure to the cold and rain.

When he finally went to Rome in the autumn of 1858 he made a deep impression on all who met him. On his return to Belfast he inaugurated some reforms and increased the number of priests in the parish there. Still this did not satisfy his critics. One element in the mistrust he inspired was that he had been too closely allied in the past with the more accommodating elements within the Irish Church, whose days were now rapidly drawing to a close. This was seen with great prescience as early as 1849 by Dr James Brown, bishop of Kilmore, who wrote to Denvir on Dr Crolly's death that it was a most distressing calamity, for 'where shall we find such a rational firmness of soul, such honest candour . . . ? You have lost a Father, indeed one dearer, and poor Dr Murray's heart will be scarcely able to bear the shock. He is an holy and great Man, but there is now no more for him for you nor for me any prospect of earthly happiness . . .'[20]

In the end Denvir was forced to have an 'active coadjutor', one who would not only seek to make sufficient catholic provision in education

---

[18] AAA, Dorrian to Dixon, 2 June 1864.

[19] A.C. Hepburn, 'Catholics in the North of Ireland, 1850–1921: The urbanization of a minority', *Historical Studies XII* (London, 1978), p. 85.

[20] ADDC, Brown to Denvir, 9 April 1849. C.49/4.

and churches but also offer more strident resistance to the protestant ethos of north-east Ulster. Patrick Dorrian was appointed to the position in July 1860. However his ability to change things was limited while Denvir remained in charge. Finally Denvir was persuaded to resign as bishop in May 1865, and he died the following year. His funeral was attended by many clergy and laity from the anglican and presbyterian communities including that scourge of Ulster catholicism the Rev. Henry Cooke.

In its internal life in the years after the famine northern catholicism consolidated its spiritual and religious strengths against a background of great economic and political change. It became more of an urban phenomenon, and increased its social and educational hold on Ulster life. There was also more self-confidence in the expression of its religious convictions than at any time since the reformation. Despite the protestant majority in Ulster as a whole, the catholic community was poised to assert itself in every aspect of Ulster life. But in doing so it was to meet with a hardening of attitude from the protestant majority whose resentment at what was perceived to be a growing catholic threat would often find expression in violence. Such violence laid the foundation for yet more strife in the twentieth century.

Social ostracism, the poor and sectarian violence

Catholicism remained a socially unacceptable phenomenon in northern life even in the last decades of the nineteenth century. Although there was a growing catholic middle class, some at least of whom were Tory supporters, their inability to make much of an impact on social affairs consonant with their strength must be attributed to the prevalence of sectarianism in every facet of Ulster life. By 1880 there was only one catholic magistrate out of a total of seventy-four in the whole of Fermanagh. Although there were many prosperous catholic families in Belfast from the 1860s on—names such as Hughes, Murray, Caffery and Hamill come to mind—there was little encouragement to integrate fully into the life of the town. It is true that Bernard Hughes, the bakery owner, had been a member of Belfast Corporation from 1857 and was soon joined by the wealthy landowner and businessman John Hamill, yet they felt that their religion excluded them from full acceptance in genteel society.

In settled circumstances and when the opportunities occurred catholics could rise to positions of eminence. By the end of the 1870s three of the forty-two professors at the Queen's College Belfast— McCoy, O'Donovan and Cuming—were catholic. Cuming had held the chair in medicine since 1865 and was most distinguished, a graduate of the College and a man of liberal views. He invented

'Cuming's powder', a stomach sedative long a feature of Belfast medicinal life. The number of catholic students at Queen's was never large and declined from 7 per cent of the student body in 1859 to 4 per cent twenty years later. The overwhelming presbyterian ethos and the opposition of the majority of northern bishops to the college meant that it was not an especially welcoming environment for catholic students.

By the end of the 1860s two Belfast newspapers were owned and run by catholics. The *Ulster Examiner*, a clearly partisan paper founded in 1868 (its first editor was a priest), competed with the then politically neutral *Belfast Morning News*, which had been founded by the Antrim brothers Robert and Daniel Read in 1855. Among the most colourful of Ulster catholic characters to rise to prominence at this time was lord Russell of Killowen. Originally from Newry, he had worked as a solicitor in Donegall Street, Belfast, before ascending through the ranks of the English judiciary to become lord chief justice of England. His brother Matthew was a Jesuit and his cousin John McAuley became the first parish priest of Ballymacarrett in 1887.

Catholic occupations in the urban centres were varied. The community numbered shopkeepers, publicans and skilled tradesmen among its members. Yet the majority remained as unskilled labourers and factory and mill workers in the towns or as poor tenant-farmers and crofters in the rural districts. The poor and unskilled were as always especially susceptible to the harsh conditions resulting from fluctuations in the market economy or to agricultural depression. Although towns such as Derry generally enjoyed relative prosperity in the period 1860-95, the depression of 1884-7 was felt most keenly by the unskilled labourers many of whom, though by no means all, were catholic. Crop failures in the early 1860s, in 1872 and 1873 and again in the late 1870s and early 1880s brought untold misery to country and town alike. Many areas experienced famine. McGettigan warned on 15 June 1863 that 'the eclipse over some of the parishes is getting darker and blacker every hour'. He confided to the archbishop of Armagh that it really was a sorry spectacle—'men women and children half-naked and evidently half famished seeking at the priest's door a little relief. . . . May God grant us never to witness such suffering again.'[21] Archbishop MacHale of Tuam, an area also affected by the distress, wrote to McGettigan in October 1862 that while the conditions of the poor in the country as a whole were gloomy, the reports from Donegal were, 'I regret to say, among the most disheartening'. Dixon in Armagh distributed relief to Dromore,

[21] AAA, McGettigan to Dixon, 15 June 1863.

Derry and Raphoe. This was in addition to aid given by the 'Central Relief Committee' in Dublin.

The potato blight of 1879–80 heralded another minor famine, yet the coming crisis tended to be dismissed in England as political propaganda. Bishop Michael Logue testified in February 1880 that as many as 60,000 people in Donegal were dependent for subsistence on the Central Relief Committee in Letterkenny. The following month McGettigan, now archbishop of Armagh, in forwarding to Logue an alms of £500 from the archbishop of Boston, commented in the face of a human tragedy that knew no discrimination: 'It is idle for me to remind Your Lordship that, in the distribution of the sum I send, no distinction should be made between protestants and catholics.'

Such intercommunal sympathy was not always a prominent feature of life in the north of Ireland. Belfast was especially prone to vicious sectarian strife accompanied by the shedding of blood and the destruction of property. The years 1857, 1864, 1872 and 1886 witnessed the most notorious incidents. The 1886 riots were probably the worst episodes of violence in nineteenth-century Ireland and spilt more blood than Emmet's rebellion, the Young Ireland rising or the Fenian disturbances of 1867. In the September riots alone four people were murdered, 371 police were injured, there was mass destruction of property including catholic and protestant churches, and 442 individuals were taken prisoner.[22] The commission set up to investigate the violence of 1857 reported: 'The celebration of that festival [Orangeman's Day, 12 July] by the Orange Party in Belfast is plainly and unmistakeably the originating cause of these riots.'[23] Too often such festivals were the occasion of drumming up antagonism against catholicism, with disastrous consequences. The specifically anti-catholic element in Orangeism, at least in its late nineteenth-century expression, is associated with the Rev. Hugh Hanna, William Johnston of Ballykillbeg and Wesley de Cobain among others. De Cobain, a member of parliament, in opening the Orange Hall at Ballynafeigh on 13 July 1886 described the pope as 'an ecclesiastical dignitary presiding over a system of sensualism, superstition and sin'. Such talk was clearly not designed to inculcate a tolerance of Roman Catholicism in his audience. But these opinions were by no means

[22] For a comprehensive treatment of sectarian disturbances in Belfast see Andrew Boyd, *Holy War in Belfast* (Tralee, 1969 and 1987). In dealing with the casualty rates for the 1886 riots Boyd observes (p. 140): '. . . as in all other years of rioting, casualties died without the cause of death being properly recorded at all. Some of them were never taken to hospital or given any medical attention. They were just carried home, there to recover or die as the case might be'.

[23] *Report of the Commission of Inquiry into the Belfast Riots*, House of Commons, 1857–8, XXVI, 3.

unusual. The *Belfast News Letter* suggested on 29 March 1897 that what was needed in Ulster was a good 'Protestant Library' since

> A thorough knowledge of the conduct of the Church of Rome in the past would be one of the greatest obstacles to the aggressive campaign of that Church. . . . In Ireland the Romanists are endeavouring to attain political supremacy. In England their aim is to draw weak Protestants within their net, and then to boast of 'the conversion of England'.

The 'Home Rule is Rome Rule' motif was at fever pitch by the 1890s and was to remain an important feature in Unionist defence of the principle of protestant supremacy in Ulster. There can be no doubt that protestant antipathy was partly inspired by political considerations. The protestant-orchestrated riots of August 1864 may well have begun as a response to the laying of the foundation-stone of O'Connell's monument in Dublin. However it is significant that not all catholics were in favour of the monument or the political sympathies consonant with the event. Patrick Dorrian, the co-adjutor bishop of Down and Connor, wrote to Dr Tobias Kirby—rector of the Irish College and agent in Rome of the Irish bishops in their dealings with the Holy See—that he had not attended the ceremony because there was 'too much Whiggery on the part of some of the leaders'.[24] The protestant fear of a politically active catholicism was matched equally by a theological detestation for the beliefs and practices of the Church of Rome.

Belfast was not alone in experiencing the virtual tyranny of Orangeism with its virulent anti-catholicism. By 1869 the Tory-Orange alliance in Derry was determined to assert what it saw as its exclusive right to parade in the Maiden City[*] in the face of growing catholic impatience at the pace of political reform. The liberal protestant newspaper *The Northern Whig* subsequently castigated the overt sectionalism of the Tory party in Ulster, accusing it of trading 'on the worst sectarian passions of the populace by a professed attachment to the Protestant ascendancy and an ostentatious encouragement of the . . . cry No-Popery.'[25]

The Derry riots of April 1869 were attributed by the official commission of inquiry to provocative Orange parades. As a result the government authorities decided to ban all demonstrations. The

---

[24] Kirby Papers, *Archivium Hibernicum*, vol. 30 (1972), p. 43.

[*] A name in use since the siege of Derry. It was first coined by the protestants of the city to indicate that it had kept its integrity in the face of the Jacobite onslaught and remained unviolated by the forces of James II.

[25] *The Northern Whig*, 27 Aug. 1872.

Apprentice Boys retaliated by inviting Johnston of Ballykillbeg to preach to them on their right to march freely anywhere in Ulster. This seems to have had the desired effect, since their traditional December parade was allowed to proceed as normal and indeed passed off peacefully. However, as one government official observed in the days leading up to the demonstration, 'the object of the Apprentice Boys is to get a proclamation and afterwards to represent the loss of life as attributable to us.'[26]

As the years wore on, the intensity of the conflict in Derry increased. On 1 November 1883 some protestants seized the Guild Hall and from this vantage fired indiscriminately into a peaceful catholic demonstration which had gathered to listen to a lecture on franchise reform. Not surprisingly this provoked major and widespread rioting lasting a week, which the civil authorities were powerless to control. The following year witnessed further sectarian conflict of a relatively minor nature.

Intercommunal strife in Fermanagh was often inspired by political considerations. This was certainly true of the rioting which tore Tempo apart on 28 August 1896 and the succeeding night, and was quelled only by the arrival of forty extra police. Orange attacks on specifically religious gatherings were not unknown. The Catholic Temperance outing in July 1895 was to have been the focus for an attack by 800 Orangemen, who assembled for that purpose at Lisbellaw. Their aim to do damage to the temperate holiday-makers was frustrated when the train carrying them discharged its passengers not at Lisbellaw but at Maguiresbridge some distance away. Even peaceful St Patrick's Day parades such as that in Lurgan in 1874 drew down the wrath of the Orangemen. The peace of the town was disturbed later that year and 200 extra police had be drafted in to cope with the riots sparked off by a protestant attack on the Lady Day march on 15 August.

Belfast was to see street fighting again in August 1872, inspired by the exhortations of the presbyterian minister Hugh Hanna. Independent observers were to suggest that this was a confrontation between 'ultra-protestantism which ran riot on the one side and ultramontane catholicism' which 'went fanatically crazy on the other'. The *Northern Whig* blamed the clergy of both churches for not doing more to prevent the disturbances: 'The special promise of blessedness to the peacemakers may not have been entirely forgotten by the clergy of all denominations' in the recent violence, 'but it was certainly not actively wrought for.'

Being the object of blatant sectarian violence was but one manifes-

---

[26] Quoted in Murphy, *Derry, Donegal and Modern Ulster*, p. 121.

tation of the insecurity of the catholic population in the north
throughout the later part of the century. More subtle but equally
humiliating was discrimination in the workplace. The local authorities in Belfast and Derry were notorious for their refusal to employ
catholics, and in the major manufacturing industries catholics
were also underrepresented. In the Belfast shipyards by 1881 they
numbered only 11 per cent of the workforce, and by 1901 their
percentage had fallen to 7. There was a growing sense that catholics
in urban areas were forced into the least desirable jobs as servants,
dock workers or publicans.[27] Even so those who had work were able
to have at least some control over their lives. The treatment of the
unfortunate poor who found themselves in institutions such as the
workhouse, where the administration was overwhelmingly protestant,
often suffered not only restrictions on their liberty but affronts to their
religion. Many insignificant restrictions were enforced which in effect
prevented catholics from attending mass on Sundays. There were
also reports of individuals being denied access to the sacraments
on their deathbeds. One of the most celebrated cases was that of
Mrs Eliza Mulholland an inmate of the Lisburn Road workhouse in
Belfast. When dying in 1897 she asked for a priest so that she might
be reconciled to the Church of her baptism. The warden Miss Megahy
told her that as long as she had been 'washed in Christ's blood' it did
not matter which Church she belonged to. A complaint was made to
the Poor House Board by the catholic chaplain and although the
superintendent admitted that she had refused the dying woman's
request for a priest the matter was dropped and no further action was
taken against Miss Megahy.

Catholics of course could be just as intolerant and bigoted. There
are many instance of catholic mobs attacking protestant churches in
retaliation for similar affronts. On the whole however the pattern was
one of political rather than religious intolerance. The general attitude
was perhaps summed by Daniel Curoe, the parish priest of Drummaul
near Randalstown, Co. Antrim. Writing to G.H.Moore in January
1853, he denounced his dissenting neighbours for their desertion from
the Liberal cause, saying that 'from this section of the community we
are not in Ireland to reckon on sympathy or co-operation. . . . There
is not on the face of the globe a greater tyrant over a dependant than
a Calvinist nor a greater more base sycophant to a superior.'[28]

[27] Sectarianism did not always succeed in keeping workers divided along party lines.
In July 1874 protestant and catholic mill workers in Belfast went on strike for better pay.
The stoppage culminated in a march from Carlisle Circus to Dunville's Field on the
Falls Road, which attracted a crowd of 10,000 men and women.

[28] Quoted in Hoppen, *Elections, Politics and Society*, p. 267.

Although protestantism was regarded as inferior and heretical, there was by this stage in the nineteenth century no equivalent in the catholic community of that overriding sense of fear and loathing of the other religion, which so marked much of the prevailing protestant attitude to catholicism both then and since. It was the question of political justice, broadly conceived, which dominated Ulster catholicism's relationship with its protestant neighbours.

Politics again

Between 1850 and 1881, no issue a part from that of the disestablishment of the Church of Ireland, which was resolved in 1869, so dominated Irish politics as that of land. The need to secure the historically important 'three Fs'—fair rent, fixity of tenure and freedom of sale—was seen as paramount for the improvement of the mass of catholic rural Ireland. The Tenant League, founded in 1850, had the enthusiastic support of bishop McNally of Clogher as well as of Cullen in Armagh. Blake of Dromore also supported the organisation, if less ardently than his two colleagues. The immediate aim of the League was to secure the passage through parliament of Sherman Crawford's bill seeking to give legislative security to the 'Ulster Custom' and extend it to the rest of Ireland. The custom ensured that any tenant could recover the investment he had made on improvements to his land by selling his interest to the highest bidder if he ever decided to move. The amounts involved could be considerable, often £10-20 per acre. Landlords were happy with the practice since it enabled improvements to be made without their being out of pocket. One of the significant factors in the movement in its early stages was that it brought together in the north catholics and protestants, clergy and laity alike. But other political considerations such as the 'independent opposition'* at Westminster and the resentment caused among catholics by lord John Russell's Ecclesiastical Titles Act† soon fractured catholic-protestant co-operation in the movement.

---

* 'Independent opposition': an attempt in 1850-9 to create an Independent Irish Party which would hold aloof from supporting in any formal way the English political groupings at Westminster. Its intention was to act only in the interests of Ireland, and its members pledged themselves not to accept government office—a principle quickly abandoned by two of its members. The full story of the movement is told by J.H. Whyte, *The Independent Irish Party* (Oxford, 1958).

† The Ecclesiastical Titles Act of 1851 was the government's response to the restoration of the English Roman Catholic hierarchy in 1850, which was seen as 'papal aggression'. The Act prohibited catholic bishops from assuming in their titles the place-names of any town or city in the kingdom. It was largely ignored by both Church and state, and rescinded in 1871.

Some of the catholic clergy were hesitant about any land reform which did not have as its immediate aim the improvement of the lot of the tenant-farmer. That hesitancy become especially marked towards the end of the century over the co-operative movement. Bishop Patrick O'Donnell of Raphoe at first welcomed the movement in Donegal in the early 1890s, but his attitude cooled as time went on. Traders were on the whole opposed to it, as were larger farmers, and since these groups contributed most to clerical income and the financial support of the Church, reform which would adversely effect those interest blocks could not be wholly welcomed by the clergy. On the other hand there was no such ambiguity over one reform movement which brought the Irish Church into direct confrontation with the Holy See and provoked perhaps the greatest single display of resistance to Roman interference in Irish affairs in the whole century. This was the Plan of Campaign.

The Plan, in brief, was aimed at resisting the unjust demands of landowners. Tenants banded together to fix what they thought was a just rent, and if the landlord refused it, the amount was then paid into a fund to be used to protect tenants against the inevitable action for eviction. Anyone taking possession of an evicted tenant's land would be 'boycotted'. The British government put pressure on Rome to condemn the movement, which was largely supported by the clergy. Leo XIII sent Mgr Persico to Ireland in 1887 to investigate the affair. Although he produced a report that was not unfavourable to the campaign, Leo issued a rescript on 20 April 1888 condemning the Plan and the boycotting as immoral. As a result the country was in uproar and despite the hierarchy's ritualistic obedience to Rome the bishops simply refused, with one notable exception, to pay much attention to the pope's pronouncement. Indeed so obvious was the perceived neglect of the decree that the papal secretary of state wrote to archbishop Logue in November 1888 complaining that it was not being observed. The situation dragged on for some time. In an exasperated letter of 7 October 1890 cardinal Simeoni remonstrated with Logue that there was a lack of unanimity among the Irish bishops and clergy over the decree. In his reply Logue politely but firmly stated his own conviction and that of the hierarchy that such were the complexities of the Irish situation that only with the greatest difficulty could they be grasped by outsiders, Rome included!

A more important and decisive intervention in Irish political affairs was the condemnation of Fenianism 'by name' issued by Pius IX in January 1870. Although never a very serious political threat in Ulster Fenianism had none the less significant support. Bishop Dorrian believed that the Catholic Institute of Belfast was being used as a front to recruit Fenian support. Because of its clandestine nature and by

1864 its quite explicit aim, as articulated by Charles Kickham and others in the *Irish People* (the Fenian newspaper founded in Dublin in 1863 and suppressed by the government in September 1865), of throwing off clerical domination as well as the British administration, the Church as a whole acted against it. The clergy used their influence in the confessional to turn would-be sympathisers away from the movement. In May 1865 Dorrian wrote to archbishop Dixon saying that the 'jubilee indulgence' proclaimed by Pius IX in that year had been the occasion of a change of heart by many Fenians: 'Your Grace will rejoice to know that the Fenians have surrendered en masse. The leaders have gone to Confession and to Holy Communion.' Dorrian also conveyed these sentiments to the agent of the Irish bishops in Rome.

Similar reports had reached Dixon from other parts of Ulster telling him of the demise of Fenianism and 'Ribbonism'. The clergy made sustained efforts in the early 1860s to blot out radical clandestine movements. Malachy O'Callaghan, writing from Forkhill, in 1864, assured the primate that 'All our artillery [is] playing upon the Ribbonmen'. Another missive from the same period confirmed that the movement had been 'crushed' by the exertions of the clergy, and urged that the bishops should take even stronger measures against such organisations. A correspondent thanking Dixon in July 1862 for his pastoral letter against secret societies, pronounced that 'No language in dealing with such people can be too severe.'

Such thinking was echoed several years later by Tobias Kirby in Rome who informed Dixon that reports of the arrests of Fenian leaders had reached the Holy See. 'God grant that the remedy may be in time. These are not the times to allow such wicked societies to grow to an adult stature with the hope of exterminating them at pleasure.'[29] Not all Irish clergy abroad had such a detached perspective on radical movements at home. When Terence Bellew McManus, one of the leaders of the 1848 rebellion and a native of Tempo, Co. Fermanagh, died in 1861 his body was brought from California to Ireland via New York. At a funeral service in New York archbishop John Hughes, originally from Annaloghan, Co. Tyrone, justified the use of force in resisting British administration in Ireland. He claimed: 'Some of the most learned and holy men of the church had laid it down with general sanction and authority that there are cases in which it is lawful to resist and overthrow a tyrannical government.' This was in sharp contrast to the attitude of most Irish prelates. Dixon called for the excommunication of Patrick Lavell, the

---

[29] AAA, Kirby to Dixon, 2 October 1865.

parish priest of Party, Co. Mayo, who presided at the interment of McManus' body in Dublin.

The overwhelming majority of clergy and bishops were opposed to Fenianism and all manifestations of radical violence. However it was not always possible for the clergy to guarantee the compliance of the laity with the teachings of their pastors and even the implacable opposition of priests and bishops was liable to fluctuation, especially in the light of the treatment of Fenian prisoners in the aftermath of the abortive 1867 rising. Of more direct concern was the fear of the spread of Fenianism among tenant-farmers after the execution of three Fenians in Manchester in November 1867, a political miscalculation of the first order by the British authorities which produced an outcry in Ireland. *The Freeman's Journal* of 28 November 1867 carried the following letter from a 'Clogher priest' which perhaps gives some idea of the strength of feeling aroused by the executions:

> The merciless butchery in Manchester on Saturday last took many Catholic clergymen by surprise. I was not of the number and have therefore the satisfaction of feeling that the Holy Sacrifice offered for them by my unworthy self was completed before their execution that morning. Many of my brother priests enjoy the same satisfaction. . . . I would venture to suggest that a public month's mind should be held in every parish of the kingdom on Monday the 23rd December . . .

A certain sympathy was generated for the Fenians among bishops and clergy alike. Dr Leahy of Dromore began to support the call for an amnesty for them, and this found an echo in bishop Dorrian's advocacy of their release. However, these moves were tactical. The bishops were aware that if Fenians were released public agitation would die down and it would be less easy for the radicals to drive a wedge between the clergy and the people on the Fenian issue. By early 1870 a petition asking for the release of Fenian prisoners had been signed by half the clergy in the whole country.

It was at precisely this moment that Cullen decided to act. He called a meeting of the bishops, then all in Rome for the first Vatican Council, and persuaded them in the interests of religion to petition the Holy See for a condemnation of the Fenians. All the Ulster bishops voted in favour of the petition. Pius IX duly obliged and the decree condemning Fenianism was issued at the end of January 1870. Its effect, at least for the time being , was to bring most of the clergy into line. The laity, however, were in a different position. When the Lady Day procession assembled in Alexander Street, Falls Road, Belfast, in 1872 many of the participants wore sashes bearing the names of Allen, Larkin and O'Brien, the 'Manchester martyrs'. Still the Holy

See had moved decisively on a complex matter, in an attempt to assert its own authority pronouncing in favour of lawful government and excoriating the machinations of revolutionaries as incompatible with membership of the catholic Church.

The clerical flirtation with Fenianism, however ambiguous and tangential, was but one facet of clerical political activity in these years. We have seen that Cullen's political sympathies were determined by issues of self-interest for the Church. Evidence can be adduced to show that such an attitude found resonances in the catholic community in Ulster. But before looking at the extent of priestly involvement, we should perhaps say something of the general political attitude of Ulster catholics in the years before the Home Rule movement assumed widespread support.

In 1878 catholics in Down supported the Tory candidate, lord Castlereagh, because he was deemed to be more favourably disposed to catholic interests on the education question than his Liberal opponent. In general, however, catholic support was almost entirely Liberal till the 1880s. The Liberals were seen to be more favourably disposed to reform, in the catholic interest, than the Tories. W.E. Gladstone, with the help of English nonconformists and Irish catholics, had carried through the legislation to disestablish the Church of Ireland, a measure which gave great satisfaction to Irish catholics but which was viewed with ambiguity in Rome. The catholics were thus indebted to the Liberals on more than one count, and apart from a brief desertion to the Tories in the 1850s, except in Ulster where catholic support remained strong, catholics continued to give their backing to the Liberal camp.

Such an alliance had its dangers for the Liberal party. Any significant shift in catholic political opinion would spell the death of Liberalism at least in the north. The Ulster Liberal representation was never large but catholics were not disposed to vote for Orange Tories. Of twenty-nine seats in the Province only six were held by the Liberals in 1874; by 1880 this had risen to nine. By the time Home Rule had caught the imagination of catholic voters, Liberalism in Ulster was at an end. The 1885 election saw the division of Ulster representation into seventeen seats for Home Rule candidates, sixteen for the Tories and obliteration for the Liberals.

From the mid-1850s the leadership of the party in the Province had come from presbyterians, Church of Ireland politics being increasingly Tory and Orange in character. This is not to suggest that there was no support for the Tory party and Orangeism in the presbyterian community. For example Belfast, from the time of Cooke's Presbyterian/Church of Ireland 'marriage', had been represented by two Tories, one from each Church. This was the price paid by the ascendancy for the pan-protestant coalition. The result was to assure the Liberals of the complete support of Belfast catholics, although by the late 1860s they accounted for only one-fifth of the electorate. Nonetheless that was to prove of great significance in the 1868 election. The appearance of William Johnston as an independent Orange candidate in that year spilt the protestant vote. Johnston was assiduously supported by Hugh Hanna, one of the few presbyterian ministers in the city who was an active member of the Orange Order, who frequently denounced Tory candidates as being 'soft' on Rome. In the contest the two Tories were defeated and Johnston was returned along with the Liberal candidate Thomas McClure, himself a protestant.

The experience of the other major urban centre, Derry, was not dissimilar to that of Belfast. The town was held by the Liberals till 1860 and after that date more often than not by the Tories. None the less catholics *en masse* continued to support the Liberal cause. By 1872 as much as 80 per cent of Derry liberal support came from the catholic community. The Reform Act of 1884 dramatically increased the catholic electorate and for the first time there was near-parity between the communities in their voting strengths. This had the unfortunate by-product of virtually abolishing the protestant liberal/conservative divide as both united in the face of growing catholic political muscle. The growing frustration of northern catholics with their exclusion from real political power eroded its support of Liberalism and made the harvest ripe for the Home Rule movement when it finally caught the public imagination.

The bishops returning to Ireland from the Vatican Council found that many clergy were already open supporters of Home Rule in some form. The active role of priests in politics had long been a feature of Irish catholicism. Although clerical political agitation was perhaps less important in Ulster than elsewhere in Ireland, it was not without significance as priests and bishops sought to give advice on how catholic votes should be cast between rival protestant candidates. Priests in Ulster lacked the political sophistication of their fellow clergy in the rest of Ireland, partly because of the relative lack of political strength of catholicism in much of Ulster. However, we have seen that the Donegal clergy played their part in 'getting out' the tenants' rights vote in that county in 1852. By 1885 they had rekindled their interest in politics to the extent of organising the registration which enabled the Home Rule candidates to capture all four seats in the election of that year. Politically Home Rule was the binding force which gave northern catholics their first taste of the exercise of power, and this did much to instil fear into their protestant neighbours.

The clergy were sensitive political animals. All six priests in Newry voted for the Liberal candidate in the 1868 election, testifying not only to their commitment to the liberal cause but also, given the property qualification for the franchise, to the size of their income. Self-interest, at least as far the Church was concerned, also played a part. In the 1851 by-election in Dungannon John Francis Maguire, a promoter of the idea of an Independent Irish Opposition in the House of Commons, was defeated partly because of the opposition of the parish priest, the Very Rev. J. Hally. Hally accused Maguire of being a supporter of the Queen's Colleges and as such unworthy of catholic votes. But there is also a sense in Ulster's troubled religious–political axis that the clergy could only lead where they felt the people wanted to go. Otherwise the results could be disastrous. The archbishops of Armagh regularly tried to influence elections in favour of the Liberals in Dundalk and Drogheda, but after 1874, with the defeat of Chichester Fortescue despite McGettigan's ardent championship of his cause, their support of any given candidate was something of a mixed blessing. Still they had more success in keeping the hotheads among the clergy at bay. The bishops too were under constant pressure from Rome to make sure that the clergy did not stir up political troubles. In December 1882 and again in January 1883 Leo XIII wrote to Logue in Raphoe and McGettigan in Armagh warning them to keep priests out of politics and the 'faithful' from secret societies. 'We do not want the cause of Ireland to be besmirched by reprehensible actions,' he said.

When Home Rule became the cry of the country, Belfast was one of the first towns to open a chapter of the association. Of course Home Rule was a movement for self-government in Ireland within the British empire. Many nineteenth-century nationalists were an entirely different breed from their twentieth-century counterparts. Parnell was no Patrick Pearse and the nationalist rhetoric which he displayed when he brought the battle for his leadership of the party back to Ireland in late 1890 must be seen for what it was, a last and desperate effort to continue to lead the movement which he had helped to create, the control of which was irrevocably slipping from his grasp with every passing day. As bishop Dorrian wrote of him to Rome in happier times, 'Parnell . . . is misrepresented by the English and Irish Press . . . [he] is bringing to the surface the misgovernment of Ireland. People howl at him; but he is cool, confident and constitutional.'[30]

---

[30] Patrick Dorrian to Tobias Kirby, 24 November 1879, Kirby Papers, *Archivium Hibernicum*, vol. 30 (1972), p. 89.

When Parnell first visited Belleek, Co. Fermanagh, in November 1880 on behalf of the Land League he was listened to by protestant and catholic alike. However by 1882 when interests switched from land to Home Rule the spectre of Rome once again stalked the land and northern protestants deserted him. Of course the irony in this is that the Home Rule movement of the 1870s was distrusted by many catholic bishops because it was seen as much too protestant and Orange in complexion. Others believed that it owed too much to Fenianism.

By 1890 politics in the north as elsewhere were dominated by the issue of Kitty O'Shea's divorce and Parnell's role as the co-respondent. The split in the Irish Parliamentary Party also reflected the fragmentation of catholic opinion along pro- and anti-Parnell lines. What seems clear however is that the bishops once again saw the opportunity to seize the political leadership in the country. Indeed this line was suggested to them by cardinal Manning, the archbishop of Westminster. Logue said that he did not see that Parnell deserved 'much consideration', and in a typically intemperate outburst he declared that 'a man having the destinies of a people in his hands and bartering it away for the company of an old woman is certainly not a person to beget confidence.'[31] Much of the opposition to Parnell was led by priests and bishops. All the northern bishops signed the hierarchy's 'address' against him. In Belfast the bishop, Patrick McAlister, went further and established his own newspaper *The Irish News* because he distrusted the pro-Parnell politics of the local catholic-owned paper *The Belfast Morning News*. Such was McAlister's influence with his flock that within a year his rivals had gone out of business. There was, as we have seen, an overriding question here of the extent of clerical influence in Irish political life. This became crystallised around the split in the anti-Parnellite majority of the Irish parliamentary party between Tim Healy who accepted the need for clerical oversight in politics, and John Dillon who wanted politics free from clerical domination.

Already in January 1890 Logue had speculated that under the leadership of the party as it then was, the struggle for Home Rule 'might leave no room for the settlement of the education question'. Logue's doubts were confirmed in 1892 by a letter from Herbert Vaughan archbishop of Westminster expressing his fears over the soundness of the Home Rule party on the issue of catholic education. Vaughan poured scorn on T.P.O'Connor, the member of parliament and president of the Home Rule federation in Britain; he accused

---

[31] Quoted in Emmet Larkin, 'The Roman Catholic Hierarchy and the Fall of Parnell', *Victorian Studies*, vol. 4 (1960–1), p. 334.

O'Connor of supporting the 'progressive and anti-denominational party' and he begged Logue to exercise his influence 'on the Home Rule party in such a way as to neutralise the conduct of such a man as this unbeliever'. In 1893 Logue was writing to Rome that the Home Rule Bill then going through parliament was 'not satisfactory to catholic interests' but that it might not be prudent for the bishops to make an open protest. 'The bill will not pass and the bishops should avoid the odium of defeating it.'[32]

Catholics and the establishment

It is something of a caricature to see Irish catholic nationalism as irredeemably 'republican' or to suppose that all catholics repudiated contact with the English ruling classes. The biographer of bishop Dorrian says that he was 'anxious as a spiritual leader to demonstrate the loyalty of catholics to the institutions of the State by his presence at public occasions where the monarchy or government was involved'.[33] At the St Patrick's day dinner of 1874 in Belfast not only did he propose the loyal toast to queen Victoria but he also spoke against Home Rule if it would lead to 'divisions and religious bitterness and altercations, or to the decay of trade or agriculture of the country'.

Cardinal Rampolla, the Vatican secretary of state, wrote to Logue in June 1897 reminding him of the duty of the Irish bishops to present an address of loyalty to queen Victoria on the occasion of her golden jubilee. Bishop Henry wrote to the lord mayor of Belfast in April stating that he had 'great pleasure in authorizing you to place my name in the list of subscribers to the proposed Victoria hospital for £100'.[34] The hospital was built by the people of Belfast to mark the queen's jubilee.

When Victoria visited Ireland in 1900 cardinal Logue went out of his way to pay his respects to the head of state—in grave contrast, it must be said, to archbishop Walsh of Dublin who 'found it necessary to leave Ireland at the moment of the Queen's arrival'.[35] The formality involved Logue first going to the Viceregal Lodge and writing his name in the 'Queen's book', after which an invitation was sent to him to dine with Her Majesty. He was shown every mark of favour and had a long private talk with the queen. Victoria found Logue 'a very charming simple man'.

[32] Logue to Kirby, 23 June 1893.

[33] Ambrose Macaulay, *Patrick Dorrian: Bishop of Down and Connor, 1865-85* (Irish Academic Press, 1987), p. 226.

[34] *Belfast News Letter*, 28 April 1897.

[35] AAA, Lord Denbigh to Rev. Dr P.J. Toner, 28 February 1927.

The cardinal, who was joined by his vicar-general Mgr Byrne, confided to lord Denbigh, a lord-in-waiting to the queen and himself a catholic, that in politics he was if anything a Conservative but that like many he had 'been driven into the arena of the Radical Party for it was felt that they were the only ones they could hope to get anything out of, but that he "wished to goodness they could shake off these English Radicals".'[36] Logue also made the astute observation that he wished the office of lord lieutenant could be made independent of party politics since under the current system he was not regarded as a true representative of the queen in Ireland and consequently 'God Save the Queen' when played in his presence came to be regarded as a 'party tune'. All of this may come as something of a revelation since Logue is generally regarded as a quintessential Irish nationalist.[37]

Such desire by Ulster catholics to associate with the great and the good was further underlined at the official opening of the new Mater hospital on 23 April 1900. The ceremony was performed by the lord mayor of Belfast R.J. McConnell, a fervent unionist. Among the other 'distinguished persons' present was the marquis of Dufferin and Ava, former viceroy of India. Sixteen years later the Irish Christian Brothers, to mark their fifty years in Belfast, solicited contributions from among others the lord lieutenant and Sir William Pirrie, the Harland and Wolff shipbuilder. In the book they published to mark their anniversary they listed all their past pupils on active service in the Great War and published a moving tribute to three Flanagan brothers, all past pupils, who had lost their lives in the service of king and country. All this is somewhat at odds with their reputation for aggressive republican nationalism. The Ulster catholic community was not an undifferentiated mass of disaffected Irish nationalists. On the whole by the end of the nineteenth century it consisted of law-abiding Home Rulers anxious to play their part in the wider British empire but wanting fair play at home. The political and constitutional events from the turn of the century to the end of the Irish civil war were dramatically to change the political outlook of the community.

---

[36] AAA, Denbigh to Toner, undated memorandum.

[37] Indeed there is some evidence that Logue's successor cardinal O'Donnell wanted this intelligence kept from the public. Dr Toner had started a biography of Logue, which was never finished, and had written to Denbigh concerning the Queen's visit in 1900. Toner showed O'Donnell Denbigh's memo and the cardinal refused Toner permission to make use of the material referred to above, as is clear from the Denbigh-Toner correspondence in the Armagh Archives.

5

THE ROAD TO PARTITION

Growing confidence and growing restriction

The religious outlook of many Ulster catholics at the turn of the century was well epitomised by an editorial in the 4 October 1897 issue of the *Irish News*. Pope Leo XIII had just issued an encyclical on the rosary stressing the importance of that devotion in the life of the faithful christian. The newspaper commented with a mixture of pride and defiance: 'In all our vicissitudes Irish catholics can still humbly claim to have preserved in a great measure the love of their forefathers for the pious and efficacious practice of which the Holy Father writes so eloquently'. Here was a confirmation of all that Ulster catholicism saw in itself: the faithful observance of a religious life handed down from of old and maintained in the face of persecution and protestant hegemony in the north-east. That fidelity was to be put to the test in the coming decades in a way which equalled any previous trial. The Ulster experience of those years was to leave the catholics of two-thirds of Ulster cut off from their co-religionists in the rest of Ireland in a state which they perceived as unbendingly hostile to their social, political and, above all, religious aspirations.

The synod of Maynooth which heralded the new century was concerned, among other issues, to insist on the need for the proper training of nuns in the arts of teaching and nursing. This rather confirmed cardinal Logue's own experience in the Armagh diocese where he found novices teaching in the schools associated with various religious communities, a practice which he believed was good neither for the aspirant nun nor for the children in her care. But despite the lack of formal teacher training, schools of the religious orders in Ulster continued to flourish. The Sacred Heart convent in Armagh numbered thirty-six nuns by 1902 and had set up a 'missionary school' in addition to its other activities. The point of the new venture was to train girls with 'religious vocations' for the foreign missions. This concern for overseas development was also to find expression in the foundation of the 'Maynooth mission to China' in 1916, in which the northern dioceses played their part in sending men and finances.

The expansion of secondary education was in the main quite restricted in Ulster in the years before partition. The Presentation Brothers opened a school for boys in Enniskillen in 1903, and this was

171

followed by convent grammar schools in Lurgan (1905), Enniskillen
(1909), Portstewart (1917), Donaghmore (1920) and Kilkeel (1921),
but despite valiant efforts the educational standards of Ulster catholics
still lagged behind those of their protestant neighbours. The 1901
census showed that 19.1 per cent of Ulster catholics were illiterate
compared with 9.8 for members of the Church of Ireland, 5.0, for
presbyterians and 4.7 for the methodists.[1] At the other end of the
scale where catholics had the benefit of secondary education they
were not slow to take their place in the middle-class professions. By
1901 there were 100 catholic doctors out of a total of 724, 10 per cent
of chemists were catholics, and catholic barristers numbered 136 out
of 595. On the other hand it must be said that these figures do not
adequately reflect the proportional strength of catholics in Ulster as
a whole. Only in school teaching does their strength begin to reflect
their numerical position and this was better for men than for women.
In the police however they were over-represented, at least in the lower
ranks, numbering 1,745 out of a total of 3,142, some of them being
posted to Ulster from other parts of the country.

Among the working classes catholics represented 33 per cent of
general labourers and 41 per cent of dockers. Recruitment to skilled
trades was so heavily weighted in favour of protestants that it was
difficult for catholics to make inroads among the artisans. This was
the legacy of nineteenth-century employment practices in the urban
centres, especially Belfast. These included the tradition of not encouraging catholic apprenticeships, which having once become established
became increasingly hard to reverse. This seems to be the genuine
reason for the lack of skilled workers in the catholic community at this
stage and is certainly a more satisfactory one than that advanced by
Henry Patterson and others—namely that protestant dominance of
the skilled workforce was a product of non-conformist culture, the
implication being that the catholic ethos militated against the acquisi-
tion of skill for the workplace.[2]

---

[1] By 1911 catholic illiteracy had been cut to 14.7%, still rather high compared to
anglicans at 6.1%, presbyterians at 2.8% and methodists at 1.4%. Cf. *Census of Ireland
1911*, summary volume. The figures for 1901 can be examined in *Census of Ireland 1901*,
part 1, vol. 3. There was tremendous variation in illiteracy levels from county to
county: In 1901 Belfast city had the lowest rate for the province at 12.2% of the catholic
population, and Cavan recorded 14%. Donegal, with 31% who could neither read nor
write, had the worst level.

[2] Patterson maintains that nonconformist dominance of the skilled labour-force was
'based on the eighteenth-century capital and initiative of the Presbyterian entrepre-
neurs, and supported by the puritan ethos of education, apprenticeship and the self-help
of the nineteenth-century non-conformist migrant'. *Class Conflict and Sectarianism*
(Belfast, 1980), p. 38. Patterson is here repeating Sybil Baker's views in 'Orange and
Green', in H.J. Dyos and M. Wolff (eds), *The Victorian City* (vol. 2: London, 1973),
p. 793.

Clearly funding for education was an enormous and constant drain on Church finances, and the lack of funds must be attributed partly to the ,absence of adequate catholic representation among the Ulster professional classes at this time. Joe Devlin was to claim in April 1914 that Belfast catholics had spent £180,000 building some seventy schools for their children in that city alone. Of course the government provided most of the monies necessary to enable the educational system to function. Since 1878 the Intermediate Education Act provided funding for secondary education based on examination results. By 1912 the better catholic schools in Ulster were able to demonstrate respectable showings in these competitions. The five top schools between them shared a total of £1,532. Yet as we have seen the bishops themselves sometimes worked against educational reforms that would have enhanced the general educational level of the community. Their opposition to the idea of compulsory attendance at National school level and their obsession with clerical control at every stage in the educational process doubtless restricted the opportunities for advancement in the wider community that catholics could have expected. Also, many of the brighter pupils became priests and nuns and this undoubted drain on the talents of the community, whatever its spiritual benefits, contributed to the overall under-representation of catholics in the professions.

Of course no satisfactory representation could be accomplished until the university question was finally settled. This was at last facilitated by the University Act of 1908. The Royal University, which had been little more than an examinations board, was dismantled and two universities were set up, the National University of Ireland and the Queen's University of Belfast. Among the Ulster bishops who supported the Act were Owens of Clogher and McHugh of Derry, although both had reservations about the fine print, particularly on funding and the position of Maynooth in the grand scheme of things. Queen's with its overwhelmingly presbyterian ethos did not readily commend itself to catholic participation. However, in the first senate of the university catholics were given some representation.[3] One of the stipulations of the 1908 Act was that no state money should be used for the promotion of any denomination. None the less

---

The thesis deserves some consideration. It is evident that religion will condition attitudes to society and the material world. But it stretches the credulity of even the most sympathetic observer of Ulster protestantism to suggest that the success of Ulster presbyterians in the skilled labour market was primarily a result of the good calvinist principle of hard work and a God-fearing outlook on life.

[3] There were four senators in all: John Burke, JP, Patrick Dempsey, JP, Charles McLorinan and Sir Peter Reilly O'Connell.

the catholic senators recommended in April 1909 that for the university to be more acceptable to catholics there should be two professorships of English, and moral philosophy and history, and that the second one in each disipline should be held by a catholic. They also suggested that a professorship of Celtic studies be established, and that the Mater hospital be a recognised teaching facility of the medical faculty. This last point was conceded and a member of the Mater staff was appointed to one of four lectureships in clinical medicine.

The university also decided to appoint a lecturer in scholastic philosophy, and the appointment was greeted by a great wave of protest from the protestant community. The Ulster Unionist Council declared that the lectureship was 'inconsistent with the constitution of a non-sectarian university'.[4] Three formal protests were lodged with the Irish privy council, two of them from presbyterian ministers and the other from lord Londonderry. Beckett and Moody[5] are at pains to stress that these protests were made solely to defend the non-denominational nature of Queen's. Whatever Londonderry's motives may have been, it is difficult, reading the proceedings of the Presbyterian Church's general assembly for June 1909, to conclude that the protests of that Church were anything other than a sectarian outcry. In the event the privy council determined that scholastic philosophy did not constitute a denominational discipline and Fr Denis O'Keefe was allowed to keep his job.

The struggle to endow a professorship of Celtic studies was similarly fraught with difficulty. The authorities agreed to appoint a lecturer, and in a determinedly ecumenical gesture gave the job to a Church of Ireland clergyman, F.W. O'Connell. However, Queen's resisted the overtures of the Gaelic League to have the position raised to the status of a professorship. Various amounts of money were offered by Gaelic enthusiasts, by 1911 ranging from £300 to £1,000, but these were turned down, the university arguing that it was too short of funds to make up the deficit for a chair. Even Beckett and Moody are forced to concede that while lack of money was a factor a similar partial endowment 'on behalf of some other subject would have been more sympathetically considered'.[6]

A Catholic dean of residence was appointed in 1909 by the bishop of Down and Connor, John Tohill, to look after the spiritual needs of catholics. In December that year bishop Tohill urged catholic students to take a full part in the life of the university, and from that time he felt free to send seminarians to Queen's for their initial

[4] Quoted in David Kennedy, *Towards a University* (Belfast, 1947), p. 64.
[5] *Queen's Belfast, 1845–1949*, vol 1, p. 408.
[6] *Ibid* p. 413.

intellectual formation before going on to theological studies in Rome or Maynooth. This, given the history of Ulster, was perhaps a curious development. It must surely be unique in the English-speaking world for would-be catholic priests to have their initial formation in a non-denominational university with a heavily presbyterian bias. By August 1911, however, the Vatican had sanctioned the arrangement and general catholic participation at Queen's. The incongruity of all this was not lost on cardinal Logue. In rather surly terms he wrote to archbishop Walsh of Dublin apropos Queen's:

> Of course our responsibility ceases when the Holy See has spoken through the H[oly] O[ffice] but it is a complete revolution of our educational traditions here in Ireland. It makes one wonder how the Queen's Colleges were so long kept under the ban and it will be simply an absurd inconsistency hence forward to interfere with students going to that College'.[7]

The Queen's Colleges problem had come full circle! The number of catholics attending Queen's before the 1950s was never very great. In 1915 there were 146, by 1920 this had risen to 208, and in 1947 they numbered 400 out of a student population of some 2,000.

Throughout the period other areas of the Church's life continued to be developed. In 1898 Bishop Henry Henry set up the Belfast Catholic Truth Society with the aim of disseminating cheap booklets on various aspects of the faith. So successful did this prove to be that two years later, with Henry's blessing, it became the Catholic Truth Society of Ireland with its headquarters in Dublin. The interior of Armagh cathedral was at last finished with the aid of a 'giant bazaar' in 1900 to which the pope sent a gift of vestments to be raffled. The cathedral was consecrated in July 1904 in the presence of a papal legate, cardinal Vincent Vannutelli, who also took the opportunity of visiting Belfast and Newry. The cathedral had been more than sixty years in building and had to wait more than another decade before its distinctive spires were added. Similar developments occurred in Newry, where the cathedral was enlarged during the episcopacy of Henry O'Neill, and in Letterkenny where St Eunan's cathedral was opened on 16 June 1901. In Derry, Long Tower Church, the site of St Colmcille's monastery, was solemnly rededicated in May 1910 after extensive renovations, made possible in part by a benefaction of £9,000 from Redmond Hannigan. In recognition of his generosity and his work for the St Vincent de Paul Society, Hannigan was made a papal knight in January 1911. At his death three years later he left most of his estate of £10,720 for 'nursing the sick Roman Catholic

[7] AAA, Logue to Walsh, 1 Sept. 1911.

Poor of Londonderry in their own homes'. It would seem that northern catholics had not by this stage developed the aversion to the planters' name for the Maiden City which was to be a marked feature of their *modus operandi* in more recent times. Hannigan's generosity was by no means rare. Hannah and Teresa Hamill gave £30,000 to enable the church of St Teresa to be built in the Hannahstown suburb of Belfast in 1911. As bishop McKenna of Clogher, the guest preacher, reminded his congregation at the opening of St Patrick's church at Upper Badoney, Co. Tyrone, in September 1912, such testimonies of faith were a demonstration of endurance witnessing against 'a powerful neighbouring nation' which in the past 'had tried to rob them of what they treasured more deeply than life—their Faith'.[8]

The desire to give the faith solid form in bricks and mortar was not merely confined to homespun ventures. In 1913 Logue, in arranging celebrations to mark the sixteenth centenary of the peace of Constantine,[9] suggested to the people of Armagh that they might have a collection to contribute towards the cost of a memorial church which Pius X was building at the Milvian bridge on the Flaminian way in Rome. His diocese promptly produced £431 towards the cost of this piece of triumphalism.

Despite this remarkable degree of self-confidence Ulster catholics could still continue to feel themselves under threat from the state and their non-catholic fellow countrymen, at times with justification. According to the 1901 census the population of Dungannon numbered 3,936 of whom 2,000 were catholics. The Urban Council had twenty-one members, fourteen protestants and seven catholics. As the *Irish News* commented on 2 January 1904, 'The Chairman of the board is a Protestant, the vice-chairman is a Protestant, the town surveyor is a Methodist, the sub-sanitary officer is a Protestant, the factory inspector is a Protestant, and the rate collector is a Presbyterian.' All this in a town where there was a Catholic majority, admittedly a small one. Discrimination was felt at both corporate and individual level. Miss Rose Sweeney, a catholic employed by the National School at Carntall, Co. Tyrone, brought an action against William Coote, the master of the local Orange Lodge and a future Northern Ireland MP, whom she alleged was conspiring to have her dismissed from her position in the presbyterian-managed school. She won the original action in May 1905 only to have the judgement overturned by the Irish court of appeal in December the same year.

Equally difficult was the inability of catholics to make bequests

---

[8] *Catholic Directory* (Dublin, 1913), p. 537.

[9] The Edict of Toleration of AD 313 had paved the way for Christianity to become the religion of the Roman empire.

for specifically catholic purposes. In 1905 Ellen McLoughlan of Portadown made a bequest in favour of the archbishop of Armagh for the celebration of masses for the repose of the souls of herself and her family. On 13 July of that year the master of the rolls declared the will invalid since this was clearly not a charity and the saying of a mass, being a private affair, could not be of benefit to the public at large. Logue was initially reluctant to lodge an appeal. However, as he explained to archbishop Walsh, 'had the Masses been ordered to be said in a public church it would settle the question. Now since the 1st Synod of Maynooth all Masses must be said in a public church unless the Bishop expressly dispenses for a special reason. Saying Masses for the dead would not be such a reason.'[10] Logue was persuaded to press the matter although he had little hope of a successful outcome. He himself argued that honoraria for masses were principally intended for the support of the clergy. Such support in his view must surely be 'an object of public interest', bringing the bequest in question into the realm of public charity. The court of appeal in February 1906 decided in Logue's favour, arguing that the pious character of the gift constituted it a charity. The lord chief baron was of the opinion that the celebration of mass was a charitable act, whether celebrated in public or in private. Even more surprisingly lord justice Fitzgibbon declared that the case involved a principle vital to religious equality beyond any denominational interest. However a similar case involving the will of John Glen of Coleraine was declared void by the high court in May 1906. Glen had left his money for 'Roman Catholic purposes'. The court declared this to be 'too vague', and pointed to the Catholic Association in Belfast.[11] While the activities of that organization involved catholics, its objectives in the court's view were political rather than religious.

A more direct threat to the community came on 6 July 1912 with the expulsion of some 2,000 catholics from the Belfast shipyards. By the end of that month more than 8,000 workers were affected, in shipbuilding and other industries. This cruel injustice was not unrelated to the political developments then under way, but it confirmed the vulnerability of catholics in north-east Ulster. In organising their own defence and appealing to the rest of the country for financial help, the Catholic Vigilance Committee asserted that 'our only object is the alleviation of distress'. Bishop Tohill who presided at the meeting which set up the committee called for more police to be sent for the protection of the catholic population. On the 7 July he cabled to the lord lieutenant, '[We] solemnly protest

[10] AAA, Logue to Walsh, 22 July 1905.
[11] The Belfast Catholic Association will be discussed below.

against the inaction of the authorities in Belfast for the last week, who have given no protection to Catholic workers or property. . . .' Catholics have been the subject of "violent intimidation, brutal attacks, and mob law".'[12]

Such violence directed against the catholic population might be thought of as the result of political rather than religious considerations. But attacks by protestants on catholics for religious reasons were not infrequent. The Belfast Protestant Association headed by its leader Arthur Trew set about breaking up a Corpus Christi procession in Belfast in May 1900. Trew and some of his companions were sent to prison because of the disturbances, which so incensed Trew's supporters that they took revenge on catholic workers in the Queen's Island shipyard. Catholics themselves could at times display a frightening intolerance of their protestant neighbours. It was after all an attack on a presbyterian Sunday school outing at Castledawson which led to the reprisals in the Belfast shipyards, mentioned above. On the other hand there is some suggestion that the Castledawson attack was in response to an attack on a catholic outing at Tullyroan, Co. Armagh, during which a number of shots were fired by protestants at the catholic holiday-makers. There had been a similar incident in June 1912 when Sisters from the Sacred Heart convent in Lisburn were attacked on an outing with some children to Ardglass. That summer the situation had become so tense throughout the north that in certain areas priests had to have police protection when administering the sacraments to their people.[13] Assaults on such easy targets were not the prerogatives of one community only.

Apart from external attacks, the Church was quite capable of inflicting damage on itself. Pius X declared war on modern thought and practice in a series of documents in the early years of the twentieth century. 'Modernism' was branded as the 'synthesis of all heresies' in the decree *Lamentabili* of 3 July 1907. This general approach was confirmed in the encyclical *Pascendi* (8 September 1907) and by a *motu proprio*, *Sacrorum antistitum* (1 September 1910) which imposed the 'anti-modernist oath'. The distrust of the modern world evinced by these documents duly resonated with many elements in Ulster catholicism. Logue used the opportunity of a preaching engagement in Derry on 29 September 1907 to speak of the dangers of socialism. In particular he warned against the perils for Irish catholics of entering into alliance with socialists and 'secularists' in England in the hope of forwarding the aims of Home Rule. In the cardinal's view it would be better not to have Home Rule than to contaminate Irish

[12] *Irish News*, 8 July 1912.
[13] *The Catholic Directory* (1913), p. 541.

catholicism with such a nefarious alliance. In February 1914 the bishops of the whole country issued a joint Lenten pastoral letter in which, while expressing sympathy 'for the conditions of workers', they made plain that socialism could not in conscience be the remedy to which catholics might resort for the betterment of harsh social conditions.

Anti-socialist rhetoric caused the bishops to view the emerging trades union movement with suspicion. Part of the difficulty here was that Jim Larkin had told the Irish Trades Union Congress in 1908 that Irish education would only improve when the clerical monopoly was ended. This confirmed Logue's worst fears about the movement and caused bishop MacKenna of Clogher to reflect that, irrespective of the material success that good education might bring, 'what would it profit a man if he gained the whole world and lost his own soul?'[14] The Lenten pastoral of February 1914 was in part a response to the Dublin lock-out of 1913. As Logue told Walsh, the challenges of trade unionism would have to be met with energy: 'It will be necessary for the bishops to make a very emphatic pronouncement to warn the people against the pernicious principles which the Larkinites are endeavouring to propagate'.[15]

The general mistrust of protestantism which pervaded Roman opinion at the time was given further impetus when *Pascendi* renewed the condemnation of Anglican orders as invalid. The direct significance of this on Ulster affairs is more difficult to judge. Patrick Buckland has advanced the view that the prevailing attitude of southern catholics towards Ulster in those years was one of open hostility: 'To many Southern Catholics Ulster Protestants were not to be conciliated but converted, for there was a strong element in Irish Catholicism which saw the achievement of home rule as a signal for a crusade for the conversion of the north.'[16] However, he does not offer supporting evidence for this assertion. Certainly one cannot detect the urge to proselytise protestants as a feature in the disposition of northern catholics towards their non-catholic neighbours. Indifference is rather the key to an understanding of their approach. Be that as it may, it is also evident that at times of greatest danger the northern bishops were able to appeal to all sides in the northern conflict on the basis of what they termed 'our common Christian civilisation', which is scarcely the language of people who aim to overthrow those with whom they disagree.

[14] David W. Miller, *Church, State and Nation in Ireland, 1898–1921* (Dublin, 1973), p. 271.
[15] AAA, Logue to Walsh, 15 Dec. 1913.
[16] Patrick Buckland, *Irish Unionism 2: Ulster Unionism and the Origins of Northern Ireland, 1886–1922* (Dublin, 1973), pp. xxxiv–xxxv.

One of the church's most remarkable self-inflicted wounds was the papal decree *Ne Temere* of 1908. In strict terms it merely confirmed the teaching of the council of Trent that catholic spouses and their partners were to adhere to the church's law on marriage. The marriage must be celebrated before a catholic priest and the children must be brought up as catholics. If one of the partners was not a catholic a dispensation had to be obtained and the standard regulations in such instances observed. The effect of the decree in Ireland was to provide ammunition for the more politically intransigent Unionists, who saw it as further evidence to justify the maxim that Home Rule would be Rome Rule.

The implementation of the decree gave rise to a *cause célèbre* in Belfast in October 1910. It was alleged that a local priest persuaded one Alexander McCann to abandon his wife and take his children away from her on the grounds that she refused to 're-marry' according to the Catholic rite. McCann's priest had persuaded him that because they had been married before a presbyterian minister they were not really husband and wife. Needless to say the case attracted widespread publicity. Mrs McCann's minister, the Rev. William Corkey, encouraged her to write to lord Aberdeen, the lord lieutenant, giving a full account of the distress caused to her by her husband's priest and the 'kidnapping' of her children. 'I bore it all', she told Aberdeen, 'hoping his old love for me would show him his error. But the power of the priests was supreme . . . .'[17] The case was mercilessly exploited by Unionist politicians for party political advantage. Even catholic public figures such as Joe Devlin recognised that *Ne Temere* was a gift to Orange propagandists.[18]

Less well known was a dispute in 1902 between the parish priests of Ballymena and Ahoghill over the exact boundaries of their respective parishes. Fr John Nolan of Ahoghill had built a hall and a house within the bounds of his neighbour's parish and Dr Henry, having set up a commission of inquiry, determined that this was illegal since the disputed territory had belonged to Ballymena 'for the past seventy years'. Nolan appealed to Logue, who after six months' investigation confirmed Henry's finding. However Logue prevailed on Henry to allow Nolan to go to America to fund raise the £1,000 he had spent on his building enterprises.[19]

Clerical life at this time was strictly regulated. The 'Rules for

[17] *Belfast News Letter*, 2 Nov. 1910.
[18] Devlin told the House of Commons that Mrs McCann was the greatest Tory party asset since William III. Cf. Parliamentary Debates (House of Commons) Series 5, XXI, 7 Feb. 1911, col. 169.
[19] The details of this dispute are preserved in Logue's archives in Armagh.

Priests on the Belfast Mission'[20] stipulated that in every presbytery a bell was to be rung at ten o'clock each night whereupon all the clergy 'with servants' were to assemble in the oratory for the recitation of the rosary. After this the doors of the house were to be locked and lights put out by 10.30. The amount of money each priest might expect from parish funds was also indicated, along with the fact that in the bishop's mensal parishes * the administrator was to receive a bonus of £5 every two months. On those occasions he was also to forward to the bishop one-third of all the revenues collected in the proceeding months. To facilitate the easy accumulation of the offerings of the parishioners the administrators in parishes were reminded of their responsibility 'for keeping up a constant staff of church-door collectors on Sundays and holidays'. Money concerns were treated very seriously at every level. The provincial synod of Armagh in 1908 laid down that a stipend for a mass was to be three shillings and sixpence. This ensured not only a minimum income for individual clergy in the exercise of the spiritual duties, but also helped to guard against avarice.

In the midst of so many life-shattering events the Ulster Church not only found time for internal squabbles which now seem tinged with both pathos and comedy, but it also mounted a vigorous campaign against alcohol and the 'flood' of irreligious, unclean and demoralising literature'. This campaign led to the setting up of 'vigilance committees' in almost every parish and diocese and, in the Irish Free State, to some of the most repressive censorship laws in Western Europe. That was still to come but in the mean time Logue saw his denunciations of such literature as being merely to protect the faith and morals of his flock.[21] By the 1910s temperance was an old chestnut in Irish and Ulster piety, but this did not prevent bishops from churning out endless pastorals and sermons on the subject. A mass gathering of 20,000 people in Armagh at a 'temperance union' in June 1909 heard the cardinal say that temperance was more important than politics in bringing about change in Ireland. Similarly bishop O'Donnell of Raphoe urged his diocese in January 1906 'for the sake of faith and fatherland' to rid Ireland of the 'woeful habit' of drinking. Ironically many catholics in Ulster depended for their living on the drink trade. Keeping a pub, which they did in both

---

[20] A copy of the rule book is preserved in Dr MacRory's hand in the Armagh Archives.

*I.e. those parishes which pay money directly to the bishop to cover his expenses and of which he is strictly the parish priest, but with the day-to-day duties being carried out by an administrator.

[21] Cf. *Catholic Directory* (1912), p. 502.

catholic and protestant areas, or running an off-licence (a spirit grocery, in the language of the day) was one of the few areas of commercial life where Catholics had a strong share of the market. Gambling was, in 1912, added to the vices against which there needed to be 'a league', with some Ulster bishops going so far as to threaten excommunication as a means of coping with 'this terrible evil'.

While in general Ulster bishops were keen to demonstrate their loyalty to the crown, this was tempered by an over-seriousness about their own position as successors of the apostles. They observed the due protocol on the death of Edward VII by sending telegrams of sympathy to the new king George V but joined with their co-religionists in Britain in asking that the oath against transubstantiation be dropped form the coronation ceremony. Cardinal Logue refused to go to that state occasion observing that he 'could not take part in a protestant ceremony'. On the other hand he did encourage his fellow bishops to attend the levées to mark George V's visit to Ireland in 1911,[22] and he presented the king and queen with a loyal address on their visit to Maynooth on 9 July that year.

However, the coronation of Edward VII in June 1902 had presented the bishops with a more pressing dilemma. Cardinal Vaughan notified Logue that the Holy See had granted a dispensation from the obligation to abstain from meat on the day of the king's crowning, that event falling on a Friday. Logue was roused to a pitch of fury. He declared that such a dispensation would shock the Irish people who were accustomed to regarding the abstinence 'not merely as a law of the church but as a test of profession of faith'. His self-righteous indignation probably had more to do with the fact that the privilege had been communicated to him through his English colleagues rather than directly from Rome. Indeed this had been an ongoing cause of complaint from Armagh for more than twenty years. When the pope granted similar dispensations for St Patrick's day 1905 and 1912 they were graciously received as tokens of the pope's 'genuine interest' in the Irish people. In fact the bishops had requested the dispensations in both instances.[23]

The political landscape

The lack of enthusiasm among many Ulster catholics for the British side in the Boer war was a product not so much of disloyalty to the

---

[22] Cf. AAA, Logue-Walsh correspondence, May 1911.

[23] A similar dispensation from abstinence was also granted for the coronation of George V on 23 July 1911. By this time the Holy See had learned its lesson and cardinal Merry del Val, the Vatican secretary of state, sent the dispensation directly to Ireland. A copy of the document is preserved in the Armagh Archives.

empire but of fellow-feeling—the sense that they and the Boers were in the same position. Both wanted a measure of control over their own affairs which the imperial parliament was reluctant to concede. When news of general Roberts's victory at Pretoria reached the north of Ireland on 5 June 1900 protestants across the Province gave themselves up to great rejoicing. Belfast, Derry and Armagh witnessed tumultuous scenes of patriotic fervour. These were often enhanced by the participation of local loyal Orange lodges who provided musical accompaniment for the festivities. In contrast the catholic reaction was by turns subdued and petulant.

The Belfast Board of Guardians voted a congratulatory message for general Roberts. One of the catholic representatives William O'Hare dissented from the general conviviality of the moment claiming that it was hardly a momentous victory given the might of the empire compared to the resources of the Boers. He was rounded on by his fellow guardians, one of whom accused him of being but the nominee of an 'ecclesiastical force'. Mr Oswald remarked that O'Hare's sentiments showed that while the people he represented 'enjoyed all the liberties and principles in connection with the British government, they were the deadliest enemies of the United Kingdom'.[24]

At root the charge against catholic politicians was that they had no minds of their own and were simply the creatures of the bishops. This charge, though not without foundation, was too simplistic. While the bishops and clergy in the north continued to wield enormous influence in the political sphere, their preferences sometimes encountered strong opposition. As early as 1900 canon McCartan had drawn to the attention of his bishop, Patrick O'Donnell, the threat posed to clerical domination by the growing popularity of the Ancient Order of Hibernians* in Donegal and other parts of Ulster. Logue attacked the organisation in 1908 and this provoked hostility between its members and many clergy particularly in mid-Ulster. Logue's views had support from the Scottish bishops who the previous year had claimed that the AOH had been placed under the ban by the Holy See in December 1882, because of its oath-bound nature. Consequently members could not be admitted to the sacraments in Scotland—a decision overturned by Rome in January 1910. Meanwhile cardinal Logue in May 1909 returned to the attack, during a visit to Carrickmore, accusing the Order of bully-boy tactics in trying

[24] *Belfast Newsletter*, 6 June 1900.
*This body owed something of its origin to the Ribbonmen tradition, and came to be regarded by some as the catholic equivalent of the Orange Order. It was aggressively catholic in composition, but it was distrusted by the Church hierarchy, which lessened its appeal to the Ulster catholic community.

to extend its influence in the catholic community. He threatened to
order his priests to withhold absolution in the confessional from the
AOH's members and implied that he would excommunicate them if
the order persisted in its forceful recruitment policy.

The veteran Belfast politician Joe Devlin as the grand master of the
Order was placed at some political disadvantage by such posturing.
His relationship with Logue was at best cold. But the quarrel over the
AOH was only one thread in a complex tapestry of clerical political
control. When the two factions of the Irish Parliamentary Party
reunited under its Parnellite leader John Redmond, the union was
solemnly blessed by bishop O'Donnell. The future cardinal acted
as a treasurer of the Parliamentary Party Fund and was to have
considerable influence on Irish Nationalist politics. The irony of
his position was that he was more closely associated with the non-
clerical than the pro-clerical elements within the party. O'Donnell
had after all publicly approved of the United Irish League in 1899
although it opposed the policies of T.M. Healy, the leader of the
anti-Parnell and clericalist faction in the Irish party. It was the
momentum created by the League which precipitated the reuniting
of the Parliamentary Party.

Because of continued differences of outlook and temperament and
his refusal to dissolve his support organisation, the People's Rights
Association, Healy was expelled from the party in December 1900.
The dean of Armagh immediately leapt to his defence with a letter
to *The Times*, claiming that Healy had fought the catholic fight at
a time when William O'Brien and John Dillon 'were skulking in
Galway gaol to escape the expression of a manly opinion on Parnell'.
The episcopal political agenda was by that stage in a state of grave
confusion. Richard Owens, bishop of Clogher, had initially supported
the United Irish League candidate in the 1 December by-election in
North Monaghan, but he quickly changed his mind when the UIL
candidate David O'Donnell was denounced by his brother the bishop
of Raphoe for opposing Healy's candidate. In the end a compromise
had to be found to prevent the seat from falling into non-nationalist
hands.

This debacle and its attendant stupefaction merely confirmed the
definite break in clerical electoral control which had been manifested
in the general election earlier that year. Healy's group had enjoyed
considerable support in the Armagh diocese and in small pockets
of lay subservience elsewhere in Ulster. Healy himself was elected
in Louth with considerable help from the cardinal, but Arthur
O'Connor his close associate was defeated in Donegal in spite of
ardent clerical backing. In the country as a whole the bishops found
it difficult to impose their will. They issued a statement on 19 June

instructing catholics to withhold support from any candidate not in favour of a catholic university funded at state expense, an unambiguous statement in favour of the Healy faction which none the less went down to defeat in the majority of cases. Healy's coterie was, in J.H. Whyte's words, 'the last group in Irish politics to put their trust in the clergy'.[25]

Not everyone was to accept the lesson so harshly learned. In Belfast bishop Henry Henry was determined to run an old-style political operation through his Belfast Catholic Association, set up in 1896. Henry was a man of decided theocratic tastes who was not above using his position to impose his political preferences on clergy and people alike. The Association was intended to consolidate the catholic political gains made under the recent borough reforms which gave catholics a representation of eight in the city corporation, their influence being confined largely to the Falls and Smithfield wards. However the seasoned politicians of the Irish National Federation objected to such clearly sectarian politics,[26] and this led to increasing intra-Catholic tension in the city.

The Association received encouragement from cardinal Logue who addressed it in April 1900. He said that it represented the principles on which their country 'could find both its spiritual and temporal welfare'. He castigated those who claimed that priests should stay out of politics since when that happened political parties ceased to flourish.[27] But already in that year even ecclesiastical authorities were concerned at Henry's policies. The Holy See wrote complaining that 'reservations [of sins] and censures in Down and Connor are yearly increasing'.[28] The politicians too became increasingly frustrated with Henry's posturing. In 1903 the Association under his direction decided not to make the updated register of electors available to Nationalist party workers. Henry's quixotic actions in the West Belfast by-election of that year helped ensure the return of H.O. Arnold-Forster, the liberal Unionist and secretary of state for war, with a majority over the Nationalist candidate of 241, amid allegations that a deal had been struck whereby Henry would not publicly oppose

[25] 'The Influence of the Catholic Clergy on Elections in Nineteenth Century Ireland', *English Historical Review*, 75 (1960), p. 256.

[26] As F.J. Whitford observed, Joe Devlin for example held firmly to the belief 'that a purely sectarian organisation should take no part in local or national politics. Dr Henry believed just as sincerely that the catholic Association should be the sole champion of Catholic interests in Belfast and that it should be supported by catholics of all classes and parties'. 'Joe Devlin and the Catholic Representation of Belfast 1895–1905', *Bulletin of the Irish Committee of Historical Sciences*, vol. 78 (1957), pp. 3–4.

[27] Cf. Miller, *Church, State and Nation in Ireland*, p. 48.

[28] AAA, Henry to Logue, 11 Oct. 1900.

the Unionist in return for a bill on university education favourable to the hierarchy's interests.

The United Irish League, as the official campaigning organisation of the parliamentary party, was determined to oppose Henry at every step. Their efforts were not always blessed with success. Henry's hold on Belfast catholics was understandably strong but it was not watertight. Although he told the electors at the January 1904 local elections that he expected 'Catholic electors . . . to vote solidly for the candidates nominated by the Catholic Association', the majorities in the wards in question, while not narrow, were by no means overwhelming: 346 out of a total of 2,734 in Falls, and 234 out of 1,962 in Smithfield.

This particular contest caused some of the laity to take matters into their own hands and appeal to Rome about Henry's relentless politicking. A petition on behalf of 'several thousand' was sent to cardinal Gotti of Propaganda by Thomas Maguire, a Belfast solicitor and United Irish League official, complaining of the bishop. Rome's response was to refer the matter to Henry's metropolitan cardinal Logue. Maguire wrote to Logue in March 1904 detailing the case against Henry. He claimed that since he had written to Rome in February the problem had been made worse by Henry's actions over the election for the water board earlier that month. Maguire told Logue: that 'This board is not concerned in any possible way with questions affecting Religion, but the occasion was nevertheless availed of by Dr Henry . . . to publicly denounce, in churches, halls, and also in the public streets Catholic citizens who . . . dared to question the exclusive privilege of his lordship . . . to the absolute nomination of candidates'. The clergy denounced Henry's opponents as 'Garibaldians', 'bad Catholics' and also, more surprisingly, as 'priest hunters', 'Jewish rabble' and 'traducers of nuns'.

On the day when the result of the water board elections was announced, the vicar-general Dr Bernard Laverty led a torchlight procession along the Falls Road, which ended in violence with twenty-five of Henry's supporters being arrested. However the *Irish News* of the following day made no reference to the violence. At the end of its long account of the proceedings it added that 'Dr Laverty called for three cheers for his lordship the Bishop, which was responded to with tremendous enthusiasm, the crowd cheering vigorously for several minutes. The proceedings then terminated'.[29]

Logue was at first inclined to support Henry since the principle involved was the degree of direct influence bishops and clergy could exercise in politics. As he explained subsequently, 'The question as

[29] *The Irish News*, 11 March 1904.

it appears to me is whether we are justified in standing by passively and seeing a brother Bishop flouted. If we do I fear the trouble will soon come home to our own doors'.[30] An added difficulty for all concerned was that bishop Henry's was a mind capable of such intellectual dexterity as in anyone else would have seemed to border on pathological deceit. When archbishop Walsh of Dublin issued a stinging condemnation of the National Catholic Association, Henry published a statement that the organisation which Walsh condemned was quite a distinct entity from the Belfast group, although the latter had been affiliated to the Dublin-based national association since March 1903.

Henry issued instructions to his clergy not to make financial contributions to the United Irish League in support of the Nationalist Party; some of them defied him. Henry then sent a letter to the priests of the diocese saying that the League had interpreted these contributions as expressions of sympathy 'with the hostile and disrespectful attitude taken up by prominent members of the Belfast Branch of the League', towards him and his political activities. The bishop then threatened with suspension any priest who in future supported the League or even sent secret contributions. This use of spiritual sanctions for political ends had also been complained of by Maguire who asserted that some priests were commanded by Henry to attend meetings of the Catholic Association 'contrary to their opinions and repugnant to their feelings'.

A further problem arose in 1905 when the whole hierarchy encouraged catholics to support the Irish Parliamentary Party fund. Henry ordered the Belfast Catholic Association as a body to organise the collection. John Redmond gave instructions that the contribution from Down and Connor be returned. By this stage even cardinal Logue was moved to tell Henry that his actions were a 'mistake in tactics'. Even senior clergy of Henry's diocese had begun to doubt the wisdom of the bishop's political policy, and the association itself was starting to fall apart.

The vicar-general of Down and Connor wrote to Logue in April asking him to intervene in Belfast to bring about political unity. A peace conference was held headed by Joe Devlin and Dr Laverty at which the UIL and the Catholic Association patched up their differences and the association went into voluntary liquidation. However there was a small rump determined to be more catholic than the pope, which remained faithful to the previous policy of the bishop. But the power structure of this group had been irrevocably broken by

[30] AAA, Logue to Walsh, 3 March 1905.

Henry's withdrawal of support, and at the January 1910 election its candidate in West Belfast received a mere seventy-five votes. Bishop Henry's story will never be fully told because of the misguided act of one of his successors, Joseph MacRory, in consigning most of his papers to the flames.

In Derry, before the reunification of the Irish Parliamentary Party, the anti-Parnell Irish National Federation was largely supported by the priests of the city. Clerical control of political life was to continue almost unchallenged throughout the 1890s, and indeed in 1899 the Nationalist candidate count Arthur Moore was selected to stand by Fr William McMenamin, a close friend and confidant of bishop O'Doherty. However, the clergy were far from being a united body and decided in 1900 to end factionalism by no longer engaging in political activity. The effect of this dramatic self-abnegation was that the nationalist political organisation all but collapsed and allowed the anti-Home Rule candidates to keep the Westminster representation uninterrupted for the next thirteen years. There was some attempt to revive catholic political hopes in 1906, when Fr Willie Doherty made valiant but unavailing efforts to unite the disparate catholic groups.

The new bishop of Derry, Charles MacHugh, a former parish priest of Strabane consecrated in September 1907, pursued a policy of pressuring the parliamentary party for a more aggressive campaign on Home Rule. Under his leadership the clergy as a group reasserted their prerogatives as political king-makers. MacHugh personally nominated the liberal protestant businessman David Hogg as the candidate in the 1913 by-election in preference to Sir Shane Leslie, the catholic convert and Irish nationalist. The presbyterian chaplain at the local prison, Samuel Patton, seconded the nomination. In this way MacHugh hoped to show that under Home Rule protestants would have nothing to fear from the catholic Church. Hogg was at best a moderate Home Ruler but he was nevertheless returned in a bitter and closely fought contest with a majority of fifty-seven.

Elsewhere in Ulster there were no such ecumenical displays. The Tyrone county council elections of 1908 were deeply sectarian. At the same time there was little support for MacHugh's more aggressive approach to the Nationalist Party. However for various reasons the clergy in south and east Tyrone had never consistently enjoyed the same political influence as their fellow-priests had in Derry. The region of mid- and north-west Ulster was on the whole fairly committed to a moderate Redmondite policy. This was probably due in part to the ecclesiastical leadership and political outlook of bishop O'Donnell. Miller in contrasting the bishops of Derry and Raphoe says that 'MacHugh represented the ghetto mentality of northern catholics far more authentically than did O'Donnell whose diocese contained only a small minority of protestants and who was capable of considerable emotional detachment in discussing the Ulster question'.[31]

Events in Ulster in the first decade of the twentieth century were causing politicians to reassess their relationship with the Church. The political need to secure Home Rule continued to be overshadowed by the religious fear that Home Rule equalled Rome Rule. In an attempt to counter such an accusation Redmond wrote an article for *Reynold's Weekly* in February 1911 outlining the number of occasions when the laity had resisted the intervention of Rome in Irish affairs. He said he agreed with Daniel O'Connell's view that the Irish would as soon take their politics from Constantinople as from Rome. The archbishop of Armagh reacted furiously, telling his counterpart in Dublin that Redmond was simply playing to the English non-conformist gallery. 'The statement he attributed to O'Connell . . . in its full significance is simply heresy. It denies the right of the Pope to interfere in politics even if they contravene the Divine or moral law'.[32] The cardinal was beginning to feel that the bishops needed to 'check present tendencies' in the Irish political scene which advocated a greater independence of the political sphere from the religious.

Political developments in the Ulster protestant community were overtaking the bishops' ability to control the political scene. The need to convince the unionists that Home Rule was not *ipso facto* inimical to their interests became the urgent task that nationalist politicians set themselves. This was precisely the background to Redmond's outburst; and to Logue's response which was all the more depressing for being predictable. Already in 1910 the Ulster Unionist Council had stressed the specifically religious objection to Home Rule in a series of pamphlets aimed at the English and Scottish market. The secretary of the Council—Robert Dawson Bates, a future Northern Ireland minister for home affairs—was anxious to note that the pamphlets were drawn up in such a way as not to offend the religious sensibilities of British catholic unionists. It was however a very narrow tightrope along which he walked.

By 1912 the unionists were preparing to use violence to frustrate the will of the majority in Ireland for Home Rule.[33] Edward Carson and the Conservative Party leader Andrew Bonar Law, together with seventy other members of parliament, reviewed on Easter Tuesday at Balmoral in Belfast some 80–100,000 Ulster Volunteer Force

---

[31] Miller, *Church, State and Nation in Ireland*, p. 299.
[32] AAA, Logue Papers, 24 Feb. 1911.
[33] After the Derry by-election of 1913 even the majority of Ulster MPs were in favour of Home Rule, 17–16.

members who were ready, in the words of the Solemn League and Covenant,* 'to use all means which may be found necessary to defeat the present conspiracy to set up a Home Rule parliament in Ireland'. The proceedings that April day were opened with prayers offered by the Church of Ireland archbishop of Armagh and the moderator of the general assembly of the presbyterian Church. A mass rally full of political bravado, held in July at Blenheim Palace in Oxfordshire, heard Carson openly support the idea of violence. Bonar Law imagined that there were no lengths to which Ulster might go which would not receive Conservative support.[34]

In these circumstances some of the catholic bishops were beginning to have second thoughts. Logue wrote to O'Donnell on 6 December 1912 that as far as the Church's interests were concerned it might be best to continue to live under an Imperial than a Home Rule parliament. Winston Churchill's speech of 8 October 1913 on the need for compromise with Ulster over Home Rule drew a sharp retort from O'Donnell that the needs of Ulster's catholics must not be overlooked in the rush to propitiate the anger of its protestants. The following March Redmond despatched Joe Devlin, Jeremiah McVeagh and J.C.R. Lardner to Ulster to meet the catholic bishops individually and assure them that catholic interests would be protected in any compromise with Unionism. Logue was not impressed and wrote to his confidant in Dublin, 'I fear the concessions on the Home Rule Bill will be a bad business for us here in this part of the North. It will leave us more than ever under the heel of the Orangemen. Worst of all it will leave them free to tamper with our education.'[35] This was to be a constantly recurring theme for the northern churchmen as they struggled to ward off a local Ulster settlement.

Given the extent of protestant lawlessness the catholic reaction in Ulster was at times subdued and even timid. A large gathering had been planned in Derry for 14 March 1914 to protest in favour of Home Rule. Redmond decided that the demonstration should not go ahead lest there be violence which would set back the cause. Bishops

---

*A declaration against Home Rule to be signed by all loyalists in Ulster on 28 September 1912, pledging the signatories to do all in their power to prevent Home Rules. Some enthusiasts signed the document in their own blood.

[34] Although the Protestant/Unionist community in Ulster has tended to portray itself as constitutional and law-abiding there can be no doubt that this is simply part of its mythological consciousness with little grounding in the realities of its history. As Michael Laffan has pointed out, 'Viewed in the long-term historical perspective Carson was the first of many in the twentieth century who proved that British Governments would yield to force or the threat of force what they denied to majority votes. Cf. *The Partition of Ireland 1911–25* (Dundalk, 1983), p. 32.

[35] AAA, Logue to Walsh, 13 March 1914.

O'Donnell and MacHugh agreed to call it off but gave vent to their sense of injustice that their peaceful protests had to be checked 'whilst their opponents were openly carrying rifles and trundling . . . field-pieces through the streets of Belfast and elsewhere'.[36]

A more serious threat was posed in Derry that same month by the determination of the Irish Volunteers, formed on a nationwide basis in 1913 at the suggestion of Eoin MacNeill in response to the UVF, to hold a demonstration. Redmond again pleaded with MacHugh to use his influence to have the parade stopped, which the bishop only succeeded in doing by threatening to have the volunteers denounced from every altar and pulpit in the city if the proposed parade was not called off. He told Redmond that the volunteers had 2,000 members in the city all armed with revolvers and that they were being drilled by ex-soldiers.[37] The following month the UVF landed in Larne, Bangor and Donagadee some 40,000 rifles and 3,500,000 rounds of ammunition which had been shipped from Hamburg. Telephone and telegraph wires were cut to ensure a smooth operation. The authorities made no effort to prevent these illegalities. By 10 July the Ulster Unionist Council had constituted itself the 'Ulster Provisional Government' and despite efforts by the king later that month there seemed to be no hope of compromise. The Home Rule Act became law on 18 September; Carson speaking in Belfast on 2 October derided it as merely 'a scrap of paper', but events in Ulster were overtaken by the Great War, which Britain had entered on 4 August, and Home Rule was put into a state of suspended animation. In 1915 the wartime coalition government was formed, and Carson became attorney-general.

The war years

On his return from the conclave which elected Giacomo della Chiesa as pope Benedict XV in September 1914, cardinal Logue gave the impression that he wholeheartedly supported the war effort. This was in spite of the fact that several Ulster divisions were formed out of the UVF from which catholics were effectively excluded. While expressing reservations about the Amending Bill on the Home Rule Act, the cardinal indicated that Irishmen were prepared to forget 'petty animosities' given the cataclysm then overtaking Europe. Bishop MacHugh, believing the Home Rule cause to have been won, took a similar view, which was also generally reflected in the general opinion of the Ulster Church during the early stages of the war. By the

[36] T.J. Campbell, *Fifty Years of Ulster, 1890–1940* (Belfast, 1941), p. 59.
[37] Cf. Bernard J. Canning, *Bishops of Ireland, 1870–1987* (Ballyshannon, 1987), p. 93.

beginning of Lent 1915 the northern bishops were writing uncompromisingly about German aggression. Logue in his pastoral letter condemned the German methods of warfare as immoral, and bishop Henry O'Neill of Dromore referred to the gallant fight carried on against 'the overwhelming forces of a ruthless despot' and the need to 'strike down the tyranny of a militarism that threatened the very existence of the British empire and other European states'. For his part Dr Patrick McKenna of Clogher blamed the war on 'the godless tendencies' of the age.

There is nothing in all this to suggest that the majority of northern catholics did not follow John Redmond's lead and fervently hope for an allied victory in a war which after all was being fought in defence of small nations. The situation in Belgium made a deep impression in Ireland and a Belgian relief fund was set up to which Ulster catholics contributed £7,800. In addition many Belgian refugees were housed and given employment in various parts of the country. By 1916 Logue drew attention to an apparent 'campaign' among Ulster protestants to proselytise the refugees; three refugee families in his diocese had been thus 'perverted'. The bishops were also deeply concerned with the need for an adequate supply of catholic chaplains for the forces. Much time and correspondence was given over to this topic throughout the various stages of the war, even after the 1916 rising and the further concessions on Home Rule which were especially ill received in the north. One issue in the affair of the chaplains was that the Irish bishops did not want the government to assume that cardinal Bourne, the archbishop of Westminster, should somehow be in charge of catholic military chaplains since many of these were Irish.[38]

Their support for the war effort did not mean that Ulster catholics lost a sense either of the urgent need for Home Rule or of the vulnerability of their position if there were to be any tampering with the arrangements outlined in the 1914 act. Nor did it mean that they took kindly to the wartime restrictions. Logue constantly complained of the tendency of the censor to open his mail, especially communications to and from the Holy See, which he regarded as 'an outrage'. He also refused to sign an appeal from the Red Cross that church collections on 3 January 1915 should be appropriated for the Red Cross ambulance service. The reason he gave for this was that the Irish bishops had not yet agreed that 3 January should be a day of general 'supplication'. He also protested that Francis Bourne was the only catholic bishop whose name appeared on the appeal; even then it was placed after that of the archbishops of Canterbury and York.

[38] This is made clear from the letters in Logue's archives. Cf. for example the bishop of Cloyne to Logue, 30 Jan. 1916.

'The late King Edward', Logue observed, 'had long since settled that matter giving Cardinal Manning precedence over the archbishop of Canterbury.'[39]

The dedication of Ulster catholics to the interests of the United Kingdom in the war was not always enthusiastic. By July 1915 the cardinal was suggesting that the systematic economic policy of the London government had forced Irishmen to go overseas to look for work, and now that same government expected Irishmen to fight in Britain's interests. By 1918 the bishops had become so disillusioned with British intentions in Ireland that they ruthlessly opposed the introduction of conscription. This had been in operation in Britain since January 1916 but the opposition of the Irish parliamentary party ensured that the general call-up was not, at that stage, extended to Ireland.

The Irish Conscription Act was passed on 16 April 1918 but it would only have affected 60,000 men since by then 130,000 had already volunteered. On April 18 the bishops met at Maynooth under Logue's presidency and issued a statement lambasting the Act as 'an oppressive and inhuman law which the Irish people had a right to resist by all means consonant with the law of God'. They ordered a national novena in honour 'of Our Lady of Lourdes'—novenas were a favourite device of Logue's in times of crisis—and a special mass to be said on April 21 in all churches and chapels in the country 'against conscription'. The administrator of Armagh cathedral Fr Joseph Brady had already begun to organise his 'Solemn League and Covenant against conscription' in which the covenanters pledged themselves to one another 'to resist conscription by the most effective means at our disposal'. An anti-conscription fund was launched which by 30 August stood at £250,000.

O'Donnell was subsequently to protest at the injustice of the proposal as he saw it, since although the government had power to conscript in Australia, South Africa and Canada it had not done so.[40] The bishop of Raphoe declared that in resisting conscription the hierarchy was 'at one with national sentiment'. Following the general strike of 23 April which brought government administration in the country to a standstill, the Conscription Act was abandoned, and the order-in-council needed to bring it into effect was never made. Lord Curzon reported to the House of Lords on 20 June that the Irish clergy had told their flocks to resist conscription under pain of eternal

---

[39] AAA, Logue to Walsh, 14 Dec. 1914. The reference here is obscure since Manning died in January 1892 and Edward did not become king till nine years later.
[40] *Irish Independent*, 24 May 1918.

damnation. Logue, MacKenna and bishop Edward Mulhern of Dromore issued a statement saying that they had done no such thing, but none the less this opposition to what, from the British perspective, was a sound operational procedure confirmed the widespread impression that Irish ecclesiastics were as disloyal as the population at large. This was the view, expressed in rather florid terms, of John Henry Bernard, the Church of Ireland archbishop of Dublin, who in writing to the archbishop of Canterbury reported of the Irish hierarchy that they were 'intensely anti-British at heart, thoroughly disloyal to the King, to Great Britain, and to the Empire. That is in their blood.'[41] A somewhat overstated conviction and not entirely true. But Bernard was more astute in his claim that by putting themselves at the head of the anti-conscription movement the bishops had 'regained the confidence of all Roman Catholic Ireland'. The change that had come about both in the catholic attitude to the war and in the relationship between prelates and people was the result of the events of Easter 1916 and its aftermath.

The 'insurrection' of Easter week while involving some northerners largely by-passed Ulster, being confined as it was to Dublin. Indeed the clergy did their best to ensure that Eoin MacNeill's countermanding order was obeyed.* Fr O'Daly, himself (unusually for a priest) a member of the Irish Republican Brotherhood, propagated the message as widely as he could in his native Co. Tyrone. Several of the bishops condemned the Rising in the weeks following the rebellion, but none of them was from Ulster. However the administrator of St Eunan's cathedral in Letterkenny denounced the rebels in no uncertain terms. By June Logue was to describe the insurrection as 'foolish and perverse'. On the whole the Rising was not well supported in the north but the ruthlessness of the leaders' execution and the wholesale internment of suspects which followed brought a wave of revulsion which caused the bishops to be more cautious in their attitude than they otherwise would have been. Speaking at the Maynooth Union meeting on 22 June, Logue described the government's policy of repression as 'the greatest act of folly any government could have been capable of'. This is not to say that the hierarchy itself had any sympathy with the insurrection. As the cardinal told his auditors no one would find fault with the government for defending

---

[41] Miller, *Church, State and Nation in Ireland*, p. 408.

*Eoin MacNeill, professor of early and medieval Irish history at University College Dublin, was Chief of Staff of the Irish Volunteers but unaware of the presence in its ranks of the secret Military Council commanded by Patrick Pearse. When he discovered that Pearse had given an order to the volunteers to begin the rising in Easter week 1916, MacNeill issued an order cancelling the rising and even put an advertisement to this effect in a national newspaper.

the rights of the state or for moderately punishing, 'within the laws of humanity', those who had violated the law.[42]

The bishops at their 19 June meeting in Maynooth were unable to reach a decision on whether or not to have a church-door collection for those who suffered in the rebellion, 'lest the bishops might incur the imputation of favouring in any way the authors of the unfortunate attempt'.[43] Logue took much the same attitude in his support for the reprieve of Roger Casement, stressing that he supported commuting Casement's death sentence 'from motives of mercy and charity, and not from any sympathy whatever with the unfortunate course' he had embarked upon. At that same meeting Patrick O'Donnell was one of four bishops, the only one from Ulster, appointed to a sub-committee to prepare a statement setting forth 'the Catholic doctrine on insurrection'. However by 9 October 'it was considered that the [proposed] statement on this subject would at this stage be inappropriate and would serve no useful purpose'.[44] The situation was simply too delicate at that time for any dramatic anti-revolutionary pronouncement to be made. The government authorities, not surprisingly, took a very different view. The military governor, general Sir John Maxwell, called on the cardinal and urged the necessity of keeping priests out of politics, convinced as he was that clerical influence had helped to precipitate the Rising. Logue robustly refuted such a suggestion and also spoke 'pretty freely of the mistake the authorities are making in keeping the whole country in a state of excitement by their wholesale arrests'.[45]

That excitement had been raised to fever pitch by the London government's proposal to enact a modified form of Home Rule immediately, as a means of restoring peace and stability to Ireland and as an attempt to keep some semblance of national unity in the United Kingdom's resistance to Germany. This scheme, the brainchild of Lloyd George the prime minister, was aimed at giving Home Rule to the three southern provinces and the counties of Cavan, Donegal and Monaghan. The remaining six counties of the north-east would continue to be governed from Westminster. Redmond again tried to reconcile the northern bishops to the scheme. In addition to sending representatives to explain it to them in private, he wrote to Logue asking for a meeting with those bishops whose dioceses would be affected by the new political arrangements. Logue wrote to bishop Joseph MacRory in Belfast on June 7:

[42] Cf. *Catholic Directory* (1917), p. 518.
[43] AAA, Logue Archives II.
[44] AAA, O'Donnell Archives IV.
[45] AAA, Logue to Walsh, 23 June 1916.

There is a project to cut off Ulster except Cavan, Monaghan and Donegal. Besides I know Carson is going in for large additional concessions in the way of patronage etc. Hence it behoves the bishops to be cautious, if they do not want to go down to posterity with a charge worse than the *veto* against them.[46]

The 'large additional concessions', as became clear, included some degree of local control over such matters as education. This the bishops could not accept since it would mean, in their eyes, catholic education being controlled by Orangemen.

Redmond had an unsuccessful meeting with the northern bishops in Dublin on 19 June at which they made clear in the strongest terms their disapproval of the new scheme. Logue argued that it would be better to live under English rule for another fifty years than to accept the current proposals.[47] Bishop MacHugh declared his 'absolute' opposition, decrying 'the perilous position in which religion and catholic education would be placed were the proposals so imperfectly understood by the public reduced to practice'. However had the concession of 'county option' been on the table, i.e. the possibility of a plebiscite county by county to determine which of the northern counties could if they wished join the rest of the country under Home Rule, it seems clear that the clergy would have accepted the surrender of the other counties to Westminster rule. This was not a concession Carson was willing to tolerate.

Meanwhile, in a preliminary meeting at Omagh on 1 June under the auspices of the parish priests of Omagh and Cappagh, Mgr W.T. O'Doherty and the Very Rev. James O'Kane, a resolution was passed condemning Lloyd George's proposal. In a letter conveying this to the bishops, the parish priests concerned added that they intended to hold a meeting of 'the clergy and representative nationalists' on the 7 June in Omagh, and asked for bishops to send messages of support. MacHugh, O'Donnell, MacRory and MacKenna did so. Similar meetings followed throughout the north in the following weeks.

The catholics of Ulster outside Belfast rejected the scheme in the run-up to a representative meeting held at St Mary's Hall, Belfast, on 23 June, but by the time of this meeting 776 representatives, including a priest from every parish in the six counties, had voted to accept the exclusion of the six Ulster counties from the jurisdiction of a Home Rule parliament on a temporary basis. This was achieved only by Redmond threatening to resign the leadership of the party. However

---

[46] AAA, MacRory archives.

[47] He had taken a not dissimilar line in 1912. He wrote to O'Donnell on 6 December that year that as far as religious interests were concerned the imperial parliament was to be preferred to a Home Rule one. AAA, O'Donnell Archives IV.

it was a pyrrhic victory since neither Redmond nor the party were again to enjoy widespread popular support. Already by the end of June bishop MacHugh was organising anti-partition rallies in Derry which by mid-July had grown into the Anti-Partition League. On July 27 the government published a white paper making clear that the 1914 Act would not apply to the six counties. Lloyd George's duplicity was clear for all to see and the scheme to grant Home Rule was immediately dropped.

By the middle of 1917 the administration had changed direction. Lloyd George announced the government's decision to call a constitutional convention involving all interests groups in the country in the hope of arriving at a compromise on Irish self-government within the empire, but also stressing that Ulster could not be coerced. Sinn Fein refused to have anything to do with it, as did bishop MacHugh who declined to be one of the hierarchy's representatives. He further wrote to various parties in the north and south condemning the forthcoming convention as 'partisan and pro-partition' and asked for a national meeting in Dublin to protest against it. This evoked a letter of rebuke from Sir Horace Plunkett, chairman of the convention, to Patrick O'Donnell saying that what he most feared was that 'if through any action of the bishops, the Convention is wrecked, the catastrophe will be regarded as a triumph for the revolutionaries, due to the support of the Church'.[48] However a petition against partition published on 7 May attracted the signatures of eighteen of the twenty-eight Irish bishops. All the Ulster bishops signed as did the Church of Ireland bishops of Tuam, Ossory and Killaloe. As a result of O'Donnell's lobbying and to avert the possible charge to which Plunkett had referred the bishops on 28 June issued an instruction stating that, as was well known to any student of theology, any organisation which plotted against the Church or state was condemned under the gravest penalties. They further argued that the authority by which temporal rulers governed was from 'the same divine source as that by which God's kingdom on earth is sustained'. Contempt for one led to disregard for the other. In addition priests were again forbidden to speak on political affairs in church, but this did not prevent the parish priest of Enniskillen and archdeacon of Clogher, Mgr Keown, writing to the commander of forces in Ireland, Sir Bryan Mahon, to upbraid him for prohibiting a Sinn Fein demonstration in the town in October. Keown derided what he took to be a blatant act of political discrimination, pointing out that although Enniskillen had a nationalist majority Sir Edward Carson and his followers had been allowed to demonstrate as often as they wished, unmolested by either catholics

---

[48] AAA, Plunkett to O'Donnell, 18 June 1917.

or the security forces.

On 25 November Logue appealed in a letter to his diocese for domestic peace, condemning as Utopian and ill-considered the agitation which had sprung up in the country for a republic. Such sentiment merely 'blasted hopes of peace'. It was an idle dream to think either that a future European peace conference would grant a republic in Ireland, or that it could be wrested from the British empire against its will. He ordered a novena in the diocese to the Virgin Mary to invoke her aid in bringing peace to the country.

Meanwhile the convention got under way with the hierarchy nominating four representatives two of whom, O'Donnell and Joseph MacRory, were from Ulster. Lord Desart, a prominent southern Unionist, told his colleagues that partition would be unworkable either for the six counties or for Ulster as a whole, since in either case it would open the way for continuous agitation by the large Catholic minority, 'the most bitter and violent in Ireland'.[49] MacRory made an early and unfavourable impression on the convention by listing all the Irish catholic grievances about English rule in Ireland and evincing bitter memories of various nineteenth-century disputes.

The grand master of the Orange Order, colonel Wallace, launched into an attack on the *Ne Temere* decree. O'Donnell gave such a nuanced and scholarly exposition of the decree that lord Oranmore asserted that the *odium theologicum* had been exchanged for the *divina caritas*. O'Donnell in fact had merely pointed out that it was a mistake to suppose that the papal decree had been aimed at protestants but that it ought rather to be thought of as the catholic Church regulating its marriage practice for its own members.[50]

The nationalists became hopelessly divided largely because of O'Donnell's political manoeuvres. Redmond found himself isolated from members of his own party, but his untimely death during the convention robbed that gathering of one who might well have steered it in a direction likely to produce its hoped-for compromise. On the other hand there is a real sense in which his brand of nationalism, which envisaged an Ireland with its own parliament under the crown, had seen its day and the fact that he clashed with O'Donnell and Joe Devlin, neither of whom had the least sympathy for Sinn Fein, is indicative of a sea-change in Irish politics to which Redmond was in some ways unable to adapt.

O'Donnell, as the *de facto* leader of the nationalists, proposed a number of possibilities for a future all-Ireland Home Rule parlia-

---

[49] Quoted in Nicholas Mansergh, *The Unresolved Question: The Anglo-Irish Settlement and its Undoing, 1912–72* (New Haven and London, 1991), pp. 126 and 226.

[50] Cf. AAA, O'Donnell Archives 'The Irish Convention', folder 24.

ment with guarantees for unionist representation in the lower house of 40 per cent. It must be admitted that some of his ideas, such as that of re-establishing the Irish House of Lords, were simply hare-brained. He, along with the other nationalists, seemed to find it impossible to understand the extent of the northern unionists refusal of any arrangement in which they were not in control of their own affairs. On the unionist side there seems to have been some willingness to consider a federal structure for the country on Canadian or Swiss lines. But time and again catholic bishops expressed the fear that in any purely northern state catholic education would suffer from being under the control of a protestant majority, a contingency they simply would not stomach. The convention's report, finally published on 20 April 1918, was scarcely a basis for a comprehensive settlement of the Irish question. The majority report, carried by 41 to 29 votes, proposed a parliament for an undivided Ireland with a Senate of 64 seats and a lower house of 160, of which 40 would be reserved for the unionists. The most controversial issue in the Convention, the control of customs and excise, were shelved until after the war. Control of police and postal services would have a similar fate. The parliament would have no role in foreign affairs or defence. A minority report signed by twenty-nine nationalists including O'Donnell and MacRory recommended that Ireland should be granted Dominion Home Rule. The government ignored it. The convention had been a white elephant, but it had shown the strength of feeling on both sides and how uncompromising the various interests groups were.

The last year of the Great War did not begin well for Sinn Fein in Ulster. Their candidates in the by-elections in south Armagh and east Tyrone were defeated at the hands of the Nationalist Party. Eamon de Valera regarded the outcome of the contests as an unmitigated disaster, describing the failure to secure South Armagh as 'a defeat for Ireland'.[51] In both cases the figure of cardinal Logue lurked as an *éminence grise* to ensure as far as possible that Sinn Fein, which he disliked intensely, would not be victorious. Both constituencies lay within his diocese and he was determined to exercise all the influence that his status as cardinal archbishop afforded. However by this stage in the troubled world of Ulster's religio-political conflict the mere will of even the archbishop of Armagh was often insufficient to bring about a ready compliance from priests and people.

Many of Logue's clergy deeply resented the Nationalist Party, and that antipathy was shared in large measure by bishop MacHugh in Derry and somewhat less by MacKenna of Clogher. However in the

---

[51] John Bowman, *De Valera and the Ulster Question, 1917–1973* (Oxford, 1983), p. 33.

January contest in south Armagh the parish priest of Carnlough, Canon Quinn, campaigned vigorously against Sinn Fein to the extent, on one famous occasion, of resorting to physical violence. Logue indicated his approval of the Nationalists by agreeing to meet their candidate at Ara Coeli, the cardinal's residence in Armagh. By March, when the east Tyrone contest got under way, Logue urged his priests to stay out of politics and concentrate on their pastoral activities. His injunctions was widely ignored as a large body of clerical opinion swung behind the 'republicans' and 'revolutionaries'. As Miller tellingly indicates, 'the Cardinal could take but small comfort from the fact that the voters had agreed with him, for the elections had made plain that a significant section of his clergy was in revolt against his political opinions'.[52]

However, the Sinn Feiners were not relying only on the democratic process to achieve their aims. On 24 May the inspector general of the Irish National Volunteers, J. Grean, sent out orders to members to maintain a volunteer force 'for the defence of Ireland and the advancement and preservation of Irish rights and the maintenance of Irish national self-government'. Copies of these orders were sent to O'Donnell in Letterkenny. The hierarchy, having entered with great gusto into the anti-conscription campaign, found itself an incongruous bedfellow with the revolutionaries whom it so publicly abhorred and condemned. The Volunteers had in fact been heavily dependent on parish organisation in the anti-conscription agitation. The passionate anti-British sentiment shown in that particular dispute strengthened the conviction of the younger clergy, especially in the north, that Sinn Fein unlike the Nationalists would not leave Ulster catholics at the mercy of a Unionist administration in Belfast. Many of the clergy were deeply sympathetic to Sinn Fein but not always as candidly as Fr Michael McCarvill who founded and organised the Sinn Fein club in Enniskillen in June 1917.

On 15 November, a few days after the end of the war, Sinn Fein wrote individually to the bishop reminding them of the stand they had taken in the late campaign and asking them for the same resolve in helping Ireland secure her freedom from British rule 'by declaring for Independence as courageously and as clearly as they declared against conscription'. The northern bishops had carefully prepared the counter-offensive by issuing a statement urging Ulster catholics to take a 'common sense' view of politics. They implored them to abandon support of Sinn Fein (without of course mentioning it by name) and its programme which was but 'a wild pursuit of visionary aims no intelligent man regarded as possible of attainment'. Having

---

[52] Miller, *Church, State and Nation in Ireland*, p. 401.

stated their opposition to what they regarded as Sinn Fein extremism, they appealed for an end to division among nationalists. In uncharacteristically forthright terms, with a political sagacity not always to be found in their pronouncements, they continued:

> The mischievous effects of division are brought very clearly home to us in this northern Province . . . If the seats to which our position on the register [of electors] be contested in a spirit of rule or ruin, by conflicting nationalist candidates, they are sure to go to our most determined opponents . . . [The result] which would harrow the tenderest feelings of every patriotic Irishman [would be] the almost certain partition and dismemberment of the country'.[53]

In addition the bishops warned the clergy once again not to meddle in politics but to 'live up to their high calling' and concentrate on their pastoral ministry.

Previously, in early October, two of the Ulster bishops had drawn attention to the danger for the nationalists of losing up to eight seats in the aftermath of the war if there was not some sort of agreement between the parties. By 16 November MacHugh of Derry decided to take matters a step further and wrote to the press proposing a strategy conference in Dungannon to be hosted by MacKenna of Clogher. The dean of Armagh, Mgr Byrne, wrote another letter on 18 November suggesting that the 27th should be the appointed day for the gathering where it would be decided who would contest the disputed Ulster seats. In the event the proposed conclave did not take place largely because John Dillon, the Nationalist leader, distrusted the clergy, whom he accused of being in the pocket of Sinn Fein. Fearing the worst, the Ulster bishops appealed to Dillon to meet and discuss the matter. A gathering did take place at the Mansion House in Dublin on 3 and 4 December between Dillon and De Valera, but they could not agree among themselves which seats should be allocated to whom, and they called on the Ulster bishops to decide the matter for them. It was left to Logue to determine the issue. In a manner reminiscent of pope Alexander VI dividing the world between Spain and Portugal (1493), the cardinal determined that Sinn Fein should be the sole contestants in Derry city, east Down, south Fermanagh and north-west Tyrone. The Nationalists were to have a similarly safe passage in south Armagh, east Donegal, south Down and north-east Tyrone.

Logue was under considerable pressure from the contestants and his task was far from easy. He wrote to bishop MacRory:

> I have not had a moment's peace since I had the misfortune to put

[53] *Catholic Directory* (Dublin, 1919), p. 623.

my finger in the ugly pie. Telegraph, telephone and post are kept busy with complaints from Sinn Feiners. I have had no complaints from the other parties though [the] Sinn Feiners are insisting on a thing to which they have no right. They are expecting what is virtually a Sinn Fein pledge from the Nationalist candidates. Neither side is coming out of the agreement honestly and it is likely to end in the Carsonists getting the seats.[54]

The cardinal's adjudication came too late to affect the nominations but it was understood that catholics would vote appropriately in the apportioned constituencies. This is what happened except in the case of east Down where the Nationalists did not keep the bargain. Logue acidly referred to east Down's loss to the Carsonites 'through the treachery of National Party followers'.[55] De Valera was humiliatingly defeated by Joe Devlin in West Belfast by 8,488 votes to 3,245. In the new parliament five of the six seats retained by the Irish Parliamentary Party were in the north as Sinn Fein swept the country. Ulster catholics were therefore at this stage by no means rabid Sinn Feiners, and there are indications that they would have been prepared even at the end of 1918 to make some sort of compromise with unionism. Such possibilities were quickly excluded owing to the abstentionist policy of Sinn Fein, the further machinations of Carson's unionists and, as ever, the intransigence of the Ulster bishops over their recurring nightmare, the education question.

Although the war years were obviously dominated by domestic and international politics, it would not be true to say that other areas of Ulster catholic life did not therefore develop, or were neglected. Bishops, priests and laity continued fervently to engage in what after all was the primary source of their identity, the practice of the catholic faith. Logue reported to Rome in December 1916 that there were parishes in his diocese where not a single member of the flock failed to fulfil the Easter obligations of confession and communion. For Lent 1917 MacRory granted factory workers a respite from the fasting customarily demanded, taking the opportunity to complain that it was the sweat of labourers which went to swell the pockets of a handful of employers. The annual 19 August pilgrimage of Ulster catholics to the mass-rock at Hilltown, Co. Down, which commemorated the massacre of a priest and his parishioners in 1649, continued to attract large crowds throughout the war years, as did that other site of pilgrimage St Patrick's Purgatory which in 1918 had 12,240 pilgrims, the largest number for a century. The upsurge in pilgrimage numbers

---

[54] AAA, Logue to MacRory, 9 Dec. 1918. The pledge to which Logue refers was to abstain from taking one's seat in Westminster in the event of being elected.

[55] AAA, Logue to Walsh, 29 Dec. 1918.

may have been connected with the publicity surrounding a legal action by Sir John Leslie in May 1917 claiming ownership of land on St Patrick's Purgatory. In the end bishop MacKenna was forced to make a settlement in Sir John's favour of £2,000.

Taking time off from politics, bishop MacHugh of Derry launched the Clerical Benefit Society in December 1917 to provide for priests 'who have broken down in the course of their ministry'. The infrastructure in Down and Connor continued to expand with the new church of St Mary's Star of the Sea which MacRory opened on 8 July 1916. The bishop of Down and Connor had also contributed to the renovation of the church at Ballyscullion in the Derry diocese which was re-opened for worship on 7 May that year. At the opening of the church of Saint Patrick and Saint Brigid in Glenariff on 30 September 1917 a collection of £900 was taken to help defray the expenses of the new church. By 1915 the debt on the principal church of the Dromore diocese in Newry stood at £13,000 owing largely to the extensive enlargements carried out by bishop Henry O'Neill before his death that year. By the end of April 1918 the Holy See had authorised the establishment of a diocesan chapter in Dromore, one of the last dioceses in the country to conform itself to the Tridentine model of Church organisation.

On an altogether different note the Irish chief secretary announced in March 1916 that he would introduce a bill to repeal those sections of the Emancipation Act of 1829 which prohibited the legal operation of religious orders in the country. Colonel James Craig, the future Northern Ireland prime minister, who in the words of the *Catholic Directory* 'was too ill to go to the Front and has relinquished his commission on that account, has given notice that he will oppose the Bill'.[56]

The Church in the north continued to function through these years of crisis much as it had always done. The spiritual life of Ulster catholics, in so far as that can be measured by external criteria, remained centred around the traditional practices which had proved of value in the past, and added to this was the whole panoply of ultramontane devotions which had merged so discreetly into the landscape of Irish catholicism that they seemed to have been there since time immemorial. The bishops, as we have seen, frequently demanded of the people a more pietistical response to the great events of the day, and recourse to novenas, fasting and benediction was often invoked as a means of bringing peace to Ireland and Europe. The community's ecclesiastical leadership, if at times unimaginative was

[56] *Catholic Directory* (Dublin, 1917), p. 508.

none the less solid since, as Logue explained at his priestly jubilee in 1916, 'when it was a question of an essential thing for the good of the people the Irish Bishops moved forward as one man'. Such unrestrained determination and dogged leadership was needed in the following years which were to see some of the bloodiest trials that Ulster and Ireland had to experience since the seventeenth century.

Setting up the new state

The 1918 elections left the country polarised along religious lines. The counties outside Ulster were solidly catholic and Sinn Fein, and Unionism had demonstrated its strength in its traditional heartland. The parameters were thus drawn up for the fragmentation of the country into the respective spheres of catholic and protestant influence. In Ulster however the picture was much more complex because of the relatively high proportion of catholics, many of whom distrusted the protestant-Unionist ascendancy. For their part the Unionists, aided it must be said by Lloyd George and other high-ranking members of the British establishment, often gave the impression of completely disregarding the political aspirations of Ulster catholics: talk of the 'homogeneity' of Ulster, as if the area were overwhelmingly protestant, helped to strengthen their conviction that in any political arrangements which cut them off from their southern co-religionists their needs and views would simply be ignored. When Sinn Fein set up the first Dail illegally in January 1919, they invited the participation of both the Unionist Party and the National Party, in which Joe Devlin's influence was by now minimal. The invitation was declined by both groups.

The country moved unstoppably into war with Britain, a war which northern protestants felt had the blessing of the catholic bishops. Thus the *Belfast News Letter* stated on 20 November 1920 that it was 'the bigotry of the [Catholic] Church and its constant efforts, open and secret, to increase its power, which have brought a large part of Ireland to the state of lawlessness . . .' While it is easy to see that in the abstract such an assertion is patently absurd, nevertheless at times the supercilious remarks of bishops and clergy provided fuel for the fires of northern protestant intolerance. At a meeting of the Catholic Truth Society of Ireland on 20 October that year, cardinal Logue remarked that outside the catholic Church any trace of christianity was becoming less and less as the days went on. To add insult to injury he added that he did not make these remarks 'in any critical spirit but simply mentioned it as a matter of fact'.[57]

[57] *The Irish News*, 21 Oct. 1920.

As we have seen, the Ulster bishops had discussed the possibility of partition as early as June 1916, and their opposition was twofold. They believed it to be against the best interests of the island as a whole, and they feared too for the future of catholic education in a protestant-dominated parliament. In an Ulster in which Cavan, Monaghan, and Donegal were cut off from the remaining six counties, there would in Logue's view be no safeguards for the rights of the minority.[58] With their colleagues in the rest of Ireland the bishops issued a statement on 27 January 1920 suggesting that the only way to ensure peace and establish friendly relations between Ireland and England was to let an undivided Ireland choose its own form of government. The previous December the Ulster prelates had considered one of the proposals emanating from Lloyd George— (a reassertion to some extent of his 1916 proposal) to give a parliament to the twenty-six counties and have the six counties ruled directly from Westminster. In the circumstances they determined that this was probably the most satisfactory compromise. On the other hand, had Ulster west of the Bann or at least Fermanagh, Tyrone and Derry city been included in the proposed Free State this would have gone a long way to satisfying many northern catholics. By this stage this was hardly a realistic possibility since, as Mansergh has pointed out, it was for the Unionists a question not of six counties or four but rather of six or nine. 'Six was the minimum, "not an inch" of which would be surrendered. In democratic terms, this was not defensible. But then the Ulster Unionists at no point suggested that was for them a consideration'.[59]

There were differences of opinion among the northern bishops over the declaration of the republic by the first Dail and how much authority it could be given and how seriously they were to take it. While several of them individually contributed to the 'national loan fund' they decided with the rest of the hierarchy that they could not sanction the handing over of what remained of the £250,000 raised in the anti-conscription drive in 1918. This did not prevent many of the lower clergy who were trustees of the fund from doing just that.

The ambiguity of their attitude towards the Dail was also seen by the fact that while in Rome for the beatification of Oliver Plunkett in May 1920, Logue, O'Donnell and a number of other Irish bishops attended a reception given by the speaker of the Dail on behalf of 'the

[57] AAA, Logue to Walsh, 7 Dec. 1920.
[59] Mansergh, *The Unresolved Question*, p. 226. One might indeed suggest that this is the very crux of the problem which has beset Irish and Ulster history for four centuries, namely the absolute refusal of the Protestant population to accept their minority status, coupled with their consistent demand for a controlling role in the country's affairs far beyond their numerical strength.

government of Ireland'. Towards the end of that gathering the
orchestra struck up 'A Nation Once Again' and 'The Soldier's Song'
at which 'archbishops, bishops, priests . . . sang the stirring anthem
amid enthusiastic scenes'.[60] This seemed to give some recognition,
even if nebulous, to the republic. As might be expected, the whole
proceedings were viewed with horror by Ulster protestants. The
Belfast News Letter commented on 3 June:

> The Pope, some of the leading officials at the Vatican, and a
> number of RC bishops from this country have spent a week in
> praising and blessing an Irish rebel who was hanged for treason,
> and there is no doubt that the proceedings were intended to
> encourage the present rebellion, although they know it is accom-
> panied by assassination and outrages of every kind.

Understandably Logue saw the matter somewhat differently.
Conveying to the pope the gratitude of bishops and laity alike, he
remarked that 'the Decree of Beatification . . . has brought great
joy to the whole Irish race'. Perhaps it could not be expected that
the *News Letter* would see the situation in any other light. On the
other hand even English catholics could display a remarkable degree
of misunderstanding in their estimate of the relation between the
Church and society in Ireland. *The Tablet* in a rather conceited editorial
on 4 December 1920 demanded that Logue set about excommuni-
cating all members of Sinn Fein and those associated with it, since
it was no more than a front for a secret organization which had
been condemned by papal rescript, namely the Irish Republican
Brotherhood. A condemnation of this nature would also have involved
such northern bishops as Mulhern of Dromore, MacRory of Down
and Connor and McHugh of Derry, who were not only keenly
sensitive to the danger of partition but who remained fairly close to
Sinn Fein up till the beginning of the civil war. It was Mulhern who
passed on to De Valera Lloyd George's letter of 25 June 1921 inviting
him to the London conference which paved the way for the treaty
negotiation and the truce in the Anglo-Irish war. MacRory was
invited by De Valera to a clandestine meeting in Dublin in January
1921 to discuss what Sinn Fein's attitude should be to the forthcoming
elections to the northern parliament. De Valera further asked him
to solicit the opinions of the other Ulster bishops on the issue.[61] As
a result of that meeting MacRory persuaded De Valera to open
negotiations with Joe Devlin to ensure a common approach in the

---

[60] *Catholic Directory* (1921), p. 519.
[61] AAA, MacRory Archives, De Valera to MacRory, 17 Jan. 1921.

north between Sinn Fein and the remnants of the Nationalist party. MacHugh of Derry described the proposals contained in the 1920 Act as intended for 'the permanent partition and plunder of Ireland and the enslavement of her people in the interests of Great Britain'.[62] At this time O'Donnell of Raphoe seems not to have been in a position to make much of an impact politically, doubtless because of his too close association in the past with Redmond's party. This did not prevent the IRA from writing to him in October 1921 asking for financial aid and telling him, in a printed cirular, 'As a Citizen of the Irish Republic, it is your duty to support and defend it.' In the following year the local secretary in Falcarragh of the Cumann Na mBan, the women's section of the Republican movement, wrote complaining of Fr MacGinley, the parish priest of St Johnston's, that he was impeding the work of her organisation in the district. She pleaded with O'Donnell to take action against the unpatriotic cleric.

For his part cardinal Logue had a pathological aversion to the idea of a republic, but he also regarded it as a political impossibility. Speaking in a confirmation service at Clonoe, Co. Tyrone, in April 1921 he declared that England would never concede a republic to Ireland as long as she had one man left to fight. The cardinal seemed genuinely to favour dominion status for the whole country. *The Times* of 27 February 1920 published an article attributing to Logue the view that Ireland should remain within the British empire with a parliament similar to that of Canada or Australia. This of course greatly annoyed Sinn Fein but it did bring encouraging communication from well-connected English catholics. James Pope-Hennessy told Logue that discussions he had had on the Irish question 'with Ministers and Members of Parliament have brought it home to me that one of the greatest obstacles in obtaining for Ireland a Dominion Constitution is the widely held opinion that the Church backs Sinn Fein and is opposed to any solution within the British Empire. That delusion Your Eminence has now dispelled.'[63]

Logue was also to prove himself an unwitting collaborator of the British propaganda machine as a result of his Advent pastoral letter of 28 November 1920. Earlier that month the Belgian hierarchy (headed by cardinal Mercier) had issued a statement severely criticising British government policy, which amounted in effect to an expression of support for the Sinn Fein analysis of what was happening in Ireland. Logue's pastoral was roundly critical of Sinn Fein, without mentioning that organisation by name. His statement was not only seen as a rebuff to Mercier and his fellow bishops but

---

[62] Cf. *Derry People*, 20 March 1920.
[63] AAA, Logue Archives, 4 March 1920.

sections of it were reproduced by the British government and distributed at the Paris peace conference in an effort to embarrass the unofficial Irish legation headed by Sean T. O'Kelly. In addition the English press agencies ensured that Logue's rebuke to those fighting in the war of independence were transmitted to foreign newspapers so that, in O'Kelly's words, 'all the press of Europe was re-echoing [Logue's] condemnations of his fellow countrymen'.[64] On the other hand Logue did not go as far as Daniel Cohalan, bishop of Cork, who on 12 December excommunicated members of the IRA operating in his diocese.

The hierarchy as a whole were however deeply critical of the government for both its conduct of the Anglo-Irish war and its obvious desire to please the northern protestant/Unionist minority. Their frustration at what they saw as glaring injustices perpetrated against the catholic community drove them to issue a joint state-ment on the Ulster question on 19 October, in which their bitterness is barely concealed. Reviewing the situation since 1914 they commented:

> The governing classes across the water, instead of encouraging Ulster Unionists to coalesce with the rest of the country, have used that section for centuries as a spear-head directed at the heart of Ireland. The whole British administration sat complacently while a provisional [Unionist] government was formed and an army drilled in Ulster. . . . [Then during the first World War] the highest offices in the gift of the State were for the contingent rebels of Ulster in contrast with the bullet for Irish insurgents. [Now government policy indicates that] all Ireland must be coerced for the sake of the North-East, and especially Tyrone, Fermanagh and Derry City . . .'[65]

As a result of the parliamentary elections in May 1921 under the terms of the Government of Ireland Act, the Unionists were returned with forty seats to the new Northern Ireland parliament. Sinn Fein and the Nationalists each had six members, but they were all deter-mined to boycott the new parliament, as indeed did the Church. When Sir James Craig invited Logue to the state opening by George V on 22 June, the cardinal pleaded a prior engagement and declined. This refusal to recognise the new state was also reflected at local level. The local government elections of January and June 1920, carried out under a system of proportional representation, left many catholic areas in Ulster under nationalist control, thus giving catholics a taste of political power. They were resolved to use this in the most effective

[64] AAA, O'Kelly to MacRory, 9 Dec. 1920.
[65] *The Catholic Directory* (1921), pp. 558–9.

way possible to demonstrate their opposition to the new political arrangements. Derry city council refused to fly the Union flag or to attend official government receptions. Many catholic education boards withheld recognition from the new Northern Ireland ministry of education and affiliated themselves to the Dail, from which they drew salaries for their teachers. The northern government did not remain idle in the face of such defiance and acted to abolish proportional representation as a way of curbing catholic power. Furthermore it introduced an oath of allegiance to the crown for every conceivable public sector job and office. A number of catholic priests who served as chaplains to prisons or workhouses lost their jobs for refusing to take the oath. Teachers in the end were forced into a working relationship with the new government when, after the assassination of Michael Collins in the Irish civil war, William T. Cosgrave made it clear that he would not continue Collins's policy of financing northern catholic defiance of the Belfast parliament.

The British government had attempted to sweeten the bitter pill of the impending division in the days before partition by the appointment for the first time since James II's reign of a catholic, lord Fitzalan of Derwent, as lord lieutenant for Ireland. This produced rounded criticism from many protestant-Unionist sources. Logue, when asked for his comment on the appointment, said that he received it in the same manner as he would the appointment of a catholic hangman. It would be wrong to give the impression that all northern catholics were as hostile to Northern Ireland as the clergy and nationalist politicians obviously were. After all the first lord chief justice of the new state was a catholic Sir Denis Stanislaus Henry, a former Unionist MP and successively solicitor-general and attorney-general for Ireland. He rendered distinguished service on the Northern Ireland bench, and his example runs counter to the normal pattern of catholic exclusion from the operations of the state. However Sir Denis was clearly not a typical product of the Ulster catholic community and his political adroitness may, in part, have been the result of his education at the English Jesuit public school Mount St Mary's in Derbyshire.

The tolerance of a catholic in such an exalted position was very much the exception. The new minister for agriculture and commerce, Edward M. Archdale, was to complain publicly of the number of catholic civil servants in his department. 'I have 109 officials, and as far as I know three or four are Roman Catholics, three of whom were civil servants turned over to me whom I had to take when we began'.[66] His associate in the home affairs office Sir Richard Dawson

[66] Campbell, *Fifty Years of Ulster, 1890–1940*, p. 97.

Bates was equally suspicious of catholics, and tried to ensure as far as possible that there were none in his department. When he discovered that a catholic had been employed as a telephonist he sent a note to a colleague asking him never to phone him at the office since there was a danger that calls might be put through by this individual.

As we have seen, the area which perhaps concerned the catholic authorities more than any other was education. Here, under the (by the standards of the day) liberal regime of lord Londonderry, a southern catholic Andrew N. Bonaparte Wyse rose in 1927 to become permanent secretary. Londonderry saw his first task as reforming the education system, and to this end the Northern Ireland parliament set up a committee of inquiry in September 1921 to examine the issue. Its report duly became, with some amendments, the basis of Londonderry's education act of 1923. It is notorious that the catholic Church refused to have anything to do with the Lynn committee, whose only catholic member (out of thirty-two) was Wyse in his capacity as a high-ranking civil servant. The Ulster bishops have been severely criticised for their failure to co-operate with the committee, and a leading authority on Northern Ireland's educational history has observed that 'in all probability the refusal of the Roman Catholic authorities to join the Lynn committee was the single most important determinant of the educational history of Northern Ireland. . . . By refusing to sit they surrendered their last shred of influence at the very time when the basic character of Ulster's educational development was being determined.'[67]

However this line of argument is somewhat naive. As we have seen many managers of catholic schools refused to recognise the authority of the new government, and were receiving their financial support from the south. Logue had told parishioners at Cookstown in June 1921 that judging by the utterances of prominent Unionists, catholics could expect nothing but persecution in the new state, adding 'There are I fear great trials before Catholic and Christian education.'[68] Furthermore Lynn was an ardent extremist whom even Sir James Craig regarded as a fanatic. In a debate in the Northern Ireland parliament soon after his appointment as chairman of the commission on education, he observed: 'There are two peoples in Ireland, one industrious, law-abiding and God-fearing, and the other slothful, murderous and disloyal.'[69] But perhaps above all catholic reluctance

---

[67] Donald H. Akenson, *Education and Enmity: The Control of Schooling in Northern Ireland, 1920–50* (New York, 1973), p. 52.

[68] *The Catholic Directory* (1922), p. 553.

[69] Quoted in Dennis Kennedy, *The Widening Gulf: Northern attitudes to the independent Irish state, 1919–49* (Belfast, 1988), p. 97. Despite the sub-title Kennedy's interest is primarily in northern protestant attitudes.

to engage with the new state was because they felt themselves to be at the mercy of a repressive and brutal ruling élite determined to suppress manifestations of political dissent. Such suppression did not exclude the use of force.

The Belfast troubles

On the occasion of the Orange rally at Finaghy of 12 July 1920 Sir Edward Carson warned that if the government did not take steps to counteract Sinn Fein 'penetration' into Ulster then the loyalist people themselves would once more have to act in self-defence. The speech was so intemperate that even *The Times* was moved to say it was a 'parade of anachronistic intolerance'. Carson's vituperations were closely followed by a series of anonymous letters to the *Belfast News Letter* which complained bitterly of outsiders from the south of Ireland infiltrating the Belfast shipyards and taking the jobs of loyal men who had fought in the Great War. This in effect became the starting point for two years of violent sectarian skirmishes throughout the north, but chiefly in the Belfast area, which were to leave 400 dead, 1,600 injured and thousands homeless and without work. The majority of those who suffered were catholics. The extent of the violence coupled with the birth of the state amid suggestions of a 'protestant parliament for a protestant people', gave the impression that a systematic pogrom had been deliberately set in train with the aim of subduing residual cath-olic opposition to what became to its supporters 'Northern Ireland' and to its opponents 'Carsonia'.

The expulsion of 5,000 catholic workers from the shipyards in July 1920 was the beginning of a two-year orgy of violence in which the authorities either would not or could not act to protect the lives and property of the catholic community in the Belfast area. The *Daily Mail* reported on 1 September that the trouble was 'simply and solely because there has been an organized attempt to deprive Catholic men of their work and to drive Catholic families from their homes.' What appeared to be a spontaneous outpouring of working-class protestant invective nevertheless had the approval of the upper echelons of the Unionist hierarchy. On 14 October at the unfurling of a Union Jack in the shipyards Sir James Craig remarked: 'I think it only fair that I should be asked a question . . . and it is "Do I approve of the action you boys have taken in the past?" I say Yes'. By the end of the year more than 8,000 had been forced from their work. It must also be said that a number of protestant socialists were also included in the early expulsions from places of work since they were seen as fellow travellers with catholics. It was alleged by a number of protestant clergy that those forced from their work were all Sinn Fein supporters, and that their exclusion was for political rather than religious reasons. By 1922 the catholic bishops had strongly refuted such a suggestion. In a statement on 26 April they noted that 'long before Sinn Fein was heard of Belfast had gained a notoriety for savage riots and the murder of Catholics in the name of religion'.[70] Many of those expelled from their jobs testified to the specifically religious nature of the grounds for expulsion. One witness reported that 'the vests and shirts of those at work were torn open to see if the men were wearing any Catholic emblems, and then woe betide the man who was'.[71] In addition the bishops indicated that the heart of the problem was the failure of democratic process in the country as a whole:

> Contrary to the best interests of the nation a section of the country has been partitioned off, apparently to give us a specimen of model government. If that government is to be judged by results, it must rank more nearly with the government of the Turk in his worst days than with anything to be found anywhere in a Christian State. . . . [Belfast Catholics were] subject to a savage persecution which is hardly paralleled by the bitterest sufferings of the Armenians.[72]

The bitterness of these remarks is hardly surprising given the situation in the north in the two preceding years. Catholic places of worship were regularly attacked, convents burned and innocent catholics emerging from churches shot dead by protestant snipers. The government propaganda machine also contrived to give the impression that the catholic population was the principal source of the violence then sweeping the six counties. There is no doubt that by 1922 catholics had begun to retaliate by launching attacks on protestant civilian targets. Before then it is also true that the IRA had been active in a campaign which seemed to the authorities to be aimed at destabilising Northern Ireland. In reality, however, much of the IRA activity was simply defensive. As the *Manchester Guardian* reported on 6 September 1921, 'the blame for beginning the trouble lies at the door of the Orangemen, and for the desperate [recent shooting] both sides must bear responsibility, with this point to be remembered in favour of the Catholics, that as they were attacked, and as there was no military protection available, the members of the IRA retaliated in kind and quite as effectively.'

At times the sheer brutality exhibited was appalling, with the added twist that much of it was meted out by members of the security forces against innocent catholics. One of the most celebrated instances of

[70] *Catholic Directory* (1923), p. 604
[71] Quoted in Michael Farrell, *Northern Ireland: The Orange State* (London, 1976), p. 28.
[72] *Catholic Directory* (1923), p. 603.

mass murder at this time was the case of the McMahon family. Seven members of the household, including an employee, were done to death in the McMahon home in the early morning of 24 March 1922. It is alleged that five men, some of them partly dressed in police uniform, burst into the house, rounded up all the men, and began to shoot them one at a time in the downstairs front room. This happened during the curfew and within five minutes' walk of Glenravel Street police barracks. One boy, the youngest, survived by hiding behind some furniture. In later life he attracted a certain notoriety by his fervent flying of the Union flag every armistice day.[73] Equally rebarbative was the 'Arnon Street massacre' of 1 April 1922. In a raid the police killed five innocent people including a seventy-year-old man and a seven-year-old boy in bed with his father and younger sister. His father was bludgeoned to death. The motive for this violence seems to have been revenge by the police for the shooting earlier that day of constable Turner on the Old Lodge Road in Belfast. Indeed the motive of revenge was a central theme for many of the police attacks in those years.

Not all the acts of violence were perpetrated by the security forces. On 13 February 1922 a bomb was thrown into a group of catholic children playing outside their home in Weaver Street. Two were killed outright and four others died later in hospital. A further sixteen were injured. In a not dissimilar outrage on 13 March the fire service was summoned to a hoax blaze at the catholic end of Foundry Street. When a crowd gathered to witness the spectacle a bomb was thrown from the protestant end of the street, and twelve people were seriously hurt in the explosion.

In response to the violence the catholic population organised itself into a defence force for mutual protection and self-help. The Catholic Protection Committee under the chairmanship of bishop Joseph MacRory sought to provide practical help to those families who had been driven from their homes and their work. In a letter to the committee in late July 1920, enclosing £100 for its relief work, MacRory noted:

> Even when allowance is made for the unholy Carsonite incitement on the 12th of July last to religious bigotry, the hard fact remains that it was by fellow-workers the victims were driven from their works and their homes wrecked and looted. These bullies and their sleek abettors talk glibly of *Civil and Religious Liberty*, but they appear

---

[73] Cf. Tim Pat Coogan, *Michael Collins: A Biography* (London, 1990), p. 355. It has not been possible to establish the veracity of this claim by Coogan. In fact the youngest McMahon boy seems to have become a barrister in London and consequently spent little time in Belfast.

from their actions not to have even the most elementary idea of what either means'.[74]

On 31 August the *Daily Herald* Irish correspondent made a similar point when he observed: 'The bloody harvest of Carsonism is being reaped in Belfast. . . . The gangs who have organised the reign of terror are the very people who protest they are afraid that *they* would, under even partial home rule, be persecuted and denied religious liberty'. On 19 June 1921 MacRory told the newspapers that 30,000 Belfast people had depended for ten months on the generosity of the civilised world for their material survival. Catholics had been as far as possible disarmed and were now at the mercy of the most unruly elements of the Unionist community. However the following February he joined with Dr Grierson, the Church of Ireland bishop of Down, Conor and Dromore, W.H. Smith, president of the Methodist conference, and Dr Lowe, moderator of the general assembly of the Presbyterian Church, in condemning violence as being of no advantage to any section of the community. In addition the joint statement declared that no amount of provocation could justify the extent of the violence Northern Ireland was then experiencing. And in his Lenten address MacRory followed the other catholic bishops in declaring that there could be no hope for the north-east if it persisted in cutting itself off politically from the rest of Ireland. When the violence finally came to an end the economic hardship continued. As late as 1923 the poverty of catholics was so acute that the pope remitted the Peter's pence collection, of £830, from the diocese of Down and Connor adding a gift of £70 with instructions to MacRory to distribute the money among the poor.

The joint statement of the church leaders in February 1922 was not the only effort made by protestants to help end the violence in the six counties. The Irish Protestant Convention held in Dublin in May provided an opportunity for many Southern protestants to dissociate themselves from the activities of their co-religionists in Belfast and called for an end to attacks on catholics. However George Russell (AE), himself a northern protestant, said of the convention that it was like a death-bed conversion 'when the sick man remembers all he has left undone and unsaid in the past, and calls his relatives round to witness his repentance in the hope of warding off the devils'.[75]

One cannot underestimate the effect of these two years of death and destruction on the perception of the catholic community in Northern

[74] Quoted in G.B. Kenna, *Facts and Figures of the Belfast Pogrom, 1920–22* (privately published, 1922), p. 18.

[75] Quoted in Patrick J. Gannon, 'In the Catacombs of Belfast', *Studies*, vol. 10 (1922), p. 293.

Ireland and its attitude to the state both then and since. The state was set up in circumstances of appalling civil strife, the scars of which were never to heal, and which left a residue of mutual hatred and recrimination. Those early troubles were coupled with the stated aim of creating political structures which favoured one socio-religious outlook almost to the exclusion of any other philosophy or way of life. In these circumstances catholic participation in the new state could not be wholehearted. Indeed what is remarkable is the extent not so much of catholic resistance as of its acquiescence in the new 'Ulster'. This was brought about partly by the creation of draconian 'security arrangements', facilitated by the setting up of the Royal Ulster Constabulary and the exclusively protestant Ulster Special Constabulary. With so many Ulster protestants under arms and the subsequent 'Emergency Provisions (Special Powers) Act' 1922, which was renewed annually until it became permanent in 1933, it was relatively easy for the government to suppress discontent. The problem of course was that the Northern Ireland government and perhaps the protestant population as a whole saw its relationship with northern catholicism as one of containment. Catholics were disloyal or potentially so; many would give their allegiance to a 'foreign' state if they had the opportunity, and so their very existence as a community had to be closely scrutinised and controlled. This became the theme of much of the government's operations in those years. Catholicism was seen as a 'security' problem. Added to this was the pervasive suspicion and intolerance of catholicism as a creed which made the policymakers in the new state continue to regard the catholic Church as the instigator of subversion. The security policy of the northern government was aimed at preserving the new state by whatever means might be necessary. Much of the violence of the security forces against the catholic community can only be explained, if not thereby excused, by their view of almost every catholic as a potential Sinn Feiner or IRA member whose avowed aim was to overthrow the organisation of the state. But it is to the northern catholic community considered as a 'security problem', that we must now turn our attention.

The security situation in Ulster

Article 7 of the Anglo-Irish treaty provided for what amounted to a federal structure of government for Ireland. The Northern Ireland parliament could however opt out of this arrangement and continue to govern its own affairs as envisaged in the 1920 Act. This it promptly did. Although the northern bishops in general supported the treaty they still looked askance at the Northern Ireland state which was beginning to show symptoms of the anti-Catholic malaise which the bishops had feared would be the hallmark of its operation since it was first mooted as a means of pacifying Unionist opinion. Patrick O'Donnell, from January 1922 co-adjutor archbishop of Armagh in addition to his duties in Raphoe, declared in the course of a speech in Drogheda on 20 May: 'The sooner that dividing line [the border] is obliterated, the better for Ireland and the better for Ulster'. Such declarations merely confirmed the Ulster Unionists' belief that all catholics encouraged by their bishops and clergy were traitorous subversives. The government of Northern Ireland was determined to act to stem such sedition.

The repressive tactics used in the war of independence and associated in particular with the Black and Tans* set the tone for Northern Ireland security policy when the new state finally came into being. Despite widespread condemnation of Black and Tan atrocities, highlighted by among others seventeen Church of England bishops in November 1920, the British government remained steadfast in its determination to use whatever means were necessary to bring peace to Ireland. Given the hostility of catholics in both parts of Ireland to the idea of partition, the northern Unionists were as resolved as their imperial masters to preserve Northern Ireland as an independent entity from incursions from without and within.

Already by mid-1920 the Unionist establishment had begun to resurrect the old Ulster Volunteer Force under various guises throughout the north of Ireland. By October that year the British government had agreed to an auxiliary police force to be known as the Ulster Special Constabulary, which as everyone understood was to be simply the UVF under a different name. Indeed the foundational plans for the new constabulary were drawn up by none other than lt.-col. W. Spender, the principal organiser of the UVF. However the government, though challenged to do so, would never reveal how many ex-UVF men actually joined the new force. Eventually the 'Specials' became a virtual law unto themselves and resisted several attempts to abolish them on the grounds of cost, which by December 1925 had totalled nearly £7,000,000. By June 1922 their numbers had risen to 48,000 and they were seen as a force used almost exclusively to contain the unruly elements within the northern catholic community. These elements included cardinal Logue and his assistant archbishop O'Donnell, who were stopped and searched several times as they went about their pastoral work in the Armagh diocese. In one

---

*The Black and Tans were reinforcements for the security forces specially recruited in Britain for the task of helping reduce Ireland to order. The name derived from the odd colouring of their uniform. R.F. Foster says of them that they 'behaved more like independent mercenaries; their brutal regime followed the IRA's policy of killing policemen, and was taken by many to vindicate it.' Cf. *Modern Ireland*, p. 498.

famous incident the aged cardinal had a rifle poked in his ribs and his name and address noted. Bishop MacHugh in Derry suffered similar affronts from the force as did the De La Salle Brothers in Falls Road, Belfast, on 26 June 1922. Their home was raided by a group of Specials in the early hours of that morning and the Brothers were made to stand in their night attire for two hours while the house was searched and ransacked. Communion bread was trampled underfoot and money and other articles were looted from the house.

Such activities were among the more innocuous actions of the Specials in the years 1920-3, yet the northern administration continued to regard them as an essential plank in the defeat of terrorism. Most members of the catholic community viewed them as little more than armed hooligans. However it is significant that the assistant under secretary for Ireland, received a deputation of catholic Justices of the Peace on 15 November 1920, headed by Dr Michael Deveny of Cookstown, on the question of catholic recruitment to the USC, and whether catholics would be given officer status. In his minutes of the meeting Clark noted that he told the delegation: 'The command of the Force must depend upon the character of its members and . . . up to now I have received no encouragement from the heads of the Church or responsible political leaders to think that any large number of Roman Catholics were likely to join'.[76]

With the division of the country new police forces became an essential pre-requisite in both parts of Ireland. In the north the Royal Ulster Constabulary was founded in 1922 to replace the old RIC. Sir Dawson Bates had set up a committee of fifteen members to make recommendations about the new force. It was suggested that one-third of its 3,000 members should be drawn from 'suitable' members of the catholic community. This particular recommendation was opposed by nine members of the committee but eventually adopted by the Belfast government. However by 1925 catholics numbered only 551 out of 2,990 men. The force made little effort in the early years to be impartial and even boasted its own Orange Lodge, founded in January 1923. A number of senior officers in the force, including Detective Inspectors Nixon and Harrison, were linked to several outrages against catholics including the McMahon murders. These individuals seem to have been given a relatively free hand in counterinsurgency operations, and it has been suggested that they had the active support of Dawson Bates and the secretary of the cabinet who were supposedly in favour of reprisals against catholics for shooting members of the security forces.[77] In addition bishop

---

[76] PRONI, Fin. 18/1/100.
[77] Coogan, *Michael Collins*, p. 353.

MacRory told the provisional government in Dublin that the Brown Street barracks at the bottom of the Shankill Road contained a number 'of notorious murderers who are immune from discipline'.

As a result of the second 'Craig-Collins' pact of March 1922, a Catholic-Police liaison committee was set up to try and bring about some communication of a non-hostile nature between nationalists and the security forces. The bishop of Down and Connor was a member of the committee. By June the arrangement had fallen apart when two of the catholic members were arrested on their way to a meeting of the committee, amid allegations that the had passed on intelligence gained at previous meetings to the IRA

One further undertaking which Craig gave to Collins but did not fulfil was to establish a catholic police force in certain specified nationalists areas. One might speculate how different the Northern Ireland political landscape might have been had this promise been kept. The setting up of the security apparatus of the state took place against the background of atrocious violence in the south of Ireland and frequent incursions into the new state by the IRA, with the active support of the head of the provisional government Michael Collins. The IRA conducted a vicious campaign against the security forces in the north which at times involved the murder of civilians who were associated with the RUC. Three police drivers and a civilian with whom they were talking were shot dead in Victoria Square, Belfast, on 11 March 1921. A number of outrages were perpetrated in the period 1920–3 against unarmed protestants on both sides of the border, most of whom from the IRA point of view were 'legitimate targets' since they had given information to the security forces on IRA operations. The problem was that such murders tended to be regarded by Ulster Unionists as direct attacks by catholics on innocent protestants and therefore excused the strong-arm tactics of the Ulster security forces in their dealings with the catholic population in Northern Ireland.

. Blanket security became the order of the day in the new state and security tended to mean the security of the Protestant-Unionist population and the subjugation of the catholic population at every level. St Mary's Hall in Belfast was commandeered by the Specials in March 1922 and not returned to the church till 1925. The imposition of the curfew affected catholic church services at Christmas, and impeded clergy in bringing the last rites to the sick and dying during the hours of darkness. Priests in such circumstance were often harassed by members of the security forces, which reinforced in the minds of many the perception that the suppression of catholicism rather than terrorism was the aim of the northern state.

The introduction of internment without trial in 1922 was likewise seen as a weapon aimed almost exclusively at the catholic community. Of 520 thus held by the end of that year over 500 were catholics. There were also allegations of mistreatment of internees. This seemed to follow the same pattern as in the days, two years earlier, when republican prisoners detained under the Defence of the Realm Act were mistreated in Belfast gaol. A move by the imperial parliament to impose martial law in Northern Ireland was blocked by Sir James Craig because he felt that it would show that the province was incapable of running its own affairs at the very outset of its existence. He told the Northern Ireland House of Commons that if martial law were imposed 'our cause in England will suffer immediately and intensely. They will say one side is as bad as the other'. Catholics tended to feel that Sir James's objections had more to do with the fact that the Unionists would not then have a free hand to pursue what was by any standard a most illiberal security policy.

From its very inception the state of Northern Ireland was obsessed, not without some justification, with its internal security. By 1923 there were some 70,000 men under arms in the province, including 20,000 British troops of whom the overwhelming majority were pro-testant, and this at a time when, as bishop MacRory complained, catholic farmers could scarcely possess shotguns to shoot menacing crows. The catholic minority were seen as 'the enemy within', and it has been estimated that by 1922 there was one armed agent of the state for every two adult catholic males in the population.[78] The northern catholics clearly faced tremendous difficulties in the years 1920–3. The political divisions in the country as a whole touched them deeply. That the bishops in general, and Logue in particular, supported the Anglo-Irish treaty came to be seen subsequently by the more ardent northern republicans as the Church's final act of betrayal of nationalist hopes, but in fact the northern minority and the IRA in the north were mostly pro-treaty. The civil war largely by-passed the north. The suffering at that time of catholics in the north-east more or less excluded interest in what was happening in the rest of the country. Of course initially both sides in the civil war were anti-partitionist but after Collins's death the pro-treaty side was willing to acquiesce in the harsh political realities of a divided Ireland. The northern Church leaders supported the excommunication of the anti-treaty faction in the civil war. The Church's action over this was in stark contrast to its attitude in the war of independence and could not be said to reflect northern catholic opinion as a whole. Increasingly catholics in the new 'Ulster'

---

[78] Michael Farrell, 'The Establishment of the Ulster Special Constabulary' in Austen Morgan and Bob Purdie (eds), *Ireland: Divided Nation Divided Class* (London, 1980), p. 134.

felt themselves to be an oppressed and isolated minority unable to draw on the support of catholics in the Free State.

The hierarchy's approval for the new political order south of the border was not without self-interest. The Church regarded itself as a national institution and the northern bishops could exercise, with the other members of the ecclesiastical establishment, considerable influence over the shape of politics in the south, the very thing that was clearly impossible for them in the north. Their influence on southern politics was partly the result of all the northern dioceses apart from Dromore and Down and Connor straddling the border. The northern bishops acted almost immediately to assert their interests in the new political possibilities now open to them. In a revealing letter to bishop Patrick MacKenna of Clogher in March 1922, cardinal Logue laid down what he saw as the role of the church in the Free State. On the construction of the new constitution he remarked:

> Those engaged in drawing up the constitution should remember that it is being drawn up for a Catholic country not for the Soviet of Russia. . . . Hence it must be submitted to the Bishops and a committee of theologians aided by a lawyer should be appointed to examine it and see that it is in accordance with the principles of Christianity and with Catholic principles as far as we are concerned.[79]

At times it is difficult to escape the conclusion that the northern bishops were content to sacrifice northern catholic interests for their enhanced position as arbiters of public policy in the south. In a certain sense Home Rule was if not Rome Rule then at least Bishops' Rule. Justification for such an outlook was provided by Pius XI's encyclical on peace of January 1923. MacKenna, in writing to his clergy ordering them to read the encyclical to their parishioners, said that 'the splendid passage, page 22, in which the authority and prerogatives of bishops are described may with great profit be frequently put before the people'. The pope had identified the causes of war as 'godless governments, godless homes, godless schools'. MacKenna was convinced that the encyclical would 'go straight to the hearts of our people and arouse them . . . to a realization of the dangers to their faith and piety to which they are being recklessly exposed'.[80] The application of the pope's sentiments to Northern Ireland were obvious.

That Northern Ireland was largely passive by the end of 1923 was

---

[79] AAA, Logue to MacKenna, 22 March 1922. In his reply two days later MacKenna in accepting Logue's suggestions also comments, 'I think the clauses dealing with education and religion are satisfactory, and as strong as they could be without arousing controversy.'

[80] PRONI, DIO(RC), 1/14/20.

a measure of the 'success' of the northern government security operations, and because southern politicians had made it clear that they would no longer finance attempts by northern catholics to destabilise the Belfast regime in any way. But the price paid for the state of 'normality' which then ensued was a lingering and burning resentment on the part of the catholic population against the Unionist administration. For their part the protestant-Unionist majority made little effort at magnanimity in their dealing with the catholic minority. The catholic population continued in many ways to withhold recognition from the Northern Ireland government and frequently organised its life in parallel to the society around it, thus giving the impression of being 'a state within the state'.

6

CATHOLICS IN THE
PROTESTANT STATE

Early alienation

In the initial stages, as we have seen, many northern catholics supported the treaty arrangements, not because they liked the idea of partition but because they shared the optimistic view that the new 'Ulster' could not long endure and that soon the border would become but a figment of protestant Unionist imagination. This attitude did not prevent them from demanding at a quite early stage the immediate inclusion of obviously nationalist areas such as Derry city, Tyrone and Fermanagh in the Irish Free State. Their hostility and indifference to the northern parliament grew out of hearty disdain for an institution they regarded as ephemeral and irrelevant to post-war Ireland. It seemed pointless for Ulster catholics to engage with a new transitory political arrangement clearly marked for an early demise.

The results of the civil war in the Irish Free State to some extent began a sense of alienation and despair among northern catholics in their dealings with both parts of Ireland. While many northerners actually fought on the Free State side, it quickly became clear that the Cosgrave government, despite the presence in it of northerners such as Ernest Blythe, did not—understandably—intend to give northern catholic affairs a high priority in Free State policy.

Setting aside their hostility in principle to what was in effect a protestant state, the catholic authorities quickly became immersed in dealings with the new political order over the question of education. The issue here was one of clerical control, coupled with a desire to secure as much money as possible from the state to support the catholic system. The Church favoured none of the various schemes on offer to deal with educational provision. It spurned the relatively liberal 'four and two system', advanced in 1925, whereby in voluntary schools four of the managers would be appointed by the Church and two by the local authority, in exchange for substantial state financial assistance. The idea that democratic control could have any place in catholic education was firmly repudiated by cardinal O'Donnell: 'It is a great fallacy to suppose that election is the only way, or always the best way to find a representative man. Among Catholics there is

222

no more representative person in the parish than the average parish priest. . .'[1]

'Lord Londonderry's Education Act of 1923 aimed at providing a system of integrated education at least at the primary level. Under its provisions catholic schools were to lose the grants they had under the national school arrangements, which amounted to two-thirds of building and equipment costs. Londonderry was determined to resist the idea of religious instruction in the new system, asserting: 'Religious instruction in a denominational sense during the hours of compulsory attendance there will not be'.[2] He did not reckon with the defiance this would meet from the protestant clergy and the Orange Order. By February 1925 Orange Lodge officials had formed an alliance with the 'United Education Committee of the Protestant Churches', to pressure the government into amending the 1923 act. In particular they wanted the power to appoint only protestant teachers to 'state' schools, or at least representation on appointments committees for protestant clergy, and a repeal of the provisions that forbade religious instruction. After some initial resistance Londonderry, under pressure also from the prime minister Sir James Craig, interpreted the amending bill of 1925 in the sense specified by the protestant-Orange alliance. He then offered his resignation.

By 1928-9 the protestant Churches again agitated for further reforms of the state system in a more specifically protestant direction, covering much the same ground as the previous demands. The 1930 act made more explicit what had been simply tolerated under the 1925 act. The intention of the new act was, in the words of the prime minister, to 'make the provided and transferred schools safe for Protestant children'.[3] Given such clear manipulation of the system by the majority population the catholic hierarchy acted decisively in its own self-interest. The bishops threatened that if the grants to catholic schools that had been abolished in 1923 were not restored then they would take legal action to refer the 1930 measure to the judicial committee of the privy council since it manifestly contravened the provision of the Government of Ireland Act of 1920, which had forbidden the endowment of any Church. On the principle that two wrongs make a right, the government offered the bishops 50 per cent grants for building and equipment costs in catholic schools—they already paid teachers' salaries in such schools.[4]

[1] *The Irish News*, 22 Feb. 1927.

[2] Quoted in Akenson, *Education and Enmity*, p. 66.

[3] Cf. Patrick Buckland, *The Factory of Grievances: Devolved Government in Northern Ireland, 1921–39* (Dublin, 1979), p. 261.

[4] Following a representation from archbishop O'Donnell in December 1924, even members of religious orders teaching in schools were to receive salaries on the same basis as other teachers. Before this they were paid only a 'maintenance allowance'.

This victory of the northern bishops over the Belfast parliament was by no means the only such triumph. As co-adjutor archbishop of Armagh, O'Donnell had assiduously lobbied lord Londonderry for specific provision for the training of catholic male teachers. In March 1923 the bishops had ruled that catholic teachers trained at the state-run Stranmillis College would not be employed in catholic schools. Not to be outdone, the government regulated that teachers trained in the Irish Free State, mostly at the catholic college of St Patrick's Drumcondra, who completed their training after 1925 would not be eligible for employment in the north. In addition Londonderry indicated that 'notwithstanding [the March 1923] warning, Catholic candidates of good educational qualifications are presenting themselves for training [at Stranmillis] in sufficient numbers to supply the vacancies for male teachers in Catholic schools'.[5]

Negotiations were entered into with a view to the Northern Ireland government paying for catholic students to train at St Mary's College, Hammersmith, London, which transferred to Strawberry Hill at Twickenham in 1925, and the Church agreed to employ the students then at Stranmillis provided the final-year students undertook a summer school in religious instruction. The first-year students moved to St Mary's with the new intake in 1925. One of the many complications in all this was a shortfall in the amount of money available to train the Northern Ireland students in London. Londonderry was able to sell the proposal to his cabinet colleagues only by assuring them that the training in London was cheaper than that provided in Belfast. In this he was more than a little economical with the truth. The principal of St Mary's wrote to O'Donnell that the English Catholic Education Council did not see why it should make up the shortfall in government funds available for Northern Ireland students.[6] Somewhat reluctantly, it has to be said, the northern bishops agreed to pay £300 a year to St Mary's Strawberry Hill for the Northern Ireland students. Such successes in the education field could not however dispel the fear of the catholic hierarchy that the Unionist government was determined to undermine the position and status of catholicism within the state. Although the 1930 Education Act was favourable to catholic interests, it was obvious to all concerned that its provisions were initially designed to placate the protestant clergy and the Orange Order on the question of the role of education as an instrument for preserving the protestant way of life in Northern Ireland. The

---

[5] AAA, Londonderry to O'Donnell, 1 Jan. 1925. Londonderry argued in this letter that his 'educational administration' had won the 'approval and confidence of the Catholic community'.

[6] AAA, Rev. J.J. Doyle to O'Donnell, 27 May 1925.

protestant Churches had set the agenda for the education debate and virtually dictated the terms for settling the question. It is also true that the hierarchy had simply refused to exert any positive influence on the development of the government's educational policy. O'Donnell had declined the offer of a place on the Northern Ireland Advisory Council on Education in November 1924. Despite the minister's pleading both he and cardinal Logue refused to recommend anyone for the post.[7]

Taken in isolation such non-cooperation might be regarded as a disastrous lost opportunity. However it would have been impossible for the officials of the Church to be seen to be working in too close harmony with the Northern Ireland state at that period in its history. Londonderry's urbane and sophisticated approach to dealing with the minority community was something of an exception among the Unionist establishment as a whole. The government, as has been noted, had already acted to impose an oath of allegiance for even the most trivial of public service jobs, and had abolished proportional representation in local government elections, and in 1923 re-drew the electoral boundaries to the severe disadvantage of nationalists in the west of the province. It is estimated that in all thirteen nationalist councils and two that were evenly balanced thereby fell into Unionist hands.[8] Internment without trial remained a cause of resentment within the catholic community. In January 1924 cardinal Logue had said that the bulk of internees were innocent of any criminal or treasonable activity, and in the circumstances of peace then prevailing there was no need for it. There were large-scale protests against internment all over the north of Ireland in September that year, and O'Donnell asserted that he was fully in sympathy with the object of such demonstrations.[9]

Given all this, it is perhaps understandable that the catholic authorities maintained a certain aloofness from the prevailing political order. On the other hand, as early as 1923 the bishops had called upon catholic politicians to abandon the official policy of abstentionism. In 1925 Joe Devlin and Thomas McAllister both took their seats in the Belfast parliament, arguably in an attempt to protect catholic educa-

[7] Londonderry had written to O'Donnell on 15 Nov. 1924: 'It would be of the greatest assistance to me if you and His Eminence would consider the matter and recommend to me a person who I might substitute for yourself upon the Council, if indeed it is impossible for you to reconsider your decision'. The full correspondence on this matter in preserved in the Armagh Archives.

[8] John Whyte, 'How much discrimination was there under the Unionist regime, 1921–68' in Tom Gallagher and James O'Connell (eds), *Contemporary Irish Studies* (Manchester, 1983), p. 5.

[9] *The Catholic Directory*, 1925, p. 595. By January 1926 all internees and political prisoners had been released, thus removing one bone of contention from the catholic complaints against the northern state.

tional interests. This was the strategy agreed upon at a meeting in St Mary's Hall, Belfast, on 21 March. That gathering, made up of clergy, politicians and other interested parties, had decided to contest the forthcoming elections. However they determined that only MPs elected in areas that would not be affected by the Boundary Commission would sit in the Belfast parliament while those affected by it would not take their seats.

The 'official' Church had supported Devlin's brand of constitutional nationalism against Sinn Fein. That party had already suffered something of a humiliation in the Westminster elections of 1924 when it took only 46,257 votes, and in the 1925 elections Sinn Fein secured only two seats while the nationalists took ten. Meanwhile the Speaker of the Northern Ireland House of Commons, Hugh O'Neill, wrote asking the archbishop of Armagh to appoint a catholic chaplain to parliament now that some catholics had taken their seats. This O'Donnell refused to do.[10] Although Devlin and McAllister found their participation in the Belfast parliament a frustrating experience[11] they were joined by other like-minded nationalists in October 1927. This move was partly facilitated by Fianna Fail having entered the Dail in August that year.

By that time the boundary commission had shown itself not to be the instrument whereby catholic grievances on the border issue would be resolved by peaceful means. The Cosgrave government had accepted partition as a *fait accompli* as early as 1924 and expected little or no adjustment in the territorial arrangements laid down in the 1920 Act. It could also be argued that catholics in the Belfast area were anxious to have as many of their co-religionists as possible kept in Northern Ireland as a means of offering some sort of mutual protection. Thus the border remained.[12]

There was some ambivalence in the attitude of the hierarchy towards the border and the Northern Ireland state. Some bishops such as O'Donnell and Joseph MacRory of Down and Connor would rail from time to time against what they took to be a deliberate policy of exclusion of catholics from official positions in the state, either in the judiciary[13] or in public employment. Others, such as Bernard

---

[10] AAA, O'Neill to O'Donnell, 29 April 1925.

[11] Devlin had complained in the Belfast House of Commons in the autumn of 1926: 'We [catholics] have no place in the administration of the province whose laws we are supposed to accept, and do accept. I do not think that the representations we make have the slightest possible effect'. Quoted in Farrell, *Northern Ireland: The Orange State*, p. 109.

[12] In J.J. Lee's words, '[It was] begot by violence. It would beget violence. It would be held by violence.' *Ireland, 1912–1985: Politics and Society* (Cambridge, 1989), p. 149.

[13] When the catholic Lord Chief Justice died in 1925, no other catholic was to sit in the Northern Ireland Supreme Court until Mr Justice Shiel was appointed in 1949.

O'Kane of Derry, preached an outright hostility and rejection of the state and all it stood for. In his consecration address in September 1926 he referred to the 'anomaly and absurdity' by which one part of his diocese 'was in one kingdom and the remainder in another state'. He undertook as a feature of his episcopacy to work for a united Ireland whether this met with approval or not![14] Of course catholic churchmen were quite capable of arguing both positions simultaneously without any hint of inconsistency, demanding both justice for catholics in Northern Ireland and the abolition of the border. Complaints and a sense of ill-treatment at the hands of the 'protestant state' became a constant feature of catholic self-understanding in relation to Northern Ireland. At an ecclesiastical level this was at times shared by catholics south of the border. The joint pastoral letter issued by all the bishops of the country from the fourth synod of Maynooth in August 1927 complained that catholics in the north were not being accorded their rights as citizens.

The abolition of proportional representation in Northern Ireland parliamentary elections in 1929 became yet one more source of catholic discontent with the northern state. On the number of seats lost by the catholic nationalist community it had negligible influence. The real purpose of its elimination was to prevent the fragmentation of unionist opinion. The 'first past the post' system ensured continuous rule for one party for as long as the northern parliament survived.

By the late 1920s the catholic community had settled down to weather the storm of opposition it had come to expect from its dealings with the protestant-Unionist populace. The climate of opinion within Ulster catholicism by the end of the decade was such that the community seemed almost content to play the part of a hard-pressed and powerless minority, which had willy nilly been forced to look inward and draw on its own religious and cultural strengths as a means of survival. Such convictions had been strengthened politically by the formation of the League of the North, an anti-partionist group formed in May 1928 and presided over by Joe Devlin and archdeacon Tierney, the parish priest of Enniskillen. This also marked the dominance of the Church in catholic political affairs, a position not surrendered till well into the 1960s. The League conducted its affairs in such a way that 'in effect it was a Catholic party claiming to represent the Catholic population without distinction of class or politics but therefore in practice representing the Catholic Church and the Catholic middle class.'[15]

---

[14] *Catholic Directory* (1927), p. 615.
[15] Farrell, *The Orange State*, p. 116.

All this is in contrast to the hopeful musing of prelates such as O'Donnell who in the mid-1920s had referred to a new generation of unionists from whom catholics could obtain their rights. At the same time he was convinced that 'when the existing order has been sufficiently tried, and good men have put forth their best endeavours in the North and South, division will cease . . . and Ireland will be one in the struggle for . . . a better existence.'[16] The Church also was experiencing a new generation of leadership. Logue died and was replaced as archbishop by O'Donnell who received the cardinal's hat in December 1925. By October 1927 he too was dead and was succeeded by Joseph MacRory, whose replacement in Down and Connor was Daniel Mageean.

These developments in ecclesiastical leadership were matched by progress in other areas of Church life. In March 1926 the Society of African Missions opened a seminary in Drumantine near Newry and gave the north the only senior theological centre that it was ever to possess. Concern for 'foreign missions' had already seen the foundation in Belfast in October 1923 of the Apostolic Work Society whose aim was to provide help for missionary activity abroad. It was affiliated to the *Opera Apostolica* in Rome in 1926, and received the benefits of various papal indulgences for its members. Another organisation which had its origins in the unionist-dominated north was the Knights of St Columbanus, whose proclaimed aim was to foster 'a Catholic conscience to be applied to all the living problems of the day, and to secure adequate recognition for Catholic doctrines and practices in all phases of life social, public, commercial and professional'.[17] Despite these admirable sentiments, the organisation often gave the impression of being little more than a professional club for the catholic business classes. The objectives of the Knights were linked to the ideals of 'Catholic Action' in Europe and America, a movement seeking to bring catholic influence to bear on every aspect of social and political life.

The 1920s saw a great mushrooming of catholic organisations in the north of Ireland doubtless as part of the process whereby the community held the state at a distance and developed its own alternative society within the Orange-dominated environment. The Catholic Arts Guild, the Catholic Young Men's Society, the Legion of Mary (introduced in 1927), the Catholic Boy Scouts, the Holy Childhood Society, even a Catholic Billiards League—these and a host of other societies contributed to the one end of preserving a distinct catholic ethos in the protestant state.

---

16 *Derry Journal*, 26 Sept. 1926.
17 *Irish News Supplement*, 1955, p. 52.

It would be wrong to suggest that throughout the 1920s the catholic Church and the Northern Ireland state were always mutually antagonistic. Lord Londonderry and archbishop O'Donnell had a warm personal relationship and dined at each other's table. When O'Donnell arrived back in Armagh on 23 December 1925 having been made a cardinal he was greeted with the sounding of a general salute by a bugler of the Royal Ulster Rifles. In August 1926 on a visit to Warrenpoint the cardinal was presented with an address by the urban district council, despite the Orange character of that body. At O'Donnell's death lord Craigavon sent a telegram of sympathy to the dean and chapter of Armagh, courtesies also shown at the time of Logue's demise.

Not all the legislative acts of the Belfast parliament met with catholic resistance. In July 1925 the Fr Matthew (temperance) Union, meeting in Armagh, praised the good effect of the recent temperance legislation in the six counties, which closed public houses on the sabbath, and hoped that the Free State government would follow the example of the northern parliament. On the whole however the 1920s were to reinforce the mutual hostility which marked the relations between the two communities for the rest of the history of the Belfast parliament. Catholic antipathy to the state was matched by protestant mistrust of the traitorous intentions of catholics. At the back of this was a continued deep-seated fear of Rome and the papacy. Protestant suspicions were thus heightened by the appointment of a Free State minister at the Vatican in July 1929, and the arrival six months later of a papal nuncio in Dublin. Cardinal MacRory was in fact opposed to the appointment of a nuncio since he felt that it would mean too much Roman interference in Irish affairs. The Free State government was also anxious to make clear to the Holy See that its envoy would not be expected to meddle in the affairs of Northern Ireland.[18]

Catholics and the state

The climate of fear and suspicion between the two communities could at times be aggravated by the injudicious pronouncements of leading churchmen. The celebrations to mark the centenary of the Catholic Emancipation Act of 1829 were fully exploited by the northern bishops, and by MacRory in particular, to attack the Northern Ireland state.[19] In an outburst against the fact that the Church of

[18] Dermot Keogh, *The Vatican, the Bishops and Irish Politics, 1919–39* (Cambridge, 1986), pp. 142 and 155.

[19] MacRory's Lenten pastoral in 1929 demonstrated the extent of his dislike of partition and the British connection. He commented on the 1829 Act: Some may regard the

Ireland claimed to be the historic successor to the legacy of St Patrick, MacRory asserted that it was doubtful if the protestant Churches were even part of the Church of Christ. This remark, delivered in a lecture at Armagh on 17 December 1931, needless to say caused widespread and bitter indignation and occasioned a long, and frankly tedious, newspaper controversy. The capacity for insult was not the preserve of one community only. Archdeacon Kerr of Dromore, among many to respond for the Church of Ireland, claimed that 'Romanism is just a gigantic institution more dangerous than any tyranny that ever menaced mankind. . . . We charge Rome with deluding people by corrupting the true faith . . .'[20]

MacRory's opinion of the protestant Churches did not represent all Irish catholic thinking on the matter. Archbishop Byrne of Dublin, defending the application of anti-divorce legislation in the Free State to protestants as well as catholics, said that it did so because protestants too were part of the Church of Christ. Many northerners however gave the cardinal's remarks an unqualified welcome.[21] In that year there had already been anti-catholic riots in Portadown, Armagh and Lisburn, and protestant Church leaders were hardly conspicuous in condemning their co-religionists for the outrages.

In October the bishops had found it necessary to issue a joint pastoral warning catholics of the dangers of communism and the militant socialist-leaning republican group Saor Eire, which had been founded the previous month, and a general injunction against the IRA. 'You have no need to be told', the bishops addressed the faithful, 'that there is in active operation amongst us a society of a militarist character, whose avowed object is to overthrow the state by force of arms.' Such activity was forbidden by catholic teaching. The pastoral was also issued to coincide with the Westminster elections, and its application to the affairs of northern Ireland was spelt out by an editorial in the *Irish News* which stipulated that only by constitutional means could governments be changed.[22]

The repudiation of both communism and the IRA was to be a constant theme of the pronouncements of northern churchmen throughout

---

right then secured of sitting in a foreign parliament as but another step towards our country's denationalization . . . while others again may maintain that especially here in the Six Counties we are not emancipated yet. . . .'

[20] Quoted in *The Irish Presbyterian*, February 1932, vol. 37, no. 2.

[21] Their attitude is well summarised in a letter from Daniel Mageean of Down and Connor to MacRory: 'I admire hugely how you are striking your enemy hip and thigh. . . . All your friends here are delighted—when they meet, they ask each other with the joy of battle in their eyes: "Did you see the Cardinal's letter?" I congratulate you most heartily'. AAA, Mageean to MacRory, 23 Dec. 1931. The letter referred to appeared in the *Belfast Telegraph* on 22 December, as did MacRory's reply to his critics.

[22] *The Irish News*, 19 October 1931.

the period. MacRory and Mageean frequently returned to the topic in pastoral letters in the 1930s. However, Mageean was also careful to lambast 'capitalist industrialism' as the cause of irreligion in Ireland and elsewhere. Bishop Patrick Finegan of Kilmore said in June 1933 that the IRA was anxious to get communism into the country, and he further disavowed the suggestion from that organisation that the catholic bishops were anti-nationalist in their politics.[23] Bishop MacKenna of Clogher argued in a similar fashion in February 1934 in a Lenten pastoral which was a sustained attack on 'the men of violence'. Political violence was, in the bishop's words 'the very gravest of sins against the law of God'. Once again he reminded catholics that organisations which promoted violence were 'sinful associations' and therefore under the 'ban' of the Church.

Not that the IRA took these challenges lying down. Several days before the October 1931 pastoral was issued the 'Secretary to the Army Council' wrote to MacRory condemning various episcopal pronouncements against militant republicanism as 'extremely uncharitable'. He further hoped that the bishops would not 'lend their aid to the enemies of the nation's freedom, nor frustrate the people in their efforts to assert their inalienable rights and liberties'.[24] Frank Aiken also wrote to MacRory to express his horror at the pastoral. He stressed that excommunication of the IRA was no real answer to the problems faced by the north. He appealed to MacRory not to be content with condemnation 'of the results of the evils but to take active and fatherly steps to deal with the root causes'. Aiken proposed a conference of all nationalist groups in Ireland including Saor Eire and the IRA, and asked MacRory to chair it.[25] This idea surfaced again in 1933 by which time De Valera was in government and Aiken, a Co. Armagh man, was the Free State minister of defence.

Edmond Rice, a Co. Tyrone solicitor, proposed a conference of leaders of all nationalist political parties as a means of settling their differences especially over the north. Like Aiken before him, Rice persuaded cardinal MacRory to be the chairman of such a conference. Fine Gael and Labour favoured the idea but De Valera refused the request saying that the people had spoken in 1932 and all parties should accept that verdict. The irony of this was not lost on Rice who remarked to the cardinal: 'What a pity that the sentiments expressed

---

[23] *Catholic Directory* (1934), p. 610. The latter charge was a fairly consistent feature of republican spokesmen. Even Sean Lemass had stated: 'The question of the political influence of the Catholic clergy, an influence that throughout our history has been used with uncanny consistency to defeat the aspiration of Irish nationality, has to be faced sooner or later.' *Irish Independent*, 14 March 1925.

[24] AAA, MacRory papers XII, folder no 5.

[25] AAA, Aiken to MacRory, 19 October 1931.

in that letter of the President were not borne out by him from 1922 onwards up to the year 1932. What a lot of destruction in life and property would have been avoided'.[26] Many northern catholics felt that De Valera would reopen negotiations on the Treaty and the boundary commission, and although he was happy to receive northern delegations which pressed him on these matters his actions never matched the intensity of his declamations against partition. He contented himself with urging abstentionism as the main weapon against the northern administration.[27]

Within Northern Ireland catholic marginalisation was further emphasised by inflammatory speeches throughout the early 1930s by leading Unionist politicians. On 12 July 1932 the prime minister had stated: 'Ours is a protestant government and I am an Orangeman'. Basil Brooke's famous declaration in July 1933 that he employed no catholics on principle was echoed the following month by Sir Joseph Davidson, grand master of the Orange Order, saying that protestant employers must realise that every catholic they employed meant one less protestant vote. Brooke returned to this theme in a speech at Derry on 19 March 1934: 'When I made that speech last "twelfth" I did so after careful consideration. What I said was justified—I recommended people not to employ Roman Catholics who are ninety nine per cent disloyal'.[28] Two years later the Rev. J. Tolland, the deputy grand chaplain of the Orange Lodge, explained to his audience in a 12 July speech that 'Popery is the key to the problem of the peace of Ireland. Popery in the past has been the curse of Ireland and there will never be peace in Ireland while this popery reigns. You must get rid of it'.[29] Brooke himself had given vent to similar attitudes in 1932: 'The fight is only beginning and it will have to go on until Italy and the Church of Rome are submerged in the waters of the Mediterranean.'[30]

Although there is no suggestion that the government systematically tried to follow such advice, it is equally clear that the Unionist administration did not at this time try to facilitate catholic participa-

[26] AAA, Rice to MacRory, 16 November 1933.

[27] In this at least he was consistent. When in 1933 he was elected MP for South Down in the Stormont parliament he refused to take his seat.

[28] In a subsequent attempt to justify his position Brooke revealed that when he was a commandant in the 'B' Specials he had been informed 'whether rightly or wrongly' that there was a plot to kidnap his eldest son. 'The inference was that the kidnapping was not going to be carried out by the people of my own party. Therefore I took every precaution and got rid of every man in my place who I thought might betray me.' *Official Report of Debates Parliament of Northern Ireland: Commons*, vol. 16, 1116-7.

[29] Qutoted by 'Ultach' in 'The Real Case against Partition', *The Capuchin Annual* (1943), p. 301.

[30] Cf. *Fermanagh Herald*, 6 February 1932.

tion in the state. It maintained draconian 'emergency measures' well after any justification for them had evaporated. The National Council of Civil Liberties recorded in 1933 that the operations of the Special Powers Act had served merely to bring the freedom of subjects into contempt. In a damning report it accused the Northern government of having used the act to secure the domination of one particular political faction and at the same time curtail the lawful activities of its opponents. It had encouraged its own supporters in 'violence and bigotry' against the catholic community.

Catholic participation in the civil service and public employment has long been a controversial subject within Northern Ireland. Whatever mitigating reasons may be offered, it remains true that ministers of the crown did from time to time boast of how they had managed as far as possible to keep catholics out of state employment. In 1933 J.M. Andrews, the minister of labour and future prime minister, remarked that he had investigated the complaint that there were too many catholics employed as porters at Stormont, and found that of thirty-one men so engaged only one was a catholic, temporarily employed.

The following year lord Craigavon in a Stormont debate remarked that 'the employment of disloyalists . . . is prejudicial to the state and takes jobs away from loyalists'.[31] The Orange Order maintained a close oversight of appointments in the civil service, and Unionist politicians, but not nationalists, were appointed to civil service selection boards. At the lower end of the scale, by 1934 10 per cent of civil servants were catholics yet by the mid-1940s catholics accounted for only a little over 5 per cent in the administrative and technical grades. Patrick Shea, who was one of only two catholics in forty-eight years to attain the rank of permanent secretary in the civil service, in an otherwise sympathetic account of the workings of the Northern Ireland administration, records being told by the financial secretary to the ministry of finance in 1939 that it would be 'injudicious' for a catholic appointment to be made in his office.[32] Unionist politicians and especially Craigavon were, in the words of his cabinet secretary, 'over-responsive to almost any non-catholic pressure group in the province'.[33] Much of that pressure was anti-catholic. This led Ernest

[31] *Offical Reports of Debates*, vol. 16, 1095.

[32] *Voices and the Sound of Drums: An Irish autobiography* (Belfast, 1986), pp. 142–3. Although Shea admits discrimination on religious grounds in the civil service he believes that the villains of the piece were politicians and the Orange Order, rather than public officials. 'The influence of Orangeism was, I believe, considerable, often malevolent, and always an impediment to good government' (p. 198).

[33] Paul Bew, Peter Gibbon, Henry Patterson, *The State in Northern Ireland, 1921–72: Political Forces and Social Classes* (Manchester, 1979), p. 83.

Blythe to remark that the 'Ulster' government was not responsible for protestant bigotry in the north, but rather it was such bigotry which created the northern government.[34]

In a famous exchange in the Stormont parliament in April 1934, Craigavon justified the bigotry by declaring: 'In the South they boast of a Catholic state. They still boast of Southern Ireland being a Catholic State. All I boast of is that we are a Protestant Parliament and a Protestant State.'[35] In the following year in a St Patrick's Day broadcast De Valera remarked that Ireland 'remains a Catholic nation'; this is taken as proof by some commentators of the sectarian nature of southern Irish society.[36] But the President was in fact contrasting the attitude of Irish people to the state with the 'state worship' then in vogue in some continental countries. Later in the same speech he adverted to the 1916 'proclamation' of independence of the Irish republic which saw Ireland as 'cherishing all its children equally'.[37] Irrespective of what the Church liked to think about the Free State, politicians often made clear that they would not tolerate an unqualified assumption that Southern Ireland was 'a catholic state'. William Cosgrave in a long letter to MacRory in March 1931 makes this clear. Whatever the desires of the bishops might be the government was determined to operate a non-sectarian policy in public appointments.[38] Cosgrave further complained of the hostility of some sections of the catholic press to this policy.

Northern protestant trepidation over the Free State and Catholicism was increased by the spectacle of the eucharistic congress in Dublin in 1932. At the opening reception in Dublin Castle, to which the governor-general was pointedly not invited, De Valera knelt to kiss the ring of the papal legate cardinal Lorenzo Lauri. The congress was an occasion for catholic triumphalism on both sides of the border. Many catholic streets in towns throughout the north were bedecked with bunting, and mini-altars were erected at which people gathered nightly for the recitation of the rosary and other prayers. The bishop of Namur, president of the permanent committee for international eucharistic congresses, told the congregation at the opening mass in the pro-cathedral in Dublin on 22 June: 'The Irish people remained true to Christ in the face of the most terrible persecutions, and bore toil and suffering, chains and death itself, rather than abandon the Faith.'[39]

---

[34] *The Capuchin Annual* (1943), p. 344.
[35] *Parliamentary Debates Northern Ireland*, vol. 16, p. 1095.
[36] Cf. Kennedy, *The Widening Gulf*, p. 167.
[37] *Irish Times*, 18 March 1935.
[38] AAA, MacRory papers, 28 March 1931.
[39] *Catholic Directory* (1933), p. 617.

It is estimated that as many as 100,000 northerners travelled to Dublin for the main mass of the congress in Phoenix Park on 26 June. The progress of some pilgrims was interrupted by violent sectarian attacks, the most serious being in Ballymena, Belfast, Larne, Lisburn and Portadown. Policing was inadequate in all cases and a number of catholics needed treatment in hospital. The attacks are significant not because of the injuries, which by Northern Ireland standards were minor, but because they revealed the obvious hatred of catholicism as such on the part of many protestants. Isolated attacks continued throughout that summer and in October bishop Mulhern of Dromore issued a strongly worded protest 'against the outrages to which the Catholic section of the people have been recently subjected in Ballynahinch and in various other parts of this diocese by assaults upon their persons, interference with the freedom of public worship and organised attempts to deprive them of the ordinary right of citizens.'[40]

There is some evidence that those arrested for their part in the attacks on the pilgrims going to the eucharistic congress were treated with undue leniency owing to an arrangement between the minister of home affairs Sir Dawson Bates and the chief crown solicitor.[41] To many in Northern Ireland the bishop of Namur's words seemed not so such a recalling of the past but a description, however overstated, of present reality.[42]

The sectarian violence which had become so much a feature of Ulster life flared again in the summer of 1935 when the silver jubilee of the accession of George V was being celebrated. In the Belfast riots that year thirteen people lost their lives, most in fact protestant, and 514 catholic families were intimidated to the extent of being forced to leave their homes. One protestant family suffered a similar fate. One of the more bizarre pronouncements that year was made by A.J. Babington, the attorney-general, at the trial of those accused of shooting dead John McKeirnan on 21 September. Babington observed that McKeirnan was 'a publican and a Roman Catholic and therefore liable to assassination'.[43] The government showed some recognition of the threat to the catholic community when it erected a physical barrier called a 'peace line' to prevent attacks on catholic areas of Belfast. It was removed after several months.

[40] *Catholic Directory* (1933), p. 657.

[41] Bew *et al.*, *The State in Northern Ireland*, p. 91.

[42] It must be noted however that at least one prominent Unionist politician, Sir Edward Archdale, repudiated the attacks on the pilgrims. In a speech on the 12 July he referred to 'the silly attacks on unoffensive people going to a great religious festival [which have] done our cause a great harm'. *Belfast News Letter*, 13 July 1932.

[43] Boyd, *Holy War in Belfast*, p. 217.

Lord Craigavon refused to hold an independent investigation into the causes of the riots, in spite of being pressed to do so by influential catholics. A delegation from Belfast which included T.J. Campbell who had become the leader of northern 'constitutional nationalists' on Joe Devlin's death in 1934, Fr Arthur Ryan a lecturer in scholastic philosophy at Queen's University, and Fr George McKillop, administrator of St Peter's Belfast, presented the case for an independent inquiry to a meeting of Westminster MPs as late as June 1936. A majority of those present voted in favour of a resolution to that effect but Stanley Baldwin the prime minister turned down the request on the grounds that it was a matter for the Northern Ireland government.

Notwithstanding the somewhat hostile conditions of northern life and the depression years, catholic Church life remained as vigorous as ever and showed signs of increasing confidence. A large congregation assembled at Clonard monastery in Belfast in June 1931 to mark the 1500th anniversary of the council of Ephesus. In March 1932 the first public procession of the blessed sacrament through the streets of Armagh attracted a crowd of 20,000. A few days previously the foundation stone was laid for a new church in Derry, to be a chapel of ease for the cathedral parish; it was to take a year and a half to build at a cost of £18,000. The cathedral itself was finally consecrated in April 1936 after nearly a hundred years of trying to pay off the debt incurred in building it. In June 1934 nineteen bishops and archbishops gathered in Belfast for the Catholic Truth Society congress held in the city to coincide with a diocesan eucharistic congress. A crowd of 120,000 attended pontifical high mass at Beechmount on the Falls Road and heard bishop Mageean praise not only the faith of northern catholics but also the Belfast police commissioner and his officers for their courtesy in carrying out their 'arduous' duties during the congress.

Such public displays and celebrations of burgeoning catholic life were at times used as a reminder of catholic alienation from Ulster society past and present. At the centenary celebrations for St John the Baptist church in Moy, Co. Tyrone, in November 1933 Canon Johnson reminded the parishioners that their ancestors had attended Mass 'at the back of a hedge in the open country and later in a tiny building with its roof of thatch'. He added that the catholics of the parish were just emerging from a 'long dark age of persecution'.[44] Against the accusation that catholics built too many churches Fr P.J. Gannon told the congregation at St John's, Gilford, Co. Down, in May 1933 that such reproaches came from 'the descendants of

---

[44] *Catholic Directory* (1934), p. 641.

those who stole and desecrated the lovely temples raised by our forefathers'.

Those descendants were still quite capable of demonstrating their opposition to catholicism. In 1932, when the Catholic Truth Society had planned a 'missionary exhibition' in the Ulster Hall in Belfast, the Ulster Protestant League organised a number of protests against the event some of which turned into large and angry protestant gatherings in the city centre. Two of those responsible for the demonstrations, including the Church of Ireland rector of Dundrum, were charged with incitement. The scale of the opposition forced the cancellation of the exhibition, but the Church of Ireland dean of Belfast the Very Rev. W.S. Kerr. denounced the 'misguided protestants' who had deprived their fellow-citizens of their right to use the Ulster Hall. He said they should be ashamed to talk of liberty if they claimed it only for themselves and denied it to others.[45]

Further antagonism to the catholic community came in 1935 with a boycott organised by the Orange Order of catholic businesses in and around Belfast and other towns in the province. This gave rise to additional feelings of frustration, expressed by bishop Mageean in a pastoral letter issued on 3 March. 'Catholics in this part of Ireland have grown accustomed to being persecuted on account of their religion . . . Within the last few months a boycott of Catholics has been openly advocated by men in authority; . . . by leaders of industry and commerce, by members of local councils and even by men holding high executive office in the State.'

When cardinal MacRory visited Derry in April 1936 there were some ugly scenes and he was greeted with booing and scuffles from some protestants. Another troublesome incident was the attempt to bomb St Teresa's church, Glen Road, Belfast, in the early morning of 21 September 1937. Little damage was done and no one was injured. Intolerance of catholicism could at times be seen to emanate directly from the governing classes. Soon after his consecration as bishop of Derry in October 1939, Neil Farren made an official visit to Strabane and was accorded a civic reception by the urban district council. The Stormont authorities took a dim view of this and surcharged the council for this 'waste' of public money. This action by the government may in part have been a reaction to Farren's address on that occasion. He had said that Strabane was the only part of his diocese in the north which had not been gerrymandered, and that 'in Derry, where we have 29,000 Catholics represented by eight, and 18,000 Protestants represented by twelve seats on the Corporation, and in Omagh where the Catholic majority is similarly pushed

[45] *Belfast Telegraph*, 4 June 1934.

aside, they envy Strabane . . .'[46]

The northern catholic community was not pre-occupied exclusively with its own affairs in those years. When the preparations were being made to adopt the 1937 constitution in the south of Ireland, some northerners attempted to have a say in the shape of the new Ireland. Cardinal MacRory was anxious that in the new constitution the catholic Church should be given every mark of recognition and favour. As is clear from the Armagh archives, he disliked acknowledgment being given to Jews and other 'sects' in the draft constitution, and he wrote to De Valera saying that the title 'the Church of Ireland' should not be allowed to remain. On this particular point the president replied: 'At this stage I am afraid it will be very difficult to make any change regarding the matter to which you refer. I will, however, give the whole question further careful consideration'.[47] Also preserved in the Armagh archives is a draft in MacRory's hand, on Nunciature paper, of his own version of the famous article 44 of the Irish constitution, now deleted, on the position of the catholic church in the state, a copy of which he sent to De Valera on 5 April 1937. There it is claimed that the state recognises catholicism as the religion of 93 per cent of the people of the twenty-six counties, and as the faith established by 'Our Divine Lord'. Wisely De Valera rejected this and persuaded Rome to do likewise.[48]

One other area of concern was the Spanish civil war. A number of the northern bishops addressed pastoral letters to their flocks on this issue. In particular they were concerned to head off any support for the socialists and communists in Spain. In March 1937 the bishop of Derry warned that a group in the catholic community was 'making every effort to draw off the sympathy of the people from the Insurgent forces and the Spanish Church. . . . They appear to be able to combine profession of the Catholic Faith with communism, a combination which Pius XI declares impossible'. In addition a substantial amount of money was raised to be sent for 'the relief of the Spanish Church'.

By 1938 northern nationalist hopes for the ending of partition were again raised by the prospect of the negotiations between De Valera and the British prime minister Neville Chamberlain over the 'treaty ports'. A letter from 'representative six county citizens' was sent to both men deploring partition and the 'useless parliament' in Belfast. It rehearsed the by now standard objections of catholics to the

---

[46] *Catholic Directory* (1940), pp. 667–8.

[47] AAA, De Valera to MacRory, 29 May 1937.

[48] MacRory pencilled a note on his draft indicating that his wording was rejected by the Free State authorities and by Pius XI 'in view [of] the Six Counties etc. . . .' Cf. also Keogh, *The Vatican, the Bishops and Irish Politics, 1919–39*, pp. 212–15.

northern state. The abolition of proportional representation, anti-catholic bias in education and employment, and the Special Powers Act all find a place in the letter.[49] A separate missive was sent to De Valera stressing that his conversations with Chamberlain should be used to 'right the grave injustice of Partition' and warning him that should that fail it would 'leave unchanged the intolerable position of almost half a million of your people in the North-East who are deprived of their natural rights as Irishmen'.[50] Bishop Mageean followed this with a pastoral letter six days later denouncing the Stormont regime and decrying its sole purpose as one of determination to keep alive 'those religious animosities that have so long disgraced the north-east corner of Ireland in the eyes of the civilised world'.

De Valera did press the partition issue in his initial meetings with Chamberlain,[51] but he quickly accepted that there was little room for manoeuvre. He was anxious to get agreement on the other outstanding differences between the Free State and Britain and was thus prepared to let the question of the border fade into the background after the first round of discussions. In February 1939 he told the Irish senate that he had definitively abandoned violence as a means of resolving the partition question. On the other hand he admitted that this was a question of feasibility rather than principle. If there was a way to rescue the catholics in the 'nationalist' areas of the six counties he would have tried to do so. Others were not to be dismayed by the magnitude of the task. The IRA, which had recently been active in Britain, now formed a northern command and with the onset of the Second World War it once again saw its opportunity to use physical force in the ongoing struggle with the 'Ulster' government.

A resort to violence

The IRA had been sporadically active since 1937. In protest against the visit of the new king and queen to Belfast in that year they burnt down twenty-eight customs posts along the border. On 11 July the following year members of that organisation took over the town of Maghera attacking the RUC station and injuring several constables. In 1939 it 'declared war' on Britain and by July it caused 127 explosions. The most serious was the Coventry bombing on 25 August which killed five and injured fifty. In Northern Ireland a raid by the

---

[49] A copy of this letter is among MacRory's papers in Armagh.

[50] *Irish News*, 21 February 1938.

[51] John Bowman, *De Valera and the Ulster Question, 1917–1973* (Oxford, 1982), pp. 160 ff.

IRA in February 1940 on the Ballykinlar military base in Co. Down was a spectacular propaganda coup and yielded a haul of 100 rifles. However only in March 1942 did the northern command settle on a systematic wartime campaign, led by Hugh McAteer brother of the future leader of the Nationalist party, which was to see the deaths of three of its members and five policemen.

IRA operations in the Free State also involved northern catholics among whom was Thomas Harte from Lurgan who in September 1940 was sentenced to death by a military tribunal for his part in IRA operations. One of the most controversial deaths in the campaign was that of the teenager Thomas Williams who was hanged in Belfast on 2 September 1942. Williams was one of six IRA members sentenced to death for their involvement in the shooting of constable Patrick Murphy on Easter Sunday, 5 April 1942. As a result of a reprieve campaign, which among other things involved the collection of 207,000 signatures on a petition, the other five had their death sentences commuted. A group of people kept vigil on the night before Williams died saying the rosary outside Crumlin Road gaol. The prison chaplain testified that Williams had gone to his death 'with the name of Jesus on his lips',[52] thus witnessing once more to the peculiar tradition of religious and ideological cohesion which was so much a mark of the 'republican movement' of those years.

The catholic authorities were not silent in the wake of the upsurge of republican violence, which was directed both at the northern state and the southern government. Bishop Farren in an address to the members of the Irish army barracks of Fort Dunree, Lough Swilly, Co. Donegal, on St Patrick's Day 1940 said that the IRA were not serving the cause of Ireland. Moreover they were against the Church and not helping to improve the lot of catholics in the six counties. However, the most vocal opposition to the IRA activity at that period came from the bishop of Waterford who in his Lenten pastoral issued on 4 February declared it to be a mortal sin to be a member of the IRA, and reminded such individuals that they could not be admitted to the sacraments.

The archbishop of Westminster, cardinal Arthur Hinsley, also felt compelled to denounce the IRA's campaign in England. In a statement issued on 25 June 1939 he said that the IRA bombings were 'savage, insane and cowardly' and he reminded catholics that because of the secret nature of the IRA its members automatically incurred excommunication. In response the 'secretary of the army council of the IRA', 'Patrick Fleming', wrote to Hinsley on 1 July saying:

[52] *Irish News*, 5 September 1942.

We are quite certain you are aware that the Cardinal Primate of Ireland [MacRory] has expressly stated that the occupation of our country by the armed troops of your country is an unwarrantable act of war . . . [and because of this] the Catholics of Ireland have been subjected to recurring campaigns of murder, arson and despoliation beside which the London incidents you condemn are insignificant.

Hinsley sent a copy of this letter to MacRory adding, 'It is true that I have publicly condemned . . . what is taking place in England. But it is not true that I have defended the Brit. Gov. or any other Gov. in Ireland'.[53]

Hinsley was obviously anxious not to ruffle the feathers of his fellow cardinal and the northern Irish bishops..For his part MacRory maintained fairly close links with the republican movement, so much so that the IRA asked him to act as an intermediary with De Valera's government. The IRA proposed that it would cease drilling and broadcasting 'War News' in the twenty-six counties and would call off the campaign in England. It also offered a three-month cessation of violence in Ireland, or longer if this was agreed to by the Irish government. In exchange it wanted all police activity against the IRA to cease and the release of IRA prisoners. It also asked for a conference with the southern government 'to explore the possibilities' of cooperation with De Valera towards achieving a republic.

MacRory submitted all these points to De Valera on 12 October 1940. In reply the Taoiseach said that before any negotiations the IRA should first recognise the government of the Irish Free State. He was also unsure if those members of the IRA who had approached MacRory actually spoke for the whole movement.[54] Even more remarkable was the IRA's approach to MacRory in the following year requesting a meeting between the cardinal and 'an accredited officer from the German Supreme Comman[d] at present in Ireland illegally'. In the margin of this letter the cardinal noted: 'I replied orally on phone to a friend of the writer that in my position as primate I couldn't see my way to agreeing to such a meeting'.[55]

At about the same time the Taoiseach and the Tanaiste, Sean T. O'Ceallaigh, received a delegation of 'north-eastern nationalists' led by a priest of the Armagh diocese, Fr Coyle, who kept the cardinal informed of what transpired. The lengthy memo which Coyle pro-

---

[53] AAA, Hinsley to MacRory, 5 July 1939.
[54] These points are marked in MacRory's hand on the document which he used to brief De Valera in October 1940 and which is among the cardinal's papers in Armagh.
[55] The letter purporting to be from 'C. Bean Cathal Brugha', sent on 20 October 1941, is kept in AAA.

duced of this meeting gives insight into both the tensions within the
northern catholic community in the early years of the war, and the
growing disillusionment of some sections of Ulster catholicism with
the republican rhetoric of Fianna Fail. The delegation identified three
strands of opinion among northern catholics. Some supported the
IRA and its current campaign, others wanted to assist the Northern
Ireland government in its defensive measures against a possible
German invasion, and a third group was content to trust Fianna Fail
and give its support to the Free State military forces. De Valera made
it clear that he was against the view that 'England's difficulty is
Ireland's opportunity', and that it was too risky to think of reuniting
the country by force. When pressed by the northerners as to what
sacrifices he was prepared to make in the interests of national unity,
he 'showed definite signs of impatience and told us he had done and
was doing all that was possible'.[56] On overall policy the Taoiseach
was very firm that northern catholics 'should not co-operate in the
defence measures or do anything that would suggest that Six County
Nationalists were prepared to make any efforts to maintain the present
regime'.[57]

That northern churchmen were not more vociferous in their condemnation of IRA violence at the outbreak of the Second World War
may be partly explained by their preoccupation with pressuring the
government not to introduce conscription into Northern Ireland, and
by their resistance to internment which the government had again
invoked as a means of dealing with the IRA threat. In December 1940
Mageean denounced the 'violation' of catholic homes by the
'representatives of what is called law and order'. The bishops suggested that those interned were allowed 'to lie there and rot in the
prisons of the Six Counties', saying that this was both tyrannical and
unjust. In his Lenten pastoral the following February he condemned
the raids on catholic homes by the police which he claimed were taking
place on a wide scale. He also claimed that individuals were detained
for hours on their way to work, and when they were finally released
and turned up at their place of employment they found that their jobs
had been given to others. MacRory's interventions through 1940 and
1941 tended to stress the injustice of partition, and on one occasion
went so far as to say that he hoped that the war would see it ended.[58]

Some historians of the period have emphasised that the German

---

[56] By 1942 bishop Mageean was voicing his concern that 'Our Catholic people in the
North have sometimes been painfully disappointed at the apparent apathy of the rest
of Ireland to their suffering and persecution . . .' *Capuchin Annual* (1943), p. 313.

[57] AAA, MacRory papers.

[58] *Catholic Directory* (1941), pp. 656–7.

bombing raids on Belfast in April and May 1940 had the effect of reducing sectarian tensions in Belfast as the communities tried to come to terms with the destruction and loss they were both enduring. The various changes in the Stormont government during the war did not however build on such goodwill. Craigavon died suddenly in November 1940 and his replacement as prime minister, J.M. Andrews, appointed two presbyterian clergymen to the cabinet, Professor R. Corkey and the Rev. Robert Moore, neither of whom was noted for sympathy with northern catholicism.

Andrews did not last long in the job and Basil Brooke succeeded to the premiership in May 1943. In 1947, speaking at a meeting in Derry, Brooke commended the local Unionist party for having set up a fund with the object of helping to prevent protestant-owned property from falling into catholic hands. Several years earlier the minister of home affairs William Lowry had been forced to make an abject apology for suggesting that an Orange hall in Portrush which had been used as a Mass centre for American servicemen would have to be fumigated.[59]

By the mid-1940s catholics were taking a more active part in the political process. Having consulted the cardinal towards the end of 1944 nationalist MPs decided to take their seats again in both Stormont and Westminster. The main concern for the Church was once more the question of education and the Northern Ireland government's intention to amend the education legislation in the province to bring it into line with the English Education Act of 1944.

The bishops condemned the government's educational proposals and were so worried about the consequences that two of them, Farren and Mageean, led a delegation to the minister of education at Stormont in September 1945 to complain that insufficient provision was being made for new school building in the proposed act. Given their experience, they disliked the idea of having to deal with local education authorities in the master of distribution of grants but they were happy to deal directly with the ministry. The idea of such a delegation was an unprecedented departure from previous practice and was uniquely galling for Mageean who tried as far as possible

---

[59] In his letter of apology to bishop Farren of Derry, Lowry said: 'Speaking with all reverence for a Faith I do not hold and with respect for what I believe to be the central mystery of that Faith, I assure your Lordship that no insult was intended by me to the American Catholic Chaplains in the exercise of their sacred functions or to those present'. Lowry to Farren, 4 Feb. 1944. While this is a most gracious letter it must also be remembered that Farren was in close touch with the American government and it was clearly important not to offend the Americans at this critical stage of the war. In 1947 he was awarded the US Medal of Freedom in recognition of his work for the spiritual welfare of Americans stationed in Northern Ireland during the war.

to have no dealings with the northern government. The minister promised to consider the points they raised.

It is important to record that there was some division among the bishops themselves in private over their attitude on the issue. Surprisingly MacRory, then approaching the end of his days, took a less strident line than the others and was willing to make some concession in return for increased monies for catholic education. He was prepared to accept the 'four and two' committee scheme if the government would give 75 per cent grants to catholic schools. The minister told him through an intermediary that the most they could expect would be 70 per cent since 'the opposition from the protestant churches who had handed over their schools would be too great for the cabinet to give 75%'.[60] In the event although the bishops condemned the white paper, it was finally enacted in 1947 and catholic schools received 65 per cent grants under its terms. The 'four and two' system which had been accepted by English catholics since 1902 was not at this stage imposed on catholic voluntary schools in northern Ireland. One casualty of the measure was the minister of education himself, who was eventually replaced in 1949 since he had seemed too disposed to listen to catholics for the taste of some of his Orange colleagues.

The Public Health Act of 1949 presented what the Church authorities took to be another challenge to the position of catholics in the state. Its intention was to introduce the national health service in line with the equivalent arrangements in England, and it was proposed that the Mater hospital in Belfast would be brought into the system. This raised a storm of protest with the Church accusing the government of 'theft', since the hospital would simply be appropriated and come under the control of the local health authority. The senior clergy of Belfast pointed out that in the English legislation there was provision for 'voluntary' hospitals, and they asked only that the Mater be treated in the same way as denominational hospitals elsewhere in the United Kingdom.[61] Although the concern was to preserve the 'catholic ethos' of the Mater, the hospital also catered for the protestant population in its immediate vicinity in the Crumlin

---

[60] AAA, Canon John Macaulay to MacRory, 16 Jan. 1945. Macaulay, who was parish priest of St Malachy's Belfast, also revealed in a subsequent letter the attitude of certain circles of the Belfast clergy and laity to the government. He told the cardinal on 29 January that from his contact with 'leading priests and laymen of unquestionable integrity' the education debate 'may be used as an occasion to raise a more fundamental issue, namely, the general attitude of the Catholic Church towards the Northern Government. Their contention is that a more conciliatory attitude on the part of the church would best promote the religious, educational, and social wellbeing of the Catholic community'.

[61] *Irish News*, 20 September 1947.

Road and Shankill Road and was also dependent, as the archbishop of Armagh pointed out, 'on the generous help of many of their non-Catholic brethren'.[62] The government capitulated to catholic pressure and allowed the hospital to remain outside the system.

Although catholics were beginning to be more active in the political life of Northern Ireland their energies were still directed against the border. The Anti-Partition League was formed at the wish of a large gathering of clergy and laity in Dungannon on 15 November 1945, to which the bishops of Derry and Dromore sent messages of support. It was the first attempt to give a coherent focus to nationalist aspirations. The APL had a Belfast headquarters and local chapters throughout the north. As was the norm at that time it was heavily dominated by the clergy. One of the ironies of its inauguration was that two weeks later one of its founding fathers T.J. Campbell accepted a county court judgeship. His place as the effective leader of the nationalist group in the Stormont parliament was taken by James McSparren.

Political developments in the rest of the island also had some bearing on the status of the Ulster catholic community. The 1948 elections returned a coalition government of Fine Gael and the recently formed Clan na Poblachta, with John A. Costello as Taoiseach. Costello indicated his intention on a visit to Canada in that year of declaring Southern Ireland a republic outside the Commonwealth. Almost immediately Basil Brooke announced elections in the north in protest. In support of anti-partition candidates in Northern Ireland the government in the south organised a country-wide 'chapel collection' which netted £46,000. The idea of the collection was ill received by the northern Unionists and the election campaign which followed was the most violent since 1921.

The late 1940s marked further growth in the self-confidence of the catholic community and witnessed yet more expansion of catholic church building and renewal. It also saw the opening of the first contemplative monastery in the north since the reformation. Our Lady of Bethlehem abbey was founded by the Cistercian monks from Mount Mellary, Co. Waterford, in the protestant heartland of Portglenone near Ballymena in Co. Antrim in 1948. On 5 June the following year the first priory of the Servite Order in Ireland was solemnly dedicated at Benburb, in Co. Tyrone, in a ceremony attended by thousands of people from all over Ireland. On 31 August 1947 40,000 people had turned up to attend the final religious festivities to mark the golden jubilee of the foundation in Clonard monastery in Belfast of the Holy Family Confraternity. The Falls

[62] *Irish News*, 1 September 1947.

Road was bedecked with religious symbols and papal flags for a week
in a display said to have been unparalleled since the Eucharistic Congress of 1932.

It was perhaps some mark of the growing rapprochement between
the catholic Church and the Northern Ireland state that at the funeral
of cardinal MacRory on 17 October 1945 the Governor of Northern
Ireland was represented by Sir Norman Stronge, the speaker of the
Stormont House of Commons. MacRory was replaced in Armagh by
John D'Alton, former president of Maynooth and bishop of Meath.
Not since the appointment of Anthony Blake in 1758 had a Connaught man succeeded to the primacy. D'Alton's tenure was to mark
a further thawing in the relations between Church and state in the
north, since on the whole he was more disposed to the northern
administration than it had been either psychologically or emotionally
possible for his predecessor to be.

Despite this increase in confidence catholics continued to feel
put upon by the Unionists, not without some justification. Addressing
a Unionist convention in Enniskillen in April 1948, the local MP,
E.C. Ferguson, reported that the nationalist majority in the county
was down by 336 and stood at 3,684. However despite this Ferguson
was able to proclaim: 'This is a Unionist county. The atmosphere is
Unionist. The boards and properties are nearly all controlled by
Unionists and still there is a millstone around our necks. [Unionists
must] take whatever steps, however drastic, to wipe out this
Nationalist majority.'[63]

Clerical ambivalence and lay contentment?

In the aftermath of the war there were some signs that the catholic
community was beginning to settle into an acceptance of the political
facts of life about its situation in the Northern Ireland state. In this
cardinal D'Alton's leadership of the community was important. For
their part however the Unionist authorities did not always respond to
the catholic community with that generosity which, given their position as an unassailable majority government having to deal with an
at times recalcitrant political minority, might have seemed prudent.
The Safeguarding of Employment Act 1947, though applying equally
to immigrants from England and Scotland, was in the first instance
intended to exclude people from the south of Ireland, in an effort to
prevent an increase in nationalist votes. This was emulated by the
Franchise Act the same year which increased the number of possible
business votes to the advantage of the protestant unionist community.

[63] Peadar Livingstone, *The Fermanagh Story* (Enniskillen, 1969), pp. 364–5.

Even in 1964 the local government franchise was smaller than the Westminster electorate by some 220,000. Catholics thus felt discriminated against in the exercise of their electoral rights.

Although the Northern Ireland Housing Trust, set up in 1945, allocated housing on a non-discriminatory basis, local authority policies in providing homes still operated on sectarian lines. The Unionist administrations in Armagh, Derry and Omagh refused to build new houses for catholics outside nationalists wards. By 1958 65 per cent of those on the housing waiting list in Belfast were catholics. In June 1956 when the minister of labour Ivan Neill announced family allowance increases in line with British legislation, he also proposed to abolish payments for fourth and subsequent children. Since catholics tended to have larger families than protestants the proposal was seen as sectarian in intention. A major political row forced the government to back down. In this instance the presbyterian Church also intervened and sent a delegation to Stormont to complain about the proposed change on the grounds of its unfairness to the catholic community.[64]

Discrimination in employment was long to remain a grievance among catholics in Northern Ireland. The department of labour accepted a religious bar as sufficient grounds for employers to turn down prospective workers, and individuals refused work on the basis of their religion would continue to qualify for state benefit if the reason for such refusal was that they were catholic. Despite higher emigration from the catholic community, unemployment among catholics in the 1950s stood as an average at 10.8 per cent, as against 4.6 per cent for Northern Ireland as a whole. West of the Bann rates were higher owing to local conditions not always related to immediate discrimination, but due partly to long neglect by the Stormont government because of the preponderance of nationalists in the area.

The church continued to feel hard done by in the matter of education. When the government pointed out in November 1953 that in giving 65 per cent grants for new intermediate schools it was being more generous to catholics in Northern Ireland than governments in other countries, bishop Eugene O'Doherty of Dromore responded that this merely 'showed less justice for catholics in those countries than here'! Despite the admittedly generous allowances made for catholic schooling the financial burden on the community was none

---

[64] *Minutes of the General Assembly of the Presbyterian Church*, 1956, pp. 20 and 43. Not all presbyterians took such an enlightened view. In a senate debate in October 1964 the former education minister Professor R. Corkey, himself a presbyterian minister of good standing, said that parents of large families ought to be fined for having so many children.

the less considerable. In opening the new St Patrick's primary school in North Queen Street, Belfast, on 15 February 1955 bishop Mageean said that although the government had paid £80,000 towards the cost of the school the parish had still to make a contribution of £49,000.[65]

Nor did the Church see the social legislation of the state as wholly beneficial. A number of the leading bishops, including cardinal D'Alton, were interested in 'the social question', but were inclined to see too much state provision as an interference with the rights of the individual. Bishop Farren launched a scathing attack on the welfare state in Northern Ireland in April 1951, in the course of which he denounced much of the prevailing social legislation as inspired by Nazi and Communist materialism.[66] Farren was also thinking of the recently enacted Public Order Act which he said was aimed against catholics. Farren had run a very successful catholic social services centre in Derry from 1947 which in time even attracted praise from unionist politicians. The key to understanding his and the other bishops' attitude was their belief that even social service provision was a realm of activity for the Church and not the state.

Cardinal D'Alton spoke at the opening of a new parish hall in Armagh in January 1955 of the state extending its control into every aspect of life with the negative consequence that society was excessively centralised. He advocated as a counterpoise the development of smaller units of political organisation such as the parish, which would enable people to have a sense of belonging to a definite community. In many ways these views were farseeing and not the conservative product of a moribund and reactionary Church as some have suggested. The underlying problem however was the issue of control in society. In this the bishops could not be said to be especially enlightened. We have seen how in practice the issue of catholic education meant control of education by the clergy though paid for by the state and the catholic laity. The bishops too often saw themselves as the sole arbitrators of all social interaction. Farren at a confirmation ceremony in May 1953 complained of the dangers of creeping 'pagan atheistic civilisation':

> 'It is the duty of Catholic men to see that when the bishops lay down a particular line of conduct as proper for christian people either in administering the Government or in the private practice of individuals, that the bishops will have behind them the full support of the right-thinking christian community'.[67]

[65] *Irish News*, 16 February 1955.

[66] J.H. Whyte, *Church and State in Modern Ireland, 1923–1979*, 2nd edn, p. 251.

[67] *Catholic Directory* (1954), p. 714. Three years later he rejected the notion that catholics could make up their minds for themselves on such issues as the amelioration

With the growth of the catholic middle classes in the 1950s some at least in that group were prepared to re-evaluate their traditional hostility to the union and moved towards an acceptance of the political *status quo*. Thus many catholics began to vote for the Northern Ireland Labour Party although it had by now shown itself to be in favour of partition. In the local government election in Belfast in the mid-1950s there were no nationalist candidates, and catholics contented themselves with voting for moderate Unionist candidates to keep out the more extreme elements. Cardinal D'Alton in a refinement of traditional catholic nationalism proposed in 1957 that a united Ireland should seek readmission to the British Commonwealth.[68] This as D'Alton saw it would be part of a wider package which envisaged a federal Ireland within the then nascent European Economic Community, and the opening of bases in Ireland to the North Atlantic Treaty Organization.[69] A growing acquiescence in the British connection was highlighted on the accession of Queen Elizabeth II when the cardinal issued a statement saying:

> I am sure that Irishmen of all shades of opinion . . . will join in good wishes to the young Queen who was called to the throne in circumstance of great personal sorrow. It is my earnest prayer that God will protect and guide her in her exalted office, and that her reign may be the opening of a new era of prosperity. . . .[70]

By the late 1950s it was suggested that many northern catholics had 'abandoned their messianic hopes' of a united Ireland: 'They prefer to use their own efforts to achieve a tolerable present rather than wait behind the barricades for a heavenly Nationalist hereafter'.[71] But not all aspects of catholic life indicated that Northern Ireland was a political paradise. In Derry city no position of major responsibility was held by a catholic. When in November 1959 a prominent Unionist politician Sir Clarence Graham suggested that 'suitable' catholics might be allowed to join the Unionist Party and even be selected as candidates for elected office he was rebuked by the grand master of the Orange Order, Sir George Clarke. Clarke declared that it was difficult to see how a catholic 'with the vast differences in our religious outlook, could be either acceptable within the Unionist

---

of social distress, saying 'private judgement' was a consequence of the reformation and led to fragmentation and disunity. *Catholic Directory*, (1957), p. 642.

[68] Bowman, *De Valera and the Ulster Question*, p. 292.

[69] Bernard J. Canning, *Bishops of Ireland*, p. 53.

[70] *The Catholic Directory* (1954), p. 717.

[71] Desmond Fennell, *The Northern Catholic: an Inquiry*, 1956 (no pagination). Fennell's booklet began as a series of articles in the *Irish Times* in the late summer of 1956.

Party as a member or for that matter, bring himself unconditionally to support its ideals'.[72]

While there were grounds for continued catholic rancour against the northern state the community was not entirely disaffected. Catholic nationalists did control local government in areas such as Downpatrick, Keady, Limavady, Newry and Strabane. Throughout the 1950s the number of catholic students at Queen's Belfast increased, as did the number of catholic doctors, lawyers and school teachers, leaving aside traditional catholic occupations such as book-making and pub ownership. In certain ways however the ability of the catholic middle class to direct the community's political fortunes was restricted by a recidivist republican element which was not prepared to have any 'accommodation' with the Unionist regime.

In the mid-Ulster by-election in 1956 the Anti-Partition League candidate was rejected in favour of the Sinn Fein prisoner Tom Mitchell even though the Church had given its undiluted support to the 'constitutional nationalists'. This had followed the pattern of the Westminster general election of 1955 when the Nationalist Party decided not to contest the general election and left the field clear for Sinn Fein. The republicans secured two seats in the west of the province on an abstentionist platform, but its two members Tom Mitchell and Phil Clarke were in prison for their part in an attack on Omagh barracks and so their seats were awarded by the electoral court to their Unionist opponents, thus giving the Unionist party all twelve Northern Ireland seats for the first time since 1924. By 1959 Sinn Fein's electoral support had dwindled from its 1955 height of 24 per cent to just 11 per cent.

By the late 1950s the constitutional nationalists were again agitating for electoral support, and one should not underestimate the negative effect of the IRA border campaign then in full swing on the decline in Sinn Fein popularity. Although there was some IRA activity in 1955 the border campaign began in earnest in 1956 and by its end in 1962 had caused the deaths of six RUC policemen and eleven IRA members. The total cost to the Northern Ireland exchequer in compensation and security in those years was in the region of £11 million. It is estimated that as many as 250 IRA men were involved in the six years of the campaign.[73]

In response the Belfast government reintroduced internment between 1956 and 1961 which affected a total of 335 men.[74] De

---

[72] *Irish News*, 10 November 1959. Cf. also Farrell, *The Orange State*, p. 223. The prime minister Lord Brookeborough supported Clarke's views in the matter.

[73] Tim Pat Coogan, *The IRA*, 3rd edn (London, 1980), p. 246.

[74] Patrick Buckland, *A History of Northern Ireland*, p. 105.

Valera's party returned to power in the Republic in 1957 and on 7 July opened the Curragh as an internment camp which by the following year had 187 internees. One of the most widely publicised events of the various border incursions was the attack on Brookeborough barracks near the prime minister's home on 1 January 1957. Two IRA men were killed, Fergal O'Hanlan from Monaghan and Sean South from Garryowen in Limerick. South had been a member of An Realt, the Irish-speaking section of the Legion of Mary, and when his coffin was taken to Limerick for burial there was an enormous outpouring of public sympathy, much of it led by the clergy.

For their part the bishops had made clear the hierarchy's continued opposition to political violence. As early as Christmas 1955 D'Alton had appealed to 'our young men' not to resort to violence as a means of achieving national unity since this could only lead to bitterness. At a midnight mass in Derry bishop Farren had spoken in a similar vein. On Thursday 19 January 1956 the hierarchy issued a statement 'to be read at all Masses on Sunday 29' solemnly denouncing violence. It reminded catholics of the conditions for a just war and stressed that private individuals could not take up arms against a state since 'sacred scripture gives the right to bear the sword and to use it against evil doers to the supreme authority and to it alone'.[75]

The day after the statement was issued the *Irish News* sought in an editorial to interpret the bishops' intentions for northern catholics:

> Ireland owes much of its greatness to its achievements as a Catholic land. It cannot hold fast by this greatness if it becomes involved in civil strife or becomes a country of private armies. The bishops' statement is a significant signpost to the road its people must continue to travel as members of a Catholic nation.

Speaking at a meeting of Orangemen in Lisbellaw, Co. Fermanagh, on 20 January Brookeborough welcomed the bishops' forthright pronouncement but regretted that 'it had not been made long ago before the outrages and bloodshed took place which horrified all rightthinking people'.[76] Even before the IRA campaign was called off, an obscure Italian cardinal had been elected to succeed pope Pius XII in 1958. The brief reign of John XXIII was to have tremendous consequences for the Church in Ulster as in the rest of the world, and linked with political developments in Northern Ireland it looked at last as if catholics might begin to accept wholeheartedly the political reality of their situation in the north.

---

[75] *Catholic Directory* (1957), pp. 632–3. Cf. also Whyte, *Church and State*, p. 308.
[76] *Irish News*, 20 January 1956.

Catholic liberalism and liberal unionism

The Second Vatican Council which met intermittently in Rome during the years 1962–5 was aimed at enabling the Church to renew and
update itself in a world which had changed beyond recognition since
the last general council of the Church had gathered in the Vatican in
the year 1869–70. The work of Vatican II caught the imagination of
the political and religious establishment in the early 1960s and
facilitated in Northern Ireland a re-evaluation by the catholic community of its relationship with the state and the protestant population.

Cardinal D'Alton had been appointed by Pope John to the
preparatory commission for the council, and he in turn relied heavily
on his assistant bishop William Conway for advice and support in the
interim stages of the commission's work. Indeed it was to Conway that
the leadership of the Ulster and Irish Church would devolve on
D'Alton's death in 1963. Conway, a former professor at Maynooth,
was made a cardinal in 1966, the first Belfast man to be so honoured.
But this was no mere automatic accolade attached to the archbishopric
of Armagh. Conway was highly regarded in the Church as a whole,
and was even talked of as candidate for the papacy. Pope Paul VI
chose him as one of three cardinals to preside over the first synod of
bishops which opened in Rome in 1967. The other two were high-
ranking Vatican officials, cardinals Felici and Villot, the latter subsequently secretary of state. For all this Conway remained at best a
'liberal conservative' and some of his speeches at Vatican II, as we
shall see, sound distinctly reactionary.

The other important figure on the episcopal bench in the north from
the early 1960s was William Philbin. Appointed to succeed the
unreconstructed old-style nationalist Daniel Mageean, Philbin was
transferred from the diocese of Clonfert to Down and Connor in June
1962. By that time the latter diocese was the second largest in the
country with 210,000 faithful and it was to grow by 30 per cent in
Philbin's time as bishop. A man of outstanding ability, he was the first
non-Ulsterman to govern the diocese in two centuries and was seen
by some as a future primate. His early interest in the social teaching
of the Church had led him in the 1950s to defend the legitimacy of
comprehensive state intervention in social and family issues when
such views, in the eyes of many Irish clergy, smacked of 'statism' or
'communism'. He was never truly at home in the north, but he set
the tone for his leadership by paying a courtesy call on alderman
Martin Wallace the lord mayor of Belfast on 1 October 1962, the first
such visit by an Ulster bishop since partition.

Conway and Philbin between them provided most of the Irish
interventions in the debates at Vatican II. Philbin was then regarded

as a theological liberal[77] and a speech that he made at the second session of the Council was described as 'one of the most remarkable talks of the entire session'.[78] Philbin believed that the proposed preparatory document for the decree *Lumen Gentium* was much too focused on heavenly things and had little to say about social justice in the world. Nor did he think that the Church could condemn artificial contraception without addressing the problems of married couples. 'As it stands now', he said 'the schema treats unrealistically of an ideal world, not of the world in which fallen man struggles and sweats to provide for his own and to win heaven.'[79] In a broadcast on Radio Telefis Eireann on 13 December 1963 Philbin described the decree on ecumenism as 'a revolutionary document', and highlighted the many admirable qualities to be found in the other christian Churches, in stark contrast to the observations of cardinal MacRory thirty years earlier. However, in his speech on the decree at the council Conway said that 'ordinary' catholics did not have sufficient knowledge of their own faith to enable them to engage in ecumenical dialogue, and that inter-church relations should be conducted under the careful guidance of the bishops.

Philbin described the draft of the document *Gaudium et Spes* as 'a laboured survey of habits and tendencies in our age conducted in a philosophic and pedantic manner' whereas it ought to be a proclamation of Christ as the only cure of the world's ills.[80] But his speech on the decree on divine Revelation showed that his churchmanship could be quite conservative; here he emphasised the historicity of the gospels and was cautious on the merits of using literary criticism in the exegesis of the text of scripture.[81]

Conway proved a model of openness in dealing with journalists at the Council and freely entered into discussions of the main issues out-

[77] Xavier Rynne, *Letters from Vatican City: Vatican II First Session Background and Debates* (London, 1965), p. 63.

[78] Michael Novak, *The Open Church: Vatican II in Act II* (London, 1964), p. 136.

[79] Novak, *The Open Church*, p. 137. Cf. also Xavier Rynne, *The Second Session: The Debates and Documents of Vatican II, September 29 to December 4, 1963* (London, 1964), p. 149. The speech had an enormous impact on the final document where a whole section is given over to underlining the points on social justice which Philbin raised. Cf. Tanner (ed.), *Decrees of the Ecumenical Councils*, vol. 2, pp. 878–9.

[80] *Irish News*, 9 Oct. 1965.

[81] Xavier Rynne, *The Third Session: The Debates and Decrees of Vatican Council II, September 14 to November 21, 1964* (London, 1965), pp. 46–7. This particular intervention caused a storm of protest in the non-latinate catholic world since in his speech on 5 October Philbin had said he wished to give scholars an *admonitio*, a reminder, of the need to be guided by the interpretation of the Church in their exegesis. This was taken by many to be a *monitum*, an admonition or warning, to do so. Cf. *The Catholic Directory* (1965), p. 754.

side the formal sessions.[82] His speeches covered quite a number of subjects ranging from religious liberty to the priesthood. His intervention on this matter caused a rethink on the relevant section of *Lumen Gentium*.[83] His speech on 'mixed marriages' was less constructive, and although he was supported by archbishop Heenan of Westminster it was among the most rigid interventions in the whole debate. Conway argued that people should be dissuaded from such marriages and suggested that protestants, the 'separated brethren', shared this view. Although gracious to protestants 'among whom I live' he pointed out that there could be serious disharmony in mixed marriages which might also lead to indifferentism. On the other hand he pleaded for an end to the practice of conducting inter-church weddings 'in the sacristy', and this recommendation was accepted.[84]

The general spirit of openness which marked the early 1960s, and on which the Council capitalised, was evident in the formation in Belfast in 1961 of the Churches Industrial Council, with the bishop of Down and Connor and the various protestant church leaders as patrons. In a statement issued on 1 May, bishop Mageean, Dr Mitchell and Dr Elliot, Church of Ireland bishops of Down and Dromore, and Connor; Dr Fulton, moderator of the Presbyterian Church, and the Very Rev. R.W. McVeigh, president of the Methodist conference, spoke of their concern as Church leaders at the level of unemployment in Northern Ireland. They called on all classes and creeds to break down barriers and co-operate fully for the common good.

Such tolerant consideration was also seen in Enniskillen in January 1964 when bishop Eugene O'Callaghan of Clogher met the Unionist mayor and other Church leaders to discuss the 'restoration of friendliness and co-operation' following recent controversy in the town on the question of housing allocation. In April that year the prime minister Terence O'Neill made his famous visit to a catholic school, Our Lady of Lourdes Intermediate, in Ballymoney, Co. Antrim. The parish priest Canon George Glenaghan, a former soldier, said to O'Neill: 'This is a step in the right direction . . . it is in keeping with the spirit of the time.' By 1966 the ecumenical movement was in full swing and in a sermon in Armagh cathedral on 16 January, cardinal Conway spoke of the need for change in the mental attitudes of individual christians if the unity of the Churches was to become a reality. Nine days later the Greenhills ecumenical conference opened

---

[82] Louis McRedmond, *The Council Reconsidered* (Dublin, 1966), p. 185.
[83] Cf. Rynne, *The Second Session*, p. 96, and Austin Flannery (ed.), *Vatican Council II: The Conciliar and Post-Conciliar Documents* (Dublin, 1981), p. 385.
[84] *Irish Times*, 21 November 1964.

in Drogheda, an event which became a regular feature of Church life in Ireland over the next two decades.

The catholic Church in the north in the 1960s was also more accommodating in its dealings with officials in the ministry of education. Philbin on more than one occasion praised the excellent spirit of cooperation that the Church experienced in its dealings with the ministry and saw this as a symbol of good neighbourliness.[85] These sentiments were repeated by Mgr P.J. Mullally at a graduation ceremony for St Mary's and St Joseph's teacher training colleges in June 1966. The admiration was mutual. When in April of that year the Christian Brothers held an exhibition in the Ulster Hall in Belfast to mark the centenary of their coming to the city, the permanent secretary at the ministry of education, John M. Benn, attended and praised the Brothers for their forward thinking in educational matters.

The presbyterian Church, through its general assembly 'committee on national and international problems', produced in the mid-1960s a report on 'discrimination in Ireland', which went some way towards recognising the extent of discrimination against catholics in the north. While suggesting that catholics could be more accepting of the state, and that the extent of discrimination was at times exaggerated, it nonetheless condemned religious discrimination in the work place, in housing allocation and in the drawing of electoral boundaries. The report praised the work of the Mater hospital in Belfast and called for government assistance for that institution which it acknowledged served all sections of the community.[86] This went some way to improving relations between the presbyterians and catholics. The presbyterian general assembly had already, in June 1964, passed a resolution, at the suggestion of the Rev. Alfred Martin from Finaghy presbyterian Church, welcoming the more tolerant attitude evident in Northern Ireland society which was emanating from both civic and religious leaders. Martin adverted to Conway's tribute to protestants on his appointment as archbishop of Armagh.[87]

It is important not to exaggerate the satisfaction that catholics were beginning to express about their position within the Northern Ireland state. There is no doubt that at a religious level catholics showed themselves more open than ever before and this in turn produced reciprocal demonstrations of acceptance by some Northern Ireland

---

[85] On 26 October 1966 Philbin blessed and opened two new secondary schools in Andersonstown in Belfast. Among the invited guests were the Rev. Hugh Scott of the Broadway presbyterian church and Nat Minford, the formerly hardline Unionist MP for South Antrim.

[86] Presbyterian Church in Ireland General Assembly, *Annual Reports* (Belfast, 1966), pp. 119 and 124–6.

[87] *Belfast Telegraph*, 4 June 1964.

protestants. There remained however a hard core of anglicans and presbyterians who still saw catholicism as essentially evil and would have nothing to do with the new ecumenical movement. For its part the catholic Church still found much in Northern Ireland society to complain of.

Fr Sean O'Kelly drew attention to the underrepresentation of catholics at Queen's University in the faculties of medicine, science and agriculture. Educationalists however tended to suggest that the fault for this lay in the lack of science provision in catholic schools rather than in discrimination *per se*. Whatever its student recruitment the university gained a reputation in catholic circles for discriminating against catholics in its employment practices. And astonishingly when the Lockwood committee was set up in 1963 to examine the question of providing a second university in the province there was no catholic representation on it.[88] When its report was published and it recommended Coleraine as the site of the new university, bishop Farren spoke of his bitter disappointment that it was not to be located in Derry. He had not 'spoken out [till now because] . . . the hidden body who are determined to keep Derry down would have sought to use [any intervention] to allege that it was the Catholic Church that was really behind the idea of a University for Derry'.[89]

For the Church education was still the main point of contention. At an ecumenical meeting in Corrymeela near Ballycastle in early April 1967 Terence O'Neill called on the catholic authorities to abandon their opposition to integrated education. Two weeks later Conway described the 'continuing pressure on Catholic education' as disquieting. When the Church asked in 1967 for a further increase in grants to catholic schools from 65 per cent to 80 per cent to bring them up to the English level, the government responded with a white paper designed to impose the 'four and two' committee scheme. Philbin claimed that the proposal amounted to 'an invasion of the established system of school management'. The imposition of representatives from the local authorities was singularly irksome. The bishop asserted that 'the attitude of many of these bodies to Catholic interests is so notorious that we can only regard with dismay their direct involvement in the running of our schools'.[90] This time however the govern-

---

[88] J.J. Lee, *Ireland, 1912–1985*, p. 417.

[89] *The Derry Journal*, 9 Feb. 1966. Such sentiments were to some extent set aside when on 26 June the following year Fr. Patrick Walsh, the chaplain at Queen's, attended the laying of the foundation stone of the new university. In the presence of the governor of Northern Ireland, lord Erskine, and the prime minister, Walsh read a letter from cardinal Conway conveying his greetings to all present and his hopes for the future of the project.

[90] *Catholic Directory* (1968), p. 842.

ment was not to be swayed from its determination to impose the scheme, and after more than forty years the catholic system in northern Ireland was brought into line with that in England. Contrary to the dire predictions of churchmen, it made little observable difference to the running of schools except that they now received more money from the state. The other outstanding source of friction between the government and the Church over support for the Mater hospital was also settled amicably when the hospital was taken into the state system but with certain guarantees that protected its 'catholic ethos'.

The pace of reform of Northern Ireland society in a more tolerant and just direction was none the less almost pathetically slow. O'Neill for all his bravado did almost nothing to bring about social and political reform. He freely admitted that he was unable to restore to catholics, because of pressure from the Orange Order and hardline Unionists, 'the rights which small minded men had removed from them during the first years of Northern Ireland's existence'.[92] He chose instead to concentrate on improving relations between catholics and protestants,[92] and between north and south. In this he had some undoubted successes, which resulted in the surprising spectacle of working-class catholics in areas such as west Belfast voting for the Unionist party in 1966 and 1969.[93]

One of the main political grievances was the local government franchise. In October 1964 the Derry Catholic Registration Association claimed that new research showed 19,297 catholic voters in the city, which should have given nationalists a majority of 9,297 at Stormont elections and 5,090 at local government elections given the dual mandate, but despite this they were in a minority on the city council. O'Neill did finally act in the matter in 1969 and carried a 'one man one vote' measure through the House of Commons with a majority of three on the Unionist benches. There is general consensus among observers that by the early 1960s the political agenda for most nor-

[91] *The Autobiography of Terence O'Neill, Prime Minister of Northern Ireland, 1963–1969* (London, 1972), p. 129.

[92] David Harkness, *Northern Ireland since 1920* (Dublin, 1983), p. 143, is inclined to see O'Neill's public condolence to Conway on the death of Pope John XXIII as especially significant in this regard. But this is probably to overstate what had become a matter of public procedure. The flying of the Union Jack at half-mast on public buildings to mark the Pope's death had been ordered by the Queen throughout the United Kingdom.

[93] Sceptics are inclined to see O'Neill's attitude as provoked by tensions within the Unionist block over economic policy rather than a principled desire to achieve a fair society. The specific political problem he faced was the potential loss of important sections of the protestant working class because of continued high unemployment. Cf. Bew et al., *The State in Northern Ireland*, pp. 132 and 151.

thern catholics was not so much an end of partition as justice for the community within Northern Ireland.[94] This was certainly the aim of the Northern Ireland Civil Rights Association when it was founded in January 1967, building as it did on the work of the Campaign for Social Justice (the latter had been started by Mrs Patricia MacCluskey and her husband in Dungannon in January 1964, and affiliated in 1965 to the National Council for Civil Liberties).

By then under the leadership of Eddie McAteer, the Nationalist Party had become Her Majesty's Official Opposition at Stormont. At Westminster too developments were under way. A group of back-bench labour MPs and others came together in June 1965 and formed the 'Campaign for Democracy in Ulster' to press for structural change in Northern Ireland. The republican movement also shifted in a more political direction with the setting up of the Republican Clubs to enable the more ardently minded nationalists to seek their objectives with the ballot rather than the bomb. The government however banned them in 1967, perhaps because it had been forced, for the first time in Northern Ireland's existence, to ban an extremist protestant private army, the UVF, which had been involved in a number of violent outrages including the murder of a young catholic barman Peter Ward in 1966.

Unionists regarded the ceremonies held to mark the fiftieth anniversary of the 1916 Rising as a threat to the stability of the Northern Ireland state. O'Neill was to opine that the extent of the celebrations in the north, which included masses for those who had died, was one of the main factors in the falling apart of Northern Ireland society in the following years. Of course by 1966 O'Neill was having severe difficulties with his own right wing, which came close to destabilising his government. By then also the maverick former baptist preacher, now describing himself as a 'Free Presbyterian' minister—the Rev. Ian Paisley—had started a personal crusade to stave off reforms and bring down O'Neill. As O'Neill himself remarked, '. . . if Ulster does not survive, then historians may well show that it was the Protestant extremists, yearning for the days of the Protestant ascendancy, who lit the fuse which blew us up.'[95] Increas-

---

[94] Tim Pat Coogan, *Ireland since the Rising* (London, 1966), p. 116. John Darby comments that 'the radical change which took place in the 1960s was that almost all opposition parties in Northern Ireland came quietly to accept—if sometimes only conditionally—the existence of the State'. *Conflict in Northern Ireland: The Development of a Polarised Community* (Dublin, 1976), p. 98.

[95] *The Autobiography of Terence O'Neill*, p. 80. This of course was coupled with the fact that for 'far too long no effort had been made to make the minority feel that they were wanted or even appreciated' (*ibid.*).

ingly bitter opposition to reform and civil rights proposals led to a massive build-up of tension within both communities in Northern Ireland, which from 1968 on would find release only in bloody street violence and confrontation in scenes of destruction unrivalled since the foundation of the state.

7

THE TROUBLES, 1969–1983

The church and civil unrest

By the late 1960s the catholic hierarchy felt sufficiently confident of its role in Northern Ireland society for cardinal Conway to declare that the bishops had given every mark of recognition and acceptance to the Northern Ireland state.[1] The cardinal himself had taken the initiative in this by paying a visit to the governor of Northern Ireland, lord Grey, but at the latter's request kept the meeting secret.[2] Conway also said that there was almost as much contact between the bishops and the Northern government as there was with the government in the Republic.[3] In private Conway was ready to admit that 80 per cent of catholics did not want a united Ireland in the short term.[4] The appointment in December 1970 of Fr Robert Murphy as the first catholic chaplain to Stormont further cemented the bonds of mutual tolerance between the hierarchy and the Stormont regime. By this time Terence O'Neill had been removed from the political scene and his superficial liberalism[5] finally exposed as a pretence in his famous remark on 5 May the previous year that if one treated catholics with due consideration and kindness they would live like protestants in spite of the authoritarian nature of their Church. Such remarks were obviously resented but none the less the hierarchy still aimed for accommodation with the state.

In the sometimes violent civil rights marches of 1968 and 1969 the police did not always deal evenhandedly with those caught up in rioting. Catholic rioters were mostly treated more harshly than their protestant counterparts, and the courts also gave the impression of a disparity of treatment of alleged offenders. This led Fr Denis Faul of Dungannon to complain of bias in the judiciary. Conway acted immediately to deprecate Faul's remarks which he considered 'both unwarranted and unfortunate'. In addition Conway temporarily forbade Faul to make public statements on the pressing issues of

---

[1] *Belfast Telegraph*, 27 March 1969.
[2] Eric Gallagher and Stanley Worrall, *Christians in Ulster, 1968–1980* (Oxford, 1982), p. 46.
[3] Whyte, *Church and State in Modern Ireland*, p. 354.
[4] Barry White, *John Hume: Statesman of the Troubles* (Belfast, 1984), p. 258.
[5] Buckland, *A History of Northern Ireland*, p. 107.

the day. Church-state rapprochement was given a further boost by Dr Philbin, bishop of Down and Connor, when he attended a Buckingham Palace garden party in the early 1970s, the first catholic bishop to do so in Northern Ireland's history, although invitations to such functions were issued annually. By then of course the north had been plunged into a devastating and bloody conflict and Philbin may have thought that his actions would in some way contribute to a spirit of reconciliation, but he clearly laid himself open to criticism from his own community.

In the early stages of its evolution Church officials supported the limited demands of the civil rights movement. As time went on senior clergy became concerned that the movement might be taken over by communists or republicans, and a number of priests began to distance themselves from the civil rights agitation. There is some suggestion that what remained of the IRA in the period 1968–9 had infiltrated the Civil Rights Association.[6] However in the early phases of the campaign for reform the hierarchy gave unqualified if cautious support to the movement. Conway for example stressed the peaceful nature of the organisation and he was also anxious to emphasise that the civil rights agenda had nothing to do with aspirations for a united Ireland. His counsels found support among the other northern bishops at the beginning of 1969, when in a joint statement they pointed out that in origin the civil rights movement was both non-sectarian and non-violent. They also regretted that the government had not taken the initiative over civil rights before 'the people took to the streets'.[7] By 1970 with intercommunal strife threatening to spill over into civil war the bishops wondered if the price to be paid for the reforms was not already too high.[8]

The catholic community as a whole felt that no reforms would be conceded without a bitter struggle with the Unionist government.[9] Although there were objective grounds for catholic complaints of their treatment in the state, the community's sense of being a hard-pressed and disadvantaged minority was not unconnected with ideological presuppositions which had as much to do with nationalist sentiment as with day-to-day experience of discrimination.[10] The violent

[6] Charles Townshend, *Political Violence in Ireland: Government and Resistance since 1848* (Oxford, 1983), p. 389, and J. Bowyer Bell, *The Secret Army: The IRA*, 4th edn (Dublin, 1989), pp. 357–8.

[7] *Irish News*, 20 Jan. 1969.

[8] Cf. Xavier Carty (ed.), *Violence and Protest* (Dublin 1970), p. 9.

[9] Paul Arthur, *Government and politics of Northern Ireland*, 2nd edn (London, 1974), p. 123.

[10] Bob Purdie, *Politics in the Streets: The Origins of the Civil Rights Movement in Northern Ireland* (Belfast, 1990), p. 1.

upsurges in August 1969 in which catholic frustration found its outlet in frontal attacks on the police and the Ulster Special Constabulary provoked bitter and widespread reactions from the protestant-Unionist community. The bishops were genuinely shocked at the extent of the violence which the catholics, particularly in Belfast, had to face. It seemed beyond question that the police had collaborated with militant protestants in invading nationalist areas in West Belfast and Ardoyne and causing injury and destruction on a scale reminiscent of the 'troubles' of the early 1920s.[11]

The catholic community was faced by mid-August 1969 with a number of interrelated problems. Among the first was the need for effective defence against what was seen as a hostile and partial police and the protestant militants. These were the days when IRA stood for 'I Ran Away'. Vigilantes banded together in 'citizens defence committees' to police their neighbourhoods and erect barricades. Thus the era of the 'no go' areas in Belfast and Derry began. In Belfast the various 'defence committees' came together to form the 'central citizens defence committee', charged with overall co-ordination of defence activities. Bishop Philbin was anxious that the CDCs should be under the leadership of the clergy but this idea was dropped when it was pointed out that they were intent on arming themselves for future confrontations.[12]

The burning of homes and expulsion of people from 'mixed areas' was ultimately to affect 15,000 families, both protestant and catholic, in what was at that time the biggest forced movement of people in Europe since the end of the Second World War.[13] Partly because of its resources and partly because of the desire to control a rapidly deteriorating situation the Church became almost solely responsible for the care of catholics forced to leave their homes.

In the absence of decisive leadership within the catholic urban areas some churchmen attempted to assert a more direct political influence over their flocks. It was after all as a result of a plea from Philbin that the British army was committed to the streets of Belfast. Soldiers and the clergy worked well together. The army disliked the idea of 'no go' areas and used well-placed churchmen in an attempt to have

---

[11] Cf. Eamon Phoenix, 'Northern Ireland: from birth pangs to disintegration, 1920–72' in C. Brady, M. O'Dowd and Brian Walker (eds), *Ulster: an Illustrated History* (London, 1989), p. 211.

[12] This at least is the allegation made by Fr Des Wilson who in August 1969 was a curate in the Ballymurphy area of West Belfast. Cf. an interview Wilson gave to Pat Buckley which is reproduced in the latter's *Faith and Fatherland: The Irish News, the Catholic Hierarchy and the Management of Dissidents* (Belfast, n.d.), p. 88.

[13] John Whyte, *Interpreting Northern Ireland* (Oxford, 1990), p. 33.

barricades in catholic districts removed. Such attempts aroused some hostility between catholics and their priests.[14]

It is some mark of the political vacuum in the catholic community in the early stages of the troubles that when the British home secretary James Callaghan tried to sell the Westminster government's reform package to northern nationalists it was to the Church, and specifically cardinal Conway, that he turned.[15] At the end of August 1969 Conway suggested that Callaghan's proposals deserved widespread support since they marked a way forward for catholics in Northern Ireland. In the following months various reforms were enacted which, coupled with those already passed, should in principle have enabled catholics to feel more at home in Northern Ireland. The 'B' Specials were abolished and replaced by the Ulster Defence Regiment, which had a 16 per cent catholic recruitment rate; the police were temporarily disarmed and the Northern Ireland government began to listen seriously to catholic grievances as articulated by leading churchmen, symbolised by the historic meeting between Conway and the Stormont premier James Chichester Clark on 25 February 1970.

The institutional Church continued to command immense respect and loyalty from ordinary catholics. Church attendance was one of the highest in Europe[16] and more than 60 per cent of catholics surveyed reported that it was important to do what their priests told them.[17] Although the ecclesiastical reforms of the Second Vatican Council had been implemented without too much difficulty, there was none of the enthusiasm which had greeted the Council's reforms in other parts of the catholic world. The balance of power both ecclesiastical and social was still weighted in favour of the clergy. However, given the upheavals the community had undergone, there were indications in some quarters of a reappraisal of the relations between lay people and clergy in the Church.

The most important manifestation of this change was the emergence of the Provisional IRA in 1970. The Provisionals posed a severe leadership threat to the clergy over the form and content of political life in the catholic working-class urban areas and the poor

[14] Cf. The Sunday Times Insight Team, *Ulster* (Harmondsworth, 1972), p. 157; *Irish News*, 22 Sept. 1969; and Gerry Adams, *Cage Eleven* (Dingle, 1990), p. 100.

[15] Gerald McElroy, *The Catholic Church and the Northern Ireland Crisis, 1968–86* (Dublin, 1991), p. 29.

[16] By 1983 almost 90 per cent of Catholics claimed that they attended mass at least once a week. Edward Moxon-Browne, *Nation, Class and Creed in Northern Ireland* (Aldershot, 1983), p. 125.

[17] Richard Rose, *Governing without Consensus: An Irish Perspective* (London, 1971), p. 479.

rural communities west of the Bann. The Church rejected the Provisionals' claim to be the defenders of the catholic community, but the organisation presented itself as a major embarrassment to the church as ecclesiastics sought to strengthen their influence with the secular authorities. The Provisionals were not slow to condemn what they took to be the pro-government position of the bishops. When Dr Philbin visited Ballymurphy in January 1971 following a week of rioting in the area, he preached in Corpus Christi church and urged catholics to stop supporting the IRA. Many of the parishioners were so outraged by the timing of the remarks that they organised a demonstration outside the bishop's house a few days later. Furthermore one of the leading lights of the republican movement has since written that their intention was to confine the Church's activity to the sacristy.[18] Notwithstanding its protestations to the contrary the Church is not content with such passivity in society.

Even the 'constitutional' wing of northern nationalism began to distance itself from ecclesiastical influence. The formation of the Social and Democratic Labour Party in August 1970 marked the end of the old alliance between the clergy and the Nationalist Party. While it is true that in the 1980s the Church would throw its influence behind the SDLP to detract from Sinn Fein, in the early '70s it was distrustful of at least some of the SDLP policies. When as part of the power-sharing executive of 1974 the party supported Basil McIvor's proposals on integrated education, Church spokesmen rejected the ideas as naive and ill-informed.

By that time the education issue was troubling the Church in other ways. One result of the intensified Unionist-nationalist struggle was that catholics began to re-discover their Gaelic identity and seek educational provision through the medium of Irish. Some Irish-language enthusiasts set up an Irish-medium primary school in Belfast, which eventually became a major educational institution outside the catholic system and controlled by the laity. None the less it prepared children for the reception of the sacraments thus depriving the bishops of one obvious justification for the clerically controlled catholic system.

In its early days there was some suggestion that the Church authorities would refuse the sacraments to children who attended the Irish school. This precise issue also forced the catholic educational authorities in the diocese of Down and Connor into a turn-about in relation to the Vere Foster state primary school in New Barnsley, West Belfast. Given the displacement of population, many protestants moved out of New Barnsley to be replaced by catholic refugees. Some

---

[18] Gerry Adams, *The Politics of Irish Freedom* (Dingle 1986), p. 122.

of the new arrivals decided to send their children to the school on the housing estate rather than to the local catholic primary school, which was some distance away across a busy main road and which in any case was already overcrowded. The diocesan education inspector told the parents concerned that their children could not be admitted to the sacraments since they were not receiving catholic religious instruction, and he demanded that their children attend catholic schools.

The parents decided to take a stand and acquired the services of a former seminarian to teach religious knowledge to their children. Eventually the Church agreed to supply a teacher of religion to the Vere Foster school and this particular crisis between clerical and lay interest and authority in the Church was defused.[19] The issue of catholic children attending 'state schools' was a continuing problem for Dr Philbin throughout the 1970s, and led to appeals to Rome from a number of parents whose children he refused to confirm because they did not attend catholic schools. The issue was exploited for sensationalist purposes by a number of newspapers including the *Irish Times*, which Philbin sued for alleging that he had fallen foul of the Roman authorities in the matter. The paper was forced to pay substantial but undisclosed damages.

By the middle of 1971 the catholic community was more fragmented than it had been for many years. Bishops and clergy were finding increasing difficulty in imposing their authority on those determined to take the law into their own hands. The desire to bring down the government and force the reunification of the country had become the priority of the IRA. Catholic and nationalist violence was on the increase and the community's alienation from its erstwhile protectors the British army had been completed by the Lower Falls curfew of July 1970, in which five people lost their lives, seventy-five were injured and 1,600 canisters of CS gas were fired. Referring to it subsequently Brian Faulkner remarked that the incidents were 'a search operation . . . which had gone wrong'.[20] This was also the beginning of the period of military 'dirty tricks' when army undercover operations helped to destablise an already chaotic situation. One curious allegation to emerge from the contorted politics of the time was the suggestion that the army used catholic chaplains to the forces in intelligence-gathering operations in catholic areas, where even army chaplains would normally receive a warm welcome. One priest involved in such activities Fr Gerry Weston was killed in an Official IRA bomb attack on Aldershot barracks.[21]

[19] A full account of this extraordinary and neglected episode is given by Ciaran de Baroid in *Ballymurphy and the Irish War* (Dublin, 1989), pp. 141 ff.

[20] *Memoirs of a Statesman* (London, 1978), p. 74.

[21] Des Wilson, *An End to Silence*, 2nd edn (Cork, 1987), pp. 79–80.

The 'chaplains affair' led to further disunity within the catholic community and to growing distrust between the people and their clergy. The Unionist government's own ineptitude was however soon to provide an issue which would serve as a focus for catholic unity and hostility to the state. At the same time internment without trial became a source of conflict between the bishops and the lower clergy over the proper means of addressing what many saw as yet another instrument of state repression.

Internment and the fall of Stormont

Preparations for internment had already been made before Brian Faulkner became prime minister in March 1971. It was his decision however to introduce the measure in August that year, in consultation with the government in Westminster. The Stormont administration was under considerable pressure from the Orange Order and from the protestant community to take firmer action against the nationalists and republicans. On 12 March more than 4,000 protestant workers from the shipyards marched on Unionist headquarters in Belfast demanding the internment of known IRA leaders. Senior politicians were aware that it would be seen—as in effect it was—a weapon aimed not only at the IRA but at the very heart of the catholic population.[22]

Catholic reaction was immediate, and many took to the streets in an orgy of violence which over two days left twenty-three dead and saw 7,000 fleeing to the Republic for safety. Constitutional nationalists launched a campaign of civil disobedience involving a rent and rate strike, which received support from more than 25 per cent of the catholic population and was to last for some three years. The response of Church leaders in the face of the violence was somewhat muted. On 15 August Conway issued a statement that internment was 'a terrible power to give any political authority'. He stressed the abhorrence of internment in the catholic community and condemned its one-sided application.[23] Although the northern bishops expressed their concern at the treatment of internees,[24] as did the Church of Ireland arch-

---

[22] The British home secretary Reginald Maudling urged Faulkner to 'lift some Protestants' in order to give the impression of an even handedness of treatment. Cf. Faulkner, *Memoirs of a Statesman*, p. 119, and Ian McAllister, *The Northern Ireland Social Democratic and Labour Party: Political opposition in a divided society* (London, 1977), p. 99.

[23] *Catholic Directory* (1972), p. 737.

[24] On 21 November the bishops issued a hard-hitting statement concerning 'the shameful use of interrogation in depth methods' on internees. They continued: 'We condemn this treatment as immoral and inhuman. It is unworthy of the British people'. They also claimed that such treatment of internees was 'contrary to the law of Christ'. *The Catholic Directory* (1972), p. 740.

bishop of Armagh Dr George Simms, they refused to denounce internment as immoral. Indeed in their public statements protesting against internment they emphasised several times that the violence of the IRA was the main, if not the only, factor in the difficulties facing Northern Ireland.

The public posturing of the hierarchy was complicated by the action of the leaders of the three main protestant Churches in issuing a statement recognising that in the circumstances internment was a necessary evil. This put the catholic leadership in a great dilemma. On the one hand the bishops wanted to maintain good relations with the protestant Churches but on the other they recognised that many innocent people were being wrongfully arrested.[25] In a strongly worded declaration on 12 September, which fell short of an outright denunciation of internment, the bishops displayed a sensitivity to the ecumenical impact of their censures of the Northern Ireland state. At the same time they sought to reassure protestants of the benevolent attitude of the catholic Church towards them.[26]

The measured reaction of the bishops was not reflected in the clerical body as a whole. On 23 September the Ulster branch of the Association of Irish Priests wrote to the whole hierarchy asking it to condemn internment unambiguously as immoral in itself and to give guidelines on how this 'violation of a basic human right' could be resisted.[27] By November 387 priests, nearly all the clergy in Northern Ireland, had signed a statement declaring internment to be immoral.

Two monks from the Cistercian monastery at Portglenone, Co. Antrim, played a more direct role in protesting against internment. Fr Thomas O'Neill and Br Joseph Skehan were arrested on 19 November with two IRA internees who had escaped from the prison ship *Maidstone*; the monks were trying to help the internees to cross the border. Their arrest sparked off a three-day search of their monastery for arms and explosives, in which nothing was found. Eventually the monks were brought to trial and although they were prepared to go to gaol their abbot Dom Aengus Dunphy decided instead to pay the fine of £600 which the magistrates imposed as an alternative to a

---

[25] Two clerical campaigners for human rights in Northern Ireland make the general point that the catholic Church has the means 'to defend the human rights of its members, but whether it will face the ecumenical misunderstandings and political flak is doubtful'. This is precisely the problem which the Church leadership tried to grapple with throughout the years of internment. Denis Faul and Raymond Murray, *The Alienation of Northern Ireland Catholics* (privately published, 1984), p. 8.

[26] *Irish News*, 13 September 1971.

[27] This letter is reproduced in McElroy, *The Catholic Church and the Northern Ireland Crisis*, p. 207.

custodial sentence.

The politicisation of the lower clergy was to reach a degree of militancy in the early 1970s unparalleled in the recent history of Ulster. In late April more than forty priests announced that they would not complete the 1971 census returns as a means of protesting against injustices in Northern Ireland society. Twenty-seven of the clergy were from the diocese of Down and Connor, but bishop Philbin refused to comment on their actions. In all some seventy-one clergy broke the law in refusing to complete census returns, and the lead of the clergy was taken up by a large number of laity. Eventually eight Belfast clergy, six from St Malachy's college and two from the neighbouring Holy Family parish, were taken to court and each fined £7, which they refused to pay, instead contributing the same amount to a human rights organisation. The priests were saved from gaol by an anonymous benefactor who paid their fines.

In December the Association of Irish Priests issued a statement supporting the aim of a united Ireland. They declared that a new constitution would have to be drawn up, but that in such circumstances it would be possible to create an environment in which both protestants and catholics could feel at home, and in which there could be lasting peace. The dissatisfaction of the lower clergy at the failure of the hierarchy to be more outspoken against state injustice in Northern Ireland was to remain an abiding feature of the ecclesiastical situation well into the 1980s. By then some 43 per cent of priests expressed unhappiness at what was perceived to be the hierarchy's failure to take a resolute stand over human rights issues, the level of disgruntlement rising to 60 per cent in the diocese of Down and Connor.[28]

The discontent among the Belfast clergy could have been due in part to a growing disaffection with the leadership of Dr Philbin, who was clearly ill at ease in the street politics of north-east Ulster. There were reports of differences between him and his episcopal colleagues over matters of ecclesiastical policy in relation to the troubles. By 1974 he was the only bishop to make an unequivocal call to catholics to support the security forces. Such demands coupled with his scholarly pursuits could have appeared almost eccentric given the unprecedented suffering in the catholic community at that time caused by both the IRA and the security forces. In 1973 he published a translation of fragments of Greek poetry and prose which had little resonance with the conditions under which many of his flock in Belfast were living. Ironically however one fragment from Anacreon which he translated could be construed as a glorification of warfare that even the IRA would have found acceptable:

[28] McElroy, *The Catholic Church and the Northern Ireland Crisis*, p. 106.

> *You also Cleanor's son are one who gave*
> *Life for your country's love; this was the reason*
> *You challenged tempests of the lawless season*
> *And left youth's flower in the disfiguring wave.*[29]

In August 1971 the violence had already claimed its first clerical victim. Fr Hugh Mullan was shot dead in Ballymurphy on the day internment was introduced, in what the army claimed was crossfire as it did battle with the Provisional IRA. This version of events was disputed by a number of eyewitnesses who suggested that the army had deliberately shot the priest as he was about to give the last rites to another victim. Even Dr Philbin, not a man to offer the IRA a propaganda advantage, called for 'a most vigorous investigation' into the shooting but at the same time he said that it would be a tragedy if Mullan's death were used as a pretext for further violence.[30] Another paradoxical consequence of the shooting was a display of sectarian intolerance by a group of Church of Ireland clergymen. The anglican bishop of Connor, Dr Arthur Butler, in a gesture of solidarity and Christian fellowship attended Mullan's funeral. He was subsequently condemned by his select vestry for conduct 'incompatible with the teaching of the Church'.[31]

Mullan was not the only priest to suffer directly in the troubles. His fellow curate in Ballymurphy Fr Noel Fitzpatrick was shot dead in July 1972 in circumstances eerily similar to Mullan's own death. Perhaps one of the most bizarre incidents of the entire period was the kidnapping of Fr Hugh Murphy the parish priest of Ahoghill, Co. Antrim, and a former naval chaplain, in June 1978 as a reprisal for the abduction by the IRA of a policeman in south Armagh. Murphy's abductors turned out to be two members of the RUC, one of whom was subsequently gaoled for the murder of a catholic. Murphy's ordeal was brought to an end by the intervention of among others the Rev. Ian Paisley.[32]

Attacks on catholic churches and even the killing of worshippers became features of the sectarian warfare that raged in the north of Ireland in the 1970s. One such attack on St Matthew's church in the Short Strand area of East Belfast on 27–28 June 1970 brought the Provisionals to the defence of the building in a gun battle resulting in the deaths of three militant loyalists and one IRA man.[33] A subse-

---

[29] William J. Philbin, *To You Simonides* (London, 1973), p. 49.
[30] *Irish News*, 11 August 1971.
[31] Gallagher and Worrall, *Christians in Ulster*, p. 63.
[32] Chris Ryder, *The RUC: A Force under fire* (London, 1989), p. 279.
[33] Michael Hall, *20 Years: A Concise Chronology of events in Northern Ireland from 1968–1988* (Newtownabbey, 1988), p. 22.

quent attack on St Anthony's catholic church in the neighbouring Woodstock Road three years later provoked a sense of outrage in the protestant community. More than 200 protestants from all over Belfast converged on the church in a clean-up operation which lasted several hours. The Church of Ireland bishop of Down and Dromore set up a fund to pay for the repair of the church.

By that time tit-for-tat sectarian assassinations were regular occurences. The catholic authorities drew attention to what they saw as a 'campaign of violence . . . being waged against the Catholic population. Already since the beginning of the year the bodies of over sixty Catholic victims of assassination have been found in the streets'.[34] The perverse logic of such killing gave rise in the mid-1970s to one of the most gruesome coteries of religious malignity ever to arise in the long history of sectarian violence in Ulster: the Shankill butchers. The sole purpose of the gang, led by Lenny Murphy, was to strike fear into the catholic community in Belfast. Its motivation, put starkly, was hatred of Roman Catholicism.[35]

From the earliest days of the troubles prominent churchmen have tried to play down the specifically religious nature of the hostilities. The leaders of the four main churches issued a statement in June 1970 denying that what was happening in Northern Ireland was a religious war. As time went on this view became fashionable among certain groups of liberal academics, who wanted to characterise the problem as social and political rather than religious. This led one observer to remark: 'We have convinced ourselves that religion is not important in Western European societies and that, therefore, it cannot and *should* not be important in Northern Ireland and cannot *really* be contributing to the violence there'.[36]

To many ordinary catholics it seemed that the forces of the 'protestant' state and the British government were directed against them. Since internment was such a devastating weapon the opposition to it was equally vehement. After the initial violence, the protests continued and catholics took to the streets of Northern Ireland in unprecedented numbers calling for an end to this most draconian measure. The shooting dead of thirteen people at an anti-internment rally in Derry on 30 January 1972 ('Bloody Sunday') united the whole catholic population—bishops, clergy and laity—as never before since

---

[34] *The Irish News* 15 November 1972. Twelve months later cardinal Conway repeated this allegation and claimed that the security forces were dragging their feet in tracking down sectarian killers. Cf. *Catholic Directory* (1974), p. 735.

[35] The full story of the bloody exploits of the gang is told by Martin Dillon in *The Shankill Butchers: A Case Study of Mass Murder* (London, 1989).

[36] John Hickey, *Religion and the Northern Ireland Problem* (Dublin and Totowa, 1984), pp. 110–11.

the start of the troubles. The sense of outrage over the deaths undoubtedly led to the fall of the Stormont parliament as the British government engaged in a damage limitation exercise to sustain its flagging international image.

The Church welcomed the sweeping away of the *ancien régime*, and saw the imposition of direct rule as a way forward for the catholic community in the north. Groups of priests in Belfast and Derry issued statements in April and May 1972 calling on the IRA to stop the fighting and allow a period of political negotiation to commence. For the first time bishops began to visit political prisoners in Long Kesh in the hope of influencing the more militant among them to give the political process a chance. For its part the British government entered on direct negotiations with the IRA in an effort to bring the violence to an end. The prime minister Edward Heath and the new secretary of state for Northern Ireland William Whitelaw offered new hope for an end to the age-old antagonisms within Northern Ireland, and the Church too was poised to exert its influence in the cause of healing and reconciliation.

Religious and political developments

The appointment in September 1971 of Dr G.B. Newe as minister of state in the prime minister's office brought a catholic into the cabinet for the first time in Northern Ireland's history. The fall of the Stormont government meant that Newe's tenure of office was brief, but it was a mark of the rapidity of change then taking place even within the Unionist Party that the move was acquiesced in by the protestant-Unionist population. By contrast, the British government's proposals to set up a power-sharing executive in which catholics and protestants would formally share the government of the province met with fierce resistance. The executive was destroyed by the determined opposition of large sections of the protestant community. Ostensibly the reason for the hostility was the Council of Ireland in which both the Northern executive and the government of the Republic would participate. Faulkner however has written that the Council of Ireland was only a convenient red herring, and that the real objection was to the principle of power-sharing itself.[37] Most protestants, at that time, simply did not want to allow catholics a say in running the affairs of Northern Ireland.

IRA violence had obviously hardened protestant antipathy towards the whole catholic population. When Daithi O'Connail the IRA chief of staff outlined the IRA bombing strategy in Britain in a television

[37] *Memoirs of a Statesman*, p. 287.

interview in November 1974, Sammy Smyth of the Ulster Defence
Association responded that his reaction was one of 'sheer unadul-
terated hatred'. 'At that moment I could have, without a twinge of
compassion, bombed every well-filled chapel in Belfast. . . . They
had nurtured this serpent, this reptile . . .'[38] All catholics were then
'legitimate' targets for militant protestant groups. John Darby has
well summarised the cause of much protestant distrust of the catholic
Church in his observation that 'many protestants regard the catholic
Church as obstinately opposed to the will of the majority in Northern
Ireland, and as adopting a frankly political role in association with
nationalist politicians and as professing doctrines which are actively
impairing the freedom and values of Protestants in Southern
Ireland'.[39]

One further area of protestant anxiety was the perception that the
altitude of the catholic Church to violence was ambivalent. Too often
it seemed that bishops equivocated in their condemnations of the IRA
and were too disposed to criticise the security forces thus encouraging
republican atrocities. In a 1971 statement the bishops while condemning IRA violence none the less admitted that many of those engaged
in violence 'may be in good faith, confused by conflicting emotions
and ideals'. Dr Cahal Daly, who was to become the Church's most
vehement and articulate critic of the republicans, wrote when bishop
of Ardagh and Clonmacnois of his conviction that 'political violence
will never be removed from Irish society, North or South, until a just
and acceptable solution is found for the problem of the North'.[40] By
1975 however the hierarchy declared: 'Our vocabulary of moral condemnation has been virtually exhausted. . . . From the very outset of
this campaign the Catholic Church has pointed out unequivocally that
it is utterly immoral'.[41]

Such forthright language notwithstanding many protestants were
still not convinced that the clergy were opposed to the violence of the
IRA. With the paraphernalia of republicanism surrounding the
funeral rites of dead terrorists, further proof was provided for those
who needed it that the catholic Church in Northern Ireland was allied
with the men and women of violence. On the other hand there were
instances in which parish priests refused burial services to dead IRA
men, and bishop Edward Daly of Derry warned the IRA that there
would be a blanket ban on funerals if republican emblems were not
removed from coffins before they were brought into church. Such facts

[38] Hall, *20 Years*, p. 55.
[39] *Conflict in Northern Ireland: The Development of a Polarised Community* (Dublin and
New York, 1976), pp. 117–18.
[40] *Violence in Ireland and Christian Conscience* (Dublin, 1973), p. 63.
[41] *Human Life is Sacred*, p. 37.

were ignored by those who sought political gains from the dilemma the Church faced in having to minister to all who were caught up in the strife of the troubles.

Protestant perceptions were by no means universally hostile. A number of protestant clergymen talked to the IRA towards the end of 1974 in the hope of persuading them to stop the killing. The ceasefire and political negotiations in 1975 can be regarded as a measure of their success. In addition the main Churches made attempts to promote intercommunal understanding by setting up the Ballymascanlon talks which in addition to the Greenhills and Glenstall Abbey conferences became a regular part of the ecclesiastical scene.

Some ecumenical endeavours which may have helped were formally frowned upon by Church authority. In the mid-1970s groups of like-minded individuals, some on the fringes of the cross-community Alliance Party whose leader Oliver Napier was a catholic, were anxious to promote integrated education as a means of helping to further understanding between catholics and protestants. The protestant Churches were as opposed to the idea in principle as the catholic Church, but it was the catholic Church which vociferously opposed any such scheme and thus earned the opprobrium of many commentators on the issue. The Church was also less than forthcoming in support of the Peace Movement begun by Betty Williams and Mairead Corrigan, which was subsequently also led by Ciaran McKeown. The reason here may have been tactical so as not to give the impression that it was a 'catholic' peace movement and thus alienate well-disposed protestants.[42] However the movement itself collapsed amid public recrimination between its founders over the movement's policies and organisation.

Thus ecumenical contacts between Church leaders did little to combat sectarianism on the ground. The main problem of political violence continued unabated. While it was true that in 1977 there were fewer deaths than in any year since 1970, none the less 112 people died through terrorist violence in that year. The IRA continued to operate with more than merely minimal levels of support from the catholic community, and its hold over alienated working-class communities seemed as firm as ever. The inability of the security forces to police catholic areas enabled the IRA to fulfil that role with a ruthless determination, and its favourite sanction in dealing with 'anti-social' elements became punishment shootings, otherwise known as 'kneecapping'.

As Northern Ireland became a major international issue it attracted

[42] McElroy, *The Catholic Church and the Northern Ireland Crisis*, pp. 52–4.

the interest of leading figures in the catholic Church outside Ireland. One of the most celebrated of these, Mother Teresa of Calcutta, sent a group of four of her Missionaries of Charity to the Springhill area of Ballymurphy on a 'mission of mercy' in November 1971. There was some resentment from the ecclesiastical establishment at the unorthodox methods used by Mother Teresa's nuns in their work in West Belfast; living in the same conditions as those to whom they ministered was a challenge to the more bourgeois life-style of most priests and religious at the time. The *Catholic Directory* of 1973 records that the nuns 'arrived unannounced' which may indicate that Mother Teresa had not sought episcopal approval for her Belfast venture.

It was the original intention of the sisters that they would live in the same house as some Church of England nuns, the Sisters of the Church, whom Mother Teresa had persuaded to come to Belfast, and although this proved impossible the two groups did work closely together. In September 1973 Mother Teresa's nuns were suddenly withdrawn amid suspicion that they had been forced out by the church authorities. One of the local clergy alleged that some priests felt it unseemly that missionary sisters from India should be working in Ireland.[43]

In the middle to late 1970s a more populist episcopal leadership emerged in the northern church, which somewhat alleviated the discontent among the lower clergy over the hierarchy's attitude to pressing social and political issues. Dr Edward Daly replaced Neil Farren as bishop of Derry in February 1974. Daly had risen to sudden prominence during the Bloody Sunday episode: the Irish government used his services by sending him on a tour of the United States to explain to the American people what had happened on that fateful day. Daly used his position as a platform from which to criticise the British Labour government for its continuing internment policy. On one famous occasion when condemning the use of military tactics to achieve political ends he suggested that internment was one such example.[44] He also suggested that the British government had betrayed the interests of the catholics in Northern Ireland to placate the army and the unionists. He maintained that the military establishment dominated otherwise sympathetic politicians such as Merlyn Rees, the Labour minister for Northern Ireland, and in consequence reduced them to political inactivity.

Daly was seen as essentially on the constitutional wing of Irish nationalism; his brother Thomas was until 1979 an important SDLP

---

[43] Michael Hall, *20 Years*, p. 46, and Des Wilson, *An End to Silence*, 2nd edn (Cork, 1987), p. 95.
[44] *Catholic Directory* (1975), p. 673.

councillor and parliamentarian, and his outspoken criticisms were regarded as within the limits of acceptability for a nationally-minded catholic bishop. The same indulgence was not extended to his colleague Dr Tomas O'Fiaich, the new archbishop of Armagh, whose unreconstructed old-style nationalism upset many Unionist and English politicians and protestant clergymen. O'Fiaich's appointment was only made possible by the fall in the Republic of Liam Cosgrave's coalition government and its replacement by Fianna Fail with one of the largest majorities any party had ever enjoyed in the history of the state.

O' Fiaich's appointment was announced on 22 August 1977 and his ordination to the episcopacy in October was attended by leading figures of Church and state from both sides of the border, including the Northern Ireland secretary Roy Mason. In January 1978 O'Fiaich gave a two-part interview to the *Irish Press* in Dublin which angered many northern protestants. He declared that the only solution to the northern problem was a British withdrawal, and regretted that this had not happened with the demise of Stormont. A veritable storm of protest was raised by these remarks which were to set the tone for the O'Fiaich episcopate and his dealings with both politicians and the clergy of other Churches. His remarks were excoriated by the English press and by the presbyterians and the Church of Ireland. Indeed the *Church of Ireland Gazette* began to imitate the practice of the calculated insult of the English *Daily Telegraph* by referring to the archbishop with the English form of his name, Thomas Fee.

Despite the attempts to portray him as an unthinking fellow-traveller of militant republicanism O'Fiaich was a man of deep culture and of great ecumenical sensitivity. He was closely attached to Canon William Arlow of the Church of Ireland, and was the first catholic bishop in the country to appoint a full-time ecumenical adviser. Because of the death of pope Paul VI and the short pontificate of John Paul I, there was some delay in O'Fiaich's appointment to the College of Cardinals. It has been suggested that after the election of the Conservative government in May 1979, Mrs Thatcher the new prime minister tried to prevent O'Fiaich from being made a cardinal, and used the good offices of cardinal Basil Hume of Westminster to this end.[45]

[45] While it is impossible to know if this is true, such a scenario is not without historical precedent. Owing to political differences between English and Irish catholics Cardinal Herbert Vaughan managed to prevent the avowed nationalist archbishop of Dublin Dr William Walsh from being elevated to the Sacred College in 1892. Cf. P.J. Walsh, *William J. Walsh, Archbishop of Dublin* (Dublin and Cork, 1928), pp. 430–2, and Vincent Alan McClelland, *Cardinal Manning: His Public Life and Influence, 1865–1892* (London, 1962), p. 198.

One of the most significant Irish ecclesiastical events of the decade was the visit in September 1979 of pope John Paul II. Cardinal O'Fiaich extended the official invitation on behalf of the catholic bishops and people of Ireland, and the pope confirmed his intention of visiting the country in a communication to O'Fiaich that was inauspiciously made public on 12 July. It was originally intended that the pope would include Ulster in his itinerary but the killing by the IRA of lord Mountbatten, a close relation of the royal family, at Mullaghmore, Co. Sligo, on 27 August and of eighteen British soldiers at Warrenpoint on the same day caused the hierarchy to think again. There had already been some opposition to the proposed visit to Armagh in certain circles in the north. The moderator of the General Assembly of the presbyterian Church Dr William Craig had announced that he would not meet the pope because of theological difficulties relating to the office of the papacy.[46] Outright opposition came from the Rev. Ian Paisley's Free Presbyterian Church. The Orange Order while not opposing the visit took the opportunity on behalf of northern protestants 'to spell out clearly their concern at the glaring silence of successive pontiffs, and the obvious acquiescence of the Roman sacramental system, in the rape of Ulster with the murder of our citizens and the destruction of our property'.[47]

The pope made a visit to Drogheda, within the archdiocese of Armagh, and spoke of violence as 'unacceptable as a solution to problems . . . Violence is a lie, [it] destroys what it claims to defend: the dignity, the life, the freedom of human beings. . . . to those engaged in violence, I appeal to you in language of passionate pleading. On my knees I beg you to turn away from the paths of violence and return to the ways of peace'.[48] Several days later the IRA rejected the pope's plea and defended its 'right' to use violence to forward its aims.

Many northern catholics had travelled south to hear the pope's words in Dublin or Drogheda, but in scenes reminiscent of the Eucharistic Congress pilgrimage of 1932 buses and trains were stoned by angry protestant mobs. The papal visit was an enormous fillip to northern catholics and in particular to O'Fiaich who seemed never to stop smiling throughout the pope's Irish visit. The following year however O'Fiaich and the northern catholic community were to face one of the most serious trials to beset the Church since 1969: the IRA hunger strikes in Long Kesh.

[46] *Belfast News Letter*, 25 July 1979.
[47] *Belfast News Letter*, 1 August 1979.
[48] *The Pope in Ireland: Addresses and Homilies* (Dublin, 1979), pp. 21–2.

A struggle for power

Throughout the 1970s catholic spokesmen often condemned the IRA
on the basis that the organisation had no popular support. From the
bishops' perspective the IRA consisted of self-appointed activists
who perversely claimed that their reign of terror was carried on in
the name of the catholic community.[49] But there were voices in the
clerical body which were not prepared simply to follow the lead of
the bishops in outright condemnation of the IRA. In January 1972 a
group of sixty priests published a statement which presented a direct
challenge to the line which the hierarchy had argued consistently
throughout the whole period. In the opinion of this group, 'it is not
true to say that armed resistance to aggression can never be justified;
it is not true to say that only bishops and priests can decide when
armed resistance has become lawful; it is not true to say that only the
"elected" leaders can decide when to resist aggression and brutality
with force. . . .'[50]

By the late 1970s fewer members of the lower clergy were prepared
to argue such a case, especially given the more outspoken leadership
of Edward Daly and Tomas O'Fiaich. Support for the republicans
was on the decline between the phasing out of internment and the rise
of the 'supergrass' system of informers. Added to this there was a
certain war-weariness in the catholic-nationalist population, and
constitutional nationalists and the clergy could point to genuine
reforms such as fair employment legislation which the government
had introduced. The bishops tended to emphasise the capacity of
Northern Ireland society to reform itself. This analysis was rejected
by the republicans and this rejection was surprisingly to receive subsequently academic respectability.[51] For its part however the IRA was
determined once again to seize the leadership of the catholic community from the clergy, or at least to reassert its influence over that
section of the community which had traditionally given it most support. The emotionally charged issue of the treatment of republican
prisoners in Long Kesh and Armagh gaols was to become the cause
above all others which the republicans sought to exploit in an

[49] Cf. *Human Life is Sacred* (Dublin, 1975), p. 37.

[50] Quoted in Joseph McVeigh, *A Wounded Church: Religion, Politics and Justice in
Ireland* (Cork and Dublin, 1989), p. 79.

[51] According to Bill Rolston 'Reformism and sectarianism can happily co-exist . . .'
Ironically reforms can simply reconstitute sectarian division in new and more pervasive
ways. Thus 'the basic structure of Northern Ireland's inequality remains remarkably
undented' despite changes in Northern Irish society since direct rule. Cf. 'Reformism
and Sectarianism: The State of the Union after Civil Rights' in John Darby (ed.),
Northern Ireland: The Background to the Conflict (Belfast and Syracuse, 1983), pp. 200–33.

ideological battle with the catholic authorities for leadership of the catholic community. Dr Cahal Daly in early 1979 had sought to disabuse the IRA and Sinn Fein of the emotive issue of human rights for republican prisoners. In his view the IRA were the last people to talk about human rights given its 'immoral and anti-national' campaign which respected no one's rights.[52]

By contrast archbishop O'Fiaich had already nailed his colours to the mast after his second visit to Long Kesh at the end of July 1978, when he compared the conditions of the 'H-Blocks' during the dirty protests to the spectacle of the homeless in Calcutta living in sewer pipes. It has been suggested that O'Fiaich's trenchant statement on that occasion[53] was a source of embarrassment to at least some of his fellow bishops.[54] Nonetheless he threw his not inconsiderable energy into the movement for reform of the 'H-Block' system. His intervention is seen as of enormous significance both in giving credibility to the prisoners' demands and in encouraging wide support for the H-Block campaign in the catholic community, which at its height was to capture an approval rating of more than 60 per cent.[55] Others were to see the H-Block committee and organisation in less benevolent terms than O'Fiaich,[56] who at the time was also meeting Sinn Fein as part of his 'open door policy' in which he committed himself to speak to anyone in Northern Ireland who was prepared to meet him.[57]

After more than four years of the 'blanket' and 'dirty' protests which had not advanced the prisoners' demands, the first hunger strike began on 27 October 1980. Observers are divided over whether this action was a decision by the prisoners themselves or whether the whole hunger strike process was carefully orchestrated by the IRA command. In any event the hunger strikes of 1980 were called off on 17 December as a compromise seemed to emerge between the

---

[52] Cahal B. Daly, *Peace the Work of Justice: Addresses on the Northern Tragedy, 1973–1979* (Dublin, 1980), p. 136.

[53] The statement is reproduced in its entirety in David Beresford, *Ten Men Dead* (London, 1987), pp. 183–5.

[54] Tom Collins, *The Irish Hunger Strike* (Dublin and Belfast), 1986, p. 217.

[55] Padraig O'Malley, *The Uncivil Wars: Ireland Today* (Belfast, 1983), p. 270.

[56] Garrett Fitzgerald describes the committee as IRA-dominated, cf. *All in a Life: An Autobiography* (Dublin, 1991), p. 373. Fitzgerald took a consistently hard line throughout the whole episode of dirty protest and hunger strikes, stressing that his administration of 1981 would not press the British government to grant the prisoners' five demands which he took to be equivalent to political status for IRA members. Cf. pp. 367ff.

[57] On 4 March 1988 he met the UVF leader Gusty Spence during an eleven-hour visit to Long Kesh.

prisoners and the government, but not before cardinal Basil Hume of Westminster had issued an Advent pastoral letter saying that hunger strikes were a 'form of violence'.

When it became clear that the compromise meant different things to the prisoners and to the government the IRA prisoners under the leadership of Bobby Sands determined to begin again their fasts to death. A part-time prison chaplain Fr Denis Faul tried to persuade Sands to postpone the fasts for six months to give him time to organise a campaign of civil disobedience to highlight the prisoners' demands. Sands rejected this proposal and Faul's arguments against the hunger strike weapon, arguing that to engage in a hunger strike in the circumstances of Long Kesh was to follow the teaching of Christ and lay down one's life for one's friends—an argument Faul is reported to have accepted as valid.[58]

Once again Daly of Derry and O'Fiaich pleaded with the hunger strikers and the British government to come to a compromise on the issue, but this time the prisoners were resolved not to be soft-soaped until they were completely certain of an acceptable compromise. As fate would have it the IRA and Sinn Fein were given an opportunity to use the sympathy generated by the second hunger strike for electoral advantage. Fifteen days after Sands began his fast the sitting MP for Fermanagh and South Tyrone, Frank Maguire, died. In the by-election which followed Sands was nominated as a candidate. There is some suggestion that the bishop of Clogher Dr Joseph Duffy persuaded Maguire's brother Noel to stand for the seat. Noel Maguire was nominated but withdrew ten minutes before the closing time for nominations, much to the chagrin of Austin Currie who would have run as an independent given that his party the SDLP had determined not to contest the seat. The political fall-out if the SDLP had fielded a candidate would simply have been too great for the party's future electoral prospects. Sinn Fein and the IRA were emerging as a powerful electoral force on the coat-tails of the life and death struggle of republican prisoners. The lessons Sinn Fein learned on this occasion were not lost on it for the future of its political activities.

Sands won the seat with a majority of 1,446 out of a total poll of 72,283. However there were 3,280 spoiled votes.[59] The situation had become critical both for the Church and the state. The empathy for

---

[58] Beresford, *Ten Men Dead*, p. 77.

[59] W.D. Flackes and Sydney Elliot, *Northern Ireland: A Political Directory, 1968–1988*, 2nd edn (Belfast, 1983), p. 338. This victory at the polls was to prove no mere flash in the pan; in the by-election following Sands' death his electoral agent Owen Carron was returned with an even greater majority of 2,230 and the number of spoiled votes was reduced to 804.

Sands and his fellow prisoners were leading the catholic population more decidedly than ever into support for the IRA. The papal nuncio in Dublin archbishop Gaetano Alibrandi had kept Rome informed of developments in the hunger strikes and cardinal O'Fiaich had earlier briefed the pope on the situation. Such was the international interest in the affair that pope John Paul sent his English language secretary Mgr John Magee, himself a Newry man, to plead with Sands and the others to end their fasts. Magee arrived in Belfast on 28 April, ten days after Sands had received the last rites. He saw Sands three times and the secretary of state, Humphrey Atkins, but all to no avail. Sands died on 5 May after a sixty-six day fast.

In exasperation on 22 May O'Fiaich issued a statement saying 'In near desperation I appeal to both sides for the fifth time for a compromise which would bring the hunger strike to an end'.[60] No compromise was forthcoming and as the hunger strikers continued their fasts there were obvious signs of stress between members of the hierarchy over the affair. Although Dr Philbin of Down and Connor made no public pronouncements on the matter, his diocesan chapter issued a statement after Sands' death saying that there were to be no public masses for him in the diocese—doubtless a reflection of Philbin's own thinking on the matter.

Once again Hume of Westminster intervened a few days before Sands died to say that in his personal opinion Sands' death would be suicide. Hume's view found an echo among other prominent English catholics and with the West Belfast MP Gerry Fitt who pleaded with Mrs Thatcher not to give in to the hunger strikers. Hume's remarks were rejected in a public statement by bishop Edward Daly on 11 May, and by the senate of priests of the Armagh diocese who wrote to the English cardinal to protest in the strongest possible terms.

Another Benedictine monk Alberic Stacpoole, a former officer in the Irish Guards from Ampleforth Abbey who had been born in Belfast but whose instincts and sympathies were entirely English, launched a severe attack on the hunger strikers and accused some relations of 'stiffening strikers' resolve to die when they began to waver'.[61] He was also severely critical of O'Fiaich's role in the whole affair. Indeed O'Fiaich became something of a hate figure for the English press at the time, including such catholic newspapers as *The Tablet*. Such was the extent of the campaign against him that the editor of the Journal of the Armagh Diocesan Historical Society, normally a scholarly publication, found it necessary to write an extraordinary editorial in O'Fiaich's defence:

[60] *Irish News*, 23 May 1981.
[61] *Sunday Telegraph*, 31 May 1981.

It is three hundred years ago since Oliver Plunkett was martyred at Tyburn. The knives and cleavers for dismembering are now out of fashion in British establishment circles but in view of the recent vitriolic and well-orchestrated attacks on Oliver's successor . . ., one is forced to conclude that, though the techniques may have become more sophisticated, the attitude in these same circles to an Irish Catholic Primate remains remarkably constant.[62]

The Irish Commission for Justice and Peace, a sub-committee associated with the episcopal conference, intervened in the hope of bringing about some compromise. Its efforts were supported by a statement from the hierarchy, meeting in Maynooth in mid-June, which also asked the hunger strikers 'and those who direct them to reflect deeply on the evils of their actions and their consequences'. For once the English bishops also supported their Irish colleagues on the issue and asked for a compromise on the basis of the proposals of the ICJP.[63] The Commission appeared to be making progress when for an unknown reason the government through a highly placed Whitehall source began to negotiate directly with the IRA. The Commission was receiving different messages from Sinn Fein and in the end its efforts disintegrated amid much acrimony over the British government's actions in negotiating with the IRA. Garrett Fitzgerald in an otherwise unsympathetic account of the whole affair records his 'shock on learning that a solution seemed to have been sabotaged by yet another . . . astonishingly ham-fisted approach on behalf of the British government to the IRA. . . .'[64] The deaths continued throughout the summer, and O'Fiaich made yet another effort to help resolve the crisis by visiting Mrs Thatcher in Downing Street on 1 July. No solution was forthcoming.

The hunger strikes were ended after the deaths of ten IRA and Irish National Liberation Army 'volunteers' by the intervention of Fr Denis Faul. Faul persuaded the families of those on hunger strike to seek medical assistance for them once they had gone into a coma. When the families agreed in principle that this was how they would proceed the strikes collapsed. The initiative had passed once again from the IRA to the Church. But from the hunger strike experience the IRA through its political wing Sinn Fein went on to develop its so-called 'dual strategy' of the ballot-box and the gun as a means of achieving its aim of a united Ireland.

The fact that the IRA now turned to politics through its political wing Sinn Fein was a further challenge to the authority of the Church

---

[62] *Seancas Ardmhacha*, vol. 10, no. 1 (1980–1), p. 1.
[63] Beresford, *Ten Men Dead*, p. 268.
[64] *All in a Life*, p. 371.

and its standing in Northern Ireland. The bishops had consistently argued that the IRA had no mandate from the people but after 1981 it was clear that a substantial number of catholics in certain areas were prepared to support Sinn Fein, which defended the IRA's 'right' to use armed force. At a stroke the hierarchy's analysis was reduced to a beating of the wind.

In the Northern Ireland Assembly elections of 1982 Sinn Fein received more than 10 per cent of all the votes cast as opposed to nearly 19 per cent for the SDLP. In the Westminster elections of 1983 Sinn Fein's share of the poll rose to 13.5 per cent and the SDLP's fell to just under 18 per cent. By that stage Sinn Fein accounted for more than 43 per cent of the catholic vote. Such support was deeply disturbing to the northern bishops since it showed that many catholics simply ignored the injunctions of their pastors and seemed prepared to give credence to the Sinn Fein appraisal of Northern Ireland's problem. By 1982 however Dr Cahal Daly had been transferred from Ardagh and Clonmacnois to the bishopric of Down and Connor. He immediately set to work to remind catholics that support for the IRA and Sinn Fein was not compatible with membership of the catholic Church. In his Lenten pastoral letter of 1983 he emphasised in unmitigated terms that from the viewpoint of catholic teaching 'No end, however good, can ever justify means which are evil. . . . The means are evil; and when the means are evil the ends they achieve will be evil also'. And he continued: 'This has nothing to do with politics. This is a question of morality'.[65]

Cahal Daly was without question the most formidable opponent that the IRA and Sinn Fein were to have among the catholic bishops. His endeavours to woo the community away from support of those organizations from his Belfast base did not meet with much initial success. The strain between him and certain members of his flock was such that members of the congregation would walk out of mass when he began to speak on controversial matters. It became a byword in West Belfast that certain Sinn Fein activists would attend Church only when Daly was present and then simply in order to stage a walkout. His relentless attacks on the Provisionals and their political wing did however indicate that the church was not prepared to surrender its influence over certain sections of Ulster catholicism to the radicals and revolutionaries. Only time will tell if the Church will succeed in its efforts.

[65] Cahal B. Daly, *Coming Back Home* (Belfast, 1983), pp. 14–15.

CONCLUSION

The troubled history of the Ulster catholic community, complex as it is, does not make for a simple summation. The community's history is full of courage, endurance and heroism but above all of faith. However as with any individual or group it is not without its dark side. The intolerance and at times brutality with which it has dealt with its protestant neighbours has been appalling. History however is more than a morality tale. In surveying the undulations of the catholic community I have not intended to draw some moral as to how the community ought now to see itself on the basis of its past. However one might be allowed a few general observations.

A consistent theme in Ulster catholic history over the centuries has been a need to belong, to give allegiance to something greater or more abstract than itself. This has found expression of course in the practices of the faith but it has also sought a more material outlet in the political sphere. Ulster protestants like to give the impression that they alone are the 'loyalists' and that the catholics by contrast are of their nature rebellious and subversive. Indeed one continuous thread in the intricate tapestry of Ulster catholic identity from the defeat of O'Neill till the early twentieth century was the attachment of catholics to the crown. Obviously for a period of some seventy years after the English had repudiated their rightful but, in parliament's eyes, errant king James II and interposed a usurper solely on the basis of his protestant religion, catholics adhered to the Stuart cause. Yet as we have seen it was the Ulstermen at Tremblestown who first advanced the idea that the fortunes of catholic Ireland lay with allegiance to the house of Hanover, and were prepared to disavow the temporal authority of the pope. Even in the twentieth century the Nationalist Party survived in any meaningful shape only in the north-east in the wake of the Sinn Fein election of 1918. The party's political displays in places such as the Falls Road in west Belfast, before partition, were invariably accompanied by the flying of the Union flag and protestations of loyalty to the monarch.

The obvious question then is: why have Ulster catholics since partition been almost universally hostile to the structures of the Northern Ireland state? The answer to this paradox is one which has formed part of the whole history of the relationship between Ulster catholics and protestants. On the protestant side there has been a deep and persistent intolerance, hatred is not too strong a word, towards catholicism which is so much a part of the very fabric of Northern Irish presbyterianism and anglicanism as almost to be the very touchstone of Northern Ireland protestant identity. This antagonism led the majority community in the 'new' Ulster to adopt a policy of deliberate exclusion of catholics from any meaningful participation. Protestant-Unionists were content to alienate catholics and cast the community in a role of troublesomeness and disloyalty which it actually played, and which in turn reinforced protestant antagonism. It could be argued that Northern Ireland protestants were acting only in their own self-interest since it was clear, at least in the early days of the state, that catholics did not want partition and were prepared if possible to destabilise the new regime. Yet as we have seen most northern catholics actually supported the pro-Treaty faction and were given no encouragement by the Cosgrave government in the Free State to think that they might have any help from that quarter in resisting the new political order. But protestant-Unionists still singularly failed to capitalise on their position and lacked either the imagination or the desire to deal magnanimously or even fairly with the catholic community in their midst.

This failure and the flagrant bigotry displayed for many years in Northern Ireland did not happen because catholics posed a political threat to the existence of the state. The same phenomenon had been at work for the previous 350 years of Ulster history. Where protestants were in positions of authority they used them to exclude catholics from the benefits of political society. The fundamentally anti-catholic constitution of Ulster protestantism, no doubt a legacy of the reformation, is the unspoken central cause of the Ulster conflict historically and as we see it today. If there is ever to be peace in Ireland this is the supreme issue on which the protestant community must examine its conscience. This is not to suggest that the Ulster protestants are somehow more venal than protestants elsewhere. On the contrary the Churches of the reformation as a whole share this characteristic. In England, as Dr Edward Norman has pointed out, only the collapse of interest in religion in general has made an acceptance of catholicism possible.[1] Historically English society, like Ulster protestant society, has been fundamentally anti-catholic.

A secularised society has not much use for the strong passions engendered by religion. It is the dogged adherence to the reformation tradition in Ulster, a quality admirable in itself, which leaves the lingering bitterness described in this book. The enduring belief in God, in a protestant guise, is what makes for the intolerance of which we have seen many examples. It would be the greatest irony of all to

[1] It is perhaps worth giving Dr Norman's exact words: 'To a quite real extent it must be true that anti-Catholic feeling has waned according to a scale set by the waning of all religious feeling in English Society'. Cf. *Anti-Catholicism in Victorian England* (London, 1968), p. 20.

suggest that only when the collapse of interest in religion becomes total will a reconciliation take place. I do not advocate that position; however if there should be a political settlement in Northern Ireland that is acceptable to all, this would not in itself address the problem identified here. In Scotland, which has bequeathed so much to both catholic and protestant Ulster and where there is no constitutional issue, the same syndrome is at work even today though, thanks to a greater openness in the Churches, much less so than in the past. However even today many elements in Scottish society still regard catholicism as a menacing and pernicious system of belief.

Can it be argued by the same token that Ulster catholicism is equally founded on a base of intolerance of protestantism? The issue here is more complex. One can point to instances of spontaneous and gratuitous violence levelled against protestants by catholics which seem to have no other motive than religious hatred. The massacre of 1641 is the classic example. But there are few others which are quite as clear and even the rising of 1641 was also alleged to have been in defence of the king's prerogatives against a puritan parliament, which is why, as has been noted, the Old English catholics of the Pale joined with the Ulstermen. The 1641 butchery is the exception rather than the norm.

Ulster catholic antagonism to protestantism tends to be motivated more by politics than by specifically religious considerations. This too is a legacy of the reformation. Although the catholic Church responded to the protestant reformation with a counter-reformation, it does not define itself over against protestantism in the way that the Churches of the reformation of their very nature must seek their identity in defiance of catholicism. This is not however to suggest that historically, in Ulster or elsewhere, catholics have tolerated protestantism. It was seen as a heresy, but generally it has not aroused that hatred of it as a religion which is too often experienced in Ulster protestant dealings with their catholic fellow countrymen. It is an important element in all this that anglicanism and presbyterianism were seen as essentially foreign creeds. Even as late as the 1860s in Monaghan Ribbonmen were refering to the Church of Ireland and, more absurdly, presbyterianism as the 'English religion'. Lingering catholic hostility to protestantism as a religion has largely been dissipated thanks to the work of the Second Vatican Council.

The Church's dealings with the protestant state both before and after partition have at times been amicable. The state has utilised the potential of the hierarchical Church as an instrument of order in society, for its own secular ends. From Plunkett's activities in the 1670s, encouraging the rapparees to leave the country, to the condemnation of Fenianism in the nineteenth century and the IRA campaign

of the 1950s and more recently, governments have looked to the
Church to do what so often they have been unable to do, namely
reduce insurgents to a sense of order. The Church for its part has
not been slow to respond. It is the deadly enemy of lawlessness and
revolution as the consistent history of the Ulster Church bears witness
time and again.

One of the consequences of this is that the church does thereby gain
a certain influence in the state even, as in Ulster, where it has often
seen the state as inimical to its interests. But it also seeks to have
influence and control in every area of its members' lives. That is its
enduring fault and is doubtless one component in protestant antipathy
to catholicism. The hierarchical church in Ireland must learn to
respect the individual conscience as an authority in determining how
individuals and the state conduct their affairs. Having had too much
influence in the past it is now in danger of losing any influence it might
have. This too has been a characteristic of the history we have
examined. It has been made manifest in the struggle between the
clergy and the laity to determine the nature of the community in its
political aspect. The hierarchical Church has asserted its right to
speak on any political or social issue, and has at times incurred the
opprobrium of its own followers who have charged it with interference
with matters not germane to its role in society. This predicament
is also raised today over the Church's stand on violence. Given the
Church's authoritarian nature, many commentators outside its
ranks question the sincerity of its injunctions against violence: if the
Church took a firmer line, so the argument runs, catholics would be
less disposed to engage in it. However, to think that 'the people will
do what their priests tell them', especially in political matters, is a
preposterous caricature. This does not mean that the church can
abrogate its right to speak up for what it believes to be the truth, or
indeed has done so.

The clerical versus lay stand-off over political considerations has
been the most divisive element in Ulster catholic history. At the time
of writing the catholic community enters the third decade of the present conflict more divided than at any time in its past. Because of
the increasing reserve with which many approach the subject of
nationalism, it is no longer fashionable to proclaim oneself in favour
of a united Ireland, and there is therefore enormous self-doubt about
northern Irish catholic identity. This self-questioning has produced an
intellectual vacuum which the Church cannot fill, and which has left
the way clear for the IRA-Sinn Fein to pose as the only group with
a clear understanding of the direction in which the catholic-nationalist
community ought to be going.

In these circumstances Church leaders find themselves forced into taking a more public and political role than is perhaps appropriate. After all the main role of the priest is to be a leader of worship and to direct his flock to the contemplation of eternal realities. But even here the history of the community has shown that the catholic faith survived in the north of Ireland under trying and difficult circumstances not because of the clergy but in many instances in the absence of direct access to sacramental ministry. There must surely be a lesson in that experience for a Church which so depends on its clergy for many aspects of its belief and practice. Ultimately the realm of the relationship between God and the individual is unmediated by any intervention save that of God himself.

These considerations are linked to another specifically religious issue which the community must also face. In its more recent history the Church has witnessed an alarming decline in practice, and at times has even appeared irrelevant to the experience of its members in what is a highly complex and divided situation. The problem then arises: can the Church survive as an institution commanding the adherence of most northern catholics? It would be unfair to see its continued existence in the last four centuries as attributable simply to its being a counterpoint to protestant and English influence, although these were undoubtedly factors in its ability to command the affection and respect of its adherents. These considerations are obviously no longer as important as they once were. But now the Church faces a much greater threat to its position in Ulster society. The process of secularisation, at work on both sides of the border, and its own inability to come to terms with changing values in Ireland may prove a more redoubtable opponent than anything it has faced previously. For the present however it continues to play as vital a role in Northern Ireland life as it has done over the whole period here examined. Its endurance thus far is indeed a testament of faith.

SELECT BIBLIOGRAPHY

Manuscripts

ARMAGH
Archives of the Archdiocese of Armagh (AAA)
  Curtis Papers
  Kelly Papers
  Crolly Papers
  Cullen Papers
  Dixon Papers
  Kieran Papers
  McGettigan Papers
  Logue Papers
  O'Donnell Papers
  MacRory Papers

BELFAST
Archives of the Diocese of Clogher (in the Public Records Office of Northern Ireland)
  Correspondence and papers of bishops and clergy including
  McDermott Papers
  Kiernan Papers
  McNally Papers
  Letter-book of Michael Blake
Archives of the Diocese of Down and Connor
  Patrick MacMullan Papers
  Crolly Papers
  Denvir Papers
  Dorrian Papers
  McAllister Papers

OXFORD
Bodleian Library
Clarendon Papers Irish Deposit

Newspapers

Belfast Morning News
Belfast News Letter
Belfast Telegraph
Church of Ireland Gazette
Daily Express (London)
Daily Telegraph (London)
Derry Journal
Erne Packett
Northern Whig
Irish Independent

Irish News
Irish Press
Irish Times
The Times (London)
Sunday Telegraph (London)
Sunday Times (London)
The Tablet (London)

Other sources

An Abstract of certain Depositions, By Virtue of His Majesties Commission, taken upon Oath, Concerning the Traitorous intention of the Rebels of Ireland . . . . *(London, 1642)*.

ADAMS, G., *The Politics of Irish Freedom* (Dingle, 1986).

——, *Cage Eleven* (Dingle, 1990).

AKENSON, D.H., *Small Differences: Irish Catholics and Irish Protestants, 1815–1922* (Dublin, 1988).

——, *The Irish Educational Experiment* (London, 1970).

ARTHUR, P., *Government and Politics of Northern Ireland*, 2nd edn (London, 1984).

——, *The People's Democracy, 1968–73* (Belfast, 1974).

—— and K. JEFFERY, *Northern Ireland since 1968* (Oxford, 1988).

BARAZILY, D., *The British Army in Ulster*, 4 vols (Belfast, 1973–81).

BARDON, J., *A History of Ulster* (Belfast, 1992).

BARKER, D. (ed.), *Schism, Heresy and Religious Protest* (Cambridge, 1972).

BARNARD, T.C., *Cromwellian Ireland: English Government and Reform in Ireland, 1649–1660* (Oxford, 1975).

BARRY, P.C., 'The Legislation of the Synod of Thurles 1850', *Irish Theological Quarterly*, vol. 26 (1959), pp. 131–66.

BARTLETT, T., *The Fall and Rise of the Irish Nation: The Catholic Question, 1690–1830* (Dublin, 1992).

BEAMES, M., *Peasants and Power: The Whiteboy Movements and their Control in Pre-Famine Ireland* (Brighton and New York, 1983).

BECKETT, J.C., *Protestant Dissent in Ireland, 1687–1780* (London, 1948).

——, 'The Confederation of Kilkenny Reviewed', *Historical Studies II* (1959), pp. 29–41.

——, *The Making of Modern Ireland, 1603–1923* (London, 1966).

——, *The Anglo-Irish Tradition* (London, 1976).

BOWYER BELL, J., *The Secret Army: The IRA, 1916–79* (Dublin, 1979).

BELL, R., R. JOHNSTONE and R. WILSON (eds), *Troubled Times: Fortnight Magazine and the Troubles in Northern Ireland 1970–1991* (Belfast, 1991).

BERESFORD, D., *Ten Dead Men* (London, 1987).

BIGGS-DAVISON, J., and G. BEST, *The Cross of St. Patrick: The Catholic Unionist Tradition in Ireland* (London, 1984).

BISHOP, P. and E. MALLIE, *The Provisional IRA* (London, 1988).

BOSSY, J. 'The Counter-Reformation and the People of Catholic Ireland', *Historical Studies VIII* (Dublin, 1971), pp. 155–69.

BOWEN, D., *The Protestant Crusade in Ireland, 1800–70* (Dublin, 1978).
——, *Paul Cardinal Cullen and the Shaping of Modern Irish Catholicism* (Dublin, 1983).
BOWMAN, J., *De Valera and the Ulster Question, 1917–73* (Oxford, 1983).
BOYD, A., *Holy War in Belfast*, 3rd edn (Belfast, 1987).
BRADY, C., M. O'DOWD and B. WALKER (eds), *Ulster: An Illustrated History* (London, 1989).
BRADY, J., 'Catholics and Catholicism in the Eighteenth Century Press', *Archivium Hibernicum*, vols 16 (1951) and 17 (1953).
BRADY, W.M., *The Episcopal Succession in England, Scotland and Ireland A.D. 1400–1875*, 3 vols (Rome, 1870–77)
BRENAN, M.J. *Ecclesiastical History of Ireland*, 2 vols (Dublin, 1864).
A Brief Declaration of the Barbarous and Inhumane Dealings of the Northern Irish Rebels . . . . (London, 1641).
BROOKE, P., *Ulster Presbyterianism: The Historical Perspective* (Dublin, 1987).
BRUCE, S., *God Save Ulster: The Religion and Politics of Paisleyism* (Oxford, 1989).
BUCKLAND, P., *Irish Unionism*, I. *The Anglo-Irish and the New Ireland 1885–1922* (Dublin and New York, 1972).
——, *Ulster Unionism*, II. *Ulster Unionism and the Origins of Northern Ireland, 1886–1922* (Dublin and New York, 1973).
——, *The Factory of Grievances: Devolved Government in Northern Ireland* (Dublin and New York, 1979).
——, *A History of Northern Ireland* (Dublin, 1981).
BUCKLEY, P., *Faith and Fatherland: The Irish News, The Catholic Hierarchy and the Management of Dissidents*, (Belfast, n.d.).
Bulletin of the Irish Committee of Historical Studies, 78 (1957).
BURKE, W.P., *The Irish Priests in Penal Times* (Waterford, 1914).
——, 'The Diocese of Derry in 1631', *Archivium Hibernicum*, vol. 5 (1917), pp. 1–6.
BURNS, R.E. 'The Belfast Letters, the Irish Volunteers 1778–79 and the Catholics', *Review of Politics*, vol. 21 (1959), pp. 678–91.
——, 'The Irish Penal Code and Some of Its Historians', *Review of Politics*, vol. 21 (1959), pp. 276–99.
——, 'Parsons, Priests and People: The Rise of Irish Anti-clericalism 1785–1789', *Church History*, vol. 31 (1962), pp. 151–63.
——, 'The Irish Popery Laws: A Study of Eighteenth Century Legislation and Behaviour', *Review of Politics*, vol. 24 (1962), pp. 485–508.
CAHILL, G.A., 'Some Nineteenth-Century Roots of the Ulster Problem, 1829–1848', *Irish University Review*, vol. 1/2 (1971), pp. 215–37.
Calendar of State Papers Ireland, 1509–1669 (London, 1860–1908).
Calendar of the Carew Manuscripts Preserved in the Archiepiscopal Library at Lambeth, 1515–1624 (London, 1867–73).
CAMPBELL, A.A., *Belfast Newspapers Past and Present* (Belfast, 1921).
CANNING, B.J., *Bishops of Ireland 1870–1987* (Ballyshannon, 1987).
CANNY, N.P., *From Reformation to Restoration: Ireland 1534–1660* (Dublin, 1987).
——, 'Hugh O'Neill, Earl of Tyrone and the Changing Face of Gaelic Ulster', *Studia Hibernica*, vol. 10 (1971), pp. 7–35.

CARLETON, W., *Traits and Stories of the Irish Peasantry*, ed. D.J. O'Donoghue, 4 vols (London, 1896).

CARTE, T., *History of the Life of James, First Duke of Ormonde*, 2nd edn, 6 vols (Oxford, 1851).

CARTY, X. (ed.), *Violence and Protest* (Dublin, 1970).

CATHOLICUS, *The Irish University Question: Its History and Solution* (London, 1905).

A Collection of the Protests of the Lords of Ireland from 1634–1770 (London, 1771).

COLLES, R. *The History of Ulster from the Earliest Times to the Present Day*, 4 vols (London, 1919–20).

COLLINS, T., *The Irish Hunger Strike* (Dublin and Belfast, 1986).

Conditions to be Observed by the British Undertakers of the Escheated Lands in Ulster (London, 1610).

CONDON, M.D., 'The Irish Church and the Reform Ministries', *Journal of British Studies*, vol. 3/2 (1964), pp. 120–42.

CONNAN, T.L., *The Irish Catholic Confederacy and the Puritan Revolution* (Dublin, 1954).

CONNOLLY, S.J., *Priests and People in Pre-Famine Ireland, 1780–1845* (Dublin, 1982).

——, *Religion and Society in Nineteenth Century Ireland* (Dundalk, 1985).

——, *Religion, Law and Power: The Making of Protestant Ireland, 1660–1760* (Oxford, 1992).

CONWAY, D., 'Guide to the Documents of Irish and British Interest in the Fondo Borghese, Series 1', *Archivium Hibernicum*, vol. 23 (1953).

COOGAN, T.P., *Michael Collins: A Biography* (London, 1990).

COONY, J., *The Crozier and the Dail: Church and State in Ireland, 1922–1986* (Dublin and Cork, 1986).

CORISH, P.J., *The Catholic Community in the Seventeenth and Eighteenth Centuries* (Dublin, 1981).

——, *The Origins of Catholic Nationalism* (Dublin, 1968).

——, 'Irish College Rome: Kirby Papers', *Archivium Hibernicum*, vols 30 (1972), 31 (1973) and 32 (1974).

——, *The Irish Catholic Experience: A Historical Survey* (Dublin, 1985).

COSGRAVE, A. & D. MCCARTNEY (eds), *Studies in Irish History presented to R. Dudley Edwards* (Dublin, 1979).

CROLLY, G., *The Life of the Most Rev. Doctor Crolly Archbishop of Armagh and Primate of Ireland* [sic] (Dublin, 1851).

CULLEN, L.M., *The Emergence of Modern Ireland 1600–1900*, 2nd. edn (Dublin, 1983).

——, *The Hidden Ireland: Reassessment of a Concept* (Mullingar, 1988).

CURRAN, D., *St. Paul's: The Story of Inner West Belfast* (Belfast, 1987).

CURTAYNE, A., *The Trial of Oliver Plunkett* (London, 1953).

CURTIS, L.P., *Coercion and Conciliation in Ireland 1886–1892* (Princeton, 1963).

DALY, C.B., *Violence in Ireland and Christian Conscience* (Dublin, 1973).

——, *Peace the Work of Justice: Addresses on the Northern Tragedy, 1973–1979* (Dublin, 1979).

——, *Coming Back Home* (Belfast, 1983).

——, *Peace a Better Way of Justice* (Belfast, 1985).

DANGERFIELD, G., *The Damnable Question*, (London, 1977).

DARBY, J., *Conflict in Northern Ireland: The Development of a Polarised Community* (Dublin and New York).

—— (ed.), *Northern Ireland: The Background to the Conflict* (Belfast and Syracuse, 1983).

DE BAROID, C., *Ballymurphy and the Irish War* (Dublin, 1989).

DE PAOR, L., *Divided Ulster* (Harmondsworth, 1970).

DEUTSCH, R. and V. MAGOWN, *Northern Ireland, 1968–74: A Chronology of Events*, 3 vols (Belfast 1975).

A Digest of the Historical Account of the Diocese of Down and Connor (Belfast, 1945).

DILLON, M. *The Shankill Butchers: A Case Study of Mass Murder* (London, 1989).

DOHERTY, J.F. and D.J. HICKEY, *A Chronology of Irish History since 1500* (Dublin, 1989).

DOWLING, E., 'Irish Seminaries in the Eighteenth Century', *Irish Ecclesiastical Record*, vol. 58 (1941), pp. 424–42.

EDWARDS, O.D., *Eamon de Valera* (Cardiff, 1987).

EDWARDS, R.D., 'The History of the Penal Laws against Catholics in Ireland from 1534 to the Treaty of Limerick (1691)', Ph.D thesis, Univ. of London, 1933.

——, *Church and State in Tudor Ireland* (London, 1935).

—— (ed.), 'The Minute Book of the Catholic Committee, 1773–92', *Archivium Hibernicum*, vol. 19 (1942), pp. 3–172.

ELLIOTT, M. 'The Origins and Transformation of Early Irish Republicanism', *International Review of Social History*, vol. 23 (1978), pp. 405–28.

——, *Partners in Revolution: The United Irishmen and France* (New Haven and London, 1982).

——, *Wolfe Tone: Prophet of Irish Independence* (New Haven and London, 1989).

FARRELL, M., *Northern Ireland: The Orange State* (London, 1976).

FAUL, D. and R. MURRAY, *The Alienation of Northern Ireland Catholics* (Belfast, 1984).

FAULKNER, B., *Memoirs of a Statesman* (London, 1978).

FENNING, H., *The Undoing of the Friars of Ireland: A study of the Novitiate Question in the Eighteenth Century* (Louvain, 1972).

——, 'Clerical Recruitment, 1735–1738: Documents from Windsor and Rome', *Archivium Hibernicum*, vol. 30 (1972), pp. 1–23.

FINEGAN, F. 'The Irish Catholic Convert Rolls', *Studies* (March, 1949), pp. 73–82.

FITZGERALD, G., *All in a Life: An Autobiography* (Dublin, 1991).

FITZPATRICK, B., *Seventeenth Century Ireland: The Wars of Religion* (Dublin, 1988).

FLACKES, W.D. and S. ELLIOTT, *Northern Ireland: A Political Directory 1968–88* (Belfast, 1980 and 83).

FOSTER, R.F., *Modern Ireland 1600–1972* (London, 1988).

FROUDE, J.A., *The English in Ireland in the Eighteenth Century*, 3 vols (London, 1887).

FULTON, J., *The Tragedy of Belief: Division, Politics and Religion in Ireland* (Oxford, 1991).

GALLAGHER, E. and S. WORRALL, *Christians in Ulster 1968-1980* (Oxford, 1982).

GANNON, P.J., 'In the Catacombs of Belfast', *Studies*, vol. 11 (1922), pp. 279-95.

GARDINER, S.R., *History of England from the Accession of James I to the Outbreak of the Civil War 1603-1642* (London, 1884).

GIBBONS, M., *Glimpes of Catholic Ireland in the Eighteenth Century* (Dublin, 1932).

GIBLIN, C., 'The "Processus Datariae" and the Appointment of Irish Bishops in the Seventeenth Century', in *Father Luke Wadding: Commemorative Volume*, ed. Franciscan Fathers (Dublin, 1957), pp. 524-44.

——, 'Stuart Nomination of Irish Bishops', *Irish Ecclesiastical Record*, vol. 5 (1966), pp. 35-47.

——, 'Catalogue of Material of Irish Interest in the Collection *Nuziatura di Fiandra*, Vatican Archives', in *Collectanea Hibernica*, vols 3 (1960), 4 (1961), 5 (1962), 9 (1966), 10 (1967), 11 (1968), 12 (1969), 13 (1970), 14 (1971), 15 (1972).

GILLESPIE, R., *'Conspiracy' Ulster Plots and Plotters in 1615* (Belfast, 1989).

GRAY, J., 'A Loyal Catholic Sermon of 1798', *Linen Hall Review*, vol. 14/4 (1987), pp. 12-3.

HALL, M., *20 Years: A Concise Chronology of Events in Northern Ireland from 1968-1988* (Newtownabbey, 1988).

HAYES, M.J., *The Mission of Rinuccini, Nuncio Extraordinary to Ireland, 1645-1649* (Louvain, 1932).

HEALY, J., *Maynooth College: Its Centenary History* (Dublin, 1895).

HEALY, T.M., *Letters and Leaders of My Day*, 2 vols (London, 1928).

HEMPTON, D. and M. HILL, *Evangelical Protestantism in Ulster Society 1740-1890* (London and New York, 1992).

HEPBURN, A.C., 'Catholics in the North of Ireland 1850-1921: the urbanization of a Minority', *Historical Studies XII* (London, 1978), pp. 84-101.

——, *The Conflict of Nationality in Modern Ireland* (London, 1980).

HERRICK, F.H., 'Gladstone, Newman and Ireland in 1881', *Catholic Historical Review*, vol. 47 (1961-2), pp. 342-50.

HICKEY, J., *Religion and the Northern Ireland Problem* (Dublin and Totowa, 1984).

HILL, C., *Intellectual Origins of the English Revolution* (Oxford, 1965).

HILL, G., *An Historical Account of the MacDonnells of Antrim* (Belfast, 1873).

HOLMES, R.F.G., *Our Presbyterian Heritage* (Belfast, 1985).

HOLT, E., *Protest in Arms: The Irish troubles, 1916-23* (London, 1960).

HOPPEN, K.T., *Election, Politics, and Society in Ireland, 1832-1885* (Oxford, 1984).

INGLIS, T., *Moral Monopoly: The Catholic Church in Modern Irish Society* (Dublin, 1987).

Irish Catholic Directory, variously titled, annual (Dublin, 1838-).

IRVINE, M., *Northern Ireland: Faith and Faction* (London 1991).

JOHNSTON, E.M., *Great Britain and Ireland, 1760–1800: A Study in Political Administration* (Edinburgh and London, 1963).

KENNA, G.B., *Facts and Figures of the Belfast Pogrom, 1920–22* (Belfast, 1922).

KENNEDY, D., *The Widening Gulf: Northern attitudes to the Independent Irish State, 1919–49* (Belfast, 1988).

KENNEDY, L. 'The Roman Catholic Church and Economic Growth in Nineteenth Century Ireland', *Economic and Social Review*, vol. 10/1 (1978), pp. 45–60.

—, 'The early Response of the Irish Catholic Clergy to the Co-Operative Movement', *Irish Historical Studies*, vol. 21 (1978–9), pp. 55–79.

KEOGH, D., *The Vatican, the Bishops and Irish Politics, 1919–39* (Cambridge, 1986).

KERR, D.A., *Peel, Priests and Politics* (Oxford, 1982).

—, 'Under the Union Flag: The Catholic Church in Ireland 1800–1870', in *Ireland after the Union* (Oxford, 1989).

—, 'Charles McNally: O'Connellite Bishop and Reforming Pastor', *Archivium Hibernicum*, vol. 37 (1982), pp. 11–20.

KILLEN, W.D., *The Ecclesiastical History of Ireland*, 2 vols (London, 1875).

LAFFAN, M., *The Partition of Ireland, 1911–25* (Dundalk, 1983).

LARKIN, E., 'The Roman Catholic Church and the Fall of Parnell', *Victorian Studies*, vol. 4 (1960–1), pp. 315–36.

—, 'The Devotional Revolution in Ireland, 1850–1875', *American Historical Review*, vol. 77 (1972), pp. 625–52.

—, *The Making of the Roman Catholic Church in Ireland, 1850–1860* (Chapel Hill, NC, 1980).

—, *The Consolidation of the Roman Catholic Church in Ireland*, (Dublin, 1987).

—, *The Roman Catholic Church and the Home Rule Movement in Ireland, 1870–74* (Dublin, 1990).

LARKIN, P.J., '"Popish Riot" in South Co. Derry 1725', in *Seanchas Ardmhacha*, vol. 8 (1976), pp. 97–110.

LECKY, W.E.H., *A History of Ireland in the Eighteenth Century*, 5 vols (London, 1892).

LEE, J.J., *Ireland 1912–1985: Politics and Society* (Cambridge, 1989).

LESLIE, S., *Henry Edward Manning: His Life and Labours* (London, 1921).

—, *St. Patrick's Purgatory* (London, 1932).

LIMPKIN, C., *The Battle of the Bogside* (Harmondsworth, 1972).

LIVINSTONE, P., *The Fermanagh Story* (Enniskillen, 1969).

LONDONDERRY, Marquess of (ed.), *Memoirs and Correspondence of Viscount Castlereagh*, vol. 4 (London, 1849).

LYNCH, J., *Cambrensis Eversus* (ed. Matthew Kelly), 3 vols (Dublin, 1848–54).

LYONS, F.L.S., *Ireland Since the Famine* (London, 1971 and 1973).

—, 'John Dillon and the Plan of Campaign 1886–90', *Irish Historical Studies*, vol. 14 (1965), pp. 313–47.

MACAULAY, A., 'Britain's New State', *Capuchin Annual* (1972), pp. 351–61.

—, 'Dr Cullen's Appointment to Armagh, 1849', *Seanchas Ardmhacha*, vol. 10/1 (1980–1) pp. 3–36.

——, *Dr Russell of Maynooth* (London, 1983).

MACCAFFREY, J., *History of the Catholic Church in the Nineteenth Century (1789-1908)*, 2 vols (Dublin, 1909).

MACCURTAIN, M., *Tudor and Stuart Ireland* (Dublin, 1972).

MACDONAGH, O., 'The Politicization of the Irish Catholic Bishops, 1800-1850', *Historical Journal*, vol. 18 (1975), pp. 37-53.

MACHIN, G.I.T., 'The Duke of Wellington and Catholic Emancipation', *Journal of Ecclesiastical History*, vol. 16 (1963), pp. 190-208.

MACINTYRE, A., *The Liberator: Daniel O'Connell and the Irish Party, 1830-1847* (London, 1965).

MACMANUS, F. (ed.), *The Years of the Great Test* (Cork, 1967).

MACOURT, M.P.A., 'The religious Inquiry in the Irish Census of 1861', *Irish Historical Studies*, vol. 21 (1978-9), pp. 168-87.

MALCOMSON, A., *John Foster: The Politics of the Anglo-Irish Ascendancy* (Oxford, 1978).

MANSERGH, N. *The Unresolved Question: The Anglo-Irish Settlement and its Undoing, 1912-72* (London and New Haven, 1991).

MASON, W.S., *A Statistical Account or Parochial Survey of Ireland*, 3 vols (Dublin, 1814-19).

MAXWELL, C., *Irish History from Contemporary Sources (1509-1610)* (London, 1923).

McCANN, E., *War and an Irish Town* (London, 1980).

McCARTHY, M.J.F., *Priests and People in Ireland* (Dublin, 1902).

McCLELLAND, V.A., *Cardinal Manning: His Public Life and Influence, 1865-1892* (London, 1962).

McDOWELL, R.B., *Irish Public Opinion, 1750-1800* (London, 1944).

——, *Ireland in the Age of Imperialism and Revolution, 1760-1801* (Oxford, 1979).

McELROY, G., *The Catholic Church and the Northern Ireland Crisis, 1968-86* (Dublin, 1991).

McLYNN, F.J., '"Good Behaviour": Irish Catholics and the Jacobite Rising of 1745', in *Eire-Ireland*, vol. 16/2 (1981), pp. 43-58.

McNAMEE, B., 'JKL's Letter on the Union of Churches', *Irish Theological Quarterly*, vol. 36 (1969), pp. 46-69.

McVEIGH, J., *A Wounded Church: Religion, Politics and Justice in Ireland* (Cork and Dublin, 1989).

MILLER, D.W., 'The Roman Catholic Church in Ireland, 1898-1918', *Eire-Ireland*, vol. 3 (1968), pp. 75-91.

——, *Church, State and Nation in Ireland, 1898-1921* (Dublin, 1973).

——, 'Irish Catholicism and the Great Famine', *Journal of Social History*, vol. 9/1 (1975), pp. 81-98.

——, *Queen's Rebels: Ulster Loyalism in Historical Perspective* (Dublin, 1978).

——, 'The Armagh Troubles, 1784-95' in Samuel Clark and James S. Donnelly, Jr. (eds), *Irish Peasants: Violence and Political Unrest, 1780-1914* (Manchester, 1983), pp. 155-91.

MILLETT, B., 'Survival and Reorganization 1650-95' in *A History of Irish Catholicism*, vol. 3, ed. P.J. Corish (Dublin, 1968).

MOLONEY, E. and A. POLLAK, *Paisley* (Swords, 1986).

MOODY, T.W., *The Londonderry Plantation, 1609-41* (Belfast, 1939).

——, *The Ulster Question, 1603–1973* (Cork, 1974).

—— and J.C. BECKETT (eds), *Ulster since 1800: A Political and Economic Survey* (London, 1955).

——, *Ulster since 1800: A Social Survey* (London, 1957).

——, *Queen's Belfast, 1845–1949. The History of a University*, 2 vols (London, 1959).

MOODY, T.W., F.X. MARTIN and F.J. BYRNE (eds), *A New History of Ireland*, vol. 3 (Oxford, 1976 and 1978).

MOONEY, C., 'Accusations Against Oliver Plunkett', in *Seanchas Ardmhacha*, vol. 2/1 (1956), pp. 119–40.

MORAN, P.F., *Spicilegium Ossoriense: Being a collection of original letters and papers of the history of the Irish Church from the Reformation to 1800*, 3 vols (Dublin, 1874–84).

——, *Memoir of the Ven. Oliver Plunkett*, 2nd edn (Dublin, 1895).

MORGAN, A, and B. PURDIE (eds), *Ireland: Divided Nation Divided Class* (London, 1980).

MOXON-BROWNE, E., *Nation, Class and Creed in Northern Ireland* (Aldershot, 1983).

MURPHY, D., *Derry, Donegal and Modern Ulster, 1790–1921* (Derry, 1981).

MURRAY, D., *Worlds Apart: Segregated Schools in Northern Ireland* (Belfast, 1985).

MURRAY, R., *The SAS in Ireland* (Cork, 1990).

MURRAY, R.H., *Ireland, 1603–1714* (London, 1920).

NELSON, S., *Ulster's Uncertain Defenders* (Belfast, 1984).

NORMAN, E.R., *The Catholic Church in Ireland in the Age of Rebellion, 1859–1873* (London, 1965).

NOWLAN, K.B., 'The Catholic Clergy and Irish Politics in the Eighteen Thirities and Forties' in *Historical Studies IX*, (London, 1974).

O'MAOLAGAIN, P., 'Clogher Diocesan Statutes, 1789', *Archivium Hibernicum*, vol. 12 (1946), pp. 62–9.

O'BRIEN, C.C., *States of Ireland* (St Albans, 1974).

O'BRIEN, G., *Anglo-Irish Politics in the Age of Grattan and Pitt* (Dublin, 1987).

O'BYRNE, E. (ed.), *The Convert Rolls* (Dublin, 1981).

O'DUFAIGH, S., 'James Murphy, Bishop of Clogher, 1801–24', *Clogher Record*, vol. 6/3 (1968), pp. 419–92.

O'FIAICH, T., 'Edmund O'Reilly, Archbishop of Armagh, 1657–1669', in *Father Luke Wadding Commemorative Volume* (Dublin, 1957), pp. 171–228.

——, 'The fall and return of John McMoyer', *Seanchas Ardmhacha*, vol. 3/1 (1958), pp. 51–86.

——, 'The Registration of the clergy in 1704', *Seanchas Ardmhacha*, vol. 6 (1971), pp. 46–69.

——, *Oliver Plunkett: Ireland's New Saint* (Dublin, 1975).

O'HALLORAN, C. ' "The Island of Saints and Scholars": Views of the Early Irish Church and Sectarian Politics in Late Eighteenth Century Ireland', in *Eighteenth Century Ireland*, vol. 5 (1990), pp. 7–20.

——, *Partition and the Limits of Irish Nationalism: An Ideology under Stress* (Dublin, 1987).

O'LAVERTY, J., *An Historical Account of the Diocese of Down and Connor, Ancient and Modern*, 5 vols (Dublin, 1878–95).

O'MALLEY, P., *The Uncivil Wars: Ireland Today* (Belfast, 1983).

O'REILLY, M., *Lives of the Irish Martyrs and Confessors* (New York, 1878).

O'ROURKE, J., *The Battle of the Faith in Ireland* (Dublin, 1887). *Ordinance Survey of the County of Londonderry* (vol. 1 Dublin, 1837).

PATTERSON, H., *Class, Conflict and Sectarianism* (Belfast, 1980).

PERCEVAL-MAXWELL, M., 'The Ulster Rising of 1641 and the Depositions', *Irish Historical Studies*, vol. 21 (1978–9), pp. 144–67.

——, *The Scottish Migration to Ulster in the Reign of James I* (London, 1973).

PHILBIN, W.J., *To You Simonides* (London, 1973).

——, *Ireland's Problem* (Manchester, 1974).

PHILIPS, W.A., *History of the Church of Ireland*, 3 vols (Oxford, 1933–4).

PHOENIX, E.G., 'The Nationalist Movement in Northern Ireland, 1914–28', unpubl. Ph. D. thesis, Queen's Univ. Belfast (1983).

PLUNKETT, O., *The Letters of Saint Oliver Plunkett*, ed. John Hanly (Dublin, 1979).

[The] Pope in Ireland: Addresses and Homilies (Dublin, 1979).

POWER, T.P. and K. WHELAN (eds), *Endurance and Emergence: Catholics in Ireland in the Eighteenth Century* (Dublin, 1990).

PUBLIC RECORDS OFFICE OF NORTHERN IRELAND, *Aspects of Irish Social History, 1750–1800* (Belfast, 1973).

PURCELL, M. (ed.), 'Dublin Diocesan Archives: Murray Papers', *Archivium Hibernicum*, vol. 37 (1982), pp. 29–121.

PURDIE, B., *Politics in the Streets: The Origins of the Civil Rights Movement in Northern Ireland* (Belfast, 1990).

RENEHAN, L.F., *Collections on Irish Church History*, ed. D.McCarthy, 2 vols (Dublin, 1861 and 1874).

'Report on the State of Popery in Ireland' in *Archivium Hibernicum*, vol. 1 (1912), pp. 10–27.

RINUCCINI, G.B., *Embassy in Ireland*, ed. Annie Hatton (Dublin, 1873).

ROCHE, K.F., 'The Relations of the Catholic Church and the State in England and Ireland, 1800–1852', *Historical Studies III* (Cork, 1961), pp. 9–24.

ROEBUCK, P. (ed.), *Plantation to Partition* (Belfast, 1981).

ROGERS, P., *The Irish Volunteers and Catholic Emancipation, 1778–1793: A Neglected Phase of Ireland's History* (London, 1934).

——, *St. Peter's Pro-Cathedral Belfast, 1866–1966* (Belfast, 1967).

—— and A. MACAULAY, *Old St. Mary's, Chapel Lane, Belfast, 1784–1984* (Belfast, 1984).

ROSE, R., *Governing Without Consensus: An Irish Perspective* (London, 1971).

RYDER, C., *The RUC: A Force Under Fire* (London, 1989).

SENIOR, H., *Orangeism in Ireland and Britain, 1795–1836* (London, 1966).

SILKE, J.J., 'Primate Peter Lombard and Hugh O'Neil', *Irish Theological Quarterly*, vol. 22 (1955), pp. 124–49.

——, 'The Roman Catholic Church in Ireland, 1800–1922: A survey of recent Historiography', *Studia Hibernica*, vol. 15 (1975), pp. 61–104.

SIMMS, J.G., *The Williamite Confiscations in Ireland 1690–1705* (London, 1956).

——, 'County Donegal in 1739', in *Donegal Annual*, vol. 4/3 (1960), pp. 203–8.

——, *Jacobite Ireland 1685–91* (London, 1969).

——, *War and Politics in Ireland, 1649–1730*, ed. D.W. Hayton and Gerard O'Brien (London, 1986).

SMITH, P.D.H., 'The Volunteers and Parliament, 1779–84' in T. Bartlett and D.W. Hatton (eds), *Penal Era and Golden Age: Essays in Irish History, 1690–1800* (Belfast, 1979).

STEELE, E.D., 'Cardinal Cullen and Irish Nationality', *Irish Historical Studies*, vol. 19 (1975), pp. 239–60.

STEWART, A.T.Q., *The Narrow Ground: Aspects of Ulster, 1609–1969* (London, 1977).

——, *The Ulster Crisis* (London, 1967).

SUNDAY TIMES INSIGHT TEAM, *Ulster* (London, 1972).

TANNER, N.P. (ed.), *Decrees of the Ecumenical Councils*, 2 vols (London and Washington, 1990).

TOHALL, P., 'The Diamond Fight of 1795 and the Resultant Expulsions', *Seanchas Ardmhacha*, vol. 3/1 (1958), pp. 17–50.

TOWNSHEND, C., *Political Violence in Ireland: Government and Resistance since 1848* (Oxford, 1983).

WALL, M., 'The Rise of the Catholic Middle Class in Eighteenth-Century Ireland', *Irish Historical Studies*, vol. 11 (1958), pp. 91–115.

——, *The Penal Laws, 1691–1760: Church and State from the Treaty of Limerick to the Accession of George III* (Dundalk, 1961).

——, *Catholic Ireland in the Eighteenth Century: Collected Essays of Maureen Wall*, ed. Gerard O'Brien (Dublin, 1989).

WALSH, P., *The History and Vindication of the Loyal Formulary* (London, 1674).

WALSH, P.J., *William J. Walsh, Archbishop of Dublin* (Dublin and Cork, 1928).

WARD, B., *The Eve of Catholic Emancipation*, 3 vols (London, 1911).

WHELAN, P., 'Anthony Blake, Archbishop of Armagh, 1758–1787', *Seanchas Ardmhacha*, vol. 5/2 (1970), pp. 289–323.

WHITE, B., *John Hume: Statesman of the Troubles* (Belfast, 1984).

WHITFORD, F.J., 'Joseph Devlin, Ulsterman and Irishman', unpubl. M.A. thesis, Univ. of London (1959).

WHYTE, J.H., *The Irish Independent Party, 1850–59* (Oxford, 1958).

——, 'The Influence of the Catholic Clergy on Elections in Nineteenth Century Ireland', *English Historical Review*, vol. 75 (1960), pp. 239–59.

——, 'The Appointment of Catholic Bishops in Nineteenth Century Ireland', *Catholic Historical Review*, vol. 48 (1962–3), pp. 13–22.

——, *Interpreting Northern Ireland* (Oxford, 1990).

WILSON, D., *An End to Silence*, 2nd edn (Cork, 1987).

WILSON, T. (ed.), *Ulster Home Rule: A Study of the Political and Economic Problems of Northern Ireland* (London, 1955).

——, *Ulster: Conflict and Consent* (Oxford, 1989).

WOODS, C.J., 'Ireland and Anglo-Papal Relations', *Irish Historical Studies*, vol. 18 (1972). pp. 29–60.

YOUNG, R.M., *Ulster in '98* (Belfast, 1893).

YOUNGER, C., *Ireland's Civil War* (London, 1968 and 1979).

INDEX